METHODS OF TEACHING BUSINESS SUBJECTS

METHODS OF TEACHING
BUSINESS SUBJECTS

SECOND EDITION

Herbert A. Tonne
Professor of Education
New York University, New York, New York

Estelle L. Popham
Assistant Professor of Education
Hunter College, New York, New York

M. Herbert Freeman
Chairman, Business Education Department
New Jersey State Teachers College
Montclair, New Jersey

GREGG PUBLISHING DIVISION
McGRAW-HILL BOOK COMPANY, INC.

New York   Chicago   San Francisco   Dallas   Toronto   London

Preface

PURPOSE OF THIS BOOK

The primary purpose of this book is to provide teaching materials for the introductory methods course in business education offered in colleges and universities. The program in most business teacher training institutions is so heavy with content courses and general-education courses that there is usually room only for a single methods course in business education. In many cases this single methods course must include curriculum making in business education and similar problems and subjects other than teaching methods. The second purpose of this book is to assist individual teachers in the classroom. This book, therefore, is planned to meet a practical need.

CHARACTERISTICS

The unique characteristic of this book is that it deals with all business subjects and yet presents a unified concept of methodology. Most books on methods of teaching business subjects offer a series of isolated chapters dealing separately with each business subject. Not infrequently the opinions given in one chapter are contradicted in another. *Methods of Teaching Business Subjects* is built around a series of principles for teaching and developing skills. These principles are adapted and illustrated for the various skill-building subjects in the chapters devoted to them. In those subjects that stress understanding and attitudes, rather than skills, careful presentation of the necessary changes in teaching procedure is made. In those subjects that combine all types of teaching, the integrated nature of the teaching procedures required is illustrated in detail. This book thus achieves the unusual character of being unified in presentation and specific in modifications suggested for teaching procedures in each subject.

v

IMPROVEMENTS

This second edition is almost a complete revision of the first edition. In the introductory part of the book, a new chapter dealing with the special problems of teaching business subjects (Chapter II) has been added. The problem of getting students interested in basic business subjects is a perennial one; therefore a new chapter on making these subjects meaningful (Chapter XVII) is presented in this edition. Throughout the book, the amount of problem-solving material has been greatly increased. Even more attention has been given to teaching techniques and to illustrations of how these techniques may be used. Human-relations problems, as they affect the teaching of business subjects, have been stressed throughout the book. Increased recognition is given to the problems of student control and to successful techniques for securing better student attention.

Here and there, brief sections that were primarily academic in their importance have been eliminated to provide increased space for illustrative problem materials that will be of direct use to the teacher.

The chapters concerned with the teaching of shorthand, typewriting, transcription, and office practice were written for the most part by Estelle L. Popham; the chapters on teaching arithmetic and distributive education, primarily by Herbert A. Tonne; the chapters on bookkeeping and basic business education, by M. Herbert Freeman and Herbert A. Tonne. In the first five chapters and in the final chapter all three authors participated to the extent that individual writing cannot be distinguished.

Grateful acknowledgment is made for the many fine suggestions that have been given by users of the first edition.

HERBERT A. TONNE
ESTELLE L. POPHAM
M. HERBERT FREEMAN

Contents

CHAPTER I

Introduction to
Business Education

IN THE SENIOR YEAR, the prospective teacher reaches the climax of his educational career—student teaching. Accounting, shorthand, business mathematics, finance, and other content courses were mastered to provide the background for this vital phase of teacher training. The business-education methods course, on the other hand, gives the specific preparation needed to teach the business subjects, first as a student teacher, and later as a regular teacher.

It is very important, therefore, to obtain a clear picture of the duties and functions performed by the business teacher. The first step in this process is to understand and appreciate the place of business education in our American system of education.

BRIEF HISTORY OF BUSINESS EDUCATION

During the Colonial period, some bookkeeping was taught in the Latin grammar schools in addition to arithmetic and penmanship. In large cities, many private teachers taught bookkeeping and penmanship. Otherwise, any business training was on an apprenticeship basis; the bookkeeper hired an assistant who learned on the job.

After the Civil War, business expanded rapidly; and bookkeeping became an important phase of business management. More bookkeepers were needed than could be trained under the slow apprenticeship system. Thus, the private business school came into the picture by providing courses in bookkeeping and penmanship.

When the typewriter was perfected in the 1870's and shorthand became a more valuable skill, the private business schools really began to flourish and expand. The enrollment in the private schools was largely masculine until the beginning of the twentieth century.

The private business schools had a virtual monopoly in the training of business students in the period up to 1910. When public high school enrollments increased, there was a demand that vocational business training be provided at public expense instead of parents having to pay tuition in private schools.

The early public high school business courses were almost carbon-copy duplicates of the private-school offerings. The first public-school business teachers were recruited from the private schools. Naturally, the methods and techniques used were also imported from the tuition-collecting schools. A course in the methods of teaching business subjects did not exist, because teacher-training institutions did not prepare business teachers.

The rapid expansion of business after World War I, in the early 1920's, brought with it rapid development of both public and private business education. Typing and stenographic courses were the most popular programs because of the constantly increasing demand for typists and stenographers in business, industry, and government.

During the depression years in the 1930's, more attention was paid to the personal-use, social, cultural, and general-education values, because so few public high school graduates could find jobs in business. Teachers were happy to find some justification for continuing the vocational courses, even though the purposes had changed. During this period typewriting became a highly desired addition to the general-education program, instead of being limited to vocational training.

PURPOSES OF BUSINESS EDUCATION

The historical development of business education pointed out that the original and major purpose of business education was to provide specific vocational training. It also showed that during the depression years business teachers found nonvocational justifications for offering business subjects. At first, the justification was referred to as a social-business objective. Business education was believed to contribute to personal-use and consumer values. Today, many business educators feel that some phases of business education contribute to the general education of all students.

Hence, the schools should provide two major types of business education: (1) training in those phases of business that concern every member of organized society, and (2) specialized instruction for those who wish to become wage earners in specified occupations. Promotional, or in-service, training for office and distributive occupations, as well as preservice training, are included in the latter category.

The following chart indicates these various goals.

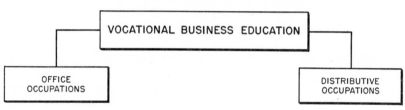

The goals of business education

THE GOALS OF BUSINESS EDUCATION

The first major purpose of business education is nontechnical and involves: (*a*) the education of persons to be intelligent consumers of the services of business and (*b*) a clear understanding of the nation's economy. The first objective is associated with the student as an individual; the second, with the student as a member of the community.

The second major purpose of business education is to provide specific vocational training. Business education for the job has two purposes: (*a*) training in specific job skills, and (*b*) achieving the ability to use these skills in the environment of business. The latter is often called "occupational intelligence." It is an aspect of social intelligence or social adaptability. For example, a stenographer must not only know how to take dictation and transcribe; she must also know how to get along with fellow employees and outsiders who deal with her company if she is to achieve job success. Although such occupational intelligence is more difficult to teach than specific job skill, it is the function of the business teacher to develop this phase of vocational training as much as possible.

Vocational business education can also be classified as follows:

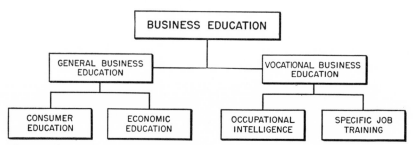

Phases of vocational business education

PHASES OF VOCATIONAL BUSINESS EDUCATION

Thus it will be seen that vocational business education is designed to prepare for two types of work: the office occupations and the distributive occupations. The need for the two phases is well illustrated by an analysis of occupational statistics in the United States.

PRESENT STATUS OF BUSINESS EDUCATION

One business subject or another is taught on almost every level of education—from the junior high school through the graduate school—in all kinds of schools—private, public, or parochial. The largest enrollments are in the public secondary schools, while the widest range of subjects would probably be found in the collegiate schools of business.

Over 33 million Americans were enrolled in private and public schools and colleges in 1952. According to a national survey in offerings and enrollments in high school subjects conducted by the U. S. Office of Education, there are over 3,000,000 individual subject enrollments in the various business subjects out of a total of almost 7,000,000 students in public, secondary day schools. This does not mean, however, that 46 per cent of all students are taking business subjects, because a considerable number of students take two, and even three, business subjects at one time. The proportion of students taking business subjects, therefore, is unquestionably less. About 50,000 business teachers are required for the 3,000,000 business students.

The principal subjects taught in the business program at present are: typewriting, shorthand, and bookkeeping, followed fairly closely by basic-business training and business arithmetic. The analysis shows that since 1933–1934 there has been some relative loss in enrollment for introduction to business; a slight decrease in the enrollment for business arithmetic, bookkeeping, and in most of the basic-business subjects. On the other hand, there has been a tremendous increase in the enrollment for typewriting. Almost one-fourth of the students in the last four years of high school were enrolled in typewriting. This heavy enrollment is probably due mainly to the emphasis on typing for "personal use."

It should be noted that when the enrollments for business law, economics, geography, and consumer education are combined, they total only 259,505. Even when the enrollments for introduction to business are added to the other basic-business subjects, they total only slightly more than the enrollment for shorthand. Adding all these subjects together, including business arithmetic and economics (listed under the social studies), the total enrollment for all basic-business subjects is much less than that for typing. In spite of our considerable emphasis upon the needs of basic-business education for all students, the fact of the matter therefore is that only a portion of all students taking traditional business subjects—typing, shorthand, and bookkeeping—are taking one or more basic-business subjects.

It will be noted that penmanship and the history of commerce are not even listed. It is to be hoped that the content of these important subjects, once so widely taught as part of the business program, is being integrated into other subjects in the high school. To what extent this is true is a matter of speculation.

Training for distributive occupations continues to be given major consideration in magazines and textbook discussions. The number of schools offering any kind of distributive training is, however, still small, although the George-Barden Act caused considerable increase in enrollments, especially on the post high school level.

The teaching of business subjects in the junior high school has not kept pace with the phenomenal growth of these institutions in recent years. Two business subjects are uniquely fitted to the junior high school program—typewriting and junior-business training; but the development of the core-curriculum concept has retarded the growth of specialized subjects. Of course, many thousands of students are enrolled in shorthand and typewriting on the post-secondary school level in junior colleges, in various forms of vocational institutes, in collegiate schools of business, and in liberal art colleges. Even more students are enrolled in accounting in these post-secondary schools. There are many additional thousands of students in management, basic business, office practice of various types, and in various forms of marketing and distributive education.

PROGRAMS FOR THE SMALL HIGH SCHOOL

In the small high school, offerings may be limited to typewriting, shorthand, and bookkeeping; for example, the business teacher may offer elementary and advanced typewriting, elementary and advanced shorthand, elementary and advanced bookkeeping, and basic business. Sometimes the course in advanced bookkeeping is dropped, and two periods of elementary typewriting are offered instead. Sometimes the course in basic business also is dropped. In order to include all subjects, two of the smaller classes not infrequently are offered at the same time. This type of program is undesirable. No teacher should give instruction for more than five periods a day. This is especially important in the small school where all the out-of-class work of the business department is done by one teacher.

A course in basic business should be basic and, therefore, should be the first subject to be presented. In many schools so many students wish to take typewriting that because of the few typewriters available, two periods of this subject must be offered. In some schools, shorthand should not be offered, because of a lack of job opportunities within the community. It must be realized, however, that many students do not stay in the local community if job opportunities are limited. In those areas shorthand should be offered to prepare students for jobs outside the community. In a small high school where facilities are limited, stenographic office practice should be offered instead of a second year of shorthand. This course should emphasize transcription and help build the basic skill. If the teacher is limited to five classes, this leaves out bookkeeping. To increase the offerings in many schools, elementary shorthand and secretarial office practice are offered in alternate years, so as to provide for a class in bookkeeping. Provision often can be made for offering stenographic office practice and a course in clerical office practice at the same time, so as to give the non-stenographic students much-needed training in adapting their learnings to the job needs. With a good course in office practice further developing the basic skills in shorthand, typewriting, and bookkeeping, there usually should not be a need for second-year courses in these subjects to bring students up to the minimum initial office requirements.

The program just presented does not provide training for merchandising. This is unfortunate; however, it is not wise for the teacher to spread himself too thin. This is all the more important in a small school. If the school is able to provide for another business teacher part time, then a more complete program may be offered. If the business teacher, however, must teach one or more other subjects, then the business program must be curtailed even more.

It must be realized that the program suggested above is far from ideal. It does, however, provide a minimum of job training with limited facilities. Of course, it should also be realized that individual adaptations can and should be made to meet community mind-set and local needs.

PROGRAMS FOR THE LARGER SCHOOLS

In large city schools there may be special curriculums in stenography, bookkeeping, merchandising, and general clerical work. In an increasing number of schools, however, formal curriculums are not so popular as they once were; and specialized sequences in business subjects are provided instead. In such a program, all students take the same academic courses like:

English	4 years
Social studies	2 or 3 years
Science	1 year
Mathematics	1 year

For the rest of his program the student may be required to take several sequences. This means he may take three years of one subject and perhaps two years of two other subjects. He may, for example, take a three-year sequence in stenographic training, one two-year sequence in bookkeeping, and a second sequence in merchandising. In a school offering this type of program, the student needs a great deal of educational guidance. There are numerous variations of business sequences. One such sequence for prospective *stenographers* might be:

Basic business	1 year
Typewriting	1 year
Bookkeeping	1 year
Shorthand	2 years
Stenographic office practice	1 year

Another for prospective *bookkeepers* might be:

Basic business	1 year
Typewriting	1 year
Business arithmetic	½ year
Bookkeeping	2 years
Clerical office practice	1 year
Salesmanship	½ year

A third for prospective *merchandising* workers might be:

Basic business	1 year
Typewriting	1 year
Business arithmetic	1 year
Bookkeeping	1 year
Salesmanship	1 year
Co-operative merchandising training	1 year

A fourth program for *general clerical* workers might be:

Basic business	1 year
Typewriting	1 year
Arithmetic	1 year
Bookkeeping	1 year
Salesmanship	1 year
Clerical office practice	1 year

It will be noted that these programs overlap considerably. Numerous variations could be suggested. For example, many business educators may insist that these programs include such subjects as the following: economic geography, business law, consumer education, advanced business training, business management, and operating a small business.

Such offerings are indeed desirable. However, it is becoming increasingly important to recognize that there must be a rich offering of core subjects in every high school student's program and that likewise there should be abundant opportunity for electives. Specific requirements, therefore, should be kept to a minimum.

The above suggestions are not offered dogmatically. Many business educators would disagree with one or more of the elements suggested. The attitudes of the administration, the community, the businessmen, the parents, and the students themselves are important.

The grade placement of business subjects may vary according to community preferences, but generally the prospective teacher may expect to find:

Typewriting—9th or 10th year
Shorthand—10th and 11th or 11th and 12th years
Bookkeeping—10th or 11th year
Basic or junior-business training—9th or 10th year
Business arithmetic—9th or 10th year
Economic geography—9th or 10th year
Business law—11th or 12th year
Salesmanship—11th or 12th year
Office training—12th year
Consumer education—11th or 12th year
Economics—11th or 12th year

The student teacher is most likely to teach:

Typewriting—elementary   Bookkeeping—elementary
Typewriting—advanced   Basic or junior-business
Shorthand—elementary   training

WHAT BUSINESS WANTS

Recently a group of businessmen were asked to list what they considered the minimum essentials of competency for beginning office workers. They suggested that a successful beginning worker should:

1. Possess skill in the fundamental processes. Beginning workers should be able to read directions understandingly, write legibly, spell correctly, solve simple arithmetic problems, and speak effectively. In addition, they should possess one business skill that has been developed to an occupational level and should have a basic understanding of business so that they can see their place in the office.

2. Use good work habits. Competent beginners should be able to do a day's work in a day and follow through to completion work that is started. They should start work promptly, organize their materials to reduce waste motion, and check carefully every piece of work to be released.

3. Have an employable personality. Beginning workers should dress appropriately for the office, exercise tact, display courtesy, and be dependable. They should have health habits that will promote job efficiency.

It is at once apparent from this list that businessmen place less emphasis than most business teachers on the building of a battery of business skills to a high level and attach more importance to maintaining and developing competency in the three R's and to implanting vocationally desirable character traits.

Businessmen want prospective workers to produce usable units of work in adequate quantity. Business teachers have failed to find out what the units of work are and what are considered adequate quantities of production. In too many cases businessmen have failed to be specific in their recommendations, partly because they do not know the answers themselves, and partly because teachers do not ask questions that require specific answers. To get more help from businessmen, teachers must be definite in the inquiries they make. It is their function to get the pertinent facts. When business teachers know what help they want in curriculum planning, businessmen are usually eager to co-operate.

QUESTIONS

1. How many high school students are taking business-education courses? How many secondary business teachers are there?

2. "The characteristic social lag is evident in the static high school program in the face of a completely different student body." Explain. Do you agree with this statement? Is the lag justified to some extent.

3. Where did business education first develop? Does this explain some of the characteristics of contemporary public-school business education? Which ones?

4. What are the objectives of business education?

5. Compare occupational statistics with high school business offerings. Why do more students take shorthand and bookkeeping than those subjects that prepare for the occupations entered by most people? Why are few students taking sales training in the schools when so many are engaged in some form of distribution?

6. Why should all workers in business have a good general education?

7. What is the contribution of basic-business subjects? Have you taken any basic-business subjects while in high school? while in college? Have they helped you get a better understanding of business? Have they made the skill subjects more meaningful? How? Be specific.

8. Do you believe that employers really are not interested in the stenographic and bookkeeping skills that students acquire in school and that all they are interested in is good character and general education? Why? Give examples.

9. What is the problem of setting up the business curriculum in the small high school?

10. A leader in business education recently said that if he were going into a small high school, he would "throw out all shorthand and bookkeeping and give the students some real business education, like business law, junior-business training, and farm bookkeeping." Do you think that he would be wise? Why?

STUDENT ACTIVITIES

1. Co-operate with a group of your fellow students and make an analysis of the various types of business workers in a local community. If the

community is quite small and the business section is primarily on one street and is not more than five blocks long, study the whole community. If the town is larger, take a similar section.

2. Work out a high school student questionnaire and ask one or more secondary-school business teachers for permission to give it to their students. Ask a few questions like the following: List the business courses you are taking. Why did you take them? Would you take salesmanship if it were given? office practice? Did you take junior-business training? Why or why not? What do you think are the values of bookkeeping? Analyze these answers in terms of the judgments made in this chapter.

3. Read what Nichols, Lyon, Lomax, and others (see Tonne, *Principles of Business Education*) give as definitions of business education. Do they agree with the statement given in this chapter? Work out your own definition and justify it.

4. Go to at least ten local businessmen and ask them what they want most in high school business graduates. Compare your results with those summarized in this chapter. Read what Tonne and Nichols give as the wants of the businessman. Compare these comments with those you obtained.

5. Inquire among at least twenty mature and respected members of your community as to their ideas of what the school should do in regard to character training in the schools. Evaluate these judgments in terms of the comments in this chapter and other readings given in the bibliography.

6. In co-operation with your fellow students obtain the business curriculums of at least five schools in the area served by your institution. Try to find out how the curriculums were determined. Evaluate them in terms of the standards presented in this chapter and other readings suggested in the bibliography.

BIBLIOGRAPHY

Business Education Program in the Secondary School, Bulletin of the National Association of Secondary School Principals. November, 1949.

Changing Business-Education Curriculum, Volume IV. The American Business Education Yearbook, 1947.

Enterline, H. G. *Trends of Thought in Business Education,* Monograph 72. Cincinnati, South-Western Publishing Company, 1949.

Harms, Harm. *Methods in Vocational Business Education.* Cincinnati, South-Western Publishing Company, 1949.

Hayden, Carlos. *Major Issues in Business Education,* Monograph 75. Cincinnati, South-Western Publishing Company, 1951.

Haynes, Benjamin R., and H. P. Jackson. *A History of Business Education in the United States.* Cincinnati, South-Western Publishing Company, 1935.

Knepper, Edwin G. "Historical Development of the Business Curriculum," *American Business Education Yearbook,* V, Chapter II, 1947.

Nichols, Frederick G. *Commercial Education in the High School.* New York, Appleton-Century Company, 1933, Chapters III and IV.

"Offerings and Enrollments in High School Subjects," *Biennial Survey of Education in the United States,* 1948–1950, U. S. Office of Education, Washington, D. C., 1951.

Principles of Business Education, Eighth Yearbook. National Business Teachers Association, 1942.

Tonne, Herbert A. *Principles of Business Education.* New York, McGraw-Hill Book Company, Inc., 1954.

Turille, Stephen S. *Principles and Methods in Business Education.* Staunton, Va., McClure Printing Company, 1949.

Walters, R. G., and C. A. Nolan. *Principles and Problems of Business Education.* Cincinnati, South-Western Publishing Company, 1950.

CHAPTER II

Introduction to

Teaching Business Subjects

THE FIRST CHAPTER introduced the prospective business teacher to the field of business education. It is the purpose of this chapter to acquaint the beginning teacher with the various elements he will work with in his business classroom. He must learn something about his students. What kind of students can he expect to find in the average high school situation? What must he know about their physical characteristics? What are their interests, desires, and needs?

After the prospective teacher knows his students, he must learn how to live with them in their daily meeting place—the classroom and the school. What are the student-teacher relationships of good teachers in the more progressive secondary schools of today? What can the teacher expect of his students, and what do they expect of him? The beginning teacher does not always know the right way and the wrong way to deal with his students in various situations. A bit of advice at this stage of his training can save him considerable grief and remorse later when he is on the firing line.

The beginning teacher must also learn how to organize and manage his classroom effectively, so that he can do his best job of teaching with the least amount of effort and lost motion. Good classroom management is primarily a matter of attending to many small details.

The beginning teacher should learn how to use the best teaching procedures and techniques. Much of teaching and learning can be fun if the teacher knows how to handle his part of the teacher-learning process.

THE HIGH SCHOOL STUDENT

What should every teacher know about every student? If he is teaching in a high school, he should know the more important characteristics that differentiate the teenager from the younger child and from the adult. In the high school of today students vary widely in ability and interests. In physical growth and development, however, they are quite alike.

Their "awkward age" is ending. The puberty period is largely completed in most cases. There may, however, be a period of glandular instability with wide fluctuations in energy level. Common ailments include headache, nosebleed, nervousness, palpitation, and acne. On the whole, girls tend to be about two years ahead of boys in physical growth and development in the early high school ages.

The behavior pattern of the high school "crowd" is very readily recognized. The high school student may have reached physiological maturity, but he lacks its experiences. He is intensely emotional. He may act as if he knew everything but inwardly he may be quite insecure. He is trying to find a place for himself in the life that surrounds and sometimes engulfs him. This may result in emotional instability at the time he is striving to understand social relationships.

The teacher must realize that the desire to conform to the standard of his group is stronger in the high school student than is his response to adult guidance. Some high school students respond more readily to the influence of a teacher than to that of a parent. There is a special tendency to form a close attachment to some adult considered to be outstanding in one respect or another. This tendency, naturally, can be used to good advantage; or it can be twisted and misdirected to the harm of both the student and the adult.

This age may also be labeled the "vain" age. The girls hunger for prettiness and beauty. The boys are eager to be tall, strong, healthy, and handsome. Both sexes are keenly aware of physical attractiveness and good grooming. Their ideas of good grooming may be based, however, on what the "gang" is wearing at that time. This keen interest in clothes and appearance brings with it a great awareness of money and wages. In average or low-income areas a large percentage of students may be employed on a part-time basis. Gone is the day when the high school student depended on parents for spending money.

Sexual manifestations in this age group frequently cause a feeling of self-consciousness. Since the girls are more mature at this age level, they seem, on the whole, to be more interested in boys than most boys are interested in girls. Many lack adequate sex information and guidance. Undue interest in sex may be caused by poor home and family relationships.

Anyone who has watched a group of teenagers in a restaurant knows that the appetite for food seems almost insatiable at this age. Nevertheless, there is a tendency toward an inadequate breakfast, if any. Adolescents are frequently concerned about "reducing" and "slimming" diets.

How does the teacher use this knowledge of his students? The younger high school students need unobtrusive adult guidance that does not take away the feeling from the student that he is an adult. He needs security and self-confidence but not at the sacrifice of freedom and independence.

The teacher must suggest worthy causes acceptable to the student, so that he will be willing to plunge his excess energy and emotions into the "cause." The school and community can profit from co-operative planning of a worth-while afterschool program. Parents may not believe it, but the rest needs of this group are about the same as those for adults—eight hours a day or longer. The teacher must remember that he is dealing with would-be adults.

STUDENT-TEACHER RELATIONSHIPS

How does the prospective teacher use his knowledge of psychological and physiological development in the process of living with teenagers in the school environment? The simplest answer to this question is, "Remember the Golden Rule." Too often, beginning teachers are likely to forget their own recent experiences as students. If they would only treat their students in the same way they wanted to be treated by their teachers, much tension would be relieved. Unfortunately most of us have very short memories. We soon forget the pet peeves we had against our teachers and commit the same mistakes we criticized when we were students.

A more detailed explanation of the Golden Rule may be very helpful to the beginning teacher at this point. Ignore the recently circulated impression that all high school students are, "crazy, mixed-up kids." That is not true. You must have faith in human nature, or you should not be a teacher. Adopt an attitude of good faith rather than one of suspicion and scorn. While it is true that no two students are alike, most of them are normal and sensible human beings. They are constantly searching for a feeling of "belonging" in any new class. They may try to cover up this craving by putting on a brave or bold front. Actually, however, the teacher who understands youth can easily earn their undying gratitude by making them feel important in that class.

The teacher must be just, courteous, and highly professional in all relations with his students. He should consider their individual differences, needs, interests, temperaments, aptitudes, and home environment. But he should be master of the classroom situation at all times. This may require a very firm hand at the beginning. It is much better to be too strict at first than to be too easy. You can relax your restrictions just as soon as you feel that the situation is under control at all times.

When the teacher is in full control of the class, the need to discipline and rebuke students constantly will disappear. Continuous disciplining is bad, because it is not fair to most of the students in the class who usually behave well. Behavior problems should not be dealt with in class. The student who is out of step with the rest of the class should not be given an opportunity to show off in public. He should be invited to come in for a private conference. A face-to-face talk in the privacy of an office is a much better way to resolve differences and misunderstandings than any open classroom battle. The teacher must appeal to the student to act like an adult, seeking a sensible solution to his behavior problems.

The beginning teacher must see each student as an individual. Learn his name as soon as possible. Always treat every student with courtesy. "Please" and "Thank you" are magic words even in the classroom. The teacher is not a master barking out orders that his slaves—the students—must obey. The classroom situation should be democratic, rather than autocratic. A teacher cannot force a student to learn. Whatever success the teacher achieves will depend on his skill in earning the respect of his students, rather than by demanding or commanding their interest and attention. Every student in a class is more important than any subject, and no student should ever be humiliated because he lacks ability in a certain subject.

A good teacher always gives praise for work well done. On the other hand, he never compares a good student and a poor one. He generally tries to help students who have been absent from class because of illness or for other good reasons. He seldom makes threats; but when he makes one, he keeps his word, because where there is a threat, there must be a penalty for the student who deviates from the rule.

The professional relationships between a teacher and his students call for the same high type of behavior that is expected of the doctor or the minister. A good teacher never discloses information obtained confidentially from his students. He does not tutor students in his classes or even in the same school for pay, nor does he refer students to members of his family for tutoring.

A good teacher never discriminates among students, either on the basis of personal likes or dislikes, or because of poverty, race, color, or creed. There are times, however, when he makes allowances for poor achievement, because the circumstances seem to warrant special consideration. He tries to develop sympathy, tolerance, patience, and understanding in his work with students.

It is very tempting for a young teacher to listen when students talk in a critical manner about other teachers or other students. A good teacher discourages such gossip and refuses to be a party to it. He never "dates" students in his school. Intimate social relationships should be avoided with students of either sex. A teacher should be friendly with pupils but must at all times retain his dignity on which none may trespass. When a teacher permits students to become too familiar with him, he makes it difficult for them to develop the proper respectful attitude toward him. He should refuse to accept favors from pupils that will put him under personal obligation to them.

A good teacher is above everything else a considerate person. He likes to know why he is asked to do a task and therefore lets his students know why they are asked to undertake a particular activity. He is considerate of their feelings. He remembers that students are at times tired, discouraged, upset, and irritable. At such times he learns "to have eyes and to see not," "to have ears and to hear not." Too many young teachers make a mountain out of a molehill.

CLASSROOM ORGANIZATION AND MANAGEMENT

Knowing how to deal with students is an important phase of the teacher's job, but he must also know how to arrange and manage the physical factors in the teaching-learning situation. Students and teacher cannot work well together when the physical conditions in a classroom are not conducive to good learning. The good teacher must also be a good housekeeper if he wants to create the best environment in which learning can take place.

Many beginning teachers do not realize that it is their responsibility to regulate the physical conditions in the classroom. The temperature of the room and its ventilation are important factors in creating and maintaining a good teaching environment. Naturally, the adjustment of natural and artificial lighting also contributes to the physical comfort of the students. Such commonplace domestic duties as removing waste from desks and floors are a part of the teacher's daily routine. On a slightly higher plane, perhaps, comes the care of chalk boards, bulletin boards, bookcases, shelves, maps, pictures, and other decorative accessories.

There are many routine duties apart from housekeeping that require the teacher's attention. Reducing this work to a minimum and using efficient procedures will preserve the teacher's time and energy for his major task of teaching.

On the very first day of class the teacher should seat students according to some plan. From many seating arrangements the teacher can select:

1. Alphabetic seating—seat according to last name.
2. Ability grouping—seat according to ability.
3. "Choose your own partner"—let students sit where they like.
4. "Buddy system"—pair a "slow" student with a "bright" one.
5. "Work station"—sit where the job is.

Many arguments can be presented for and against each plan. Suffice it to say that the teacher should use the system he feels will save him the most time and energy in conducting a particular class. One of the reasons for a definite plan is to help the teacher to learn and to remember every student's name just as soon as possible. Pointing at students is awkward and sometimes confusing.

The wise teacher uses student assistants at every possible opportunity to help with such routine tasks as collecting and distributing materials and supplies. Some teachers even use students to help grade test papers and, on some occasions, to help other students who are having difficulty in learning certain procedures. The final responsibility rests on the teacher; but students like to help, and doing this work may even motivate the better students to become teachers.

TEACHING TECHNIQUES

Every class should start promptly and continue at full operating speed until the bell rings (or some other signal is given) at the end of the period. Experienced teachers have the work so well planned that students get busy as soon as they enter the room. The new assignment is on the board, which they must copy. A review problem is on the board which must be solved at once. While the student is occupied, the teacher has an opportunity to take attendance and get organized for the job at hand.

The good teacher knows that he must provide continuous activity of one kind or another for every student in the class, or he may have trouble on his hands. Keeping everybody busy is the simplest way to reduce and eliminate discipline problems.

The experienced teacher knows that the average beginning teacher talks too much. A good teacher talks only when his students are listening. He talks only when he has something important to say. He talks in specific terms illustrating every point he makes. He talks in the simplest language possible but with dignity and authority in his tone. He talks clearly and at a moderate rate of speed, but he talks vividly and dramatically. He gives his students every opportunity to talk while he listens.

The good teacher plans every lesson carefully in advance, so that every period is adequately and constructively filled with learning activity. As he acquires teaching experience, his lesson plans become shorter and less complete; but he plans in advance for each class period no matter how many years he has taught the same subject.

The good teacher has learned the art and science of watching his class every minute of every period. He is constantly alert to anything and everything going on all around the classroom. He can spot a potential troublemaker before the resolution to create a problem is more than a gleam in his eye. He knows that he must control the class from the first minute of the first period in September to the last minute of the closing day in June. There is no royal road to good classroom control except through constant vigilance and intelligent action by the teacher. Knowing that every student question deserves immediate attention, the good teacher never fails to recognize a raised hand.

The good teacher uses the chalk boards constantly. He also uses all the teaching aids that are available in his school. He makes it his business to find out what resources are available, and then he makes good use of them.

The experienced teacher knows that the average class period is not long enough to provide for the total learning situation. Consequently, he finds it necessary to make homework assignments from time to time. He makes sure, however, that every assignment is essential. He does not make it unless it is to serve a useful learning purpose and not just to punish a class or to provide busywork. When he must give an assignment, he makes it clear and definite. He tells the students exactly what is to be done and how it should be completed. He previews the assignment carefully in class before the students start on it. He may actually do some of the assignment with the students. The next day he makes sure that the assignment is reviewed thoroughly. He seldom grades homework, because it is a learning and not an evaluating device. If many students had difficulty in doing the assignment, the teacher will reteach the new material presented previously.

The experienced teacher knows that he must proceed very slowly, because the average high school student of today is not a fast learner. The teacher must be sure that the whole class is with him before he starts a new unit. He also knows that no two classes are alike. He has discovered that it is almost impossible to keep two sections of the same subject at exactly the same point day after day. Every new class presents a new challenge.

It is this constantly renewed challenge that makes teaching such an exciting adventure for the real teacher. He is constantly on the alert to find better ways of improving instruction. He learns every day he teaches; when he stops learning, he has already stopped teaching.

HUMAN RELATIONS

Teachers are rarely failures because of inadequate knowledge of subject matter. The outstanding reason for failure in teaching is inability to get along with fellow teachers. The second most frequent reason is inability to get along with students. The third most frequent reason is inability to get along with the administration.

Teaching is often a process of doing what the administrator wants you to do and getting students to do what you want them to do. Of course, the important thing in both cases is that these things be done willingly and with enthusiasm. The field of business for which we are training students is primarily a matter of human relations. Business is a process of supplying people with their wants. These wants are supplied in terms of people's emotions and wishes rather than in terms of cold and inhuman commodities.

The administrator of a school—the principal or the superintendent—is primarily concerned with human relations. It is his job to get the board of education to realize the problems of students and teachers. It is his problem to get teachers to recognize the problems of the community in supplying the school with taxes. Even more important, it is his problem to get students to work with teachers, parents to co-operate with the school, and teachers to understand the problems of students and parents.

In human relations there are no perfect solutions. We can find a perfect answer in working out a bookkeeping problem, at least in the textbook problem, but this result is not possible in human relations. There are no perfect human relations; there are poor human relations and poorer human relations, good human relations and better human relations.

It has been said that nine-tenths of getting along on the job is personality, and one-tenth ability. Like most half-truths this statement can sometimes be more false than correct. For example, it has been said that a stenographer is successful primarily because of good personality and only incidentally because of ability to take dictation. This is basically unsound. The reason why personality seems more important is that, once a person has the minimum ability in shorthand needed for the job, the personality factors on the job loom larger. If the person does not have competency in stenography, the person is dismissed; and personality does not get a chance to operate. Personality and competency in doing the job are equally important. The tendency to minimize competency results from a failure to understand the elements of competency in getting along with people. There is truth, however, in the statement to the extent that we have given much attention to teaching people the work of the job and comparatively little attention to learning how to get along with people while they are doing the job. We must, therefore, emphasize human relations; that is, ability to get along with people, in accomplishing the work of business and the work of teaching for business in the school.

Individual Differences

If there is any single key to good human relations, it is treating each person as an individual. Each child, each teacher, and every supervisor and administrator lives an individual life and has interests other than those with which the teacher is immediately concerned. These other interests affect his conduct in the classroom and in the office. If we are to acquire the good will of another person, we must recognize that he is the center of a universe different from ours, just as he must, in order to get along with us, recognize that we live in a universe of our own.

Sometimes it is very difficult for us to understand the nature of another person's personal universe. Each of us has different purposes. Sometimes we, of necessity, mask the kind of inner life we have. In certain respects we are all alike in that we want food, sleep, adventure of some kind, recognition from other people, security, and the like. But when we interpret these different needs, each of us is different from the other. It is, therefore, all the more important that we have great tolerance for other people. This is especially important when we do not understand the causes that make them act as they do. That is why psychiatry has become so important in contemporary life. The psychiatrist is a skilled technician in discovering why people act the way they do. As a consequence, the psychiatrist is often able to help people to accomplish more effectively what they really want to do in relation to other people.

It is necessary for us to attempt to develop understanding of other people's problems. That is why we must go out of our way to be fair with other people and yet recognize that it is almost impossible to be completely fair. Beware of the person who says: "I am always fair with other people. I never try to put anything over on other people." That person is very naïve, because it is almost impossible to be always fair with others, simply because we do not understand that other person's mentality, that other person's motivations. The person who recognizes that he is often unreasonable with people is in a far better position to be fair and reasonable and have an understanding of other people than the person who assumes he is always fair to other people.

Sometimes we must accept partial failure in coping with other people. We must recognize that time solves many problems for us. This is particularly true in a classroom. Sometimes we want to solve a problem in a single period. If we would just have patience, the next day would bring a solution. Sometimes we get overwrought because students are irritable or restless. They may be restless just because the weather is bad or because they have been excited in another class. The following day the weather may be better, and the preceding period may have been peaceful. It is therefore wise not to try to rush solutions to problems; although on the other hand, we must not let things carry on too long.

In establishing good human relations, then, we must have respect for others. Even the least able student in the classroom must be treated with consideration. If he feels that students and teacher have lost respect for him, then he is lost indeed. We must accept students as they are, not as we would like them to be; but at the same time we must work for improvement. Teachers sometimes say when students are not in school, "Isn't it peaceful, isn't it wonderful without the kids?" Yes, it is peaceful, but the very purpose of the school is lost if the students are not there. The school exists only for the very purpose of working with students. If there were no learning problems, there would be no school.

Obviously also in working with people, we cannot be dogmatic. We must recognize the infinite varieties in human conduct. We must always realize that each person has a different series of causations that make him act the way he does. Nevertheless, in not being dogmatic we must still insist on standards that are adjusted to the individual for whom we have provided the standards.

Handling Human-Relations Problems

It is important for teachers not to tempt students into mischievous conduct. For example, when we threaten students time and time again and do not carry out our threat, we are simply tempting them into trying us the more. Students will naturally see how far they can go; and if they know the threat is just a threat, they will keep on acting up until the teacher is completely exasperated and attempts a form of punishment that is basically unwise.

Our great grandfathers said, "Spare the rod and spoil the child." There was possibly a grain of truth in this statement; but carried to its rigorous conclusion it is not only a dangerous, but also a false, precept. Children need recognition and attention. They respond far more to reward than to punishment. "Children should be seen and not heard" was another adage of our great grandparents. It also has a germ of truth in it. There is a time for quiet in a classroom and a time for excitement. Unless students are heard, unless they react positively, learning does not take place. The process of learning is an active process, not a passive one. Students, therefore, should be heard as well as seen. It is far more important for the students to do much talking and undertake much work than for the teacher to talk.

The foundation for solving individual human-relations problems is to get the facts before judgments are made. Without an understanding of the facts, we are likely to be failures in human relations because we do not make our decisions in terms of the purposes. In order to get relevant facts, we need to know what we are trying to accomplish. When we are disciplining a child, are we disciplining in order to get personal satisfaction? Are we disciplining the child for the sake of discipline, or in order to accomplish worth-while learning? First, we must decide what we are trying to accomplish; and if the accomplishment is one that is meaningless, it is wise to skip it. We should create problems for ourselves only when there are real problems. Far too many of us make problems that are unnecessary, problems that will solve themselves in time and place. In getting the facts, then, to solve a problem, provided it is a problem worth solving, we must review the record of the student. We must find out what kind of individual he is. We must talk with the student himself and cautiously with the other students who may be concerned in a particular problem. We must find out the rules by which the students operate. As we know, the principles and rules that students practice are quite different from those that teachers think are right. It is inevitable that students having different purposes in schoolwork will have different standards. We must be certain we have the whole story before we even try to think about making a decision.

After we have all the facts that bear on the specific problem, we must put the facts together. We must ask ourselves to what extent the school practices and policies are being contradicted or the extent to which any specific practices and policies relate to the problem. Then we must consider all possible methods that we can use in solving a problem. We must consider the effect upon the individual, upon the group, and upon achievement of classroom learning. Above all we must not jump to conclusions. After we have decided on the type of action to take, if any action is to be taken, we must ask ourselves whether we should undertake the action ourselves or ask some other teacher, the principal, or some of the students to undertake the action. Do we need help in undertaking the action? Is this the right time to undertake the action? Above all, if we have decided that we are the ones who should undertake the action, we must not pass on our responsibility to somebody else.

Finally, after we have taken this action, we must check to see its effect. What have we accomplished? Have we done more harm than good in taking the action? Has it helped to achieve better teaching conditions for us and better learning conditions for the students?

Only if it does this and still helps to develop the total personality of the individual is a particular disciplinary action effective.

In dealing with students at school, we must let them know how they are getting along. We must let them know what they are expected to do and point out ways of improvement. Obviously we must give credit when due. If someone does an extra-good job, we must let him know immediately and publicly, if possible, that he has done something worth while. The influence on the individual is much greater if he is praised immediately rather than if the praise is delayed.

If we are going to change our assignment or going to ask students to change their seats, we must let them know, if at all possible, about changes that will affect them and why they are being made. We must give them a chance to accept the change quite willingly. Obviously we must make use of each person's ability in terms of his total capacity. We must constantly observe whether students' abilities are being used. If we have a student who has an ability that is not being used, we must try to bring it into the classroom situation; above all, we must never stand in the way of a student's reasonable expectations. If students are ambitious, even though the ambition is not the kind we approve, provided it is reasonably acceptable, we must help to develop that ambition rather than hinder it. As indicated at the beginning of this chapter, we must always treat people as individuals.

Getting along with students in school, getting along with other teachers, and getting along with the administration is a never-ending task. We sometimes say, "Wouldn't it be wonderful if we didn't have to work with other people?" No, it would not be wonderful; it would be terrible. We must get along with other people if we are to be happy. This is true of children; it is true of adults; and, of course, it is most true of ourselves. Not all students can like us all the time, but most of the children should like us most of the time. If not, we are not successful teachers.

There is no easy answer for good human relations in a school. Sometimes there are problems that cannot be solved. If there is no solution to a particular difficulty, we must accept it and not let it bother us too much. However, the technique presented above will often give at least a partial solution. If there is no solution, we must just do the best we can.

In many of the chapters that follow, you will notice many more suggestions for good human relations. Emphasize them in your thinking. Try to practice them as a student right now and when you go out to do your practice teaching, try to follow them as much as possible.

Effective practice is just as important in developing good human relations as it is in learning shorthand or bookkeeping. Remember whenever you work with another teacher, student, or administrator, you must ask yourself, "Did my action help to improve my teaching and the student's learning? Did it help me to get along with others and, more important, did it help the student to get along better with his fellow students in attaining better learning?"

QUESTIONS

1. How does the "Golden Rule" apply to teaching?

2. In what respect is the role of the teacher similar to that of a doctor or a minister?

3. What are some of the routines connected with good classroom management?

4. What is your opinion of the statement, "Learning is an active and not a passive process"?

5. Does the old saying, "Variety is the spice of life," apply to the classroom situation?

6. Do you agree that the good teacher must first be a good policeman?

7. What should the good teacher know about homework assignments?

8. Should a beginning teacher keep two sections of the same subject together? Why?

9. Is a teacher with ten years of teaching experience necessarily a better teacher than a first-year teacher?

10. How can a good teacher provide for individual differences?

11. What is the relationship between good discipline and good teaching? Suggest five business-classroom activities not mentioned in this chapter that should become basic routines.

STUDENT ACTIVITIES

1. Prepare a report on, "My Favorite Teachers and Why I Liked Them."

2. Prepare a report on, "The Teachers I Disliked and Why."

3. Develop a report on, "The Teacher's Code of Ethics for Dealing with His Students."

4. Select any five of the basic principles of teaching and elaborate on them.

5. Read Harold Spears, *Some Principles of Teaching,* and list at least ten additional principles that appeal to you.

BIBLIOGRAPHY

Alcorn, M., R. Houseman, J. Schunert. *Better Teaching in Secondary Schools.* New York, Henry Holt, 1954.

Bahr, Gladys. "Suggested Classroom Teaching Methods and Techniques in Basic Business Education," *Improved Methods of Teaching the Business Subjects,* Monograph 63. Cincinnati, South-Western Publishing Company, 1945.

Dvorak, Earl A. "Orientation of Newly Graduated Business Teachers," *Balance Sheet,* XXXVI (November, 1954), pp. 106–107.

Engeman, Donald R. "Some Problems of the Beginning Teacher," *Tri-State Business Educator* (November, 1954), pp. 16–25.

Fields, Harold. "A New Teaching Rating Record," *Business Education World,* XXXV (November, 1954), 20–23.

Forkner, Hamden L. "A Self-Scoring Checklist of Professional Competency for Business Teachers," *Balance Sheet* (October, 1944), pp. 52–54.

Gress, John. *Teaching Difficulties of Beginning Business Teachers,* Monograph 78. Cincinnati, South-Western Publishing Company, 1952.

Grim, P. R., and J. U. Michaeles. *The Student Teacher in the Secondary School.* New York, Prentice-Hall, Inc., 1953.

Hosler, Russell J. "Factors Involved in the Selection of Prospective Business Education Teachers," *NABTTI Bulletin J8,* 1953, pp. 15–18.

Satlow, I. David. "What Does the Supervisor Look for in His Classroom Visits?" *Balance Sheet,* XXXV (April, 1954), pp. 349–350.

Schorling, Raleigh. *Student Teaching.* New York, McGraw-Hill Book Company, Inc., 1949.

Spears, Harold. *Some Principles of Teaching.* New York, Prentice-Hall, Inc., 1949.

Supervising Student Teachers in Business Education, National Association of Business Teacher-Training Institutions, Bulletin 60, 1954.

CHAPTER III

Effective Procedures in Teaching Business Subjects

IN THE PREVIOUS CHAPTERS the prospective business teacher was introduced to the field of business education and to some of the general elements that make up the classroom situation. He is now ready to study some of the specific competencies he must develop if he is to become a successful teacher.

LESSON PLANNING

A good teacher will not insult the intelligence of a class by not being fully prepared to make the best use of every minute of every period. This goal can be accomplished best by making a written plan for each period to be taught. Because many teachers frown on the formalistic type of lesson plan, they go to the opposite extreme and make inadequate plans. A simple lesson plan can be a good one.

A lesson plan is the individual teacher's road map. An experienced teacher may need only brief notes to remind him of the key points in the journey. The inexperienced teacher, on the other hand, must make as many and as detailed notes as he will need to make his daily lesson a smooth and successful teaching and learning expedition. Sometimes the lesson plan may be brief enough to put on a card.

This suggested plan is no great burden on the teacher, and yet it contains the essential elements of the lesson. Remember that a beginner may need far more specific details in the presentation section.

OUTLINE OF LESSON PLAN

1. *Subject, Period, and Date*
   Bookkeeping I, 3d period, Sept. 23.
2. *Purpose*
   To teach posting procedure
3. *Previous Learnings*
   What do we know about journalizing?
4. *Presentation*
   a. Use journal entries completed at home.
   b. Point out the need for classifying the entries into accounts.
   c. Demonstrate how to set up accounts.
   d. Demonstrate how to post.
   e. Post with the class the journal entries completed at home.
   f. Summarize the important points in this lesson.
5. *Assignment*
   a. Read pages 0–00 about posting procedure to review today's lesson.
   b. Complete Problem xx on page 00 started in class on the same paper.
   c. Read carefully the questions on page 00 but do not write answers. Be ready to discuss the questions in class.

Must a teacher always stick 100 per cent to the lesson plan? No. The lesson plan is only a guide; it must not become the master. It is usually wise for beginners to plan more material than can probably be covered in a period, and in this way never run out of ammunition in an emergency. Most beginners accelerate their teaching pace when they are being supervised. The experienced teacher can improvise easily; but the beginner, like a boy scout, must always be prepared.

CHOOSING A TEXTBOOK

Despite all the criticism that has been directed at the misuse of textbooks, the fact remains that a beginning teacher usually needs and should use a good basic text. Unfortunately, many schools do not provide beginning teachers with the best teaching materials available. Very often, also, the beginning teacher is given the responsibility of selecting a new textbook for his course.

Any attempt to evaluate a textbook in terms of exact number of points is as unscientific and probably as meaningless as attempts to give one person, for example, a rating of 89 in personality and another the rating of 79. There are too many immeasurables, too many varying factors to be evaluated, and too many local conditions to be considered.

Nevertheless there are some general questions that the teacher can ask himself in deciding which of several textbooks to use. Here are four areas that should be considered.

1. *Subject Matter.* Does the book in your judgment appeal to the student? Does it have flexibility, so that it can be adapted to various purposes? Most important, is the wording of the subject matter suitable to the high school student? Is it neither too elementary nor too advanced? Is it realistic in its terminology? Is the subject matter expressed in terms of students' interests and backgrounds? Does the textbook offer opportunities for differences in assignment? Is the subject matter up to date; that is, does it recognize current practices, or, for example, does the text still talk about 2/10, net/30 discounts, which were characteristic of the 1920's, and are most unusual now?

2. *Content and Format.* Is there a good index? Does the table of contents have a good outline? Are the topics arranged in an intelligent sequence that appeals to you and one that goes from the simple to the complex? Are there periodic summaries? Are the discussion questions meaningful? Are there enough questions? Are some of them really significant questions? Are they related to the subject? Are there enough problems? Do the problems vary in difficulty? Are they sufficiently comprehensive? If a glossary is in order, is it complete and related to the subject? If charts and drawings are included, are they varied? Do they appeal to the students? Can they be used to further develop the subject? Are the pictures and illustrations clear and appealing? Are the supplementary assignments meaningful?

3. *Aids to Learning and Teaching.* Are the tests adequate? Are they appropriately priced? Are they reasonably standardized? Can

they be graded easily? In other words, do they follow the criteria for tests set up later in this chapter? Are the workbooks worth while? Do they cost too much? Do they repeat themselves? Do the manuals really help the teacher present the subject adequately? Are they readily available to teachers but not available to students? Is there a helpful teacher's manual with suggestions for teaching, as well as a key?

4. *Physical Make-up of Textbook.* Is the binding attractive, and will it wear? Is the book of correct size? Is the type clear and readable? Will the paper wear well, or will it rip as soon as it is used? And finally, what is the cost of the textbook in relation to other textbooks that might be bought for the same subject?

QUESTIONING

A good teacher knows how to stimulate the learning process by asking good questions. There is a definite art in asking questions. Beginning teachers will experience much success and joy in teaching if they practice and acquire competency in this area.

1. Ask the question first—then call on the student.

2. State the question clearly, concisely, and in terms suitable for the students in that class. Most beginning teachers use college-level vocabulary.

3. Try to avoid vague and general questions like, "What about insurance?" or "Are there any questions?"

4. Ask questions that require more than a "Yes" or "No" reply.

5. Try to pull in all members of the class. Solicit volunteers and call on those who are reluctant to answer questions.

6. Allow enough time to let students think about the answer. Do not ask and answer your own questions.

7. As a rule, do not repeat questions.

8. Do not repeat student answers. Force the student to speak up if he cannot be heard.

9. Ask questions in a calm and patient manner. Do not frighten students with questions fired like bullets.

10. Encourage students to ask pertinent questions.

11. Be courteous in conducting a question period. Try not to cut off student discussion. Avoid discourteous interruptions.

12. If possible, try to answer a question when the student asks it, rather than at some later time.

13. Encourage shy students to ask questions and give praise for good questions or replies.

14. Encourage students to question your statements when they disagree with you. Do not sound as if your answer is the final word on the subject.

15. When you do not know the answer to a question, do not be ashamed to admit it. The students know when you do not know the answer even if you do not tell them.

16. Answers should be made to the class and not to the teacher.

17. Always relate questions to student interests and experiences.

18. Do not give grades for the answers to questions.

19. Vary the questions you ask. The following are suggested types of questions:

    a. *Comparison or contrasts*
    What is the difference between a check and a note?

    b. *Decision for or against*
    Do you think it is right to say that banking is essential in American business?

    c. *Application in new situations*
    Suggest ways of using multicolumn journals in a small business.

    d. *Classification*
    What do the following written statements have in common— blank, full, restrictive, or qualified?

    e. *Relationships including cause and effect*
    How does the failure to record depreciation affect capital?

    f. *Example or illustration*
    Describe instances of good manners.

    g. *Statement of aim*
    Why do we teach posting before journalizing in the equation approach?

    h. *Criticism*
    What are the most common errors usually made in typing figures?

    i. *Inference*
    What would happen to a business that continues to show a net loss?

    j. *Discussion*
    What would happen in Hometown if all banks closed?

    k. *Outline*

What are the steps in making a bank reconciliation?

l. Definition and explanation

What is a liability? Give examples of business liabilities.

m. Recall

Who was the father of modern bookkeeping?

n. Summary

What steps would you take if you had to mail a large package?

o. Observation

What were the bookkeepers doing in Hometown Department Store?

ASSIGNMENTS

In former days the teacher was not so much a teacher as a lesson hearer. While this condition still prevails to a certain extent in many schools, it has been largely remedied. The instructor is becoming less and less a task setter and more and more a teacher. Within recent years, the assignment given the class has been receiving increasing attention, so that now some educators consider the assignment to be the most important part of the lesson. In fact, it may often be looked upon as *the* lesson. When, however, the entire lesson is viewed as the assignment, the term loses much of its significance. Perhaps it should be considered only a part of the classwork, that part in which the students under their own guidance prepare for the complete understanding, or mastery, of the lesson. The assignment involves the idea of completion of the work already studied, as well as the preparation for the unit that is to be developed in class.

It is probably still a rather common procedure for a teacher to assign the next ten to twenty pages without motivating the lesson or indicating the objectives to be achieved during the study period, although both should be included. The assignment should be specific and definite, so that the student knows exactly what is expected of him. If teachers themselves would prepare the exercises before assigning them, their requirements might sometimes be more reasonable.

Assignments should be made with the psychology of the subject well in mind: *The learner must know toward what he is working.* Just telling the student to write five lines or ten lines of a typewriting drill will accomplish little. He should know what the copying is expected to achieve. He may be using the same material, but at one time he is striving for stroking facility only; at another he is working for the elimination of errors.

PROVIDING FOR INDIVIDUAL DIFFERENCES

Even in classes that are arranged on some basis of homogeneous grouping according to ability, there are wide variations in learning ability. This means that the teacher must recognize these variations and teach accordingly.

Slow Learners

There are many reasons for classifying some students as slow learners:

Reading difficulty	Difficulty in generalizing
Failure complex	Poor health
Fear of school	Emotional disturbances
Fear of the teacher	Physical or mental overload
Fear of the subject	Inadequate background of skill or
Immaturity	information
Lack of interest	Poor home conditions
Lack of initiative	Unreasonable standards
Inability to handle abstract ideas	Personality conflicts with teacher or
Inadequate memory	students
Limited imagination	Frequent absences
Short-attention span	Inferiority complex

The slow learner can be helped if the teacher wants to help him. Here are some suggestions:

1. Find out why he does not learn.
2. Show a personal interest in the student.
3. Simplify the instructions, so he can understand them.
4. Give him a feeling of success.
5. Never make disparaging remarks about him.
6. Explain each assignment very carefully.
7. Provide remedial reading assistance.

8. Give short, but frequent, tests.
9. Give him plenty of time and help.
10. Modify the standards, so he can hope to meet them.

Gifted Learner

The child with unusual academic or special abilities is usually neglected in public schools because mass education must provide for so many average or slow learners. A good teacher can help the gifted child even in a large class.

1. Expect the gifted child to do better work than you accept from other students in the class. This may not seem fair, but it is for his benefit.
2. Give the gifted student an opportunity to assist you as a teacher. This may take the form of tutoring, helping with demonstrations, preparing special reports, or building collections and displays.
3. Encourage gifted students to volunteer for school-service projects. They may even be released from class for this purpose.
4. Encourage gifted students to participate in extracurricular activities.
5. Find out from parents or administrators what you can do to help the gifted child.

USING AUDIO-VISUAL AIDS AND COMMUNITY RESOURCES

It would take many pages to sketch even briefly the many teaching aids that are now available to the business teacher. The following list is intended merely to give some indication of the types of material available.

Doing Materials

1. *Specimens and models.* Many real business forms and materials can be collected for class use.
2. *Mock-ups.* A simple telephone can be constructed to show the principle behind a real telephone instrument.
3. *Exhibits.* Displays of advertisements, sample products, bookkeeping records, and other business materials make interesting class exhibits.
4. *Demonstrations.* How checks are cleared by banks or how to sell ties can be easily demonstrated in class.

Seeing Materials

1. Pictures, sketches, cartoons, posters, diagrams
2. Chalk boards
3. Bulletin boards
4. Charts
5. Graphs
6. Maps
7. Globes
8. Filmstrips
9. Opaque projectors

Hearing Materials

1. Tape recordings   2. Disc recordings   3. Radio

Seeing and Hearing Materials

1. Sound motion pictures
2. Combination of filmstrip and tape recordings
3. Television

Field Trips

The business field trip is a carefully planned activity in which students leave the classroom to study a business organization or activity in the community. It has great value to:

1. Bridge the gap between school and community
2. Correlate book learning with reality
3. Provide source material for additional study in the classroom
4. Stimulate interest in various industries
5. Lead to possible vocational choices
6. Help the class work together in planning, conducting, and evaluating the field trip
7. Create interest in classroom work

Community Surveys and Service Projects

Many business teachers extend the work of their classroom to the community by co-operating in making community surveys. Other business teachers supervise the completion of community service projects. The typewriting teacher may direct students who type Community Chest envelopes or March of Dimes literature.

TESTING

Tests are the tools of the teacher by which he measures his students' knowledges and skills. Tests also yield very useful information about learning difficulties and may be used as a basis for further teaching. One of the outstanding deficiencies of testing is that it has been used too much as a means of measuring rote learning rather than as a foundation for diagnosis of further learning needs.

Testing is an integral part of the entire teaching process; and testing that is looked upon as a climax rather than as a phase of the teaching process is, by its very nature, merely a basis for grading and record keeping. While the keeping of records and the giving of credit for accomplishment have their places in today's schools, they should not be allowed to take the place of the primary function of testing: diagnosis as a basis for readaptation of teaching in order to improve learning.

A warning about testing should be given, especially to the beginning teacher. Testing is not teaching and should not be substituted for it. Many business teachers do not differentiate between the two. The recitation is not lesson hearing; it is a part of the learning process. In a skill-building course, the teacher should concentrate on the development of the techniques that produce the skill, not on too frequent speed tests that measure the skill. In social-business classes, study and recitation time are devoted to organization and assimilation of the material prior to testing.

Pretesting. Instruction in any class should begin at the level at which the teacher finds the student. Tests, then, are useful in determining that level. Whenever subject matter is of a general information type, such as that found in most of the business-background classes, a pretest serves to enlighten the teacher as to the amount of subject matter already known to his class and also as to the confusion existing in the minds of the learners. He recognizes areas that will require special emphasis. A second value of the pretest is that it reveals to the student his weaknesses and awakens in him readiness to learn. For instance, the review of grammar in a business English class may not appeal to students at first; they may feel that they have studied English for seven or eight years and review is not necessary.

Yet, if they are given a pretest, they are made aware of their need for learning. If the test at the end of the course covers the same points as the pretest, the teacher can measure the effectiveness of his teaching; and the student can measure the effectiveness of his learning.

Theory and Performance Tests. Tests in business subjects may be of two types. One measures the student's information about the subject; the other measures his ability to apply his information in a use situation. In a bookkeeping-theory test, for example, the student is asked to check a certain square if increases in assets are recorded as debits and another square if they are recorded as credits. In a performance test he is asked to journalize transactions involving increases in assets, and his knowledge of increases is measured in this way. In a performance test, too, he completes blocks rather than segments of actual work.

The advantage of the theory test is that the teacher can cover more subject matter during the testing period. The disadvantage is that test conditions do not approximate work conditions, that a student who knows the theory answers may be such a slow and inaccurate worker that he cannot take a trial balance within a reasonable time, and therefore he cannot keep books.

Probably the teacher should use both types of tests during the training period, gradually increasing the relative number of performance tests as the student approaches the end of the course.

Objective Tests. The making of a reliable objective test requires a great deal of time and effort. Often the services of the textbook companies in business education include tests based on their textbooks. Many excellent tests are available, and the teacher should develop a file of useful ones. He should, however, adapt the test so that it actually measures his teaching. If he is going to use a test including a section on proofreading, then he should teach proofreading before he gives it. If he is going to test for mailable transcripts of dictation that is given over a sustained period, then prior to the test his class should be trained in the substitution of words that make sense in the taking of untimed dictation over a longer period than the traditional five minutes.

For many purposes the self-constructed objective test is better than the printed one. Perhaps several printed tests can be adapted to the needs of the occasion, but the teacher should remember that copyrighted tests may not be duplicated.

STEPS IN PREPARING AN OBJECTIVE TEST

1. Determine the aims for which the subject has been taught.

2. Set up a table of specifications of the materials to be measured.

3. Obtain a list of questions in great excess, if possible, of the number finally to be used. This list may be developed while the daily teaching goes on. As the teacher prepares his lesson and as he checks over his work to see whether the topic has been fully treated, he will come across many valuable question items.

4. Select from this basic material those items to be used.

5. Classify them according to the specific type of test, such as true-false, recall, and so on. This will be an easy step if each question in the tentative list of items is put on library-size cards.

6. Decide on the length of time to be devoted to the test and choose the number of questions to conform. Perhaps there will be enough questions for two forms of the test.

7. Organize the test material and work out specific instructions.

8. Set up a key for the test.

9. Develop a basis for transforming into grades the scores that result.

10. Plan for diagnosis as a basis for remedial teaching.

After an informal objective test has been given, it may be standardized. It is not assumed that the usual teacher will standardize tests. The following steps are given as a basis for further study.

1. On the basis of a sufficient number of test results, determine the central tendency and the deviation.

2. Determine the correlation of the two forms used and of the odd items of each test with the even items.

3. Eliminate the weak items that decrease the correlation.

4. Check in some manner or in several ways for validity.

5. Continue Steps 1 to 3 to achieve additional refinement.

Comparatively few formal and printed tests have been developed in basic-business subjects. Several workbooks have been published in connection with textbooks, which give the basis for organizing testing material and may in part themselves serve the purpose of measuring student achievement.

Essay Tests. Although the new-type test has certain advantages, such as objectivity and ease of grading, many people favor the essay type of examination because it enables the student to organize his subject matter, to receive credit for information in excess of average standards, and to improve his expression.

In the construction of the traditional written examination, the teacher will find his work considerably improved if he observes the following points:

1. Check work to see that as many of the major topics as possible are covered. Nonessential details should not be asked at the expense of the vital points. Leave out catch questions.

2. As far as possible, ask questions that involve thought rather than a mere tabulation of facts.

3. Provide opportunity for everybody to answer something. There should be material difficult enough to make even the brightest student do his very best.

4. Set up the questions in simple form, so that they will have the same meaning for all students.

5. Allow ample time for the test, so that students are not penalized for being slow unless time is a factor in the test.

6. Give careful directions. The teacher is not trying to test the students' ability to take tests; he is attempting to measure their attitudes toward, and abilities in, business.

7. Write out correct answers before beginning to check papers. This will give the teacher a standard against which to rate the papers.

8. Mark question one on all papers before question two is taken up.

9. Use a comparative system of grading, such as excellent, good, fair, poor, bad; and do not attempt further differentiation of results than this. Remember the distinction between a score and a grade. A student may have received a score of ninety points out of a possible hundred and still have one of the poorest papers in the class. He should, then, receive a low grade.

10. Make notes of the students' errors. These notes will serve as a basis for remedial teaching.

If these suggestions are observed, the essay examination will be found satisfactory for most classroom purposes when supported by the judgment of classroom work and occasional new-type tests.

Grades. Typewriting teachers formerly utilized most of the class period in checking papers, not realizing that the cause of the error and not the error itself should be the point of attack. In the beginning stages of any skill-building subject, probably few papers should be graded. The assignment of a grade shifts the emphasis from the development of correct techniques to the acquisition of accuracy at the expense of both technique and speed. On the other hand, it is obvious that a teacher cannot chart his students' course without looking over their daily work to determine their progress and their needs. In any skill-building course, the work is divided into drills for improvement in technique, speed, or accuracy and into exercises in which the application of the skill is made. Probably drills should never be graded—they are learning activities, not testing devices. Let the measurement come from the exercises.

Teachers can easily become slaves to their students' papers and may even decrease their classroom efficiency by wearing themselves out by carrying papers home every night. It cannot be denied, however, that the teacher who shirks this part of his obligation will find unchecked errors on typewriting and transcription papers, *f's* written for *p's* in shorthand assignments, and incorrect totals on bookkeeping trial balances that, when added, do not yield the totals recorded. However, all through the course more and more of the responsibility for checking student work should be placed on the student himself. Businessmen complain constantly that employees cannot see their errors. How can they be expected to discover them if, when they were in school, the teacher always found them?

Checking student work in class can constitute an effective learning exercise if the work is expeditiously done. Some teachers assign a fellow classmate to each student as his proofreader; and each paper is supposedly read by its author and by its proofreader, who signs it before it is submitted to the teacher.

After work has been checked, it represents a valuable indication of the student's learning needs and should serve as the basis of individual assignment for the correction of errors. Unless such use is made of the returned papers, they serve little purpose and will be tossed into the wastebasket without further study. It seems only logical to assume that if correcting the papers was worth the teacher's time, then the student has an obligation to learn from the corrected paper. One successful teacher requires that all corrected papers be resubmitted to him at the end of the semester with the stipulated corrections made. For example, if a necessary comma was omitted on a transcription paper, the student in his corrections states the rule or principle involved and gives two original sentences illustrating its application.

In skill-building courses, teachers often overlook the importance of grading their students on technique—they think that a student's written work only should be measured—and as a result poor basic techniques are acquired. They overlook the fact that what the drill does to the student is of greater importance than what the student does to the drill.

In basic-business classes, too, grades have been assigned too often for written work only. Yet an oral report may be just as worthy of a mark as a written test.

In other words, many components are included in a grade. For that reason, some teachers have found the point system a satisfactory method of grading. Points are assigned for all the elements that comprise the grade. At the end of the semester the cumulative points are added and the grades are assigned.

COLLECTION OF INSTRUCTIONAL MATERIALS

Another element of good teaching is the development and filing of instructional materials. Business education is a dynamic, living, and changing thing. No sooner is a social-business textbook published than part of it becomes obsolete. The successful teacher, then, must be an avid reader who uses his scissors constantly to clip materials from current publications, who keeps an up-to-date bulletin board, who encourages his students to bring in outside supplementary material, who keeps some post cards on hand for ordering it, who evaluates what he finds, discarding some things and keeping others. He maintains contact with the business life around him.

Perhaps the most essential piece of equipment for the business classroom is some type of filing cabinet. The filing that a business teacher practices is not necessarily the alphabetic arrangement of a series of miniature letters; it might better consist of building up a functional subject file for use in his classes.

Manila folders are used. The captions on the index tabs should be the most likely names or subjects by which the material will be called for. The names of the various subjects taught usually form the best general headings. Then the particular aspect of the subject dealt with forms the first subdivision. Other subdivisions may follow. For instance, the Turse Prognostic Test in Shorthand might be filed "Shorthand, Tests, Turse Prognostic." Obviously this material would be found more readily than if it were filed under "Turse." A pamphlet named "Using Advertising Effectively" might be filed under "General Business, Advertising, Using Advertising Effectively."

Suggested instructional materials that might be included in the business teacher's file are: a collection of actual business forms used in the community; such as, checks, leases, ledgers and journals, notes, Social Security cards, income tax forms, simple contracts, various types of insurance policies, and charge plates; newspaper reports of Congressional action on postal regulations, telegraph service, or taxes; cartoons stressing office behavior or dress; copies of unusual business letters or direct mail advertising; old school programs and athletic schedules that may be used for tabulation assignments; publications of the local chamber of commerce; and successful lesson plans.

QUESTIONS

1. How can the teacher avoid the confusion of activity and learning? Give an example of an activity that you feel was busywork, unrelated to learning.

2. What should be included in the lesson plan? How can time be conserved in planning lessons?

3. What are the requirements of a good assignment?

4. What is the result of the teacher's failure to differentiate between testing and teaching?

5. Explain the difference between a theory test and a performance

test. What are the advantages and disadvantages of each type? When should each be used?

6. What steps should be followed in constructing the objective test?

7. What papers should be graded in a beginning skill subject? Which ones should be checked? Why should the teacher grade technique rather than students' work?

8. How can students be taught to assume much of the responsibility for checking their work?

9. What current materials may be contained in a business-teacher's files? How are they filed?

10. What is the place of audio-visual aids in teaching? What cautions should be observed in using them?

11. Suggest specific instances in which the following visual aids would be effective: chalk board, maps, charts, graphs, films, slides.

12. What are some of the items that should be considered in evaluating the subject matter of a new textbook?

13. What are some types of questions that can be used by a business teacher?

14. What are the characteristics of a slow learner, and how should a slow learner be handled by a teacher?

15. What can a business teacher do for gifted students?

STUDENT ACTIVITIES

1. How would you provide motivation for a lesson on (a) introducing of disjoined prefixes in shorthand, (b) matching transcription rate with copying rate, (c) introducing the special cashbook in bookkeeping, and (d) developing criteria for the selection of a place to put your savings?

2. Examine the files in your college business-education department. Prepare a class report on the teaching materials that you found there and the filing methods used.

3. List the elements that you would consider in assigning grades for the first semester's work in typewriting, shorthand, basic business, and bookkeeping.

4. Prepare a list of ten audio-visual aids you think would be effective in a particular situation. If possible, see the films and slides before listing them.

5. Construct twenty-five objective test questions based on the subject matter of this chapter.

6. Collect five pieces of instructional material to be used next year and index them properly.

BIBLIOGRAPHY

Bell, Robert P. "Professional Education Courses and Beginning Teachers' Problems," *The National Business Education Quarterly,* XXII, No. 3 (Spring, 1954), pp. 36–40.

Gress, John J. *Teaching Difficulties of Beginning Business Teachers,* Monograph 78. Cincinnati, South-Western Publishing Company, 1952, 105 p.

Hall, J. Curtis. "Stimulating Future Professional Growth Among Student Teachers," *NABTTI Bulletin LX,* 1955, pp. 56–61.

Hardaway, Mathilde, and Thomas Maier. *Tests and Measurements in Business Education.* Cincinnati, South-Western Publishing Company, 1952, 434 p.

Toll, Lewis R. "Advance Planning for Modern Teaching Aids," *United Business Education Association Forum,* VIII (January, 1954), p. 6.

Young, William M. "Some Standards for Good Teaching," *Journal of Business Education,* XXX (October, 1954), pp. 17–18.

CHAPTER IV

Basic Skill-Building Procedures

WHILE PREPARING FOR TEACHING, the student reads a great deal of educational philosophy, visits a number of classes, and discusses the various educational theories. He also takes a number of courses in psychology and tries to determine how all these materials can be assimilated to serve him best in the classroom.

Naturally he has heard a great deal about democracy in education, the need for teacher-pupil planning, and the importance of the pupil-centered classroom. In all probability he subscribes completely to the need for developing better citizens and for fostering democratic practices. He realizes that pupils learn best through activity and that they assimilate subject matter best when they are solving their problems. He recognizes that knowledge is not something that is poured in and that pupils are not passive receptacles into which the teacher empties wisdom. He understands that learning takes place when the learner is pushing back the horizons of his environment and discovering his place in the world around him.

He probably abhors the old concept of the authoritarian classroom presided over by the autocratic teacher. He has a genuine desire to become a teacher who implements the theories and philosophies to which he subscribes. But how? He wants to learn the best methods for achieving this goal.

DEFINITION OF METHOD

"Method" has been variously defined and discussed. Methods courses have been taught, and many words have been written and spoken on the subject. In business education much has been said about the "whole" method versus the "part" method, the "traditional" method, the "functional" method, and dozens of other methods. "Methods" to some people mean tricks of the trade. That, however, is a very narrow view, as method in the best sense involves a great deal of "why" and leaves much of the "how" to the individual teacher. Method is irrevocably tied up with psychology and the study of the learning process. It is the procedure by which the teacher meets the learner at his level, starting with his interests and his problems, and then establishes conditions that enable him to proceed to reach set goals in as effective a manner as possible. It is the application by the teacher of principles by which learning takes place.

THE NATURE OF SUBJECT MATTER

Before a teacher can determine the best method of presenting material for learning, he must analyze subject matter, which falls into two categories. In one category, the teacher is developing skills —how to swim, how to typewrite, how to play golf, how to take shorthand notes, how to change a typewriter ribbon, how to pilot an airplane—all in expeditious ways that will bring satisfaction to the performers. According to *Webster's New International Dictionary,* Second Edition, Unabridged, skill is defined as "the ability to use one's knowledge effectively and readily in execution or performance; technical expertness; a power or habit of doing any particular thing competently."

In the other category, in fact, in most cases, the teacher is developing knowledges, understandings, and attitudes. His method in business classes is to provide background experiences relating to the business world in general and to the local business community in particular. He plans various enrichment materials for his students in terms of their interests; he develops with them standards for evaluating their field trips, outside readings, visual aids, panel discussions, and other teacher-pupil planned activities that characterize the class period.

Even in the skill-building courses, before a student can use his acquired skills, he must have attained the knowledges, understandings, and attitudes acceptable in the business world or in his own circle, depending on where he is planning to use the skill.

No one course is mutually exclusive. Typewriting is not entirely a skill-building course. Certain parts of typewriting, however, *are* skill building and should be taught in accordance with the principles of skill building. One can hardly believe that a student would elect a course in typewriting unless he was interested in developing basic skill in typewriting. Of course, he can and should learn democratic procedures in typewriting class; he can and should use typewriting to work assignments and to perform activities that he and not the teacher initiates; but in most cases the primary reason for his electing to study typewriting is to develop "competent excellence in performance." Primary emphasis should be placed on teacher-directed sessions devoted to building skills that can later be used in solving problems in teacher-pupil planned activities.

The same statement may be made of shorthand. Even more than typewriting, shorthand attracts students who want to acquire a skill, the ability to take dictation. The shorthand teacher who succeeds best will be the one who employs the principles of skill building; but certainly shorthand would be incomplete without knowledges, understandings, and attitudes. A person cannot be a successful stenographer unless he *understands* English usage and punctuation, unless he *understands* form and arrangement, unless he has developed self- and class-imposed, rather than teacher-imposed, standards of mailability, unless he has learned how to work with other people. All these elements are part of the shorthand course, but they do not alter the fact that it is necessary for the shorthand teacher to adhere to the principles of skill building when dealing with the skill aspects of the subject. Basic skill must be developed before problem solving is introduced.

To the business teacher in training, then, it is important that these principles be presented and analyzed thoroughly. After the discussion of skill development in any field (equally applicable to typewriting, filing, roller skating, piano playing, jujitsu) skill building relating to specific business subjects will be discussed in chapters relating to these subjects.

While some consideration will be given to methods of teaching knowledges, understandings, and attitudes in the introductory chapters, the primary consideration of these topics will appear in later chapters.

TEACHING FOR MASTERY

Mastery is necessary before a skill can function. A typewriting teacher tells of a boy in one of his classes who consistently typed until the machine locked at the end of the line and then threw the carriage. He would type "si-" on the first line and "ze" on the next. When he was admonished both to listen for his bell and to use his margin release so that he would divide words only at the end of syllables, he said, "Oh, yes, I know all about the theory of the margin release, but I just never have used it." While this is an extreme example of the need for overlearning, it is indicative of a weakness in much of our business teaching—too much theory and too little application.

In business classes, however, not all facts that are brought to a student's attention need to be mastered. For instance, in a class in basic business, the teacher may attempt to develop criteria for selecting a savings institution. In illustrating the techniques to be used, students may discover that the local building and loan association paid 3½ per cent interest last year. Obviously this fact is incidental to creating adequate atmosphere and broader comprehension. To require that students remember this bit of information is not only wasteful but actually may interfere with the complete learning of those facts that have been selected for mastery. The teacher's first job is to differentiate the subject matter that is of basic importance from that which is to be used for illustrative and enrichment purposes.

Necessity for Mastery. When it has been decided what subject matter is to be taught for mastery in the schools, the material should not be pursued merely to the threshold of learning. If it is, it will soon be forgotten. It must be so thoroughly mastered that it will remain with the learner. Perhaps the idea may best be illustrated diagrammatically. Refer to the diagram with explanation at the top of page 52.

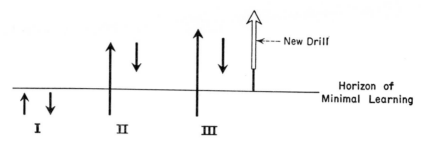

Explanation

I. If the student learns only to the horizon of minimal learning, the law of forgetting becomes operative at once, and he soon loses what he has learned.

II. However, if he overlearned well above the horizon of knowing, he will still forget but will not fall below the level of minimal learning.

III. In a related learning unit, application is made of the skill learned in II; and with new drill provided, the student not only reaches his primary competence but may go beyond it.

The Mastery Formula. Securing mastery in learning is accomplished by using, in some form or other, the basic mastery formula: [1] *pretest, teach, test the result, adapt procedure, teach, test again, and continue to the point of actual learning.* By pretesting, the teacher determines the needs of the students. Then he presents the required subject matter and tests students to determine their mastery of it. If he finds that they have not yet learned, he realizes that he has not yet taught and carefully adapts his procedures before his second presentation. The effectiveness of this reteaching is tested again. If mastery has not yet been achieved, the process is repeated.

Sometimes a test is not a test in the formal sense in which a teacher usually thinks of it. For instance, in shorthand the reading of homework that contains a review of the principles and brief forms previously covered in the course is the teacher's test and is a very adequate basis for determining the need for further teaching. Observation of transcription or typewriting technique may be a test in the sense of the mastery formula, and need for further teaching is predicated on such observation.

[1] Henry C. Morrison, *The Practice of Teaching in the Secondary School*, p. 79.

Many teachers stop short of mastery. In their classes, education is on a take-it-or-leave-it basis. Without pretesting or diagnosing needs, they teach and test; they fail to adapt their procedures and reteach; they do not retest. Of the six steps in the mastery formula, they use only two, *teach* and *test;* and they certainly do not achieve mastery. The beginning teacher who wants a guiding principle for his lesson planning may well adopt this formula.

BUILDING SKILLS

Much of the current philosophy in education is based on the idea that the educative process is largely training in problem solving. The student is presented with a situation in which he needs to learn how to do a certain thing; he realizes a felt need; consequently, learning takes place.

A teacher of skills who subscribes fully to this view might on the first day in a typewriting class direct the discussion to the uses to be derived from the course; the students decide that they should have a typed class schedule pasted inside their notebooks or a typed bus schedule posted on their bedroom wall, so that they will not be late for school. The typewriting class, then, would begin its training with an exercise in tabulation. Or in shorthand, the students might on the first day wish to learn to write each other's names in shorthand. The course would start with the writing of any new word in which the students expressed interest.

These examples are, of course, absurd illustrations of the theory that all learning is problem solving. They do, however, serve to emphasize the point that should be clearly understood by all skills teachers at the outset: *Before problems requiring the application of a skill can be solved, the learner must acquire a certain facility in the skill.* The first step in the solution of his problem is the formation of habits that best initiate the skill. Any attempt to apply nonexistent skill to practical situations fails of its purpose and even cripples the student's ultimate capacity. While problem solving is a very important part of the occupational-skills program, it is preceded by drill, which forms the habits upon which the skill is based. The skills classroom is the place where the elements comprising the skill are isolated for development before being put into a composite situation. Any successful teacher of skills must reconcile this point of view with the educational theory of problem solving. Otherwise he will, like Sancho Panza, ride off in all directions at once.

When has a skill been mastered? Mastery has been achieved when the skill can be exercised although something else is uppermost in the mind. Walking has been mastered when a person can walk while carrying on a conversation. Typing has been mastered when a person can type a letter without giving active attention to the location of the letter "y," when he can set up a tabulation without directing his thought to the correct fingering of the numerals. A learner has mastered shorthand when he can take dictation while his mind is occupied with the thought involved in the material being dictated. When shorthand has really been mastered, there will be no more senseless transcripts in which notes are misread because one character resembles another. A master of shorthand would have his mind free to absorb the meaning, even to correct minor errors in dictation.

The real test, then, of a skill is the ability to use it in problem solving. Mastery of a skill is measured by this criterion.

Achieving Mastery. It was pointed out previously that six steps are necessary to achieve mastery: pretest, teach, test the result, adapt the procedure, reteach, retest, and continue to the point of actual mastery. Basically this is the technique employed in the successful teaching of skills. Sometimes, when entirely new material, such as tabulation, is first introduced, the pretest is not used. After the initial presentation of the techniques, however, succeeding lessons dealing with tabulation start with a pretest. The pretest may often be oral.

The use of the mastery formula is fundamental to the skills teacher. Much of his teaching is done through demonstration. He shows rather than tells; then the students practice the demonstrated technique. After they have practiced, the teacher can test the effectiveness of their learning.

Before skills are sufficiently automatized, they usually must be retaught several times. In typewriting, for example, when the teacher is attempting to build technique he may determine the weaknesses of his students by observing them at work (a form of testing their technique). Then he redemonstrates the basic drills, such as carriage return or capitalization, to improve responses until mastery is attained.

The rest of this chapter deals with the principles of skill building that the teacher should observe in adapting the mastery formula to his teaching.

Order of Emphasis. In attempting to build a skill, teachers have probably been placing the emphases in the wrong order. Many of them concentrate first on accuracy, second on speed, and third on technique. In grading they certainly follow this sequence.

There is considerable evidence to indicate that the order of emphasis should be reversed, so that at all times technique is of paramount importance. If technique is developed, speed and accuracy are natural concomitants. The correct order of emphasis in teaching any skill should be: first, technique; second, speed and accuracy. Speed and accuracy are not ends in themselves; they come as the result of control.

Motion Pattern of the Expert. The business of the learner is to analyze the motion pattern of the expert and develop in himself that pattern. All efforts in a skill-building course should be directed toward developing in the student a concept of what that pattern is. One experienced teacher testifies that she learned her typewriting under the old "perfect copy" routine. This meant handing in every day a set number of lines of drill material containing not more than two errors to the page. She really never knew what the pattern of the expert was; she had never *seen* a teacher demonstration of good technique; she had never *heard* correct key stroking; she had never *felt* a word pattern. As she studied courses in the improvement of instruction in typewriting, as she saw performances of teachers and expert demonstrators, as she studied rhythm patterns of superior typists, she gained the concept of the action pattern of the expert; and her copying rate increased fifteen words a minute with hardly any practice. In other words, as soon as she knew what she was striving for, she began to achieve her goal.

A parallel may be drawn in the other skill courses. The learner must know the correct "get away" of an expert shorthand writer; how he holds his writing instrument; how he turns the page. Results in transcription have been disappointing because the subject has scarcely been "taught" until very, very recently. Students were given shorthand dictation and herded into the typewriting room to transcribe without any instruction in reading in thought groups, handling of materials, placement, or any of the many other aspects of this very complex process. Few teachers demonstrated correct transcription techniques, probably because they did not possess such techniques; they did not themselves know the action pattern of the expert.

In vocational bookkeeping, which is largely a skill-building subject the action pattern of the expert is also necessary. How can the learner most expeditiously journalize, post routine entries, and strike a trial balance? He should analyze the action pattern of the expert. It seems paradoxical that typewriting classes are largely devoted to the development of basic skill without enough emphasis on occupational skill, while bookkeeping classes seldom strive to develop any speed. In bookkeeping, the completion of trial balances and work sheets as well as other timed exercises is a valuable activity.

Enough has been said about the need for acquiring the pattern of the expert. Are there general characteristics of this action pattern? The answer is emphatically "Yes." The main features of all expert performances, as they have been revealed in many scientific studies, are:

1. Establishment and maintenance of a steady, even flow of motion. All practice should be directed toward the acquisition of such a flow, even in the initial stages, at the expense of accuracy.

2. Easy and economical movements.

3. Relaxed performance unhampered by nervous tension and hurry.

4. Concentration upon the task at hand.

5. Intelligent use of the senses. The expert sees, hears, and feels each correct technique employed.

All experts do not have exactly the same techniques, but all expert performance has these broad elements in common. Of course, "expert" in this connection does not mean exclusively the speed champions. The word refers to the person who achieves superior performance. Any teacher of skills will supposedly be "expert" in the sense that he can show his students the pattern they are trying to achieve.

TECHNIQUES IN TEACHING THE EXPERT'S PATTERN

It is essential that proper techniques by which the learner may acquire the pattern of the expert be employed. The most important of these techniques are discussed below.

1. *The Teacher Must Recognize the Factors Comprising the Pattern.* Obviously, he cannot make himself articulate to his pupils, so that they can understand what they are trying to do, if he himself does not recognize the components of good technique. He cannot help them analyze their practice efforts if he does not recognize which of the movements used are aiding them in mastering the skill and which are impeding their progress. Without this discernment, he cannot guard the learner against wrong approaches and direct him toward right ones.

2. *The Teacher Should Be Able to Demonstrate the Pattern That the Learner Is Trying to Attain.* Teacher demonstration is the most economical method of presenting a skill subject. A good skills teacher is characterized by the talking he does *not* do. Too much talk by the teacher is possibly the greatest hindrance to successful teaching of skills. Hours are saved by demonstration, for it is quicker and clearer to show how than to tell how. Furthermore, students have confidence in the teacher who can perform and give tangible evidence of mastery of his subject matter. How much more respected is the expert typist than the teacher who said to his students when they asked for a demonstration, "Certainly not. I have been all through the learning of typewriting. It's up to you to do all the typing that is done around here."

The typewriting teacher should be able to type at the levels that he demands of his students; the shorthand teacher should be able to write correct and fluent chalk-board outlines and take dictation with his classes. The transcription teacher should be able to demonstrate correct transcription techniques before the group; the office-machines teacher should be able to display occupational competency in the operation of the dictating machine or the calculator.

The teacher should remember, however, that the real learning process involves pupil activity and that his demonstration is for the purpose of showing *how* and not for the purpose of showing *off*. He should avoid the use of any demonstration that does not contribute to better student practices. As the course progresses, he will need to demonstrate techniques less and will assume a more passive role as he points out either basic or supplementary student techniques that require correction.

3. *In Presenting Subject Matter, the Teacher Must Appeal to as Many Senses as Possible.* In that way he can increase the number of stimuli to correct student responses. Also, it is a well-known psychological fact that everybody does not learn in the same way. Some people are visual minded; in fact, most people are visual minded; and appeals that involve seeing are usually effective. Others learn best through hearing; and still others have a strongly developed kinesthetic sense. For these reasons, the instructor should teach through the use of as many senses as he can. In shorthand, for instance, the student hears a word; he watches the action of the teacher in writing it; he observes the written word; he sometimes traces the word as he spells it out. In typewriting he learns correct stroking by seeing the demonstrator's hand and arm position, by hearing a clean-cut stroke, by looking at the keyboard and getting the "feel" of the reaches before he attempts touch typewriting.

4. *Group Drills Are Useful Only to Establish the Desired Patterns; Individual Drill Is More Beneficial After the Learner Understands What He Is Working to Attain.* Many skills teachers use group or unison drills extensively. However, it is believed by authorities in the field that group drill is valuable only to set the action pattern of the expert. After brief unison drill to establish the desired pattern for the work that is to follow, students should proceed to work out, under the teacher's constant supervision, their own best methods of practice. Two reasons may be given for this. In the first place, few students have the same rate at which optimum results may be achieved; and the teacher's standard may be too slow for the best students whereas it is too fast for the slowest workers. Secondly, there is no one best way for *all* students to practice. What produces effective results with one type of learner may not be the best procedure for another. One student may need to drill on one type of material while another needs to focus his attention upon entirely different subject matter that is difficult for him.

Even in shorthand this principle can be followed to some degree. With dictation records and tapes available for dictation, the class can be divided into groups working at drill levels best suited to their individual abilities.

5. *Students Should Work at the Speed Just Below That at Which Confusions Begin to Appear and Just Above That Which Is Characterized by Labored, Detailed Movements.* The question of the rate at which a skill should be practiced is a highly controversial issue. Many beginning teachers make the mistake of encouraging practice that is too fast and of trying to force a nonexistent skill. Probably more err in the opposite direction and allow their students to practice too slowly.

The solution to the problem lies in the basic concept that the learner should strive for the action pattern of the expert. This pattern involves working easily and rhythmically without stoppages or hesitations. That is why typewriting textbooks caution beginners to "Keep the carriage moving." That is why, before students write shorthand as they are taught by the Functional Method, they have seen the teacher demonstrating rhythmical chalk-board writing and have studied rapidly written plates. That is why suggested timings are given in most skill-building textbooks. That is why unison drill precedes individual drill. A satisfactory speed, then, is "any rate that just reaches the point above which confusions begin . . . and below which laborious detailed movements appear." It must not be forgotten that speed itself is not the objective; control is. When control is achieved, speed will develop.

It must be admitted that the early diffuse movements of a learner are not yet expert movements. Constant refinements in technique are necessary before expert motions are really achieved; but practice sessions in which drill is directed toward such action patterns will go far toward eliminating the key puncher in typewriting, the "looker-upper" in transcription, the drawer of shorthand notes.

6. *Each Period, Indeed Each Segment of the Period, Should Have a Definite Objective of Which the Students, as Well as the Teacher, Are Aware.* The students' needs for different types of drill change. When classes merely drill, however, without knowing the expected outcomes, they do not have so great an incentive for their practice nor do they approach it so intelligently as when they have been told the reason for their participation in the assigned activity. The purpose of the drill should always be kept before them.

The first few minutes may be spent on the reconstruction of the subject matter of the previous day. This may be followed by speed-up practice. The next part of the hour may be devoted to the consolidation of the material into composite use. The time just before the bell rings may be used for the introduction of new material that requires a certain length of time before it can be absorbed. Or, in developing a skill, the teacher may use a cycle of drills in which one technique is emphasized each day. Or, in using a textbook, the class may use the same material at one time for speed emphasis; at another, for accuracy drill; at still another, for technique practice. The important thing is that everybody should know toward what he is striving while he is practicing; otherwise students may be attempting to attain diametrically opposed objectives at one and the same time.

Recently a student teacher was observed conducting a drill to increase typewriting stroking speed. After the first writing, he instructed his class, "Now, this time try to increase your rate two words a minute and also reduce your errors." Here was a confusion of objectives. Of course, the teacher would have liked to obtain increased speed as well as increased accuracy; but the chances are that he was unable to achieve these two goals through the same drill. When he was driving for speed, he had to concentrate on that objective. Accuracy, on the other hand, is usually increased through control drills in which the class is expected to reduce its speed below "spurt" rates.

7. *Repetition Without Conscious Direction Is of Little Value.* Although repetitive practice is very important to the building of any skill, mere repetition does not guarantee learning. It simply affords an opportunity for learning.

When shorthand teachers ask their students to write five lines of each brief form in the lesson as homework, they discover the truth of the above statement. The last lines are not so well executed as the first ones. In fact, they are often illegible. There is much of the psychology of skill in the old story of the student who was required to stay after school to write the correct perfect tense of "go" on the chalk board two hundred times. After the two hundredth "have gone," he wrote at the bottom of the chalk board, "Teacher, I have finished and have went home."

Attention must be focused on the goal to be achieved if repetition is to be worth while. Members of a shorthand class complained that they had to spend so much time in writing drills to be handed in that they had no time to study the subject matter. When it was suggested that the assignment had been made to facilitate learning, each student testified that he wrote the drills first and then went back over the material to study it as time permitted.

Repetitive practice as a speed-building device is, however, very, very important. The repetition of a paragraph in typewriting when the learner is striving for a definite and attainable goal is one of his most effective means of achievement. It is only when the repetition is not purposeful that it is useless and sometimes even harmful.

8. *Practice Time Must Be Broken into Short Drill Periods.* In learning a skill, practice time must be distributed. Ten short periods of drill are more effective than one period ten times as long as the short period. Research studies have shown that in high schools results achieved in double periods of typewriting are not commensurate with the extra time spent in the learning process.

When World War II started and stenographers were badly needed for Government work, some men in charge of speed-up suggested to business educators that shorthand be taught for eight hours a day. It is obvious that the authors of such proposals did not understand the psychology of skill. A period of absorption is necessary before the fixing of any skill can be accomplished. The time factor must have a chance to operate.

This is true even in segments of lessons, as examination of almost any skill-building textbook will show. For instance, in typewriting the location drills are presented near the end of the day's lesson because of the maturation period that is necessary before the new keys become familiar to the learner. These location drills give the student a sense of what is to be acquired rather than final and perfect results. On the following day, the lesson opens with a review or reconstruction of the learning of the previous day, now placed in a new framework or setting. Practically the same parallel can be drawn from shorthand textbooks.

9. *Drills Must Be Varied Before the Law of Diminishing Returns Starts to Operate.* If a single type of drill is continued for too long a period, attention begins to wander; and expected gains are not forthcoming. For this reason practice time must be carefully dis-

tributed within the single learning period. Examination of a recent textbook in an elementary skill will show what is meant. In typewriting, for example, a short time is given to reconstruction drill on the previous day's work. Then some time is given to sustained writing, followed by speed-emphasis drill. This, in turn, is supplanted by location drill. Suggested timings are given to insure the distribution of practice time.

In shorthand, the first part of the period may be used to sample homework. This is followed by the assignment of the next day's work. After chalk-board drill on the new principles, time may be devoted to dictation of homework with particular emphasis on increased speed. A shorthand drill on a new group of brief forms may be placed on the chalk board at the beginning of the period, and the teacher may return to short drills on them as many as four times during the period.

The teacher must always be alert to the deadliness of meaningless drill, which involves mere repetition and nothing else. Always he must strive for enough variety to fix the learner's mind on the desired objective and to keep him on his toes. Much of skill building is necessarily drill; but the teacher must give direction and variation to that drill, so that it does not become monotonous.

10. *Training in Skill Building Should Be Directed Toward Development of Emotional Stability in the Learner.* Skill cannot be developed to a high degree unless the learner also acquires emotional control and poise. The student's mind-set is at least as important as his physical position. The atmosphere of the classroom should be businesslike but not strained. The teacher should be co-operative in attitude, quick to praise a student's success, anxious to help him overcome his failures. Above all, he can demonstrate that he himself has mental poise and control. By displaying a sense of humor, he can do much to ease tensions that develop in the classroom.

The tense, unrelaxed student who is superior in academic achievement but who encounters difficulties in learning skills is a constant problem. Dealing with this student requires great patience and understanding on the part of both the teacher and the learner. If the learner becomes tense and discouraged, the teacher must be alert to his opportunities to give tactful encouragement and individual help. He must try to develop in the student the kind of relaxation that leaves him poised and free to work without the interference of taut muscles.

Emotional stability may also be promoted by variation of procedures so that flexibility and adaptability are secured. The day's learning should be applied to new situations. Leaders in business education have for years pointed out the discrepancy between the ability to take the dictation given by the teacher with stop watch in hand and the ability to take untimed dictation that is required on the job. Variation in procedures is necessary to provide for the adaptations that are essential to success in the business world. The good skills teacher is always alert to possibilities for presenting subject matter in new settings.

11. *Attainable Goals Should Be Set for Each Learner.* Just as the pole vaulter starts with his rod set low and raises it gradually as his vaulting improves, so should the learner of any other skill work toward attainable goals. His progress is measured in terms of his own past performance, not in terms of what the best or worst student in the class can do, or even in terms of what the entire group can do. Both he and his teacher set their goals for the individual in terms of his potentialities. Interesting as the records of the expert or the fellow student may be, they have little incentive value for the amateur. He improves in terms of his own past performance.

A device that serves as an incentive to the learner is the individual graph on which the student may chart his gains and thereby evaluate his practice procedures. The keeping of a graph stimulates the learner's interest in skill building. At the end of a grading period, it provides the teacher with a criterion for judging the student's work.

In recording typewriting- and transcription-rate gains, the graph is very effective. In shorthand dictation, the step-by-step speed progression may be shown by a different chart. Possibly there is space for recording "takes" passed at 60 words a minute, at 80 words, and at 100 words. The student is motivated to complete his chart.

12. *Skills Must Be Automatized, Not Intellectualized.* Skills must be overlearned to the point that they can be exercised when something else is uppermost in the attention of the learner. Otherwise they are not skills.

The test of any skill is the ability to use it, not the knowledge a person may have about it. If a student knows how to form shorthand outlines correctly according to rule but cannot take dictation, he has not mastered shorthand. If a student knows thoroughly the theory of debit and credit in bookkeeping and yet cannot journalize correctly a set of entries, he has not mastered bookkeeping. If a typist knows the setup of fifteen styles of business letters but cannot type an acceptable number of letters within a given time, he has not mastered typewriting.

There is considerable difference of opinion about the degree of intellectualization necessary as a basis for automatization, but there is universal agreement that automatization is the goal of the skills course. There is also agreement that the learner who gives too much attention to the details involved in the skill is actually hampered by his analysis. Teachers need to understand fully the psychology of skill and the components of the pattern of the expert. If the learner knows too much about mechanical details, however, his progress is hindered. He develops inhibitions that impede the growth of the skill.

13. *The Teacher Must Make a Positive Rather Than a Negative Approach to Skill Building.* Frequently the instructor thinks that he is teaching when, in reality, he is only preaching. Before the pattern of the expert can be developed, the teacher will have to teach rather than criticize.

Although much of the teacher's role is to point out wrong techniques, he must realize, too, that a positive psychology usually functions more effectively than a negative one. In correcting wrong techniques, he must have something better to offer and must be able to convince the student of its superiority. He must show the student what to do and must build up correct responses to be substituted for poor ones.

Plateaus in learning of skills can be reduced if teachers and students properly analyze deficiencies in technique. A student may have acquired a generally good over-all technique, but subordinate techniques are so poor that further progress is impeded until they are corrected. Just like a first-rate coach, the teacher of business skills helps the learner to correct poor subordinate techniques and to rise from the plateau where he has been stalled.

A typist, for example, may have developed very good stroking facility and may have reached a fairly high rate of speed although he brings his hand away from the keyboard when shifting. If the teacher points out to him the need for improving his operation of the shift key, he may say, "But that way is awkward. I can do it much faster this way." Obviously, the change-over will impede progress until the new skill is brought to the level of the old one. The task of the teacher is to show the learner that the ultimate gain will be worth the effort.

A similar parallel may be cited in shorthand. A student may be able to take dictation at 80 words a minute but cannot progress to a higher level of 100 words. Analysis of his notes reveals that he is not using the phrasing principles sufficiently. When the student becomes aware of his weakness, he is again given the 100-word dictation on material involving the practiced phrases. By analyzing in this way the poor subordinate techniques, he is brought above the plateau on which he found himself.

In applying this principle, the teacher should remember an admonition given earlier in this chapter: Too much attention to the mechanics will deter the learner's progress.

14. *The Teacher and Student Must Keep in Mind That Error Is the Result of Lack of Proper Technique and That Development of Technique Is the Primary Point of Attack.* As has already been indicated, accuracy was formerly regarded as the first point of emphasis in teaching skills. Today many teachers who subscribe to the theories set forth here are still in actual practice placing their primary emphasis on it, especially in transcription training.

Merely checking errors, however, is futile. A skills teacher who spends his evenings in marking papers is accomplishing little good; perhaps the time might be spent more profitably in relaxing. As an antidote to emphasizing accuracy at the expense of technique, many authorities in the teaching of skill-building courses recommend that no papers should be checked during the formative stages of the learning process. Of course, the teacher may collect papers in order to see the types of errors being made. He should remember, however, that the error is the symptom and not the disease itself. The cause of the error is the important point, and merely calling attention to the fact that it was made is not enough.

Errors may be classified as constant or variable. If an error is constant (*f* habitually written for *p* in shorthand, *i* struck for *e* in typewriting, the introductory clause never punctuated with a comma when transcribing), obviously remedial drill is necessary. If, on the other hand, errors vary and result from lack of control, the cause of the learner's emotional instability should be considered because drill upon specific subject matter would be futile. Teacher and student should work together in error analysis.

15. *Too Much Formal Testing Is a Hindrance to the Effective Building of Skill.* This is especially true of the beginning teacher who has been likened to the gardener who pulls up his plants by the roots to see if they are growing and thus ruins his crop. Teachers are prone, particularly in typewriting classes, to spend much of their effort in timing speed tests without giving adequate drill in the techniques upon which the desired speed is built. When a student teacher is asked what he did in the typewriting class to which he was called as a substitute for the regular instructor, the usual answer is, "I gave a speed test." Of course, this technique may quiet an otherwise obstreperous class; but it will hardly serve any other purpose. As previously indicated, testing is an important part of the teaching process; but it can never be substituted for teaching.

QUESTIONS

1. What is "method"?

2. Differentiate between subject matter that should be mastered and that which is used for enrichment purposes by citing examples from business courses.

3. When can it be said that a skill has been mastered?

4. When should problem solving be introduced in the learning of a skill?

5. Show how the mastery formula is adapted to the teaching of skills.

6. What is the correct order of emphasis in building a skill?

7. What are the characteristics of the action pattern of the expert? In what ways are experts alike? In what ways do they differ?

8. Why is it necessary that the teacher recognize the components of the pattern of the expert?

9. What two important reasons can be advanced for teacher demonstration? What cautions should be exercised by the teacher demonstrator?

10. How can the teacher appeal to various senses while teaching skills? Give examples.

11. What is the purpose of group or unison drill? individual drill? When should individual drill supplant group drill? Why?

12. How fast should students be required to perform drills in a skill subject?

13. Is the objective the same during an entire class period? What is the teacher's responsibility to the class in regard to this objective?

14. Of what value is repetition in skill building? When does it lose its value?

15. What is meant by saying that an absorption period is necessary before a skill can be fixed?

16. In what ways may the skills teacher develop emotional stability in the learner?

17. How does a teacher decide upon attainable goals? Illustrate in the field of typewriting, shorthand, transcription.

18. What is the advantage of the progress graph? Should students be permitted to record their own rates? How can the teacher be assured of accuracy in their records?

19. Why should learners not know too much about the psychology of skill?

20. What is meant by a positive rather than a negative approach to skill building? Give an example of using both the positive and the negative approach in building a skill.

21. How should an error be regarded in the initial stages of skill development?

22. Should papers be checked during the early stages of learning a skill? Why?

23. What causes plateaus in learning of skills? How may they be reduced?

STUDENT ACTIVITIES

1. Select a business skill in which you feel that you have developed competency—typewriting, shorthand, or transcription. Prepare a written analysis of your acquisition of this skill in terms of the fifteen techniques discussed in this chapter. Which procedures contributed most in your case to skill development? Which were least effective? Which were disregarded? Which do you feel would have improved your learning?

2. In each of the following teaching situations some of the skill-building principles are violated, and some are followed. Indicate for each case the conformities and the violations. Rewrite each situation, so that

the teacher would have been following more of the principles of skill building.

a. During the third week of school a typewriting teacher came into the room, wrote the assignment "Type five lines of each sentence on page 4" on the chalk board. Then he moved about the room distributing graded papers, checking technique as students typed, and taking the roll. This took about 10 minutes. After this he asked students to turn to Drill 17. He called each letter aloud in staccato tones while each student typed with him. This drill took 15 minutes. Then he asked the students to type the sentence as many times as possible while he timed them. At the end of ten minutes he asked the students to report their net rates, which he recorded on the chalk board in rank order with the names of the students achieving them.

b. After devoting half of the period to drill in a typewriting class at the end of five weeks, the teacher assigned a short business letter to be typed according to the model in the textbook. Students knew that they were not permitted to erase and that the letter would be graded on the basis of the number of typographic errors.

c. An office-practice student was given a manual, was seated at a calculator, given a list of problems to be solved, and left to his own initiative to complete fifty addition problems during a 40-minute period.

d. In a shorthand class the teacher explained a new principle and wrote on the chalk board a list of words illustrating the principle. Then he called on students at random to spell the words aloud and repeat the rule that the word illustrated.

BIBLIOGRAPHY

Anderson, Ruth I. "A Good Lesson in a Skill Subject," *Business Teacher* (September-October, 1949), pp. 24–25.

Book, William F. *The Psychology of Skill.* New York, Gregg Publishing Company, 1925.

Buege, Marvin. "Applying Psychology to Typewriting," *Journal of Business Education* (April, 1941), p. 25.

Leslie, Louis A. "Psychology for Shorthand and Typewriting," *Business Education World* (November, 1942), pp. 121–122; (January 1943), pp. 252–253; (February, 1943), pp. 373–374; (March, 1943), pp. 418–419; (April, 1943), pp. 475–476; (May, 1943), pp. 541–542.

————. "Ten Commandments for Skill Building," *Business Education World* (September, 1943), pp. 19–20.

Lessenberry, D. D., and James Crawford. *Psychological Principles of Teaching Typewriting*. A leaflet to accompany *20th Century Typewriting*, Sixth Edition. 1955. 18 p.

Morrison, Henry C. *The Practice of Teaching in the Secondary School*. Chicago, University of Chicago Press, 1931.

Munchel, Alvin J. "Educational Psychology Applied to Business Education," *Journal of Business Education* (September, 1949), pp. 15–17.

Mursell, James L. "The Acquisition of Skill," *Business Education World*, XVII (November, 1936), pp. 157–160.

————. "Creation, Not Routine, Is the Secret of Learning," *Business Education World,* XXI (April, 1941), pp. 663–666.

————. "How to Budget Practice Time," *Business Education World*, XXII (March, 1942), pp. 573–576.

————. "The Rhythm of Learning," *Business Education World*, XXII (October, 1941), pp. 91–95.

————, and Charles E. Benson, "Comments on Ten Commandments for Skill Building by Louis A. Leslie," *Business Education World*, XXIV (October, 1943), pp. 63–66.

————. *Developmental Teaching*. New York, McGraw-Hill Book Company, Inc., 1949.

————, et al. *Psychology Applied to Skill Building. Business Education World,* Service Booklet 23.

Nanassy, Louis C., and Julius Nelson. "Some Principles of Learning Applied to Typing," *Business Education World* (June, 1949), pp. 610–611.

Ragsdale, C. E. "How Children Learn Motor Types of Activities," *National Society for the Study of Education 49th Yearbook,* Part I, *Learning and Instruction,* 1950, pp. 69–91.

Rowe, John L. "Some Principles of Teaching Motor Skills," *Business Teacher* (September-October, 1949), pp. 12–15.

Tidwell, Fred. "The Psychological Aspects and Conflicting Practices in the Methodology of Typewriting," *National Business Education Quarterly* (March, 1948), pp. 44–51.

CHAPTER V

Preparing to Teach Typewriting

CLOSE TO THREE MILLION PERSONS are studying typewriting today in approximately twenty-three thousand schools of various types, and it is estimated by the typewriter manufacturers that, on the average, seven hundred thousand typewriters are used for four periods a day in these schools.[1] The typewriter has become a tool in such common use that it seems hardly believable that it is only about seventy-five years old. Sholes, a printer and editor, together with Carlos Glidden, attorney, patented the typewriter on July 14, 1868.

As is often the case, however, the two collaborators needed additional capital and a promotion man before they could get their invention into production. This combination they found in a successful Pennsylvania oilman, James Densmore, who not only invested his money in the project but planned and executed the sales strategy that induced the firm of E. Remington & Sons, Ilion, New York, to undertake the commercial manufacture of the "Type-Writer" in 1873 along with its other products—sewing machines, firearms, and agricultural implements.

Since that date, many other companies, both here and abroad, have manufactured typewriters. Numerous improvements have been made from the very beginning, such as the addition of the shift key, the modern paper-feed and line-spacing mechanisms, two- and even three-color ribbons, interchangeable paper cylinders (platens), the decimal tabulator, automatic ribbon-reversing mechanisms, visible

[1] Bruce Bliven, Jr., *The Wonderful Writing Machine*, pp. 139–140.

writing, variable line spacers, back spacers, the key-set tabulator with its key-set stops and clearing devices, improved margin-setting and many other devices.

Easily portable typewriters have been developed. Noiseless typewriters were marketed first in 1915, and most typewriters have been modified to reduce noise and clatter. Partly or wholly electrified typewriters have been available since early in this century. Typewriters have been built with carriages of many different lengths (up to six feet), and time- and laborsaving devices have been invented and installed on machines used in billing, statistical, and accounting work.

Special keyboards for nearly all languages and for special fields have been made available, as well as pinpoint type for check writing and special characters for scientific, mathematical, and engineering work. At least one typewriter has been adapted to the writing of standard music.

One of the first problems met in selling the first typewriter was the necessity of giving instructions for its use to the buyer. E. Remington & Sons met this need about 1875, in a circular that has come to be known as "The First Typewriter Catalogue," by illustrating the keyboard (full size) and printing briefly below it:

Practice upon the above by touching each letter (one at a time) in any desired word, and the "space-key" after the word. One or two hour's (sic) practice, daily, will soon enable you to write from 50 to 100 words per minute, upon the machine.

Several individuals of note who had co-operated with Sholes in testing his early models of the Type-Writer contributed to its further development. Charles E. Weller, chief operator in the Western Union telegraph office at Milwaukee, Wisconsin, and also a shorthand student, later a nationally famous court reporter of St. Louis, Missouri, mastered the operation of the various models entrusted to him and reported his experiences in *The Early History of the Typewriter*. E. Payson Porter, of Chicago, long the dean of American telegraphers, also mastered the operation of early models so that, after a thorough trial, "the typewriter was taken into the operating room." [2]

[2] Herkimer County Historical Society, *The Story of the Typewriter*, 1923, p. 46.

Weller reports that about 1870 he learned of a typewriter "that was manufactured under the name of Densmore & Porter and was being used in a commercial school in Chicago, of which Mr. Porter was the principal." [3] This machine may have been used for instructional purposes.

DEVELOPMENT OF TYPEWRITING INSTRUCTION

The author of *The Story of the Typewriter* declares that "The first school which taught typewriting, of which there is positive record, was opened by D. L. Scott-Browne at 737 Broadway, New York, in 1878." [4] This same year saw the introduction of the No. 2 Remington Typewriter with the first shift key, permitting the use of both capital and small letters. Also in that year Frank E. McGurrin, of Grand Rapids, Michigan, invented a system whereby he could use all his fingers in operating the keyboard of a No. 1 Remington. This system made it almost immediately possible for him to type *without looking at the keyboard*. Bates Torrey, of Portland, Maine, was to call this system the "touch" method for the first time in a printed typewriting manual in 1889.

From these beginnings, typewriting in the United States was at first self-learned by the purchasers and users of typewriters. Soon it was taught by court reporters and telegraphers who needed typists; later by both private and public schools. Throughout the rest of the world, the typewriter companies were forced to establish practice rooms and business schools of their own in order to supply the typists needed to operate the machines they sold. In British countries, beginning in 1874, both the companies and private schools (later, also municipal schools) trained typists and stenographers.

The Business School of the Young Women's Christian Association in New York graduated its first class of eight young women typists in 1881. This school still exists as the Ballard School, Central Branch Y.W.C.A. Thus began the rapidly expanding opportunities for women in the business world, a third occupational choice for economic independence thenceforth to be added to nursing and teaching.

[3] Charles E. Weller, *The Early History of the Typewriter*, p. 47.
[4] *Ibid*, p. 81.

Learning methods and courses were very crude, most typists using only one or two fingers of each hand and practicing without the benefit of real instruction. The success of Frank E. McGurrin in learning to type skillfully "without looking" as a result of using all his fingers was publicized by such worthies as Theodore C. Rose, vice-president of the International Convention of Shorthand Writers, who testified at a meeting in Chicago, September, 1881, that he had seen McGurrin doing practical work "on a test" at the rate of "97 words a minute" while he, Rose, "held the watch."

McGurrin and his young brother, Charles H. McGurrin, became famous as demonstrators and contestants in the '80's and '90's. In the Metropolitan Typewriting Contest, New York, in August, 1888, Frank McGurrin apparently copied 494 words in 5 consecutive minutes (98.8 words a minute) and took dictation blindfolded "at the rate of 101 words a minute." Several other expert operators were reported in public demonstrations and contests, the highest figures being those of A. H. Briggs, Bay City, Michigan, 125 words a minute copying and 116 words a minute blindfolded. McGurrin later reached "as high a speed as 125 words a minute on unfamiliar matter."

The first known teacher-advocate of the all-finger method was Mrs. M. V. Longley, wife of Elias Longley, a well-known author of shorthand texts. In 1881, Mrs. Longley introduced the all-finger method to her students in the Longley Shorthand and Typewriter Institute of Cincinnati. Soon afterwards she frankly featured "typing without looking." In 1882, she read a paper at the Fifth Annual Congress of Shorthand Writers in Cincinnati, openly advocating the superiority of the all-finger method without looking. In the same year, Mrs. Longley's *Remington Typewriter Lessons* was published, "the first printed system for teaching the all-finger method." Her example inspired a few teachers and some farsighted typewriter officials to advocate the more general use of her method. Remington managers, H. V. Rowell, Boston, and C. P. Judd, Omaha, encouraged teachers to train more skillful typists by the all-finger method. These progressive sales officials provided almost the sole means of professional communication among progressive teachers of the day.

The first school boldly to announce in 1889 that all its students would henceforth learn touch typewriting was the private school in Springfield, Massachusetts, conducted by the late B. J. Griffin. Before his death in 1929, he conceived and helped to create the Rational Rhythm (phonograph) Records as an aid in teaching typewriting.

As late as 1901 the Remington Company reported that a complete canvass of American schools showed that only half of them had begun to instruct by the touch method, but most of them claimed to teach that method by 1910. A former typewriter demonstrator, Harold H. Smith, reported as late as 1926 that in the British Isles and Europe there was widespread doubt as to the feasibility and efficiency of the touch method, many schools making no attempt to teach it. In 1924, J. M. Lahy, a teacher in France, wrote a pamphlet, *Motion Study in Typewriting,* published by the International Labour Office of the League of Nations, Geneva, in which he ridiculed the ideas of all-finger and touch typing, notwithstanding their long acceptance and proof in American schools, offices, and contests. No doubt these differences in attitude can mainly be explained by the fact that between 1906 and 1926 American typewriter manufacturers had trained many young men and women experts who had given public exhibitions of their skill in schools and offices and in official championship contests. Their demonstrations stimulated teachers and typists to aim for greater skill, and their official records were matters of common knowledge. Only three or four American experts, however, went abroad; hence skill possibilities remained in the realm of argumentative theory as far as foreign groups were concerned.

Over the United States as a whole, before 1900, typewriting, like many other business skills, was usually "picked up" by learners at home or in offices. A few private business schools and an occasional private or public "academy," the forerunner of our free public high school, offered typewriting in day or evening courses. Very few public day and evening schools offered typing before 1900. Accurate data on public high school enrollments are not available prior to 1922, when the United States Office of Education inaugurated its reporting service. Since then, the trends are interesting, as may be seen from the table on page 75.

ENROLLMENTS IN TYPEWRITING IN PUBLIC HIGH SCHOOLS

Year	Students
1922	280,000
1928	440,000
1934	750,000
1940	1,000,000
1950	1,226,000

Enrollments in typewriting increased nearly five times in a period of less than thirty years. This may be due in part to the more universal distribution of standard and portable typewriters in homes, schools, professional work, and offices. Today one out of every three persons in the high school has regular access to a typewriter. Many regard typing skill as a part of their *general,* rather than their vocational, education. Typewriting for both personal and vocational use has long since invaded colleges, the educational programs of clubs, business and industrial organizations.

Prior to our entry into World War I, typewriting was generally learned by what has been loosely called the individual method. The student practiced individually under nominal teacher supervision; often in the absence of the teacher. There was little group instruction and rarely any individual supervision. With the coming of the War, however, the need for typists was so great that huge classes were formed; and solely individual instruction was no longer practicable. The group method of teaching received its first great impetus after at least twenty-five years of enthusiastic support by a few successful teachers.

The effect of World War II will long be felt in the teaching of typewriting. Expert teachers, who for many years had advocated improved teaching procedures, were given opportunities to plan instructional materials and courses for typists, both in the military services and in government offices. They helped to train many teachers in the use of effective teaching procedures. Their contributions included initial emphasis on technique rather than on speed or accuracy, demonstration by the teacher, greatly improved unison drills, and "flash" practice on frequent combinations, words, and short phrases. These improvements have been widely disseminated and accepted among teachers because of their success during the War.

An examination of the championship copying rates since the first contest in 1888 provides an indication of the improvement of two factors that contribute to speed: better machines and better-trained contestants.[5]

1. The winner of the first typing contest of which there is any record was Frank McGurrin, with an approximate speed of 96.5 words a minute in 1888.

2. The winner of the first official contest was Rose L. Fritz, on the Underwood, in 1906, with a speed of 82 words a minute. She is considered the first World's Champion Typist and held that honor for four years.

3. The best Novice record was made by Hortense S. Stollnitz, on the Remington, in 1915, 114 words a minute (5-word penalty).

4. The best Open Novice record was made by Helen M. Sayer in 1941, on the Electromatic, in a 20-minute contest, 129 words a minute.

5. The best Amateur record on the manual machine was made by George L. Hossfield, on the Underwood, in 1917, 145 words a minute (5-word penalty).

6. The best Amateur record ever made was that of Margaret Hamma in 1941, on the Electromatic, 149 words a minute. On the same day she won the Professional Contest.

7. The best Professional record up to 1930 was made by Albert Tangora, on the Underwood, in 1923, 147 words a minute (10-word penalty).

8. The best Professional record ever made was Margaret Hamma's in 1941, on the Electromatic, 149 words a minute.

9. The highest speed for one minute was made by Margaret B. Owen, on the Underwood, in 1918, 170 words without error (actual word count).

10. The best Open Portable record was made by Cortez W. Peters, on a Royal portable, in 1941, in a 20-minute test, 115 words a minute.

With the years, our concept of the typewriting course has greatly expanded. The initial phase, of course, remains the mastery of the technique of machine operation. However, such matters as type-

[5] Harold H. Smith, "Holders of Typewriting Records," *Business Education World* (January, 1945), pp. 259–262. There are no important speed contests today.

writing form, correct English usage, ability to compose at the machine, and the efficient production of all kinds of typed material are now regarded as desirable components of the course. If administrators who object to granting full credit for typewriting were given some idea of the scope of the present-day course, it is probable that their points of view could be quickly changed. Teachers realize that the copying test, valuable though it may be as a speed-building device, must be relegated to a position of relatively little importance toward the end of the course when sustained production of practical work becomes the major determinant of the typist's vocational efficiency.

GOALS OF TYPEWRITING INSTRUCTION

When typewriting was first introduced into the high schools, the aim was largely vocational; but from the beginning many students enrolled for purely personal reasons. Now those taking typewriting for personal use sometimes outnumber those studying for vocational purposes. Some expect to use the skill in other high school courses or in college as a supplementary writing technique beneficial in whatever type of curriculum they enter. This group needs to know basic operating technique and matters of simple form. They need not reach occupational levels of competency in speed nor develop specialized business techniques. It is not necessary, for instance, to include in a personal-use course a unit in typing a legal document or an invoice. Such subject matter properly belongs in a class preparing to type in a business office.

Personal-use typewriting need not be continued beyond the one-year course, and in some high schools a one-semester offering has been found to be very attractive. Usually it is not possible to separate the vocational group from the personal-use group; and it is even questionable whether such segregation is desirable during the first semester, at least. Operative techniques and subject-matter objectives are the same for both groups in the early stages of the course, and usually it is administratively economical to conduct undifferentiated classes.

What are the expected outcomes in a high school typewriting class? Since this is not a course of study and since the outcomes each

teacher and student will seek must depend on local needs and practices, it follows that outcomes will vary in degree from school to
school and from course to course. The teacher and student in
beginning classes may work toward the following goals in developing skills, knowledges, and attitudes:

1. To develop the ability to operate and maintain the typewriter
efficiently:

   a. The student should display good technique in key stroking
   and in machine manipulation. The correct key stroke is the
   basis of typewriting power and must be developed at the outset of the course before typewriting applications are attempted.

   b. He should understand the mechanical features of his machine, so that he utilizes fully all devices that save time and
   increase operating efficiency. For example, he should use the
   print-control lever on noiseless typewriters, the card or envelope holder, the paper release, the tabulator, and the ratchet
   release—all skillfully.

   c. He should arrange his material so that there is an orderly
   steady flow of work through his machine.

   d. He should care for his typewriter properly. As part of his
   regular typewriting behavior, he should always move the
   carriage to extreme right or left so that he does not erase
   over the type basket; and he should voluntarily exercise his
   responsibility for keeping his machine clean and properly
   oiled.

   e. He should be able to change ribbons quickly.

   f. He should know when his machine is out of order and report
   the facts intelligently, so that it may be repaired with minimum delay and maximum efficiency.

2. To build a fund of applicable knowledge of correct English and
acceptable typographical usage relative to typewritten materials:

   a. The student should know the rules for spacing after all punctuation marks and the correct styles for expressing numbers
   under various circumstances.

   b. He should know how to set up the parts of a personal letter
   and a business letter.

   c. He should know how to place punctuation marks in relation
   to quotation marks and parentheses, how to indicate the time

of day, and how to type titles of books and periodicals in order to differentiate them from chapters or articles in books or periodicals.

    d. He should be able to apply the rules for word division at the end of the line.

    e. He should be able to type special characters not found on the keyboard, such as the division sign.

    f. He should be able to set up simple manuscript copy.

3. To develop the ability to use the typewriter as a writing tool:

    a. The student should be able to compose effectively at the typewriter, to correct copy while typing it, and to think as he types.

    b. He should be able to type "while something else is focal in his consciousness."

    c. He should be able to correct his errors by making neat erasures and by crowding or spreading letters.

4. To develop the habit of proofreading accurately:

    a. The student should learn the techniques that will improve his skill as a proofreader. He should be held responsible for finding all errors in every piece of production work he does.

    b. He should acquire a critical attitude toward spelling, punctuation, syllabication, and grammar. He should develop strong habits and skills in the use of the necessary reference books.

    c. He should develop high standards for acceptable work.

5. To learn to arrange material attractively:

    a. The student should be able to center a title or exercise.

    b. He should be able to place a letter attractively—at first perhaps by using a placement chart or rule; later by estimating its length and using judgment placement.

    c. He should be able to set up material on postal cards.

    d. He should be able to set up letters on paper of varying dimensions, on executive-size stationery as well as on 8½″ by 11″ sheets.

    e. He should be able to arrange a simple tabulation quickly and correctly the first time he attempts it.

    f. He should be able to address envelopes in standard block, semiblock, and indented styles.

    g. He should be able to type from rough draft.

    h. He should be able to make simple outlines.

6. To prepare duplicate copies:
   a. The student should be able to prepare carbon copies.
   b. He should be able to cut mimeograph stencils and prepare master sheets for fluid duplicators.

7. To form good work habits:
   a. The student should learn how to work industriously and effectively.
   b. He should learn to complete every job acceptably the first time he attempts it.
   c. He should establish timesaving work routines.
   d. He should develop ability to work with relaxed poise and without emotional tension.
   e. He should acquire a co-operative attitude, which enables him to work well with fellow students and to adopt suggestions for improvement readily.
   f. He should become self-analytic, so that he can develop his potentialities in typewriting.

8. To integrate typewriting skills and knowledges:
   a. The student should be able to apply his typewriting skill to problem situations.
   b. He should be able to maintain a steady production rate over a longer period than that consumed by the usual speed test, which involves copying only.

For *advanced* courses preparatory to vocational use, the preceding goals should be greatly improved, and the following goals should be added:

9. To develop a production speed commensurate with the standards of competency of the employing community:
   a. The student should reach a copying speed of 50–60 words a minute on straight paragraph material for a minimum of 15 minutes.
   b. He should build a speed of 40–45 words a minute in letter-writing exercises, sustaining that rate for a minimum of 15 minutes.
   c. He should be able to set up problem material, such as tabulations and fill-ins, without losing time.

   d. He should be able to chain-feed envelopes and cards expeditiously.

   e. He should be able to prepare multiple carbons swiftly and without hesitancy.

10. To develop an understanding of the forms used in business:

   a. The student should be able to prepare common business papers used in today's offices.

   b. He should know the meaning of terms used in business typewriting; such as, lease, chattel, contract, mortgage, notary public, quitclaim deed, conveyance, warranty deed, abstract of title, jobber, creditor, intrastate, interoffice, balance sheet, debits, or cashier's check.

   c. He should understand the purpose and routine use of each business paper prepared, including order bill of lading, straight bill of lading, invoice, credit memorandum, statement of account, sight or time draft, check, bank draft, note, will, lease, or bill of sale.

   d. He should understand the legal effects of his inaccuracies.

   e. He should develop a sense of responsibility for the verification of any arithmetical computations in material he types.

SUBJECT MATTER OF THE TYPEWRITING COURSE

The typewriting course naturally falls into units of study, but certain elements are continuously emphasized. Throughout the course students should strive to improve their skill techniques, so as to increase their basic typewriting skill. A regular cycle of improvement practice should be maintained. Students should devote some portion of each period to skill building or effective recall of skill. In accordance with the principles governing the development of skill, no attempt should be made to use typewriting in difficult practical situations until good basic techniques have been developed. *Many authorities urge the student to attempt no practical typing problems, such as letter writing, before he possesses a speed of at least 200 strokes, about 40 words, a minute.* This means a stroking rate of 40 words a minute, and not a net word rate on a 5-minute test.

The following subject-matter outline is a suggested unit organization of the course:

Unit I.   Initiating Correct Responses

Learning the keyboard and developing good techniques of key stroking and machine manipulation are emphasized.

The keyboard is introduced, and a cycle of planned drills to build
operative technique is developed.

Mastering the basic rules of spacing and arrangement applicable to
simple typewritten forms follows the introduction of the keyboard.

Copying exercises may be followed by dictation exercises containing
similar applications.

Unit II.   Strengthening Basic Techniques

A skill-building cycle is followed.

Emphasis is placed on increasing the speed of each typing motion and
on improving control of mind and hand.

The typing of facile stroke groups as unit responses is emphasized.
Some short words may be typed as one or more such unit responses;
other words, as a combination of unit responses and separately
struck motions.

Exercises in erasing and aligning material may be introduced; crowding and spreading of letters, as well as reinserting paper, can be
practiced.

Unit III.   Typing Business and Personal Letters

The use of the placement chart or rule may be taught. Later, the
student learns the practical judgment-placement method of displaying letters. Judgment replaces charts and rules in determining
margins.

Unit IV.   Learning to Tabulate

Simple listing and tabulations are followed by exercises requiring
columnar headings.

Materials involving the student's own experiences are arranged, such
as assembly programs, basketball schedules, and announcements of
class meetings.

The typing of simple tabulations is timed.

Considerable time is spent on developing high facility in planning the
arrangement of tabulations, and judgment placements are introduced.

Unit V.   Typing Manuscripts

Experience is provided in typing from longhand and in setting up
manuscripts with title and contents pages.

Whether the typing of footnotes and bibliographies is included depends on the needs of the students.

Copying from simple rough draft is taught, but elaborate study of proofreaders' marks is omitted.

Unit VI. Duplicating

The preparation of stencils and master copies is taught. Limited experience is provided in "running off" mimeographed and duplicator copies.

Unit VII. Completing Office Forms (Optional)

Form letters are adapted to particular situations.

Telegrams are introduced. Cablegrams, code messages, and radiograms are included if local offices use them.

Students are taught to fill in blank forms such as checks, notes, invoices, statements, bills of lading, and leases.

Unit VIII. Integrating Typewriting Habits

Problems are introduced in which sustained production skills are emphasized. Students follow through business transactions from their inception to their completion, typing all essential papers, letters, and forms.

EQUIPMENT AND SUPPLIES

Good working conditions must prevail if good results are to be obtained. The best available lighting and equipment should be found in the typewriting room.

Lighting. Poor lighting causes fatigue and mounting tension in the typist. It lowers the level of effort, causes many errors, and slows down all progress. There should be plenty of natural light in the typewriting room, preferably coming over the left shoulder of the typist from the back of the room. The typist should never face strong light. The windows should be equipped with shades. A satisfactory shade is the natural-colored one that rolls up and down from the center of the window.

In many modern classrooms light goes on automatically when the room begins to grow too dark for efficient work. The typewriting teacher is not expected to be an efficient lighting engineer, but he may find a valuable, free service provided by the local electric company, which will send an engineer to measure the light in the classroom and make suggestions for improvement. If a teacher's request for improved lighting is backed by actual figures vouched for by authorities, it stands a much better chance of being approved by his administrators. The Research Division of the National Education Association also does a great deal of work on the best lighting for the classroom, and its publications may prove useful to the typewriting teacher with a lighting problem.

Demonstration Table and Machine. Since the modern typing teacher demonstrates when teaching instead of talking, it is imperative that he have a demonstration machine within view of the entire class. This machine may be placed on a demonstration stand that is

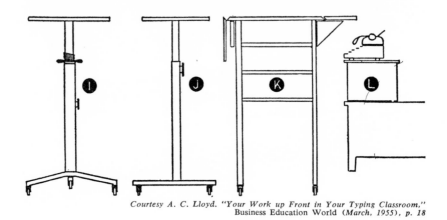

Courtesy A. C. Lloyd. "Your Work up Front in Your Typing Classroom,"
Business Education World (*March, 1955*), *p. 18*

Demonstration Stands

Type I has a tripod base, a swivel for raising or lowering the top, and a locking handle at the side.

Type J has a square, four-caster base, with a locking handle at the side. Both types are available in several models, with none, one, or two side leaves. Both stands are of metal. Both are widely used.

Type K, a wood model available from many school-equipment companies, is not adjustable in height. The simplest type of stand to make in a school woodworking shop, it is often duplicated—with or without side leaves, shelves, or casters. But, if professionally made stands are not immediately available, the ingenious teacher will improvise one. Many a teacher has made temporary, but nonetheless effective, use of something as simple as a sturdy wooden box (like L) placed on the corner of his own desk.

mounted on casters so that it may be moved about the room easily. Many teachers prefer an inexpensive demonstration box that may be placed on the teacher's desk in order to raise the demonstration machine to a height where it may be seen from any point in the room. Usually it is more convenient for the teacher to stand while demonstrating. He should be careful to have the machine high enough to maintain the proper position of his hands and forearms at the keyboard. If he sits while demonstrating, his desk and chair must be placed on a raised platform.

Some administrators feel that typewriters are so expensive that they cannot afford to reserve a demonstration machine for the teacher. The more practical view is that they cannot afford *not* to provide him with one.

Typewriter Desks. Desks should be spaced so that the teacher can get to each typist's side without disturbing other students. Arrangement of desks or tables in rows of more than two should be avoided unless wide aisles are laid out between rows. If desks are crowded, the students who do not sit at the end of a row are definitely at a disadvantage and cannot receive the necessary individual attention.

The traditional height of standard typewriter tables, as listed in furniture catalogues, is 26 inches, probably because the manufacturers of the first typewriters also made sewing machines. Their first typewriters were mounted on the sewing-machine tables that were 26 inches high.

Expert typists and industrial engineers, however, have known since 1910 that this height is too low for most writers on manual typewriters. In correct typing position both the hands and the forearms slant upward at approximately the angle of the keyboard itself. Most tables and desks should be raised to 28, 29, 30 or even 31 inches for manual typewriters, depending on the stature of the typist. During the last thirty years, attention to this factor has led to the manufacture of several adjustable desks and tables. On one of these the shelf holding the typewriter may be raised or lowered by a hand-operated screw as shown on table A. On table B a knob under the flat top, when rotated, extends or contracts the legs uniformly, so that the entire top of the table goes up and down. One type uses a wooden platform to which the typewriter is attached. The platform is slid into any one of three grooves placed two inches apart as shown on table C. The tray, or platform, may be readily withdrawn and reinserted on any pair of supports, thus making the height of the machine adjustable.

In many situations where new desks cannot be purchased, wooden lift boxes may be made, sometimes in the manual-arts department. The typewriters are placed on lift boxes of different heights to raise them 2, 3, 4, or 5 inches, or as shown in illustration D and E by placing wooden boosters under the legs, sometimes (as in D) using a heavy piece of wood connected by metal brackets to the pair of legs at each end of the table, and sometimes (as in E) by wooden "shoes" fastened to each table leg.

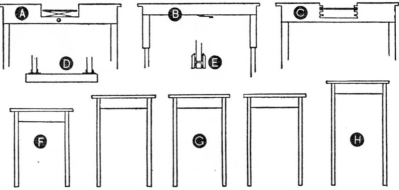

Courtesy A. C. Lloyd. "Making the Most of Your Typing Classroom,"
Business Education World *(February, 1955), p. 17*

Some schools, buying new equipment but unable to afford the superior adjustable-height tables, at least order tables of diversified height. A minimum diversification (shown by F, G, and H) would be 20 per cent of the tables, 27 inches high; 60 per cent, 29 inches; and 20 per cent, 31 inches. Even better would be 10 per cent, 26 inches high; 20 per cent each, 27, 28, 29, and 30 inches; and 10 per cent, 31 inches.

Chairs. Chair heights, too, should conform to student needs. If nonadjustable chairs are used, they should be purchased in at least two heights—16½ inches to 18½ inches. Local carpenters, even properly supervised students, can easily saw off chair legs to desired heights when permitted to do so.

Typewriters. The question arises as to what kinds of typewriters should be purchased for the classroom. If separate rooms are provided for beginners and advanced learners, all machines in the beginners' room should be of one kind, so as to simplify the teacher's task. Machine directions will be uniform for all students, and less confusion and waste of students' time will be evident. This condition, however, does not prevail in most schools. If all students use a single typewriting room, it is well to purchase machines from all major companies. Many offices are buying at least as many typewriters with elite type as with pica type, and students should be given an opportunity to use both elite and pica type during their training period.

Usually a service contract for the typewriters is desirable. At any rate, machines should be kept in good condition; and an expert repairman should call regularly. Teachers who want to develop high standards of quality among their students will see that well-inked, nonbattered ribbons are always used on school machines and that type is kept clean.

Other Equipment and Supplies. The teacher of skills who is required to time performance often will find a watch with a sweep second hand a great convenience. The stop watch, too, which has two hands, one for registering seconds and the other for minutes, is useful. An interval timer can conserve the teacher's time, for it signals the end of a timing period by ringing a bell. The teacher who uses it can devote the time, formerly used in watching the clock during a timing, to checking students' techniques and to other duties. Also, if an interval timer is used, there is less chance of running overtime and having to discard papers or complicate the computation of test results. It is recommended that the typewriting room be equipped with several such timers, so that students may occasionally time their own performance.

Individual lockers in which students store their supplies are desirable; and a storage cabinet for cleaning equipment, ribbons, paper, and similar items is necessary. A timesaver and great convenience in the typewriting room is a lavatory with hot and cold running water, pumice and hand soap, and towels. Adequate chalk boards, clearly visible from every typist's seat, should be provided. A bulletin board is essential for the display of student work and other timely material. A stapling machine, scissors, paper cutter, and screw drivers are also standard equipment. Letter trays, card and letter files are almost indispensable. An unabridged dictionary, style books, and the *Postal Manual* should be at hand, so that the teacher can develop in the learner the habit of "looking it up now" rather than guessing. Many schools ask advanced typists to use their own pocket-size dictionaries or special word books, such as *20,000 Words,* which is common practice in offices.

Copyholders. There is some evidence in favor of equipping school typewriters with Line-a-Time copyholders. However, if the school finds it undesirable to buy this equipment, two simple, handmade copyholders are recommended. Two buttons or two pieces of wood may be fastened to either end of a piece of tape about 8 or 10 inches long. When the typewriting book is opened, it fits between the two end pieces and is held securely. A piece of corrugated cardboard cut into a rectangle about the size of a sheeet of typewriting paper also makes an efficient copyholder. The cover of the book fits into the corrugated grooves in the cardboard and is held open.

TRENDS IN TYPEWRITERS

Sholes's original keyboard arrangement remains with few changes, except for foreign languages and special uses. Many have experimented with "scientific" keyboards. The best-known recent work is a "simplified keyboard" introduced by Dvorak and Dealey in 1936. After a word analysis, they rearranged the letters so that more typing is done on the home row than on the row above, as now. Their claim that this arrangement better distributes the hand and finger load has been sharply challenged. Whether any other keyboard will ever displace the present one is doubtful because of the many problems involved in such a change-over, but typewriting teachers will watch the situation with interest.

The electric typewriter is another interesting development. A light touch, a key depression of about an eighth of an inch, and an electric impulse complete each operation: no more letters that are too light or too heavy. A touch of a key, and the carriage returns swiftly. Because the typist expends much less energy in operation, he can type faster and produce more work on electric machines. Most manufacturers now produce electric typewriters, and for office

Tie a button or any small object to each end of a tape or string to hold up the copy.

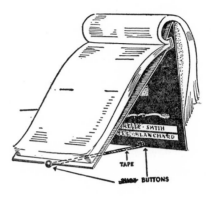

The Liberty copyholder

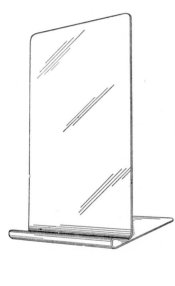

Corrugated paper serves as a copyholder

use today one electric typewriter is being purchased for every four or five manual machines.

The change-over in business came much faster than was expected, and this factor also is affecting the purchase of electric machines for schools. Formerly a business department would purchase one electric typewriter for the office-practice laboratory and try to give each student bare acquaintance with it. Today, however, there are high schools—only a few, it is true—in which the entire installation in the typewriting room is electric; while it is not uncommon to find a few electric typewriters among the manual machines in many schools. The typewriting teacher may, then, be confronted with three possible problems: (1) teaching beginners on the electric machine, (2) teaching typists trained on the electric machine to use the manual machine, and (3) teaching students trained on the manual typewriter to change over to the electric machine.

So far as methodology is concerned, there is little difference between teaching manual and electric typewriting. The teacher still uses the principles of skill building—demonstration teaching, repetitive practice, attainable goals, unison drill; however, he must teach additional machine parts. He must guard against a student's burning out the motor or in any way abusing equipment costing about three times what the manual machines cost. He must teach a lighter touch than is used on the manual machine, a different finger position, and a different alignment of the hand with the keyboard. He must give special drill to prevent the student from interspersing home-row letters among those in the copy because of resting his fingers too heavily on the home keys.

All manufacturers of electric typewriters have prepared materials to aid the teacher in the various kinds of change-overs, and the teacher should avail himself of any services offered by these companies to improve his teaching.

It is recommended that students do not change from one kind of machine to another until a certain amount of basic skill has been acquired on the first machine. It seems that about ten periods of typewriting are required for the student to make the change from the manual to the electric typewriter or *vice versa*.

The automatic typewriter provides a typewritten letter by use of the same principle that operates the electric sorting machine or player piano. Form letters are typed automatically, and the typist merely fills in special information, such as the address or a particular amount of money. One typist can keep several automatic typewriters in continuous operation.

TEACHING AIDS AND DEVICES

The typewriting teacher will find the following teaching aids and devices helpful.

Demonstration. The most effective device for the teaching of skills is teacher demonstration. The teacher who *shows how* to type saves time and presents his students with more useful practice tips than he can give by merely talking. Psychologists today believe that insight into the correct techniques to be employed is much more important than verbal understanding and mere practice. Before the learner has grasped the visual or sound pattern he is trying to attain, repetition can accomplish little. The typewriting teacher who subscribes to this psychology attaches great importance to demonstration as a teaching aid because he knows that the student both *sees* how he is to practice a particular drill and *hears* how it should sound. The teacher can increase the sound of the demonstration machine while demonstrating by leaving the paper bail up and by using either a cushion sheet from the back of a stencil or a part of a manila folder behind his paper.

Most typewriter companies employ expert typists as demonstrators, and it is sometimes possible to schedule their programs in the school.

The Textbook. The textbook is a very important element in the typewriting course.

Before choosing a book, the instructor will ask himself questions similar to these: Does the textbook cover all the topics to be taught? Are the explanations clear and simple? Are the illustrations clear, attractive, and authoritatively correct? Does the presentation conform to the principles of skill building? Is a time schedule suggested to serve as a guidepost to the teacher in handling the parts of each lesson? Are the authors of the book recognized leaders in the field of typewriting? Is the material set up to provide for individual differences (differentiated assignments)? Are the mechanical production standards of the book high as to binding, paper, English style, size and readability of type, length of line, and so on? Are the practices taught in conformity with the best usages in business? Is the copy appealing to a high school student?

The practice of purchasing one textbook for each typewriter and attaching it to the machine is not to be condoned. Typewriting subject matter should be studied just as English or history books are studied. Teachers of typewriting too often overlook the value of the textbook for teaching purposes and use only the exercises it contains. Textbook illustrations and subject matter contribute greatly to the effectiveness of the teaching of typewriting.

Curricular and extracurricular school activities can often provide supplementary teaching materials, and the alert teacher is constantly looking for subject matter in school life that he can adapt to his classroom situation.

The Chalk Board. The chalk board can help the typewriting teacher as he presents such subject matter as letter writing or tabulation. He should plan his chalk-board presentation carefully, however, before the class period and eliminate anything that does not contribute to learning.

The chalk board can also be an aid in helping students follow instructions about assignments. If the beginning teacher writes the number of the exercise to be typed as he gives the instruction, he can often avoid questions such as, "What did you say we are to type? How many carbons? What are we supposed to be doing?" Such crutchlike methods should not be carried into advanced courses, because students must be taught to hear and remember oral instructions the first and only time they are given.

During intensive drill periods, students' records of gains made can be ranked on the chalk board as a vivid motivating device, something like the illustration on page 93.

If the teacher has a rough room chart on the chalk board, each student can locate himself (but the other students will not bother to do so), and a check mark can be used to indicate the students who need to improve the technique on which the class is working. For instance, if a sustained writing reveals that some students look up, the chart might look like the one on page 94.

Films. Many excellent films are available to typewriting classes, often as a free service from the typewriter manufacturer or at a nominal rental charge. Formerly these films portrayed speed demonstrations only, but recently films showing excellent close-up demonstrations of desirable techniques have been produced.

No. Words Gained	No. of Students
10	//
6	7HH //
5	7HH /
4	///
3	7HH /
2	///
1	/
0	//

A chalk-board presentation of students' gains

The Bulletin Board. The bulletin board can be used very effectively in the typewriting class. The teacher collects suitable illustrations, then classifies and files them until he is ready to use them in connection with a unit of work. After he prepares a title and brief description for each illustration, he arranges an attractive display relating to the subject matter being presented and uses the bulletin-board illustrations during the development of the lesson, being careful to change the display when it has served its purpose. Better yet, a committee of students can be responsible for the bulletin-board displays. Outstanding student work may also be posted on the bulletin board—perfect timed writings, for example, attractive tabulations, or letters.

The Individual Student's Graph. The graph can be one of the best and also one of the most misleading devices in typewriting.

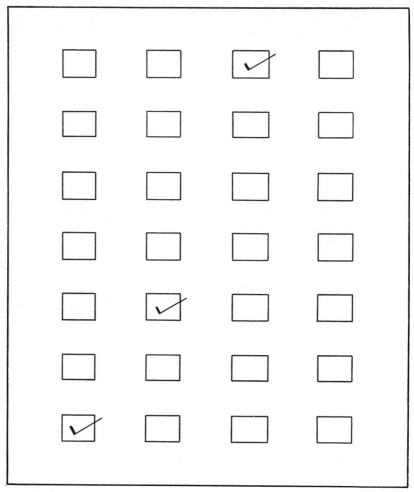

A rough seating chart showing by check mark the students who need to improve their technique

Some teachers spend hours in charting class performance from week to week. One such graph shows the class divided into three groups (the upper, middle, and lower thirds), and the line is plotted on the basis of one test a week. For several reasons this graph accomplishes little. The learner is interested in his own progress rather than that of the class; and some students in the lower brackets will only be discouraged by seeing class records, although they may have made outstanding improvement in the group during the week. The better students, on the other hand, may see that they stand high in the group and decide that they need not improve to maintain a high relative standing. The class graph has value for the teacher, it is true, but it will accomplish little in motivating the individual learner. He is interested only when he can follow his own progress in terms of his own past record recorded on his individual graph.

As the learner sees his progress—or lack of it—he accepts his individual graph as one of the logical bases for semester grading. If

BEST RECORDS

Date	Perfect 1 Minute	Highest Speed with Errors	Perfect Final Writing
9/7	21	36	23
9/8	-	38	24
9/9	25	39	27
9/10	26	-	28
9/11	27	40	—

This chart is adapted from Philip Pepe's demonstrations. The blanks indicate that the student was unable to surpass the previous day's record.

Individual student's typewriting record

he finds that he is not making satisfactory gains, he will soon ask for suggested technique drills that will help him to improve. The graph also indicates to the teacher those who need special help.

Performance cannot be based on a single test because of the variation in the difficulty of material used in testing. Unless copy is graded according to difficulty—such as word frequency, syllable intensity, sentence structure and length, and other factors—no single test or even two or three tests can be used safely as a basis for grading. A selection with a syllable intensity (average number of syllables per word) of 1.43 would obviously be easier than one with a syllable intensity of 1.89, and the students should make higher scores on it. Two methods are used for determining syllable intensity. By one method the total number of syllables in a selection is divided by the total number of words. If a long selection is used, this method may be misleading, for some parts may be very easy and other parts very difficult. The second method, therefore, is preferred: the syllable intensity being graded according to each hundred running words.

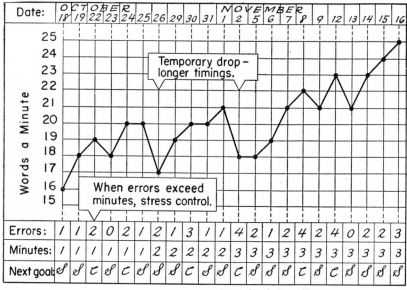

Courtesy Rowe, Lloyd, Gregg Typing, New Series, p. 41

Typewriting progress record

Daily Speed Record

Recording Progress. The illustrated record form shows one student's achievements on his timed writings. Each day he selected his most successful, longest timed writing and recorded—

1. The Date. He wrote the date on the top line of the form, as the illustration shows.

2. Words a Minute. On October 18 he typed 16 words a minute. He showed this by putting a large dot where the 16-wam (horizontal) line meets the October 18 (vertical) line.

3. Errors. On October 18 he made 1 error on the writing that he recorded. So he showed this by inserting 1 in the first box below the dot, on the line opposite *Errors.*

4. Minutes. In the box below the number-of-errors entry, he inserted each day the number of minutes he had been timed. His 2-minute timings began on October 26.

5. *Next Goal.* After comparing his number of errors and number of minutes, he selected the goal he would emphasize in all his practice in the next session. On October 18 he wrote "S" in the bottom box, opposite *Next goal*, to show that he had selected *more speed* for his practice efforts on October 19.

The next goal is always speed (S) unless the number of errors is greater than the number of minutes. Whenever the number of errors is more than the number of minutes, the next goal must be for surer control (C), with stress on typing more accurately instead of more rapidly.

When a student is attempting to gain speed through repetition of a single paragraph or sentence, the operative difficulties level off, but the inherent difficulty of material remains and defies absolute comparison. Gains may be recorded on the basis of the average of several best tests on the same or similar material. Students may keep their own records and check their own papers for such graphs; but about once a week the teacher should collect test papers so that he can determine the accuracy of student checking and record his evaluation in ink on their graphs. The first individual graphs may be set up for 1-, 2-, or 3-minute timings, and as gains are made on short timings, 5- or even 10-minute timings should be added. However, 5-minute rates should not be compared directly with 1-minute rates.

THE ACTION PATTERN OF THE EXPERT TYPIST

Fifteen general techniques to be used in developing any business skill were discussed on pages 57–66 and should be reviewed before plans for teaching typewriting are studied. It will be recalled that the skill teacher must recognize and transmit to his students a concept of the pattern of the expert typist. One of the most important steps in preparing to teach typewriting, then, is to develop this concept, for the learner must emulate it, and the teacher must be able to evaluate his students' work in terms of it.

The performance of the expert typist has the following characteristics:

Posture. The expert maintains a position of "alert relaxation." At first glance this description sounds paradoxical, but actually it represents a happy compromise between tension and relaxation. The typist is physically at ease, but he is ready to work without the hindrance of too taut muscles and mind. He does not slump in his chair; neither does he assume an unnaturally rigid position. His shoulders, arms, wrists, and fingers are relaxed when not typing; and the palms of his hands may even rest on the carriage frame at such times. His fingers, however, and, to some extent, his hands are completely tense at the moment of delivering power on each correctly made stroke, and only partly tense during the rest of each such stroke. His wrists are held low, just clearing the machine; and his hands slant upward from the wrists. The slant is less at the electric typewriter, for the keyboard slants less.

The fingers are curved lightly over the keys, so that the key is struck as nearly as possible with the ball of the finger. The anatomy of the hand is such, however, that some mobility of the muscles of the forearm is desirable in order to get the proper amount of leverage behind the fingers and, at the same time, to position the hand and fingers for following strokes. The teacher who conducts exercises in which students stroke the keys while balancing pennies on the wrist or even a glass of water, is impeding progress. The expert lets his fingers do *most* of the work. Some teachers describe correct finger position by saying that the fingers "hug" the keys. Others say that the curve of the finger resembles the kitten's paw as it pounces on a ball.

Occasionally students will be found who have double joints where their fingers extend out from the hand. The greater flexibility of this joint gives them greater fingering speed and mobility, but they risk greater inaccuracy unless their posture chairs are higher than those of normal students. Their foreams should slant but slightly upwards toward the wrist, and their hands will usually be less curved in operation.

Key Stroke. On the manual typewriter, the key stroke is backed by vibratory force without key punching or mashing. The finger movements must be powerful and vigorous, with a quick release immediately after the momentary delivery of the stroke. The finger does not follow the key far in its downward movement. After a quick getaway, the hand prepares for the following stroke without pause. The force of the stroke should be great enough to propel the type bar against the platen under its own momentum. The movement has been compared to pushing a child in a swing. The operator does not go all the way with the child; but the greater the push, the higher he swings. The stroke is directed toward the center of the key; it is not normally a glancing blow.

On electric typewriters, the same quickly released finger strokes are used but without the great force required on manually operated machines.

Contrary to popular opinion, the typist's fingers should not return to the home row after each stroke except at very slow tapping speeds. The fingers of the good typist go directly to successive keys from his working position just above the home row, combining reach, stroke, recovery, and following reach in one sweeping or blended motion.

Manipulative Motions. The expert operates the typewriter with great economy of motion. He works calmly and unhurriedly. His hands are quiet; his wrist is a loose but stationary hinge; and his arms and elbows are almost motionless, for he knows that unnecessary elbow, forearm, and hand movements are definite handicaps to the development of typewriting skill.

He *throws* the carriage without losing his basic operative position; but at the end of the throw, he gives a fling of the forefinger as his hand leaves the lever and races back to strike the first character on the next line by the time the carriage arrives at its destination. He does not return to home position unless he needs to pause and think. He operates the space bar with his thumb, not allowing the fingers and wrist to jump more than necessary in sympathy with the thumb when it strikes the bar. In shifting, he uses a wrist-hinge and stretching motion of the little finger, not permitting the rest of the hand to be diverted far from its normal working position.

Patternizing. The expert writes rhythmically; that is, there is a flow of sound in his typing, which may be compared roughly to the beats in a piece of music. Every stroke is not made in metronomic time, but there is still a rhythmic pattern to the sound of his typing even though the interval between some beats may be half that between others. Obviously it should not take the same length of time to write *fo* that it takes for the *mu* or the *$9* reaches. The expert, however, blends his slower and faster strokes into a rhythmic sounding whole. Beyond this, the making of the motions and their combination into grouped sequences must be executed with a continuity of rhythmic motion without sharp stops and starts. This rhythm of *motion* in the action of each hand is *more important* than the rhythm of the resulting sounds. The typist who does not master this fights his machine.

r ep o r t s   to   me   th a t   h e

e   x pe c   t s   t o   t a ke

ba ck t we l v e   q ua r t s

Courtesy William R. Odell and Harold H. Smith, unpublished testing material

Patterns in typewriting rhythm

As early as 1890 experts knew that in order to type rapidly it was necessary to write many words or combinations within words as wholes—to type at the *combination* level rather than at the *letter* level. They have automatized the combinations that, for them, bring the quickest responses. Experiments have been conducted by which the length of time elasping between strokes of expert typists were measured. Conclusions indicate four things:

1. Experts use a similar pattern in successive writings of any given word.
2. The context exerts considerable influence on the pattern.
3. The individual pattern is peculiar to the typist, but agrees in general for those using the same fingering methods and operating at approximately the same speeds.
4. The pattern usually involves fast combinations of letters rather than whole words, although short common words such as *the* and *and* may form a pattern. The operator speeds up when automatized combinations occur and drops back to the letter level when difficulties are encountered.

The implications of such research are that the individual typist should work toward developing facility with the combinations which, for him, are fastest. Speed is dependent on cutting down the time spent between strokes; and if patterns that reduce the time can be developed and automatized, the typist can become expert.

Reading. The mean reading rate of adults is probably over 200 words a minute; however, most individuals do not read for typewriting at a rate beyond 70 words a minute. A research study [6] of the reading habits of typewriting experts indicates that the eyes normally keep about one second ahead of the hand to supply copy as it is needed; more rapid reading is likely to cause errors. Reading for typewriting requires attention to details, not skimming. Since most mechanical errors in typewriting seem to involve the central letters of words and since in ordinary reading the most common word errors are likewise in the center of words, is it not safe to assume that teachers err in telling their typewriting students to read faster, to read by word-wholes, and to read for meaning when seeking to improve or test their maximum typing speed?

Finger Gymnastics. Experts usually employ informal finger gymnastics to relax their muscles and free finger joints before they type. In many schools such exercises are given to strengthen the fingers rather than for their true purpose, which is to limber up and improve control of the fingers. Teachers should give finger gymnastics, but their objectives should be correct.

Development of a Routine. An expert handles his materials in an orderly way. If he picks up materials, he has them positioned at a definite place on his desk, and his time- and energy-conserving movements are similar each time as he brings materials to the machine and as he removes the completed work from the typewriter. His routine includes checking of machine adjustments before writing.

He always practices some kind of brief warmup before he begins his actual work. Harold H. Smith has repeatedly described the steps in this warmup as (1) recall of best posture, stroke, rhythm, and control through the Experts' Rhythm Drill, or a similar drill, (2) recall of reach-stroking ability by typing an alphabetic sentence or right-hand left-hand words, and (3) recall of control of eye movements and thoughtful control of typing at all rates from 25 words a minute to top speeds.

[6] Donald C. Fuller, "How to Read for Typewriting," *The National Business Education Quarterly* (Winter, 1943), pp. 35–42.

QUESTIONS

1. Trace the development of the typewriter from its invention to its present position in business and in daily life.

2. Trace the development of typewriting instruction from its introduction into the high school up to the present. Include enrollment trends.

3. What effects have the World Wars had on typewriting instruction?

4. List ten possible goals of the high school typewriting course.

5. When should problem solving be introduced in typewriting?

6. Describe improvements in physical conditions that would help the typewriting teacher to achieve better results.

7. How can visual aids be used to improve the teaching of typewriting?

8. What suggestions would you make for keeping student graphs in typewriting?

9. Describe the action pattern of the expert as to position, key stroke, manipulative motions, patternizing, reading, finger gymnastics, and development of a routine.

10. What four conclusions may be drawn from a study of research about patternizing?

11. Distinguish between reading for content and reading for typewriting.

12. What is the purpose of finger gymnastics? What erroneous opinion about their purpose is held by many teachers?

13. Why should the typewriting room be equipped with a demonstration desk and table? Why should demonstration precede practice of a skill?

STUDENT ACTIVITIES

One of the major purposes of this course is to help you to familiarize yourself with the teaching materials available to you. Examine three high school typewriting textbooks. On a sheet of paper set up three column heads: *Textbook A, Textbook B, Textbook C.* Answer the following questions with regard to each book in the column of the respective book. On the basis of your analysis, select the one you would prefer in your classes. Defend your choice.

1. Are explanations clear?

2. Are suggested time schedules given for the teacher to follow during each part of typewriting period?

    Is the method for computing rate on timed copy easy? How?

3. What is the length of period for which each lesson is planned?
4. Is provision made for individual differences in each assignment?
5. Is goal always known to typist?
6. Are interests of pupil taking course for personal use served as well as those of pupil preparing for business?
7. Is practice material within experience of high school pupil?
8. Has "fun" material been included?
9. How long does the book take to introduce the alphabet?
10. When does the author introduce the figures and special characters?
11. What is the method of introducing keys (home row first, first-finger reaches first, first words alternating right- and left-hand letters)?
12. Is the presentation of rules of English applicable to typewriting adequate?
13. Is the drill on English rules applicable to typewriting adequate?
14. When is timed writing introduced?
15. Has copy been set up to develop speed and accuracy concurrently?
16. Has provision been made for developing ability to compose at typewriter? When is it introduced?
17. Has speed-development practice cycle been explained? What cycle? What devices for building speed are given?
18. When is problem solving introduced?
19. Is production work challenging to the student?
20. Does subject matter develop understanding of business procedures?
21. Does subject matter develop desirable personal traits?

BIBLIOGRAPHY

Blackstone, Earl G., and S. L. Smith. *Improvement of Instruction in Typewriting,* Second Edition. New York, Prentice-Hall, Inc., 1949.

Bliven, Bruce, Jr. *The Wonderful Writing Machine.* New York, Random House, 1954.

Clem, Jane. *Techniques of Teaching Typewriting,* Second Edition. New York, Gregg Publishing Division, McGraw-Hill Book Co., Inc., 1955.

Delaney, Opal H. "25 Suggestions on Planning the One-Room Business Department," *Business Teacher* (March, 1950), pp. 192–195.

DuFrain, Viola. "The Practicability of Emphasizing Speed before Accuracy in Teaching Typewriting," *Journal of Business* of the University of Chicago (July, 1945). Also abstracted in *Review of Business Education,* Oklahoma A and M publications, 1945, and in *National Business Education Quarterly* (Summer, 1946), pp. 3–8.

Dvorak, August. "There Is a Better Typing Keyboard," *National Business Education Quarterly* (December, 1943), pp. 51–58.

———, and Others. *Typewriting Behavior.* New York, American Book Company, 1936.

Lamb, Marion. *Your First Year of Teaching Typewriting.* Cincinnati, South-Western Publishing Company, 1947.

Leslie, Louis A., and Philip S. Pepe. "New Discoveries in the Teaching of Typewriting," *Journal of Business Education,* XXVII (October, 1951), pp. 55–56, 77; (November, 1951), pp. 114–116, (December, 1951), pp. 153–154; (January, 1952), pp. 194–196; (February, 1952), pp. 243–244, 256.

———. *Methods of Teaching Typing Simplified.* New York, American Book Company, 1952.

Lessenberry, D. D., and James Crawford. Manual for *20th Century Typewriting,* Sixth Edition. Cincinnati, South-Western Publishing Company, 1952.

———. *The Seven Basic Techniques for Typewriting,* Monograph 71. Cincinnati, South-Western Publishing Company, 1949.

Lloyd, Alan. "Typewriting Classroom Management," a series of three articles in *Business Education World* (February, March, and April, 1955).

Rowe, John. "How and When to Use Drills in Typing," *Business Education World* (April, May, June, 1952).

———, and Alan C. Lloyd. *Gregg Typing. New Series.* New York, Gregg Publishing Division, McGraw-Hill Book Company, Inc., 1953.

———. *Teacher's Manual for Gregg Typing. New Series.* New York, Gregg Publishing Division, McGraw-Hill Book Company, Inc., 1954.

Smith, Harold H. "How to Build Typing Skill Quickly," *Business Education World* (March, 1942), pp. 614–615.

———. Teacher's Manual for *Gregg Typing,* Third Edition. New York, Gregg Publishing Company, 1943.

CHAPTER VI

Teaching Typewriting

THE AVERAGE RATE OF TYPING of many second-year pupils is little above the gross copying speed of many well-taught beginners who are writing 40 words a minute on short timings at the end of six weeks. Yet it is claimed that most young people have the manual dexterity to achieve a straight copying speed of 70 to 100 words a minute.

The implications are that in many schools the job of teaching typewriting is not being done well and that, with better teaching, better results can be obtained. As the typewriting teacher approaches his class with high resolution to help learners to achieve more nearly their potential skill, he must plan his procedures carefully. He must realize that every minute spent in the typewriting classroom should be used to promote their skill, and that the effectiveness of any technique or device is measured by how well its use builds greater typewriting power. He must apply the principles of skill building and of effective teaching previously set forth. He must realize, too, that in the typewriting course three types of teaching are required:

1. The teaching of skills
2. The teaching of knowledges that are required in order to produce useful typewritten work of acceptable quality and quantity
3. Teaching the integration of these skills and knowledges into the process of solving problems requiring the use of the typewriter

HELPING STUDENTS BUILD BASIC TYPEWRITING SKILL

Before the first class period, the teacher checks all typewriters to be sure that they are in proper working condition and that he understands the mechanism of each one; he also checks the ribbons to see that they give clear impressions. He should preset the left or both margin stops. (If the paper guide is set at *0* on the elite machines and at *7* on the pica machines, they will have the same centering point—50. A 60-space line on both machines will be 20–80.) He locates the high and low desks and chairs. If he is going to use lift boxes to adjust the height of the machine for the operator, he places the boxes in a convenient place. He distributes copyholders. He experiments with the location of the demonstration stand until he is sure that his movements can be observed from all student positions in the room.

It goes without saying that the teacher will have prepared a definite lesson plan, preferably in outline form.

In general, the typewriting teacher uses the Morrison mastery formula to help his learners develop typing skill. He pretests, teaches, tests, adapts his procedures, reteaches, and retests, continuing to the point of actual mastery, always planning his work with the principles of skill building in mind. Application of the techniques to be used will be made to six teaching situations in each of which the goal is the building of a specific phase of typewriting skill:

1. Introducing the keyboard
2. Developing correct stroking habits
3. Teaching the figures and special characters
4. Building manipulative skill
5. Increasing speed
6. Developing control

To avoid misunderstanding, it should not be thought that these six teaching situations are six separate and distinct teaching problems. On the contrary, they overlap at many points. The responses taught in introducing the student to the keyboard should definitely include correct stroking habits, the techniques of increasing speed and control, and so on.

Introducing the Keyboard. Some authorities in the typewriting field introduce the entire keyboard in one period. Others contend that such a procedure causes confusions in responses that prevent development of techniques; they feel that it is better to present one or two keys a day and let the students approach expert performance on them. One widely used textbook introduces the keyboard in five lessons, another in six, and a third in nine. In training service personnel, instructors introduced the keyboard in two to six clock hours, by using twenty-six three-letter words that included every letter: *fur fun gun gum guy buy but hut jut jug vug jim dim kid red cue my, lot sit wet tex co. fat pat zip qt.* [1]

Nevertheless, there are schools today in which three months are required for covering the keyboard; and many schools do not consider six weeks, devoted to this phase of typewriting, excessive. There is, of course, no arbitrary rule to follow as to the length of time required for this work. The inexperienced teacher, however, will do well to follow the teacher's manual accompanying his textbook, especially if suggested time schedules are included. Studies indicate that classes spending longer than the suggested time on assignments do not show any greater proficiency than those following the time schedules; instruction, therefore, should be speeded up.

In most textbooks the letters are presented according to fingering —the first-finger letters first because the *f* and *j* fingers are the strongest, the most independent, and the easiest to control. The second-finger letters come next, followed by the hard-to-control third-finger letters, and finally by the characters typed by the weaker and untrained little fingers. There are two good reasons for this presentation. In the first place, it emphasizes the controlling finger for each group of keys; and the typist learns to think in terms of the correct vertical finger reaches. In the second place, faster progress is made by working from the easy fingering controls to the more difficult ones.

On the first day the beginner has no knowledge to pretest, so the teacher starts with Step 2, *Teach*. He demonstrates correct paper insertion and removal at his demonstration machine. Students then practice *with the demonstrator*. As the teacher uses the machine

---

[1] Catharine Stevens. "Know How, Show How," *Business Education World* (September, 1945), pp. 16–19. The word *jug* may be omitted, thus introducing the entire alphabet with but twenty-five three-stroke words.

parts, he calls out their names; the students then name the part they are using. The following parts are taught in this way: cylinder or platen, paper table, cylinder knob, paper-release lever. The entire drill takes no more than three minutes.

The home-row position for each finger is then taught. The demonstrator places his hands on the keys, calling attention to the fact that two keys are left uncovered between the hands. He calls out the left-hand letters, then the right-hand letters. The learners then name them. The teacher demonstrates correct hand position—both the rest or home position and the working position. Students assume the rest position. The teacher drops his hands away from the machine and very quickly brings them back to home position. He then looks to see that he made the correct reach, suggesting that home is where we go when we are not visiting and that home is where we go for rest and relaxation. The students try the drill, first with the demonstrator and then individually, dropping their hands to their laps several times and trying by kinesthetic sensation to establish ability to locate the home row and also the correct hand-rest position. This drill takes no more than two minutes.

The teacher writes the word *fur* on the clean chalk board in large letters. He then demonstrates the correct stroking of the first-finger letters he wishes to introduce. As he strokes *f* five times, he calls out in clipped syllables "fffff" and repeats it rapidly. The students hear as well as see the correct strokes. They then imitate the demonstration, calling the strokes with the teacher. The teacher calls out "frf space," as he makes the four strokes rapidly, pointing out that the finger, not the hand, makes the reach. The students type the drill with the teacher, calling out the letters as well as typing them to insure needed mental training and mind-hand co-ordination. In this way *juj* is introduced, and the students are ready to type the word *fur*.

The teacher demonstrates, typing *fur* twice, once slowly to make clear what he is doing and then fast, in expert fashion. He calls each letter as a command at both slow and fast rates. Between words, the demonstrator relaxes his hands by resting his palms on the frame of the typewriter. Relaxation is so important that one of the textbooks prints two or three red signals in each line of copy to help the beginner establish the practice of relaxing. Students practice the word in unison until they prove that they know what they are expected to do. Then they work individually to gain proficiency in typing it. (The description of this teaching routine is necessarily greatly condensed. Details may be obtained from magazine articles and teacher's manuals.)

The teacher now progresses to Step 3, *Test*. He walks around the room, checking the technique of individuals and giving assistance where needed; he cannot teach effectively and stay in the front of the room during the period. If he finds that students are not typing according to the pattern set, he redemonstrates, either at his own or the student's typewriter. Of course, if he uses his demonstration typewriter, more learners will be benefited; but the entire group may not require redemonstration. Obviously, the teacher is now following Steps 4, 5, and 6—*Adapt Procedures, Reteach,* and *Retest.* As soon as he is satisfied with student achievement, the teacher introduces additional subject matter—using new strokes and words.

The technique used here, like that employed in all teaching to build typewriting skill, may be summarized thus:

1. The teacher demonstrates, at first rapidly, then slowly.
2. The students imitate the demonstration, typing with the teacher in unison drill.
3. The students practice the routine; the teacher observes.
4. If necessary, the teacher redemonstrates.
5. The students again practice the drill in unison if the teacher feels that they have not yet learned how to achieve what they are striving to accomplish.
6. When the students learn the practice pattern, they work individually.

Developing Correct Stroking Habits. The most important objective of the first few days of work is developing the correct concept of the typewriting stroke and achieving its execution by the class. On the second day the teacher adds a step to the above routine. He pretests to determine whether each learner is acquiring a good stroke. As he listens to, and observes, their typing, he analyzes their learning needs and decides how much, and what kinds of, demonstration are necessary.

He requires rapid responses even on single isolated strokes from the start, for he realizes that the motions involved in correct technique are not those used in slow typing. That is why he types and calls out "fffff" rapidly. That is why he writes the words rapidly after he first demonstrates their formation slowly. He shows the students how to do "flash" practice and from the first day trains them to build expert speed on short words (two- and three-letter combinations). That is why he encourages them to patternize from the beginning. Early in the course he introduces the expert typist's warming-up drill or "in-and-out" drill, *a;sldkfjghfjdksla;* in order to develop the "feel" of, and insight into, the nature of rapid stroking and correct hand position. He remembers, however, that any pace at which confusion appears is too fast; and he tries to adjust the rate of practice and the length of the practice unit to the ability of the individual student.

The teacher's method of calling commands during demonstration and unison drill can help to increase the vigor of student responses.[2] He should call the strokes in snappy, staccato fashion with marked pauses for relaxation between groups of letters and between words. As students type, it is good practice to require that they, too, call out the strokes. In this way their attention is focused on the particular motions that they are trying to learn, and their actions become more decisive. If they call their strokes with snap, they will naturally use a snappy stroke. They will co-ordinate mind and hand more nearly perfectly. Even when they are trying to type on the word level, saying the word helps them type it a little faster and with surer control. During unison drill, there is no time to look up at the end of the line; learners have to keep their eyes on the copy in order to keep the carriage moving.

A word as to the nature of the drills is appropriate. Very little attention is given to reach drills outside of words—drills like *frftfgf* or *jujyjhj*—except occasionally as brief warmups. There is a tendency toward the word approach; and, in order to develop even rhythm and fast stroking, many of the early words chosen for drill

---

[2] Alan Lloyd demonstrates a useful drill to increase the alertness of a typing group and make it responsive to teacher commands. He calls out the letters of the alphabet in very erratic fashion. The typists, thinking that they know the next letter, will type it before the signal is given. Keeping with the dictator becomes a game, creates fun in the classroom, establishes the teacher as the one in charge of the drill, and improves the quality of the key stroke.

require the use of alternate hands. Such words as *fur, for, and, the, pale* encourage fast fingering, hence superior technique, in repetitive practice. Although most textbooks make this approach, one notable exception introduces many double-letter words (such as *feed, weed, tell, teem*) for early practice because they are easy for beginners.

Sentence practice is inaugurated during the first few days, and paragraph practice on easy copy soon follows; but the teacher will discover that beginners naturally fall into a slow, steady rhythm on all sentence matter. In order to maintain this steady rhythm, the beginner fits his typing of such flash words that he has practiced into the predominantly one-stroke-at-a-time style he must use until his typing on the lower level has been strengthened. He will then be able to raise and lower his rate successfully and smoothly and with full control.

Teaching the Figures and Special Characters. The problem of securing mastery of the numbers and special characters is often not solved by the typewriting teacher. One textbook postpones their introduction until eight weeks of instruction have passed. Another stresses the "pipe organ" method, which disregards the return to home row in typing any characters on the top row of the keyboard. A modification of this method is found in the "we-23" drills in which the typist works from the last row of alphabet keys rather than the home row in making reaches.

The teacher will probably introduce numbers and special characters as the textbook introduces them. He may find, however, that students will still look up when a number is encountered in context and will still use incorrect fingering on the top row. In that case he may welcome the following drill: Dictate the location drills as a review: "s2s, d3d, f4f, f5f, j6j, j7j, k8k, 191, ;0;."

After the location drills, the teacher dictates approximately two lines of isolated numbers, such as "627, 864, 129, 737, 896, 2340," and one student reads back the numbers as the others check their accuracy. If this test yields good results, the drill may be discontinued. If not, the location drills should be repeated and additional isolated numbers dictated. A variation in figure drill is the dictation of sentences containing numbers, such as "I live at 839 North 125 Street," or "I bought 8 oranges, 6 lemons, and 21 grapefruit for $2.45."

During this drill it is imperative that the teacher do a great deal of floor work, for he will find some typists using incorrect fingering and looking at the keyboard. In fact, close check on technique determines the effectiveness of this drill; and most number drills fail in this respect.

Drills for learning the special characters are set up like figure drills. Along with acquiring skill in stroking these characters, students will also learn the correct use of the special characters.

Building Manipulative Skill. At the same time that the typist is developing stroking facility, he is also building manipulative skill—in checking and setting his margins, in inserting and removing paper, in shifting for capital letters, and in returning the carriage. As time can be saved by perfecting these techniques, they should be isolated for periodic corrective drill.

Carriage-Return Drill. A drill that has been used a long time to improve carriage-return technique consists of typing the last few words in a line, returning the carriage as quickly as possible, and typing one word on the next line. The tabulator rack should be cleared of stops, and a single stop set 10 or 15 spaces from the end of a 60- or 70-space line in order to save time in resetting the carriage.

A completed drill of this kind will look like this:

```
                            at the big
    desk                    at the big
    desk                    at the big
    desk
```

Shifting Drill. Even though the wrist-hinge motion may have been demonstrated by the teacher and practiced in unison drill, teachers often find learners bringing the entire hand over to the shift key. They may be shifting with a thumb or a wrong finger, and their capitals will be out of line. Obviously special shifting drills should be prescribed. One simple assignment often used is to have students capitalize each word in some practice sentence, such as the following:

```
Do Not Start A Test Until You Finish Warming Up
```

Increasing Speed. In a significant study in typewriting, DuFrain [3] reports teaching two groups of students by two methods. One group was taught by the traditional method. The other group emphasized speed for several lessons and then worked only to improve accuracy for several lessons. After that a second speed drive was made for several lessons and thereafter the class worked only toward improving speed. The results of this study indicate that emphasizing speed before accuracy in elementary typewriting is practicable and that many of the early errors are due to chance and can be reduced by subsequent drives for control. After the keyboard has been covered and development of manipulative skills initiated, the next unit is concerned with increasing speed. Intensive drill is given until the learner has gained enough proficiency to execute the mechanical aspects of typewriting fluently—possibly until he can stroke 40 words a minute or type 30–35 words a minute on 5-minute writings.

Patternizing drills on the combination and word levels continue. Rather than dictating "t-h-e" during unison drill, the teacher calls "the" and types it as a unit. The class then calls the word as a clipped command and types it in a flash, repeating it clearly with each writing in order to automatize it. Students soon learn that they cannot type all words as wholes and will, with proper training, drop back to the letter level or to the letter-and-combination levels when they encounter difficulties.

Skill-Improvement Drills. These flash-practice drills are used as skill-improvement drills. The learner attempts to increase his speed of writing on a particular sentence. After preliminary timings, he isolates troublesome words for flash practice. Then he practices typing one word at a time until he feels out the best motion pattern for it and can type it with fluency and speed. He types each word once or twice at fairly slow metronomic rates before trying to "flash" it. The teacher suggests that students try to strike the center of each key with precision in slow practice. After flash practice, the words are put back into the sentence without timing; then the effectiveness of the drill is tested by one or two more timings on the sentence. The

[3] Viola DuFrain, "The Practicability of Emphasizing Speed before Accuracy in Typewriting," *Journal of Business* of the University of Chicago (July, 1945); also in *National Business Education Quarterly* (Summer, 1946), pp. 3–8.

teacher can measure his teaching ability by the intelligence that his learners show in choosing words for flash practice.

"Call-the-throw" Drills. This type of drill provides opportunity to build speed at individual levels. Each learner selects from a list of sentences of increasing length the one that he hopes to complete in 20 seconds. The teacher starts the class typing on signal, calls "Throw" for the carriage return after 20 seconds, 40 seconds, and "Time" after 60 seconds. The student tries to complete the sentence once and to return the carriage in each 20-second period. If he types three full lines without error in 1 minute, he advances to the next sentence, which must be typed one word a minute faster.

Intensive Paragraph Practice. One of the best ways to build stroking speed is to repeat a simple paragraph. Typists enjoy this drill when properly handled and become anxious to try again and again in the hope of experiencing the satisfaction of attaining faster rates and superior accuracy. Students become bored and derive little benefit when this drill is used incorrectly because they soon discover that mere repetition does not insure improvement.

In handling repetitive practice, the teacher should conduct perhaps three 1-minute timings, allowing not more than 5 seconds between trials. Students then check their most accurate and their fastest trials, selecting a few words for flash practice. Flash practice may require 1 or 2 minutes; then they get two or three more timed 1-minute trials on the same paragraph. They report the best of their efforts only, some teachers permitting a report only if a gain is made. Practically all textbooks have devices for establishing rates of writing without the old time-consuming and complicated mathematical computations.

The teacher asks, "How many gained as many as five words? Four? Three? Two? One?" and ranks the gains on the chalk board so that students can compare their improvement with that of others. If these trials are called "timings" rather than "speed tests," students may do better work. Whatever they are called, their purpose is to put pressure on the student to strive to do his best, a requisite of all skill learning.

Developing Control. Authors of most typewriting textbooks agree that in all learning stages a student may push for speed as long as he is not making more than one error during every half minute of

```
          1   |  2  |  3  |  4  |  5  |  6  |  7  |  8  |  9  |  10
2-Min.   0  If you were to hear a fast typist at work, one of   10
Writings  5  the things that you would note would be the sound   20
         10  of his work.  It has a steady flow, with many ups   30
         15  and downs; it is not an even jog trot.  Each time   40
         20  he comes to a short word or a group of strokes he   50
         25  has typed many times, his fingers flash the group   60
         30  of letters in a spurt, with no spelling.  When he   70
         35  comes to a long word or a hard one, he slows down   80
         40  and spells out the letters.  If you would like to   90
         45  build speed, learn to flash all the common words.  100
        PLUS ♦   1    |    2    |    3    |    4    |    5
```

Courtesy Lloyd, Rowe, Winger. Gregg Typewriting for Colleges, p. 75

Speed-measuring Device

1. At the right and above the copy is a word-counting device. The student notes the number at the end of the last line he completed and adds to it the figure under *which he stops. A student who stops after typing the word* short *in the fifth line, for example, will have typed 40 + 4 = 44 words.*

2. At the left and below the copy is a speed-measuring device. The student notes the figure at the start of the line and adds to it the figure above which he stops. The student who stops at the word short *in the fifth line, to use him again as an example, will have typed 20 + 2 = 22 words a minute.*

---

writing. Along with speed, however, he must also develop control. He must learn how to type without unnecessary tension; he must be comfortable while typing. After intelligent speed-building efforts, students should type at their best controlled rates, learning early in the course to regulate their rates consciously through recognition and maintenance of the sound of the rate they are striving to attain. In this kind of drill, studied effort is usually made to reduce or increase typing rates in stages of about 5 or 10 words a minute.

In drilling for speed gains, the teacher should not say, "Now try to type accurately this time while you increase your rate," for these two objectives are opposed. At one time the teacher drills for speed; at another, for accuracy. Finally, the students combine what they have learned from both drills into a superior technique involving improved speed and the desired degree of accuracy. The learner is told to work for "control," not for "accuracy."

Observing the Techniques of Typists. In building basic typing techniques, the teacher should constantly test his results by observing students at work. He must realize that hoped-for gains will appear only if individual techniques are steadily improved. Checking techniques serves as his guide for lesson planning. In analyzing typing techniques, the teacher should look for the following common weaknesses in unhandicapped students:[4]

1. Punching the keys with a shoulder stroke
   Caused by stiffening the arm or shoulder.
2. Mashing the keys
   Characterized by pushing the key instead of hitting it forcefully and releasing it at once. Caused primarily by a lack of understanding of the correct stroke. Learners often say, "When I mash the key . . ."
3. Striking a glancing or hesitant blow
   Caused by uncertainty of fingering, improper position of the hand in relation to the keyboard, or by failure to coordinate the thought ordering the stroke with the striking.
4. Striking keys with the wrong part of the finger
   Caused by not keeping the fingers curved. Dogmatic ideas, however, may be dangerous. Ultraspeed motion pictures of top experts in typing prove that skill may require many variations of finger-key relationships. Individual differences, such as very short little fingers, which often must be straightened out to reach keys, require consideration.
5. Clashing two keys in the type basket.
   Caused by fingers depressing home keys instead of resting lightly on them, by failing to release keys rapidly enough, or by poor timing (rhythm) of strokes.
6. Lifting the shoulders
   Caused by inability to relax and to let the fingers do most of the work.
7. Using too much arm, wrist, and hand movement
   Caused by failure to develop and emphasize correct finger action; wrists held too high and too rigid.

[4] Adapted from various materials prepared by D. D. Lessenberry.

8. Swinging the elbow out, especially on fourth-finger keys
     Caused by too rigid adherence to home-row position, particularly to "anchoring" the little fingers on *a* and

9. Slamming the carriage against the left margin stop
     Caused by too forceful a motion or not releasing carriage-return (line-space) lever soon enough.

10. Fighting the machine
     Caused by failure to relax and get a rhythmic flow of effort and motion into the work.

11. Shifting with the wrong finger (any finger but the little finger), often with fist doubled under
     Caused by insufficient specialized drill; often by an entirely wrong attitude toward skill learning.

12. Typing capital letters too high or too low
     Caused by not depressing shift key hard enough, releasing it too slowly or too quickly, or by poor timing of shifting motions; also, from poor adjustment of shifting mechanism.

13. Returning to home row after each stroke
     Caused by a misunderstanding of correct operating technique; also by too slow stroke rates.

14. Looking up at the end of each line
     Caused by lack of self-confidence, insufficient drill on steady continuity, or too many one-line drills. Can be corrected most easily by flash-drill practice on words, followed by typing paragraph matter containing flash words as half-minute and 1-minute timings.

15. Not isolating the elements which, for the individual typist, require special drill
     Caused by failure to understand and use best methods of practice. Can be corrected only by teaching each individual the whys and wherefores of typing difficulties and how to practice in order to overcome them.

16. Not using timesaving devices on machine. (The student does not check margins before beginning work, uses the space bar for indentions instead of the tabulator, does not use the paper release or the margin release properly.)
     Caused by insufficient demonstration and drill on these points.

DEVELOPING SUPPLEMENTARY TECHNIQUES

Before students are ready to put typewriting into use situations, they must learn supplementary techniques not concerned with basic copying or manipulative skills. These include cleaning the typewriter, changing the ribbon, erasing, reinserting paper and retyping copy to obtain the effect of boldfaced type, typing on ruled lines, crowding and spreading letters, proofreading, and making carbon copies. A true sense of a personal need for doing these things well generally springs from the typist's pride in the quality of his work.

Cleaning the Typewriter. Businessmen constantly complain that office workers do not keep their typewriters clean. Probably typists do not accept the responsibility for cleaning their machines because in school they cleaned them only when told to do so. Caring for the typewriter should be as much a part of the day's routine as the warmup drill or the timed writing; and students should do this daily chore automatically, without prompting from the teacher.

The teacher gives a step-by-step demonstration of cleaning and oiling the machine. He checks the students while they clean and oil their typewriters, following his demonstration of each step. If necessary, he reteaches a correct procedure before advancing to the next step. The instructor follows up by checking students' machines regularly, without previous warning.

Changing the Ribbon. One ribbon-changing experience is never sufficient to insure mastery. One very successful teacher requires each student at some time during each semester to change his ribbon within 1 minute. Without practice, he cannot meet this standard; and the teacher knows that anyone who can change ribbons in 1 minute has really mastered that technique. This skill should be acquired on all standard typewriters if at all possible.

Erasing. Students should be taught how to erase before they try to produce mailable or usable copy. It is unwise to erase drill work; but when learners start typing copy that is to be evaluated, they should know how to correct errors. The teacher demonstrates erasing; then the students follow through step by step, being sure to move the carriage over first, so that no eraser crumbs fall into the type basket. Timed writings, on which the typist corrects his errors instead of being penalized for them, provide the teacher near the end of the term with a realistic estimate of the pupil's ability to produce usable work.

Reinserting Paper and Writing in Boldface. A good typist should be able to reinsert typed papers into the machine so that characters to be inserted will appear as though they were a part of the original copy. Learning this technique takes practice and demands intimate knowledge of the particular typewriter used. The learner writes a word, removes his paper, reinserts and positions it with the aid of the paper release, ratchet release, or variable line spacer, line scales, and printing point; then retypes the same word over the first one. Repeated trials should be made to get the knack, and frequent reviews are essential to maintain this skill.

In learning to write on ruled lines, the typist makes an unbroken line with the underscore. He removes the paper, reinserts it, and types a sentence on the line. Repetitions are highly desirable. If made over the same line of typing, they will appear in boldface. By not removing and reinserting the paper, the typist will be practicing the method used in offices of typing boldface characters for emphasis.

After these preliminary drills, there should be supervised practice in erasing, reinserting paper, and inserting corrected material.

Crowding and Spreading Letters. No instruction should be given about crowding and spreading until students can erase a single letter or word and insert skillfully another letter or word containing the same number of spaces. Then the teacher should provide students with a clear idea of what successful crowding and spreading are through the display of selected examples kept for that purpose. Practically all textbooks provide adequate explanations of techniques required on the various typewriters as well as adequate drill to develop this skill.

Proofreading. The error is not the sin; the uncorrected error is. Students must be taught to proofread their work. They must be taught to read syllable by syllable—sometimes aloud—and not to skim as they do ordinarily. Many textbooks now provide exercises on proofreading. An example is:

```
        If the lesson is prepared in time, you are usally able to
master it.  However, if you are hurried in you last-min-
ute preparation, you may encounter diffuculty.  You should at-
tempt to devote enought time to it to each assignment to mast-
er it.
```

Good proofreading is not done automatically; it must be taught. The teacher should appoint a classmate as proofreader for each student, as at first it is often easier to find the errors of the other person than your own. The proofreader, as well as the typist, is then held responsible for the accuracy of the paper.

A careless typist is likely to omit an entire line. Ample copy like the following should be provided that requires close attention, especially at the beginning and end of the line where successive lines are alike:

```
        Let us pay less attention to errors in work and more attention
to the student at work.  After all, it is this very close attention
to the student while he is working which is going to be responsible
for his gains.
```

When copy such as a mailing list has been completed, students should proofread in pairs, one reading aloud and spelling the copy while the other checks him from the original. A bonus may be given for all errors corrected, or the negative incentive of counting each unchecked error as two mistakes may be used.

Making Carbon Copies. The most efficient ways of assembling carbon packs and of inserting them into the machine should be carefully demonstrated by the teacher. Care should be taken to show how failure to align sheets with each other and with the paper side guide and to depress the paper release occasionally causes the carbon to crease and consequently to mar the copy. The teacher should erase both on the original and on carbon sheets, being careful to use a pencil eraser on carbons and to clean the eraser under the desk or on clean paper before each erasure. He should show how the insertion of a card between the top sheet and the dull side of the carbon results in an erasure superior to that obtained by the insertion of a slip of paper between the shiny side of the carbon and the copy being erased.

In vocational classes, the teacher stresses the idea that the carbon copy becomes the file copy and thus the one by which the employer really judges a typist's abilities. On the other hand, the teacher should recognize that on occasions an erasure on a carbon copy is a waste of time. For instance, if a person is keeping a copy for personal use, erasures are unnecessary—just another example of how judgment can be taught in typewriting classes.

TEACHING RELATED INFORMATION

Before anyone can turn out acceptable typewritten copy, he must acquire knowledge related to typewriting. This subject matter includes the rules for spacing and the use of punctuation marks as well as an understanding of the principles involved in display, such as centering and tabulating. It also includes a fund of information about the choice of materials for different kinds of typewriting jobs. If the typist is studying vocational typewriting, he should also understand the business forms he prepares, the terms used, the situation in which the form functions, and how it is handled. Every typist needs constantly to review grammar and English style. He should practice using style manuals, dictionaries, and wordbooks.

This type of teaching has not been done too successfully in the past because typing teachers do not stress sufficiently the special drills on segregated materials that are required for mastery. For example, a student will not learn satisfactorily the rules for writing numbers by merely reading the rules and then copying an exercise in which numbers are correctly written. A planned application of the mastery formula is necessary—drill in which the typist's mental abilities are challenged, drill in which teacher demonstration has no part, drill in which the learner must apply knowledge and not merely use motor skill. These aspects of typewriting require study, perhaps home assignments. In this respect, typewriting is a prepared subject, just as English is a prepared subject. Indeed, the needed teaching methods are those for written English expression, not those for developing basic typewriting skills.

Applying the Rules. Rules to be mastered include spacing after medial and terminal punctuation marks; writing numbers; underscoring material; the sequence and spacing of punctuation marks used together, as with quotation marks and parentheses; expressing the time of day; typing sums of money; indicating titles of publications and of articles in these publications; using commercial characters; and dividing words correctly at the end of lines.

After the teacher pretests to determine the learning needs of his class, he teaches the needed points by discussing the rules and having the students type an exercise in which correct applications are made. He checks the effectiveness of his teaching by an informal test in which he dictates sentences that the students type as they apply the rules. After the students check their papers, the teacher again discusses the rules and reteaches the material in the light of any difficulties disclosed by the test. In the event that the class still seems greatly confused, he may ask the members to type original sentences illustrating the principles involved. Then follows a second dictation test. If the results indicate mastery, the material of the test may then be incorporated into timings, for the students are now ready for pressure drills to build skill—speed and accuracy—in typing problem material.

Centering and Tabulating. Before students become expert in centering and tabulating material, they must master thoroughly the information about the number of spaces to the inch vertically and horizontally on pica and elite machines and the size or sizes of typewriting paper.

Formerly the teaching of tabulation involved complicated arithmetic computations, and many a typewriting teacher despaired of ever obtaining desired results with students who were unable to do and verify the involved calculations required to set up a table before typing it. Today by the simple backspace centering method [5] and later by judgment placement, the student can learn to arrange tables and titles attractively with relatively painless effort. The exercises at the end of this chapter involve your learning the techniques that you can use in teaching what used to be a very complicated topic.

When the class understands the processes used in centering and tabulating, the teacher should advance these skills from the learning standards to job standards by introducing timings.

Selecting Materials. All typists should know the qualities to be sought in typewriting paper, in mimeograph paper, in paper for use with a gelatin or fluid duplicator. They should know the difference between 24-pound and 9-pound paper, between sulphite and rag-content paper, between bond and wove or laid finish. They should know which weights of paper and carbon paper to select in making multiple copies. They should know which size of envelope to use under particular circumstances. They should know the qualities of

[5] Rowe and Lloyd, *Gregg Typing, New Series,* 1953, p. 69.

typewriter ribbons on the market and the kinds of type cleaner that give the best results.

The teacher teaches this subject matter and informally tests his teaching. If the results are unsatisfactory, he adapts his procedures and reteaches before a second test.

Understanding Business Forms. Assignments should include the study, sometimes from supplementary nontypewriting textbooks, of the uses of the business forms and terms employed. Students should be tested not only on their ability to prepare the forms but also on their comprehension of these papers.

INTEGRATING SKILLS AND INFORMATION

Typewriting has been mastered only when it can be used as a tool while something else is uppermost in the typist's mind. For that reason, exercises should be provided in which students apply their skills and knowledges in problem situations.

Letter Writing. After students have developed facility in basic typewriting skill, letter writing is introduced. The teacher may block out a letter style on the chalk board, or the class may discuss briefly the sample letter illustrated in the textbook before copying it.

As there is considerable subject matter to be learned at this point, many teachers assign as homework the reference material in the textbook. After the class has discussed the subject matter, an informal, but informing, test on letter parts and placement should be given.

As each letter style is introduced, the student copies the model letter from the textbook and then types unarranged letters in the same style. In this way the common letter and envelope styles are introduced, including the typed friendly letter and semisocial styles. In a personal-use class, little attention should be given to styles other than the conventional, or semiblock, form.

A word should be said about how to teach letter placement without the use of complicated charts and without knowing how many words are in the letter. The teacher will want to avoid graduating a student like the beginning typist who spent her first morning on her new job counting the number of words in a letter, in order to set it up according to the chart that she had always followed in school.

Modern textbooks contain devices for estimating placement of letters of three lengths—long, medium, and short.

After the class becomes familiar with letter forms, the timed typing of letters should become regular class procedure. The teacher should be determined that basic techniques do not deteriorate during letter-writing instruction. He should insist that the typist check

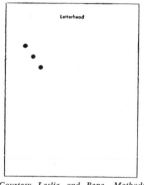

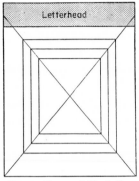

Courtesy Leslie and Pepe. Methods of Teaching Typing Simplified, p. 67 *Courtesy Rowe and Lloyd. Gregg Typing, New Series, p. 95*

Two devices for the placement of long, medium, and short letters

his machine adjustments before starting the letter; that there be no looking up at the end of the line, between paragraphs, or while writing closing lines; that the carriage is always moved over to extreme right or left before erasures are made; and that economy of movement and effort is observed while papers are being inserted and removed.

A simple but excellent drill to increase letter production is a letter-typing drill in which the sole objective is to type through the entire letter without looking up—regardless of consequences. Timed work on letter writing should be continued until the production rate, with one carbon copy, equals at least 75 per cent of the student's copying speed for periods of equal length.

If desired gains are not achieved, the teacher should check the techniques of the class and isolate troublesome items for special drill. For instance, a drill in assembling and inserting carbon copies may increase production. If looking up at the end of the line is slow-ing speed, this factor should be corrected through special drill on the particular lines where looking up occurred.

During drill to increase speed in letter writing, teachers can call attention to many simplifications in form that will increase production: using the National Office Management Association simplified letter form, using lines of a fixed, standard length, writing titles of books in capitals rather than having to look up to underscore them, using the simplest forms of reference initials, blocking addresses and closing lines, and using the tabulator whenever possible. Students will be quite willing to practice these techniques if they realize that some companies have increased letter-writing speed as much as 30 per cent by such practices. In any event, they must be impressed with their need to please future employers by being able to set up work in any form required.

Along with letter writing, students should type postal cards. The experienced teacher knows that a postal card feeds into the typewriter differently than a piece of paper cut to post-card size. He will use a real postal card or light cardboard cut to size.

Machine Composition. In order to develop the ability to think at the machine, the teacher asks simple questions, requesting that students answer them by composing complete sentences at the machine. Here are some suggested questions for first drills in this work:

1. How old are you?
2. Where do you live?
3. What subjects are you studying in school?
4. How many times do you space following a comma?
5. What did you eat for lunch?

When the student has become acquainted with the idea of composing at the typewriter, letter composition is introduced. A definite situation should be set up as the basis of the letter, but the learner should be allowed some originality in composing it. For example, as a first attempt the class may be told to order the *Reader's Digest* to be sent to a friend for one year. The proper address of the magazine publisher and the subscription price should be written on the chalk board. As the class names the essential elements of the order letter, the teacher writes them on the chalk board before typing begins.

If possible, the first draft should be a mailable one; but attention should also be given to composing rough drafts on the typewriter. Some students will want to write their letters in longhand and copy them on the typewriter, but this should not be allowed. They should be permitted to cross out material in the rough draft that they decide not to include, and they may retype from their original copy if necessary. This is the realistic way.

A time limit should be set for such exercises. At the expiration of the time, the papers should be collected and exhibited to the class for comments about placement and form. Several letters are then read and discussed, and a similar exercise is assigned.

Copies of a letter requiring a simple answer may be distributed. The proper reply may be discussed and students asked to write it within a given time.

In an assignment involving the composition of a friendly letter, the teacher may suggest that the student invite a friend to spend the week end with him or lend him a popular book. In order to instill interest in using the typewriter as a tool and also to get away from an artificial situation, the teacher may tell students that they are to type a letter for actual mailing, that he will come by to check for form, but that he will not read the letter. Pupils may be asked to compose short papers at the typewriter, using library notes on assigned readings. A possible subject would be "Qualities to Look for in Buying Typewriting Paper." Some teachers expect their classes to write short essay-type answers to examination questions at the typewriter.

Manuscript Typing. Much typewritten material is copied from unarranged longhand composition. When Frisch [6] analyzed 1,004 samples of copy from which office clerks typed business materials, he found that well over half of the copy was either completely or partially handwritten. Yet when he analyzed typewriting textbooks, he found that less than 10 per cent of the copy contained any handwriting. Obviously the student should acquire more familiarity with

---

[6] Vern Frisch, "An Analysis of Clerical Business Typing Papers and Forms for the Improvement of Instructional Materials," Ed. D. Dissertation, New York University, 1953.

handwritten and rough-draft copy than he has in the past. Manuscript typewriting should probably begin with copying from longhand and progress to more difficult rough draft involving the use of simple proofreader's marks, such as those indicating capital or lower-case letters, transpositions, and paragraphs. It is very doubtful, however, whether much attention should be given in a high school course to the more complicated proofreader's marks found in the exercises in many textbooks. After the student has done a few simple rough-draft exercises, he should be timed on this type of work.

If students intend to use their typewriting in college or in preparing research papers in high school, they should be taught to type manuscripts containing footnotes, title pages, bibliographies, and outlines. It is possible that this material could be given as a differentiated assignment for the students who seem likely to use it.

Suggested Projects for Building Sustained Speed. At the beginning of the course, much attention should be given to the building of "spurt" or "flash" speed. As the work progresses, however, increasing attention should be devoted to production speed, the rate at which the typist can work while doing typewriting jobs over a sustained period. The goal is the development of a steady, rapid pace at which usable work can be turned out. Frequent timings of 20 or 30 minutes' duration are made on material involving typewriting in use situations. Some projects for practice of this type include:

1. Letter writing that consists of copying a series of unarranged letters, some with one, others with up to six carbon copies; others without carbons.

2. Planning and setting up within a reasonable period a tabulation short enough to insure that the first calculations are correct.

3. Writing a series of letters from an address list, using a form letter requiring insertion of specific data in the blanks.

4. Alphabetizing and tabulating a list of names within a given period.

5. Composing routine letters in answer to duplicated letters, which are given to students with notations as to the nature of the reply but without the exact wording.

6. Copying an exercise in which students are asked to raise or lower the amounts involved by a certain number. For example, the class may be told to raise all prices in a price list by 10 cents while they copy it.

7. Typing exercises involving spelling demons, some of which are incorrectly spelled, and making corrections during the timing.

8. Typing exercises containing grammatical and punctuation errors, all corrections to be made during the timed writings.

CLASSROOM ORGANIZATION AND MANAGEMENT

Division of the Period. Practice time in skill building must be broken into short drill periods, providing varied practice interspersed with rest periods. Students are not capable of sustained attention over a long period of time, and there should be frequent breaks in the drills. The practice should also be varied to reduce fatigue and to prevent attention from wandering. For example, after a speed drill that has tired those students who have exerted considerable effort, the teacher may give a drill on machine adjustments before typing is resumed. After an intensive drill, the students who have exerted themselves may have an opportunity to relax while the teacher demonstrates.

During any given period, drills will vary; and the objectives of the drills will vary. At one time the drill may be directed toward achieving rhythm; at another, location of new reaches or a review of infrequent reaches may be the goal; or in a third drill, better control may be obtained by reducing the stroke rate below the level of previous attempts. Students should be aware of the objective for which they are trying, and they should work actively toward the accomplishment of the set goal *for a short time.* After a vigorous effort, however, time should be provided for relaxation before the next work is started.

The routine for a period early in the course might follow a pattern similar to this:

1. A quick check of machine adjustments
2. A brief easy drill on previous day's work for review
3. A balanced rhythm drill of three- or four-letter words for the purpose of developing correct stroking habits
4. A sentence drill—two or three copies at varying rates
5. A flash drill on words in the sentence drill that caused difficulty or on which skill improvement seems possible
6. A period of repetition practice broken into relatively short practice

efforts on the sentence typed in Step 4. The purpose of this repetition is to consolidate the gains made in flash practice, to prove those gains, and to get the student to exert himself to the utmost to improve his speed and control of flash words and sentence continuity. Flash practice and most copying to improve control should be untimed; speed-forcing practice should be of ½- and 1-minute durations and, generally, not more than four or five timed efforts in succession.

7. Introduction of new reaches and drills on them at the end of the period to provide for absorption before the next day.

How to Practice Effectively. Early in the course the aim of the teacher is to develop effective practice habits. The learners check machine adjustments in unison before starting to write. They cannot keep up with the group unless they keep their eyes on their copy, keep the carriage moving, complete each exercise they start. They cannot show desired gains unless they practice intelligently, vigorously, and observantly.

Recently a class of beginning typists was observed at work. During the first half of the period they worked under close direction of the teacher. Their technique was superior. During the second half of the period they typed individually on exercises to be handed in for grading. The rapid deterioration in technique was amazing. They did not type rhythmically or keep their carriages moving; they snatched the paper out of the machine and started over when they made mistakes. They looked up at the end of lines—and often in the middle of the line if they thought they had made errors. They violated most of the principles of good typing that they had displayed five minutes earlier. Why?

The teacher had shifted objectives too soon and had relaxed his control of the learning situation. Students were trying for a grade, not for typewriting skill. Early in the course, learners need to work on short units with the teacher, until they learn how to practice effectively; and even later in the course, the teacher should continue frequently to emphasize effective practice procedures.

During the period in which the class objective is to increase speed and develop control, the practice of many teachers is to devote at least a part of the period to budget work. In this connection it is interesting to hear what one of the leaders in the field of typewriting instruction says: "It is my considered belief that the elimination of the budget (except for an occasional long-time assignment) will do as much to improve the opportunity for good teaching as any other single factor." [7]

The teacher should retain control of group activities and *teach* during the class period until near the end of the course. The assignment of short, closely supervised projects in which there is no opportunity for deterioration should supplant the budget.

Assignments. The typewriting teacher has one advantage over most teachers: his students usually prepare the assignment immediately after it is made. Beginning teachers have great difficulty in giving definite and clear instructions and in getting their classes to listen carefully enough to follow them. The teacher should never attempt to give class instruction while a typewriter is being used. From the first day he should make this one rule clear to the class, and he should never deviate from it. When he has the attention of the group, he should give his instructions, possibly requiring the students to indicate them in their textbooks or notebooks. In order to clarify his directions, it is wise to write them out before class. He should avoid prefacing the instructions with, "I want you to—"

Checking Work. The teacher should grade only in terms of his objectives at the time he gives the grade. For that reason, while he is building technique during the first six weeks of the course, it is doubtful if he should grade *any* copy submitted. Just as soon as he does, he changes his objective from perfection of technique to perfect copies. Of course, as the objective shifts to the production of mailable copy, these exercises (not the drills) should be checked.

Teaching Electric Typewriting. Most teachers feel that electric typewriters do not change the basic pattern of typewriting instruction to a large extent. A perusal of the *Business Education Index,* however, will provide the teacher with an excellent bibliography of articles on how to teach electric typewriting. It is unlikely, however, that many teachers will be so fortunate as to have a classroom completely equipped with electrics. For the teacher with one or two such typewriters, a tape-recorded lesson of 35 minutes has been prepared by Marion Wood and is available from International

---

[7] D. D. Lessenberry, "Suggested Methods of Teaching Typewriting," *Balance Sheet* (January, 1943), p. 230

Business Machines Corporation. Companies manufacturing electric typewriters have recently developed excellent materials for teaching electric typewriting.

Testing. Obviously, timed writings measure only one aspect of typewriting skill: the ability to copy. A satisfactory test of typewriting also should measure other elements of competency, notably the knowledges to be mastered in the course. Most textbooks now contain exercises that can be used to measure knowledges, and the resourceful teacher can locate or develop for himself from the textbook satisfactory timed tests of ability to punctuate, divide words, express numbers and symbols, center and tabulate, produce letters and manuscripts, and prepare business forms. In addition to such material to be found in textbooks, published tests are available, and the teacher's attention is directed especially to the following sources:

1. Tests of skill only
   Competent Typist Tests. These tests are published monthly in *Today's Secretary* and are available in loose-leaf reprint. Students may copy these tests as many times as they wish. Certificates are awarded for 10-minute tests at rates up to 50 words a minute with fewer than five errors, and pins are given for rates of 50 words a minute and higher. These tests are valuable in motivating interest in repetitive practice.
2. Tests measuring progress in copying facility, knowledge of correct typewriting form, and application of typewriting to problem situations *Rowe New-Type Typewriter Tests.* The H. M. Rowe Company, Baltimore 17, Maryland
   Rowe-Lloyd *Production Tests for Gregg Typing, New Series,* 1953, Gregg Publishing Division, McGraw-Hill Book Co., Inc., 330 West 42 Street, New York 36, New York
   Twentieth Century Touch Typewriting Tests, Sixth Edition, 1952, South-Western Publishing Company, Cincinnati, Ohio
3. Tests measuring occupational competency
   National Business Entrance Tests in Typewriting. A production test requiring completion of a reasonable amount of usable copy involving preparation of form letters, simple tabulations, alphabetized lists, and business papers. Information may be obtained from National Office Management Association, 12 East Chelten Avenue, Philadelphia, 14, Pennsylvania.

Grading. The typewriting grade should be based on a composite of the student's total typewriting ability; [8] not alone his speed at the end of the grading period. Yet when teachers ask, "What do you require of your typewriting students at the end of the first year?" they usually mean but one thing, "What speed or what speed and accuracy do you require on 5-, 10-, or 15-minute copying tests?"

For the benefit of the latter teachers—although they are again cautioned that speed should be only one factor in setting up the typewriting grade—the following grading standards attained on at least three 10-minute writings by high school students are presented:

First Year	*Second Year*
A, 50 net words or more	*A,* 60 net words or more
B, 45–49 net words	*B,* 55–59 net words
C, 40–44 net words	*C,* 50–54 net words
D, 35–39 net words	*D,* 45–49 net words
F, under 35 words	*F,* under 45 words

These are absolute speed requirements. However, after the first semester, it is suggested that weekly speed-improvement and control-improvement (accuracy) grades be given. These improvement grades are extremely encouraging to the poorer students of the class, who thus are given as good or even a better chance than the good students of obtaining a high weekly grade. These grades also stimulate the better students to greater effort than they might otherwise put forth.

The speed-improvement grade is computed by averaging the three best tests of one week and comparing this average with the previous week's average. The number of words improved is put in rank order for each member of the class. The median improvement is located, and grades are assigned approximating the normal curve of distribution. For control-improvement grades, the decrease in errors is compared in the same way.

Teachers sometimes use the point system for assigning typewriting grades. They weigh the importance of the various elements in the course—technique, speed, objective and performance tests, im-

---

[8] The beginning teacher especially will be interested in two suggested evaluation sheets prepared at the end of the first semester which are found in Marion Lamb's *Your First Year of Teaching Typewriting,* pp. 105–106.

provement, class exercises submitted with points given according to the number of errors, supplementary work—and grade periodically on the basis of these items. At the end of the semester, total points are collected and grades are then computed on that basis.

QUESTIONS

1. What three types of teaching are involved in typewriting instruction? How do they differ?

2. How should the teacher prepare for the first class period?

3. Describe the techniques used in introducing the keyboard.

4. Show how the mastery formula is used in building skill in the use of numbers and special characters.

5. Describe two drills for building manipulative skill.

6. Describe four devices to help students increase their speed.

7. How can typists develop control?

8. What should the teacher look for in checking poor techniques? What causes each of these lapses?

9. What areas of information should students master along with their typewriting skill?

10. How does teaching for knowledge differ from teaching for skill?

11. Describe a series of exercises designed to develop ability to think at the typewriter, progressing from the simple to the more complicated types.

12. Suggest projects that will develop production speed over a sustained period.

13. Why should budgets be eliminated in the early part of the typewriting course?

14. What steps can the teacher take to insure that his students understand assignments?

15. What should a typewriting grade include? Is an improvement grade a fair grade?

STUDENT ACTIVITIES

1. Assume that you have observed a general need for specialized drill in one of the following areas because students were not making satisfactory gains. Prepare and teach a suitable 10-minute drill for this purpose. Use all typewriting materials available and any pertinent material suggested in the bibliography or in the *Business Education Index*. Be sure to provide motivation, and make sure each student is

aware of the objective for which the drill is intended. Let this be a drill for the sake of definite improvement, not just a drill for drill's sake.

    a. Students use sluggish carriage return.

    b. Students shift with second finger or turn the entire hand under while shifting.

    c. Students backspace with second finger.

    d. Students cannot type figures without looking up, and many of them are using incorrect fingering for the figures.

    e. Students are pushing the keys and do not have enough force behind their strokes.

    f. Students write spasmodically and unrhythmically.

2. Teach a class for 10 minutes in new techniques.

    a. Teach the students to center their names on a half sheet of paper and fold the paper vertically and horizontally to check the accuracy of their centering.

    b. Teach the students to tabulate in three columns the word "then" written fifteen times.

    c. Teach a call-the-throw drill.

    d. Teach students to clean their typewriters.

3. Plan three typewriting lessons—one for use during the first month, one during the third month, and one near the end of the year. Include goals, suggested timings, and techniques.

4. Compare the three speed-development cycles presented in Leslie and Pepe's *Methods of Teaching Typing Simplified,* p. 54; Rowe-Lloyd's *Gregg Typing, New Series,* p. 18; and *Twentieth Century Typewriting, Sixth Edition,* p. 48.

5. Two weeks before the end of the term a college typewriting teacher gave the following duplicated sheet to his class. Comment on this approach in terms of the principles of skill building.

Standards in Beginning Typewriting

    I. Speed Goals (established by class performance before the examination)

        a. Type 50 wam net on three 5-minute tests.

        b. Type 40 wam net on three 5-minute tests.

        c. Type 30 wam net on three 5-minute tests.

        d. Type 25 wam net on three 5-minute tests.

    II. Parts Test (before the examination)

    Point to and identify each working part of your typewriter to the instructor in an oral test.

 III. Ribbon-Changing Test (before the examination)

  Change the ribbon on your typewriter within a 2-minute period. When you are ready to pass this test, raise your hand and ask for a timing.

 IV. Final examination will be based on the following abilities only:

  a. Write as many mailable letters as possible within a 20 minute period in the modified block form on p. 75. Correct all errors.

  b. Type three examples showing how you crowd letters (such as substituting *this* for *the*). The quality of correction is important.

  c. Type three examples showing how you spread letters (such as substituting *the* for *this*).

  d. Type three examples showing how to insert an initial letter which has been omitted (such as *the etter*).

  e. Divide twenty-five words correctly as dictated (pp. 68–70).

  f. Center vertically and horizontally a simple announcement such as that found on page 65 (7 minutes).

  g. Set up a three-column tabulation of three, four, or five lines correctly (7 minutes).

  h. Type from dictation sentences based on the points of typewriter usage covered on pages 66–67, 73, 76, 78, 81, 82.

  i. Answer questions on points in letter writing given on pp. 86, 117–19.

  Bring your typewriting textbook to the final examination.

BIBLIOGRAPHY

Barrord, Sara. "How I Teach the Ribbon Change," *Business Education World* (November, 1953), p. 25.

Hayden, Carlos. "The First Two Weeks of Typewriting," *Balance Sheet* (March, 1953), pp. 292–295.

Klein, Abraham. "Fallacies in Teaching Typewriting," *Business Education World* (January, 1952), pp. 231–232; (February, 1952), p. 291; (March, 1952), pp. 330–331.

Lamb, Marion. *Your First Year of Teaching Typewriting.* Cincinnati, South-Western Publishing Company, 1947. 213 pp.

Lessenberry, D. D. *Methods of Teaching Typewriting,* Monograph 71. Cincinnati, South-Western Publishing Company, 1949. 32 pp.

———. "Providing for Individual Differences in Typewriting," *Balance Sheet* (December, 1951), pp. 148–150.

Smith, Harold H. "How to Build Typing Skill Quickly," *Business Education World* (March, 1942), pp. 614–615.

Winger, Fred. "What the Tachistoscope Is and How It May Be Used in the Typewriting Classroom," *Business Education World* (December, 1952), pp. 165–167.

Wood, Marion. "Teaching the Use of Electric and Manual Typewriters in the Same Class," *UBEA Forum* (November, 1953), p. 24.

CHAPTER VII

Preparing to Teach Shorthand

DEVELOPMENT OF SHORTHAND TEACHING

XENOPHON, THE GREEK HISTORIAN AND WARRIOR (431–353 B.C), was an early inventor of a shorthand system. Though others had developed means of rapid writing even before him, he was so eager not to lose a single word uttered by Socrates, his master, that he devised a system of speedy writing by means of which he took down the addresses of his teacher. Since that time, more than a thousand systems have been developed.

In *David Copperfield*, Charles Dickens gives an exaggerated and highly colored account of the difficulties of learning shorthand, an outgrowth of his own experience as a shorthand writer. Defoe and the Wesley brothers wrote shorthand. Many of the early colonial leaders in America knew and used shorthand: John Winthrop, Junior; Jonathan Edwards; and Roger Williams, for instance; and a surprising amount of source material for American history comes from records written in shorthand.

In modern times, too, shorthand has been the tool of many men who rose to prominence. George Bernard Shaw was a shorthand writer. Woodrow Wilson found shorthand very useful, as did James Byrnes during his term as Secretary of State. Even so colorful a figure as Billy Rose at one time earned his livelihood by writing shorthand.

Many systems are in use today. Some of them are hybrids—part longhand and part shorthand, such as Speedwriting or Hy-speed. Of the true shorthand types, most of those in use today are script,

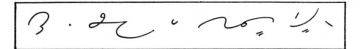

This is an example of Gregg Shorthand.

This is an example of Pitman Shorthand.

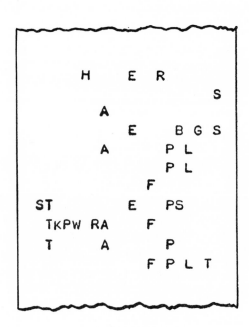

Here is an example of Stenotype.

rather than geometric, systems; that is, they are written so that the signs can be joined together as longhand writing is joined.

The teaching suggestions used in this book are based on Gregg Shorthand materials. Since Gregg is the system taught in more than 98 per cent of the schools in the United States that offer shorthand instruction, the chances are that most of the students who use this textbook and then enter teaching will teach Gregg Shorthand. The procedures recommended are applicable, however, to the teaching of any system of shorthand; and a Pitman teacher or a Thomas teacher or a teacher of any of the scores of other systems can adapt the recommended methods to his own situation.

Stenographic courses were first brought into our educational system through the business schools, probably around 1863. Pitman shorthand was introduced into this country in 1844, and Gregg Shorthand was first published in 1888. The development of shorthand courses in the business schools followed closely upon the introduction of the typewriter. One of the first attempts to attract young women to a career as an "amanuensis" was the offering of scholarships to young ladies by the Packard School in New York. An interesting aspect of this first training is that the young women who finished the course drew capsules from a fish bowl to find their first positions and were committed to accept their lot. Later acceptance of shorthand by business was rapid, and stenographic courses soon became very popular.

Because of increased demand, high schools began to offer shorthand as well as other business courses. Today it is generally thought that the student on this level should study the subject for two years to attain vocational competency. The usual high school course includes about three hundred hours of class instruction. Most leaders in the field of shorthand teaching, however, deplore the excessive length of time devoted by many teachers to covering the theory of the system. They state that, regardless of the teaching method used, this part of the course should be completed, or very nearly completed, during the first semester of instruction. Since shorthand is primarily a vocational course, it should be placed in the curriculum as close to the time of its use as possible. It should not be begun before the junior year in high school.

GOALS OF SHORTHAND INSTRUCTION

Thirty-eight leaders in business education were asked to indicate with which of the two following statements they were more nearly in agreement:

a. Shorthand has sufficient personal-use value to justify it as a part of the educational programs of many students who do not expect to use it vocationally or as an adjunct to their vocational training.

b. Shorthand must be justified on a purely vocational basis inasmuch as the length of time required for mastery is out of proportion to the personal-use value attained for most students.

Thirty-five of the respondents checked alternative *b*; only three checked alternative *a*.[1] In other words, 92 per cent believed that shorthand in the secondary school must be justified on a purely vocational basis. Ten years earlier when the same question was asked of business-education leaders, only 80 per cent of them chose alternative *b*, 12 per cent fewer.[2]

The primary aim, then, of shorthand instruction is to develop the ability to take the dictation that is encountered in a business situation with sufficient speed to insure getting it down and with sufficient accuracy to produce a mailable transcript.

It is obvious that research is necessary to determine the nature of business dictation, what causes hesitation in writing shorthand, what degree of accuracy of notes will yield correct letters, and what vocabulary is found in business writing.

An analysis of the office dictation of 72 different businessmen by Green[3] gives an indication to the schools of the shorthand speeds necessary for success in stenographic positions. He found that the speed at which a businessman dictates varies in relation to (1) whether he is a slow, average, rapid, or very fast speaker, and (2) whether he is in the groping, thoughtful, confident, or sprinting

---

[1] Carlos Hayden, *Major Issues in Business Education,* Monograph 75. South-Western Publishing Company, 1951, p. 75.

[2] J Marshall Hanna, *Fundamental Issues in Business Education,* Monograph 48. South-Western Publishing Company, 1940, p. 39.

[3] Harold H. Green, "The Nature of Business Dictation," Ph.D. thesis, University of Pittsburgh, 1951.

phase of dictation. The following table shows the dictation speeds for each type in each phase:

PHASE OF DICTATION	SLOW DICTATORS	AVERAGE DICTATORS	RAPID DICTATORS	VERY FAST DICTATORS
Groping (15% of time)	0–30 wam	0–40 wam	0–40 wam	0–50 wam
Thoughtful (45% of time)	40–60 wam	50–80 wam	50–90 wam	60–100 wam
Confident (30% of time)	75–90 wam	85–105 wam	100–130 wam	110–140 wam
Sprinting (10% of time)	100 wam up	120 wam up	140 wam up	150 wam up

According to this study, a stenographer must be a 100 wam writer in order to "take" even 75 per cent of all dictation. The average dictation period is at least 10 or 11 minutes. In that time the dictator will give four or five consecutive letters—the average letter taking 1.66 minutes for dictation.

Klein [4] analyzed motion pictures of three court reporters and of several 140-word student writers. He found that students paused about five times as frequently as the experts in writing the combinations included in the study. In other words, inability to *think* shorthand rather than inability to develop motor skills for writing at great speed determines the performance of the shorthand writer. This study emphasizes the importance of automatization of shorthand rather than intellectualization of the skill.

Phillips and Saunders, King, Lockwood, and others found that notes only 71 per cent accurate would produce transcripts that are at least 95 per cent correct. In other words, extreme attention to the accuracy of notes, which has been emphasized very greatly in the past, is hardly justified. Of course, the teacher should not forget that, when a person is taking dictation, his notes will not be as accurate as they are during practice periods and that a much higher degree of accuracy must be required at the practice level in order to attain 71 per cent accuracy of notes under dictation conditions.

[4] Abraham Klein, "Variations in the Speed of Writing of Symbol Combinations in Gregg Shorthand," Ph. D. dissertation, New York University, 1949.

Grossman asked approximately one hundred stenographers the characteristics of their shorthand dictators. The resulting list is valuable to the shorthand teacher who wants to develop teaching materials approaching office standards.[5]

MY EMPLOYER:	PERCENTAGE OF REPLIES		
	ALWAYS	SOMETIMES	NEVER
1. Walks around the room while dictating to me	3	40	57
2. Dictates while making or receiving telephone calls	11	49	40
3. Dictates while smoking	25	40	35
4. Dictates while chewing gum or eating	4	28	68
5. Dictates at an uneven rate of speed	62	34	4
6. Dictates slower than my teacher does	40	49	11
7. Dictates the name but not the full inside address	35	49	16
8. Watches me and dictates at the speed I am able to take	26	46	28
9. Makes comments to me that he does not want included in the letter	34	48	18
10. Changes words after they have been dictated	38	60	2
11. Tells me where paragraphs are to be placed	36	42	22
12. Tells me where he wishes commas placed	22	40	38
13. Tells me where he wishes periods placed	20	32	48
14. Spells words for me	8	52	40
15. Has me read back to him	20	64	16
16. Explains the meanings of words to me	9	36	55
17. Asks me whether the sentence dictated sounds all right to me	16	47	37
18. Asks me to substitute a word of my own for the one dictated	7	41	52
19. Hands me the letter from which he has been dictating	48	30	22
20. Asks me to make up the letter myself	4	57	39
21. Makes errors in grammar, figures, etc.	13	50	37
22. Leaves the dictation in the middle and returns to it later	1	52	47
23. Dictates in English and asks me to transcribe in another language (Spanish, etc.)	2	5	93
24. Asks me to write a letter like another that had been previously dictated (form letter)	12	67	21
25. Tries out a sentence before he dictates it	7	47	46
26. Asks me to leave space in my notes for information to be given later	7	42	51

[5] Jack Grossman, "46 Characteristics of Real Office Dictation," *Business Education World* (September, 1950), pp. 33–34.

	ALWAYS	SOMETIMES	NEVER
	PERCENTAGE OF REPLIES		
27. Tells me, during dictation, to get something from the files	6	46	48
28. Repeats himself and expects me to correct the error without being told	27	41	32
29. Dictates a great many letters at one time to be transcribed later that day	32	44	24
30. Dictates one letter at a time for transcription	10	34	56
31. Dictates as clearly as my teacher does	39	34	27
32. Dictates very short letters	5	84	11
33. Dictates very long letters	7	78	15
34. Dictates to me while I stand	3	33	64
35. Dictates to me while I rest the notebook on my lap	17	38	45
36. Gives me time out between the dictation of letters	17	42	41
37. Objects when I substitute my word for his	10	29	61
38. Inserts extra words after the sentence has been dictated	21	66	13
39. Permits me to stop him when he is dictating too fast	56	22	22
40. Dictates with a foreign accent	16	16	68
41. Dictates as I type directly on the typewriter		41	59
42. Dictates a letter to me with the help of another dictator	3	28	69
43. Leaves out important dates, descriptions, names, etc., and asks me to secure them	10	48	42
44. Uses the same general vocabulary in all dictation	24	55	21
45. Omits the closing of letters	34	39	27
46. Asks me whether I was able to get the dictation	23	35	42

Vocabulary analysts Ayers, Horn, Thorndike, and Dewey indicate that approximately 1,000 words comprise 90 per cent of our vocabularies. In an analysis of dictated material, Harrison found that 89 per cent is composed of brief forms and special forms. Mastery of the frequently used words would solve most of the student's problems; but, of course, the other 10 or 11 per cent of dictation vocabulary causes a disproportionate amount of difficulty.

Subordinate Objectives. In order to achieve the primary objective —writing shorthand rapidly enough and accurately enough to provide material for a mailable transcript—the teacher needs to break down his purposes:

1. Development of ability to recognize sounds and to record in shorthand the sounds heard
2. Automatization of the commonly used words and phrases
3. The building of a business vocabulary
4. Development of fluency in writing and in reading shorthand
5. Formation of well-contrasted outlines in which (*a*) straight lines are straight, (*b*) curved lines are curved, and (*c*) hooks and circles are completed
6. Development of the ability to generalize to the extent that is required in constructing new outlines
7. Improvement of English, spelling, and punctuation prior to the introduction of transcription
8. Development of desirable stenographic traits and habits, including the realization that the production of a transcript is a co-operative, not a competitive, endeavor of the dictator and stenographer
9. Understanding of the place of stenography in the business world, its possible promotional lanes, its opportunities, and its limitations

The first semester is dovoted to the study of theory. The second semester continues dictation of material for which the student has available model notes. New-matter dictation is introduced only in the second semester, at first with chalk-board previews of all outlines that may cause confusion. New-matter dictation without previews is given only after students have developed a writing vocabulary that will take care of most dictation.

METHODS OF TEACHING SHORTHAND

Few subjects in the curriculum have as many "methods" proposed for their presentation as shorthand. In fact, it is sometimes confusing to hear the discussions of the relative merits of these methods; and the question may well be asked, "Are we teaching learners or methods?"

Basically, the controversy over method in shorthand teaching hinges on the viewpoint of the teacher as to the nature of the subject. Is it a knowledge, or is it a skill? Does it involve what Morrison calls "science-type" learning in which the student's first objective is to understand the principles on which the system is built? Or is it primarily what Morrison considers a "language art" in which the learner automatizes his responses so that he can take dictation without thinking about the rule that determines the correct way of writing a word?

TIME SCHEDULE FOR LEARNING SHORTHAND IN THE PUBLIC HIGH SCHOOL.[6]

FIRST SEMESTER

Completion of 70 lessons covering theory of Gregg Shorthand (1949 and 1955 *Manuals.* Theory actually covered in first 53 lessons with last 17 lessons devoted to complete review of the system.

SECOND SEMESTER

Which Students	Standard 5-minute Business-Letter Dictation Test from The Business Teacher	Accuracy Standard.
Few	80 wam	20 errors or fewer
Most of group	60 wam	15 errors or fewer
Few	60 wam	16–40 errors

THIRD SEMESTER

Few	100 wam	25 errors or fewer
Most of group	80 wam	20 errors or fewer
Few	60 wam	15 errors or fewer

Introduction of transcription

FOURTH SEMESTER

Few	120 wam	30 errors or fewer
Most of group	100 wam	25 errors or fewer

Transcription emphasis during this semester

---

[6] Suggested by Leslie and Zoubek.

Shorthand as a Science-Type of Learning

If the teacher believes that shorthand is a science type of subject, he stresses rules or verbal generalizations of the principles of the system first and lays a solid foundation of understanding upon which speed drill can be built later. He feels that without this background of knowledge the learner cannot write new words or generalize about the system. Those who disagree with this concept say that the student who learns by this method develops mental blocking while he tries to remember the rule about whether to put the circle on the inside or the outside of the single curve and will be slower in developing facility in taking dictation than the student who does not think about the rule as such.

Shorthand as a Language Art

The teacher who believes that shorthand is a language art tries to automatize responses without intellectualizing them. The rules or principles are not verbalized; in fact, the learner does not know that there are generalizations. He writes the circle inside the single curve "because that is the easy way to write it." By the time that he has completed the textbook covering the theory of the system, he has seen and written so many words constructed properly according to the principles of the system that he writes them naturally in the correct way. If properly taught, he has developed generalizations upon which the outlines are based, unverbalized though they may be.

Those who disagree with this point of view say that correct responses can best be built on an understanding of principles and that seeing and copying correct shorthand does not insure that the learner will construct new outlines according to rules that he does not understand. They feel that verbalizing the generalizations leads to comprehension of them and that facility in taking dictation will come sooner if the learner has an understanding of the principles upon which the system is based.

GREGG SHORTHAND

Gregg Shorthand materials were originally prepared for science-type presentation only. The texts presented the principles or rules in word-list arrangement with very few shorthand plates showing connected practice material. The first edition was published in 1888, with a second edition (first American edition) in 1892, a third edition in 1898, a fourth edition in 1902, a fifth edition in 1916, the Anniversary Edition in 1929, the Functional Method edition in 1934, *Gregg Shorthand Simplified* in 1949, and the first revision of *Gregg Shorthand Simplified in* 1955. The revisions represent either modifications in the system itself or in its presentation. The publication of *Gregg Speed Studies* in 1917 was the first attempt to provide teaching material for language-art presentation. This book contained an abundance of connected reading and writing material in Gregg Shorthand and was to be used as supplementary to the *Manual.*

In 1934 Louis A. Leslie introduced the Functional Method based on the concept that shorthand is a language art. In this method shorthand is taught by the reading-writing approach to shorthand in context rather than in isolated word lists; no rules as such are stressed; students take dictation with their books open and with good shorthand notes before them. Leslie tells the interesting story of how his mother learned to write shorthand largely by learning how to read his letters written in Gregg Shorthand and how this surprising fact suggested to him the possibility of developing the reading-approach method.[7]

Because teachers hold divergent views about the nature of shorthand learning (whether it is a science type or a language-art type of subject), Leslie and Zoubek decided to publish the 1949 and 1955 *Manuals* in two forms: *Gregg Shorthand Manual Simplified* (commonly called the Basic *Manual*), an inductive-deductive presentation emphasizing the teaching of the principles of shorthand outline construction, and *Gregg Shorthand Manual Simplified, Functional Method* (commonly called the Functional *Manual*). The Basic *Manual* is intended for the teacher who believes that shorthand is science-type learning; the Functional *Manual* is for the teacher who believes that shorthand is a language art.

To help the beginning teacher of shorthand, the Basic and Functional Methods will be analyzed in terms of the principles of skill building outlined in Chapter IV; and sample patterns for teaching

[7] Louis A. Leslie, *Methods of Teaching Gregg Shorthand*, pp. 31–32.

each method will be presented. Inasmuch as other methods for teaching the Simplified Shorthand are not available at this time, only Functional and Basic Methods are discussed here.

Before an impartial analysis can be made of the methods in terms of the psychology of skill building, it seems wise to say, however, that all teachers do not teach alike and all students do not learn alike. The method that helps the individual teacher best to achieve the final objective—the automatization of correct shorthand responses—is the one for him to adopt. Actually, there is less and less difference between methods as they follow the basic principles of skill building more and more; and many of the teaching procedures recommended in this chapter are applicable to the teaching of shorthand by either method. Also, attention is called to the fact that this is not a teacher's handbook. When the teacher adopts a method, he should study and follow carefully the procedures outlined in the handbook for the method chosen.

Points of Similarity Between the Basic Method and the Functional Method in the 1955 Edition. In several ways the two methods are alike in their presentation of shorthand. The following points of similarity should be noted:

1. More and more connected matter is provided for the learner. Word lists are used only to focus attention on a new symbol or generalization; long word lists are omitted. The connected matter provides graded material packed with more than the normal percentage of examples of the theory just presented and also examples of the points of theory covered in previous lessons as a recall or reminder. The material approximates natural speech texture and the rhythm of ordinary business-office dictation.

About 30 per cent more shorthand context material is contained in the Functional *Manual* than is found in the Basic *Manual*. A reader's key for the first 54 lessons is printed at the back of the Functional *Manual,* and a separate *Student's Transcript* for all 70 lessons of the Basic *Manual* may be purchased by students whose teachers approve its use. It is believed that students will learn shorthand theory more rapidly by reading and writing shorthand in context than by repetitive work on isolated words.

2. The chalk board is used extensively. The teacher presents new principles, brief forms, and word drills on the chalk board, placing

the drills in planned arrangement and referring to them again and again. Believing that "more think, less ink" will produce better results, the teacher uses the chalk board to call attention to the construction of the forms. For instance, the dip at the beginning of the *r* is exaggerated in writing very large examples; and attention is called to other characteristics of good writing that are not quickly perceptible to the beginning reader of plates.

Courtesy Text-Films for the Teaching of Gregg Shorthand Simplified

The teacher points out characteristics of good shorthand writing.

3. Homework is based on reading and writing much context material once or twice; when the Basic Method is used, isolated word lists are to be written. Limited reading of plates in class is usually done for the purpose of checking homework, but the greater part of class time is used for taking dictation of practiced material, an activity that the student cannot engage in at home.

4. Dictation begins as soon as the student starts writing. The material for dictation is taken from current homework, which has been read just prior to the dictation. Students are forced for speed

from the beginning of dictation. They are taught, however, in shorthand just as in typewriting, to work at two levels: fast writing for verbatim recording of dictation regardless of outline quality, and occasional slow dictation for good outline quality.

5. The authors recommend that new-matter dictation be delayed until after the completion of the theory of shorthand. Even after the theory has been covered and new matter is used, previews are given of words on which errors are likely to be made.

6. The test of shorthand is a person's ability to use shorthand, not what he knows about shorthand. For this reason, the error in the application of theory is disregarded in grading; and the transcription of connected-matter dictation is the measure of the writer's skill. Tests consisting of isolated word lists are not recommended, as the authors feel that a word incorrectly written but correctly transcribed is, for stenographic purposes, correct. Ability to state rules verbatim and to construct outlines identical with those in the textbook is not an indication of the learner's ability to use shorthand. The ability to write correctly new words based on the rule just learned indicates the student's facility in problem solving, but problem solving should follow the development of basic skill. Word-list tests focus the learner's attention on the details of outline construction so strongly that the development of the learner's writing speed is retarded. Shorthand is not an end in itself; it is the basis of transcription.

7. Speed should be a factor in any shorthand test. More credit should be given for speed in writing an outline and for speed in transcribing it accurately than for mere correctness of the shorthand outline.

8. Correct outlines of dictated matter are available to the writer at all times. With the Functional Method, the textbook is kept open as the student writes. With the Basic Method, too, the recommended procedure is that the plate being dictated be before the writer; but latitude is allowed the teacher who prefers that the dictation be taken without reliance upon notes.

9. Pretranscription training is stressed during the theory phase of learning. The rules for punctuation of simple letters are given in the context preceding the plates, and reminders are inserted in red in the margins of the plates calling attention to the punctuation mark required along with the key word explaining the reason for its

use. For example, the marginal reminder says, "Comma, apposition." Marginal reminders also stress spelling words that are likely to present transcription problems. Realizing that merely including marginal reminders does not insure that teachers and students will use them, the authors have provided Pretranscription Quiz letters beginning with Chapter VIII. In them the student is told to write the necessary punctuation and the reason for its insertion when copying his homework. For example, he is told, "The correct punctuation of the following letter calls for 6 commas: 1 comma conjunction, 2 commas parenthetical, and 3 commas introductory." An additional pretranscription help is the inclusion of vocabulary studies preceding shorthand plates.

Specific Characteristics of the Basic Method. There are three specific characteristics of the Basic Method.

1. The Basic *Manual* provides verbalized generalizations. If the teacher wants to teach inductively (proceeding from examples to generalizations), the joinings and abbreviating devices are presented to the learner, and he is encouraged to verbalize for himself the generalization. If the teacher prefers to teach deductively (proceeding from the rule to the examples), he supplies the generalization first and then introduces the joinings and abbreviating devices illustrating the rule. The Basic *Manual* is set up for either presentation. Lessons 1–5, 7–11, and 13–17 contain the material upon which the rules are based. Lessons 6, 12, and 18 contain the generalizations or rules. The teacher who presents the material inductively teaches the five lessons applying the principle, trying to get the learner to formulate the rule. If he has not done so by the time the sixth lesson is reached, the generalization is made for him. At this point the teacher may place on the chalk board the words from previous assignments that illustrate the rules and ask the class to identify each circle and hook rule illustrated. (Not more than five minutes)

If the teacher prefers, he may turn first to the rule and teach it deductively, using the joinings and abbreviating devices as examples of the rule. In case the deductive method is used, the student is not required to give the rule verbatim. Instead, as the teacher points to the word on the chalk board, the class responds, "Inside the curve."

2. Writing is introduced earlier with the Basic Method than with

the Functional Method. The authors recommend that the reading approach be used for the first five lessons, but they provide also for the teacher who wants to introduce writing on the first day.

3. Penmanship drills are given in Lessons 24, 30, 36, 42, 48, and 54. These drills are provided for classroom practice, not for homework, as their purpose is to call attention to distinguishing characteristics of good shorthand. It is felt that penmanship drills should be deferred for about five weeks until the student has built up enough background to recognize the factors being emphasized. The penmanship drills, then, are the basis of remedial teaching rather than original teaching. They are a refining process by which students improve technique.

Specific Characteristics of the Functional Method. The Functional Method has two specific characteristics.

1. The reading approach is basic to the Functional Method. The student reads well-constructed, fluent outlines for twenty lessons before he attempts to write. At the back of the book are keys to the plates; and when a student does not recognize a word, he consults the key *immediately.* As he uses the key, he keeps the forefinger of each hand on the copy he is following, the left forefinger on the shorthand copy and the right forefinger on the printed transcript. After he looks up a word, he spells the shorthand and pronounces the word before he passes rapidly to the next outline.

2. The method is directed toward the automatization of correct shorthand responses without the student's learning verbalized rules, or without his even knowing that there are rules, principles, or generalizations. The author of the method, Louis A. Leslie, believes that after the student has seen and copied correct shorthand outlines during the first year of the shorthand course, he will automatically write the circle inside the single curve or the circle on the back of the opposite curve. He will make the joining that is the easiest and the most natural. By having a copy of correct shorthand before him as he writes, he is not permitted to develop bad habits and thus the good habits will eventually be automatized.

Analysis of the Two Methods of Teaching Shorthand in Terms of the Principles of Skill Building. Any skill-building course should be taught according to the principles of skill building found in Chapte· IV, pages 57–66. An analysis of the two methods, then, in terms of these principles, should be helpful to the teacher. Principles 4, 10, 11, and 13 are not included in the discussion because they do not relate particularly to method or because they are discussed elsewhere in the chapters on shorthand.

Principles 1 and 2. The teacher must recognize the pattern of the expert and be able to demonstrate that pattern. A quantity of well-written shorthand is constantly kept before the learner as a pattern. Chalk-board writing of shorthand, too, is essential to both methods. The writer must see not only the outlines, but also the movements that produce them. Unless he sees the *t, d, nd, th,* and capitalization marks written with an upward stroke; unless he sees the *sh, s,* and *b* written with a downstroke, he is likely to practice writing them in the wrong direction. Unless the teacher writes fluently with a quick getaway stroke, the student does not know what he is expected to do in writing. In presenting principles on the chalk board, the teacher exaggerates points that he wants to emphasize both as to what the character looks like and how it is formed. The teacher must understand that the *r* is written more slowly at the beginning and then ends with a fast stroke, that *m* starts rather slowly and ends with an accelerated and lighter stroke. Unless the teacher knows that the *f* is about three times as tall as the *s* and occupies approximately half the height of a line space, he cannot help the students with proportion effectively the first day they write.

The Functional Method is probably more concerned with the pattern of the expert in the mind of the reader, as writing is delayed until the concept of the pattern has been formed. The student keeps the textbook open when he is taking dictation so that the pattern of the expert is always before him. With the Functional Method, too, previews are placed on the chalk board before new-matter dictation is given. The penmanship drills in the Basic Method may act to counterbalance this criticism of the Basic Method, as they train the eye and mind of the learner to comprehend exactly what is to be written. They emphasize refinement in the concept of the pattern of the expert at the time when the learner can understand fine points more readily than is possible in the first stages of the course.

Principle 3. The teacher must appeal to as many senses as possible. When the first character is presented, the student is introduced to something he already knows, *s* or the comma. He is also shown that the *s* in shorthand is the lower half of the longhand *s*. Not one, but two appeals to sight have been made. As the teacher writes *r* or *m,* he appeals to hearing as he asks the class to listen to the sound of starting relatively slowly and accelerating, of heavy pressure at the beginning of the letter that lightens with the getaway stroke. As chalk-board drills are presented, the class spells first, then says the word. The appeal to hearing is supplementary to the appeal to sight. When the class starts to write, an appeal is made to a third sense, touch. It "feels right" to place the circle where it belongs.

Principle 5. Students should work at a speed just below that at which confusions begin to appear and just above that which is characterized by labored, detailed movements. By both methods of teaching shorthand, speed work is started the first day; and most dictation is directed toward forcing speed. To force nonexistent speed too soon, however, only leads to confusions. With the Basic Method especially, care must be taken that students do not draw their outlines. If too much attention is given to application of rules, the writer will sacrifice fluency in writing and will develop a hesitating approach to writing. Too much striving for perfection of outlines will also hinder the learner's progress. This possibility of slow, labored movements in writing shorthand by the Basic Method can be eliminated if the teacher follows the *Teacher's Handbook* and if the students read and write much shorthand in context. The Functional Method is designed to overcome this difficulty because the student has a better mental picture of what he is going to write before he starts to write it.

An innovation in the 1955 *Manuals* is the introduction of suggested timings for reading plates and also for reading word lists. These timings will help the student speed up his responses.

Principle 6. Each period, and each part of the period, should have an objective known to students as well as to the teacher. The material in the *Manuals* is set up in such a way that the teacher can easily indicate to the class the objective of each part of the lesson. In this way, work will not be mere busywork, but the reason for doing it will be apparent. The "Talks to Students" and "Did you notice—" pointers increase the student's understanding of objectives.

Principle 7. Repetition without conscious direction is worthless. Contrary to older methods of presenting shorthand, the Functional

Method involves only one reading of word lists and one writing of connected matter in homework. With the Basic Method, too, more attention is given to writing connected material. Students cover an extensive amount of material that requires conscious direction rather than the intensive constant repetition of outlines resulting in the deterioration of the quality of the outlines as well as in the quality of the attention given to the copying. It was formerly thought that repetition induces learning. Today it is recognized that repetition can only bring about conditions under which learning may or may not take place. Research has definitely established the conclusion that repetitive copying of words lists is not the best way to learn shorthand; it can best be learned through reading and writing connected matter.

Principles 8 and 9. Practice time must be broken into short drills, which must be varied before the law of diminishing returns starts to operate. In a typical period in which either the Basic or the Functional Method is used, the first part of the period is probably devoted to sampling homework, introducing new principles, possibly presenting a list of nine brief forms, and then driving for dictation speed. The dictation unit is probably from one to three minutes in length, although it can profitably be shorter in speed building. Instead of drilling for a long period on the brief forms, the teacher leaves them on the chalk board for several recalls, realizing that four drills will produce better permanent results than one long drill. Instead of staying too long on one letter in repetitive dictation, the wise teacher will move along to new material, for he knows that the gains on "retakes" may soon reach a diminishing point.

Principle 12. Skills should be automatized, not intellectualized. The Functional Method rests on the premise that students need not be able to verbalize the principles upon which shorthand is based and that thinking about the principle deters the writer. The Basic Method, if improperly taught, may intellectualize the skill so that the learner is impeded in using shorthand by too much knowledge of rules or too much consciousness of them. If adaptations had not been made in the Basic Method, this criticism would surely obtain. With the adaptations, however, the degree to which the skill is intellectualized should not slow the learner.

Principle 14. The teacher and student must keep in mind that error is the result of lack of proper technique and that development of technique is the primary point of attack. With both methods few tests of shorthand knowledge are given; tests of ability to use shorthand as a tool are substituted. Since tests of word lists are not recommended, the error of incorrectly writing an outline is not regarded too seriously. It simply indicates the need for emphasis on the generalization that will reduce similar errors. In shorthand, too, the constant and the variable error appear. An occasional circle placed on the outside of the single curve would not require attention; the constant error of this type should receive remedial drill. In any case, the real aim of the shorthand course is the development of ability to take dictation; and the real error is inability to take down shorthand that can be used in a satisfactory transcript.

Principle 15. Too much formal testing is a hindrance to effective skill building. Few tests are given, and these measure the ultimate objective of shorthand. Daily drills provide an informal test upon which teachers can base further teaching needs.

EQUIPMENT AND SUPPLIES

Location of the Shorthand Room. The shorthand room should be adjacent to the typewriting room; and, after the first year, typewriters should be available to shorthand students during their class period.

Lighting. The light in the room should be adequate for students who are reading both from their books, their notes, and the chalk board. The seating arrangement should insure an unobstructed view of the chalk board by each student in the room. Because the chalk board is used so often, the installation of a gallery light over the board is sometimes desirable. The use of soft chalk also increases the legibility of chalk-board shorthand.

Desks. Students should not be crowded at their desks or tables. There should be ample space for their open books and their notebooks during dictation periods. Desks should be high enough to preclude any necessity for bad posture when writing under strain.

Notebooks. Notebooks with spiral bindings are recommended. A stiff back that can be used with a copyholder during transcription is desirable.

Writing Media. Students should be urged to use the pen in taking dictation. At the beginning of the period, as part of their daily routine, students should check to see (1) that the pen has sufficient ink for the entire period, (2) that they have reserve pencils, and (3) that the pencils are well sharpened.

Supplementary Material. In addition to the textbook, students may use *Today's Secretary,* a monthly magazine containing material written in shorthand and inspirational articles about successful secretaries. Transcripts for the shorthand plates in *Today's Secretary* are printed each month in the *Business Education World,* counted in units of twenty standard words each for dictation at any desired speed.

The monthly *Business Teacher,* free to business teachers, contains 5-minute shorthand dictation tests at 60, 80, 100, and 120 words a minute as well as the new *Transcription Award Tests.* Students who pass the dictation tests with at least 95 per cent accuracy during the month of their issue may qualify for certificates from the Gregg Publishing Division, McGraw-Hill Book Company, Inc. The monthly set of tests also includes a Complete Theory Test of 100 words, which the student must pass with 90 per cent accuracy in order to qualify for a certificate.

Pitman shorthand teachers may use the *Pitmanite* for supplementary material.

Actual letters received together with their replies, excerpts from the school paper, the program of school activities, or other material of current interest to students may be used to supplement the textbook presentations.

Dictation records and dictation tapes are available for use with the Gregg *Manuals.* Connected material for Lessons 3–54 in the *Manuals* is included on these tapes. The dictation rate increases from 50 wam on the first ones to 90 wam for the final lessons. Records and tapes are also available for the second-semester course, based on the material in *Previewed Dictation.* The dictation rate on these tapes increases from 60 wam to 120 wam.

Use of these mechanical aids frees the teacher for administrative detail, observation of the problems of the students, and special instruction for those who need it. It may be possible to arrange for students to use the records and tapes during their study periods.

QUESTIONS

1. What is the primary aim of shorthand instruction? With the simplification of shorthand systems, do you think that this aim will change?

2. Of what value is Green's study of business dictation to the classroom teacher? Of what value is Grossman's study? Do you think that present-day shorthand teachers take cognizance of their findings?

3. What does Klein's study indicate in terms of the principles of skill building? What is its implication for the classroom teacher?

4. How accurate must shorthand be to produce 95 per cent accurate transcripts? What is the significance of studies of this problem?

5. What are the nine secondary goals of shorthand instruction? As you analyze your own instruction in shorthand, do you feel that these goals were achieved? In what ways could they have been more nearly met?

6. What is the suggested time schedule for learning shorthand? Does it seem reasonable to you?

7. Do you think that shorthand is a science type of subject, or do you think that it is a language art? Defend your point of view in detail. (Read Henry C. Morrison's *The Practice of Teaching in the Secondary School* for complete discussion.)

8. In what nine ways are the Basic Method and the Functional Method alike? In what ways do they differ?

9. Show how the Basic Method conforms to the principles of skill building. Show how the Functional Method conforms.

10. Describe physical conditions that will improve shorthand teaching.

11. What help will the shorthand teacher receive from *Business Teacher? Today's Secretary? Business Education World?*

STUDENT ACTIVITIES

1. Begin your study of the Gregg sound films on how to teach shorthand: the first lesson, a typical lesson, marginal reminders, shorthand speed development, and homework. They will give you a better concept of method than hours of reading about it.

2. Examine the Gregg Awards Leaflet and prepare a class report on the entire program of tests in shorthand, typewriting, transcription, and bookkeeping. Include information about the source of the tests, instructions for administering, cost, value. Qualify for as many Gregg awards as you can earn. Arrange them in the Credentials Booklet for display next year.

3. Prepare a bulletin-board display for the shorthand room. (You will find *Today's Secretary* useful.)

4. Analyze the various methods of teaching shorthand described in Chapters II, III, and IV of Lamb's *Your First Year of Teaching Shorthand and Transcription* in terms of the principles of skill building.

5. Familiarize yourself with the Gregg dictation records and tapes by listening to them. Experiment with preparing your own tapes.

6. In terms of the discussion in this textbook and in your readings, evaluate the following practices found in many schools: (*a*) giving the Gregg Complete Theory Test, (*b*) using the 120-word and 140-word tests based on *Congressional Record* material, (*c*) dictating a word-list test containing every brief form, (*d*) using penmanship drills, (*e*) requiring 98 per cent accuracy on Gregg *Business Teacher* tests before the student progresses to the next speed level.

BIBLIOGRAPHY

Cleary, Joseph. "Suggestions to Beginning Teachers of Shorthand and Typing," *Journal of Business Education* (May, 1951), pp. 387–389.

Condon, Arnold, and Rowena Wellman. "A Challenge to Some Commonly Accepted Shorthand Teaching Practices," *UBEA Forum* (October, 1954), pp. 9–11.

Duchan, Simon. "How I Get My Students to Do Their Homework," *Business Education World* (October, 1952), pp. 72–73.

Hosler, Russell. "Psychology of Skill Development Related to Beginning Shorthand," *American Business Education* (October, 1951), pp. 31–34.

Lamb, Marion. *Your First Year of Teaching Shorthand and Transcription.* Cincinnati, South-Western Publishing Company, 1950. 300 p.

Leslie, Louis A. *Methods of Teaching Gregg Shorthand.* New York, Gregg Publishing Division, McGraw-Hill Book Co., Inc., 1953. 497 p.

———, and Charles E. Zoubek. *Gregg Shorthand Manual Simplified, Teacher's Handbook,* Second Edition. New York, Gregg Publishing Division, McGraw-Hill Book Co., Inc., 1955. 90 p.

———, *Gregg Shorthand Manual Simplified, Functional Method, Teacher's Handbook,* Second Edition. New York, Gregg Publishing Division, McGraw-Hill Book Co., Inc., 1955. 121 p.

Reynolds, Helen. "Some Suggestions to Young Shorthand Teachers," *Yearbook* of the Commercial Education Association of New York City and Vicinity, 1951, pp. 33–38.

Rowe, Margaret. "To Shorthand Teachers, Especially Beginners!" *UBEA Forum* (April, 1953), p. 28.

CHAPTER VIII

Teaching Shorthand

TEACHING TECHNIQUES

SHORTHAND IS A TEXTBOOK COURSE, and the class instruction usually follows the textbook presentation closely until the complete theory of the system has been covered. Then follows a period devoted to advanced dictation. The difficult words in new-matter dictation are previewed on the chalk board by the teacher. When students can take dictation with a fairly high degree of competency, the typewritten transcript is introduced. The final step in the shorthand program is progression from the learning standards that have been met to job standards involving office-style dictation and office standards.

The possible profitable activities in the first-semester shorthand class have been reduced by the authors [1] of the *Manuals* to these:

1. Concerted reading and spelling of teacher's chalk-board outlines (both methods)
2. Copying from teacher's chalk-board outlines (Basic Method)
3. Individual spelling and reading of outlines from the chalk board (both methods)
4. Individual reading of connected matter from the *Manual* (both methods)
5. Individual reading of brief-form charts and similar matter from the *Manual* (both methods)

[1] Adapted from *Teacher's Handbook* for both methods, *Gregg Shorthand Manual Simplified,* Second Edition, p. 36, and *Gregg Shorthand Manual Simplified, Functional Method,* Second Edition, p. 32.

160

6. The taking of dictation (practiced matter only with the Functional Method)

7. Individual reading back of dictation (both methods)

8. Brief discussion of new theory learning and generalization drills (Basic Method only)

9. Shorthand penmanship practice (Basic Method)

During the second semester the list would be expanded to include:

10. Chalk-board preview of new-matter dictation (oral reading, no writing)

11. Dictation of new matter

DEVELOPING THE CORRECT STUDY HABITS
FOR LEARNING SHORTHAND

It is not uncommon for shorthand students to come to class the second day and report that they spent two hours on the assignment and still were not able to complete it. Skill-building techniques are different from the techniques they are accustomed to using, and the first job of the shorthand teacher is to develop effective study habits. Students must be helped to study intelligently, to eliminate time-consuming steps in learning, to make rapid responses from the start, and, above all, to automatize rather than intellectualize shorthand. Use in shorthand classes of the Text-Films for the Teaching of Gregg Shorthand Simplified, Film No. 6 *Doing Homework in Gregg Shorthand Simplified, Functional Method,* is strongly recommended.

If they are learning by the Functional Method, a part of two or three periods may well be devoted to teaching students how to use the key. Some will feel that it is a bit dishonest to look up the word instead of figuring it out for themselves. They will waste time in trying to spell the word without consulting the key, or they will lose their places either in the shorthand copy or in the key and spend too much time in going from one to the other before they learn the "two-finger" method of keeping the place on both pages. They will not spell the word after they look it up in the key and thus fail to gain a better understanding of the principles through their reading.

If they are learning by the Basic Method, they may draw their characters at first, or they may write characters incorrectly. The teacher using the Basic Method will be wise to follow the suggestion of the authors to defer homework assignments until he has devoted some time to teaching students how to study effectively so that, whether they are reading or writing, they make rapid responses from the first. Sometimes the suggestion that students study their oral homework together is a very effective device for pushing them to cover more territory in a shorter time.

Much can be done through class drills at the chalk board in pacing the responses to shorthand. If the teacher insists on rapid, staccato recitation in daily classwork, the chances for such responses during the study period are good. Another device that will force speed of reaction during study periods is the inclusion of reading-rate checkups throughout the texts.

Courtesy Leslie and Zoubek, Gregg Shorthand Manual Simplified,
Functional Method, p. 89.

Keeping the place with the left hand while writing with the right hand.

Ibid., p. 35.

Keeping the place by the "two-finger" method

USING THE CHALK BOARD

If properly used, the chalk board is one of the best devices available for teaching shorthand. Through demonstration the teacher can show exaggerated forms that bring out contrasts and principles to be observed in writing. He can call attention to the correct slant of characters (which seems to need special attention in every class) and correct proportions. He can show which strokes are written upward and which are written downward. He can show how outlines are executed with a quick getaway stroke, and he can present word lists to students for concerted drill over which he can exercise control.

The beginning teacher is timid about using the chalk board and often will not use it frequently enough. He is afraid of making a mistake in front of his students and after a sad experience or two with writing on the chalk board when his notes were not so well constructed as those in his notebook, he may feel that he cannot use this device. He should, however, take a common-sense view of his writing. Of course, the outlines will be less perfect than those on the textbook plates. To be sure, he will make an occasional mistake, but he should not sacrifice fluency for correct outlines that have been drawn. If a character does not come up to standards, he should not erase it; he should draw a line through it quickly and write it again. If a teacher makes a mistake, he will probably gain the admiration of the class by being big enough to admit it. An occasional error may even be good for class morale. Practice and preplanning will soon bring chalk-board work up to an acceptable level.

Class drills should be very carefully arranged on the chalk board, each drill occupying a block to which the teacher can refer several times during the period for quick recall. A block is usually made up of from three to five lines, each containing not more than four to six characters.

The following drill which is used to introduce the first group of brief forms illustrates the technique that the teacher follows:

Teacher: K is the brief form for *can* (writing it on the chalk board). Just read the word—you don't need to spell the brief forms. What is it (pointing)?

Class: Can, can, can (as the teacher points several times to the outline).

Teacher: The next outline stands for two words, *go* and *good* (writing in shorthand). When I point like this, say the two words together quickly without the *and.* What is it (pointing)?

Class: Go, good, go, good; (as teacher points) *go, good; can; go, good; can; go, good.*

Teacher: The letter *r* (writing) stands for *are, our, hour* (writing these words in longhand on another part of the chalk board). Let us just say *are, our,* but remember that it means two kinds of *our.*

Class: (Reading as the teacher points with increasing rapidity) *Go, good; can; go, good; are, our; can; are, our; go, good; are, hour; go, good; can.*

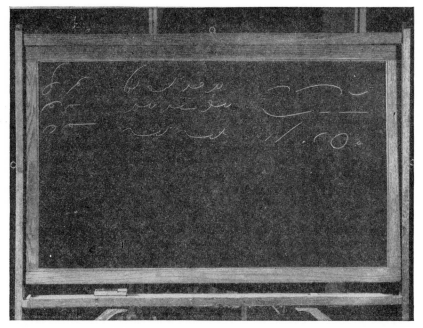

A chalk-board presentation of the TH *stroke and the brief forms of Lesson 3 in* GREGG SHORTHAND MANUAL SIMPLIFIED, *Second Edition.*

The presentation of the brief forms one by one is continued in this manner. As each new form is placed on the chalk board, every brief form previously presented is read and reread rapidly in random order as indicated by the teacher's pointing finger. The emphasis will be put on the forms most recently presented, but each form will be reread at least once or twice in each recall.

With the arrangement of the brief forms in blocks of four to six words to the line, the teacher can point at random with short jumps for the eye and hand so that the learner is not confused. This drill takes about half a minute and can be repeated as many as four times during a period with profit. The teacher quickly develops techniques for speeding up student responses and controlling the situation with the minimum of talk. Just as calling out drills in typewriting in staccato fashion develops better stroking responses, pointing in staccato fashion with firm and decisive movements quickly develops the "I point; you read" reaction so that no time is lost. Chalk-board reading and spelling should be developed in terms of the following five adjectives: *rapid, repetitive, random, unaided* (students reading, not the teacher), and *concerted*.

If the writing approach is used, there is some difference of opinion as to whether the entire oral drill should be presented before the student writes the word. Perhaps better results can be obtained by most teachers by completing the oral drill first, but some teachers find it more satisfactory to let the student write each word as it is presented.

The only difference in technique for presenting drills to introduce brief forms and drills on words illustrating theory is that with the theory drills the student spells the word aloud before he pronounces it. By oral spelling he is fixing in his mind the alphabet, the first step in mastering theory.

READING CONNECTED MATTER

It is probably better to use most of the class period for taking dictation. Some reading back of homework is necessary, however, to check on preparation, to evaluate study habits of the class, and to impress the group with the necessity for writing legible notes. Occasional sight reading of the following day's assignment is desirable, for in this way the teacher can quickly get an idea of his students' ability. When such reading drills are given, the teacher calls upon students in random order, permitting each to read not more than two or three sentences, and passing on to the next student rapidly, not stopping for the occasional inattentive person who loses his place. In case the reader has difficulty, the teacher prompts him quickly, so that the whole class is not delayed unduly.

Much pretranscription training can be brought into class reading if students are trained to give the correct form or spelling of material that might present a transcription problem. For instance, the student would read, "Mr. Jones asked—quote—capital W-Will the principal—p-r-i-n-c-i-p-a-l—source—s-o-u-r-c-e—of our supply be available—question—unquote."

The Gregg *Manuals* contain marginal pretranscription reminders that will aid classes in developing skill in "oral transcription."

INTRODUCTION TO WRITING

The students read an exercise one lesson before the present day's assignment. The teacher then tells them to watch him while he dictates to himself and writes the first sentence on the chalk board. He dictates very slowly and writes very large outlines for part of the first sentence. The students are told to watch the copy in their textbooks while they write the same material from dictation. The teacher dictates to himself as he writes on the chalk board another portion of the sentence. The students then write the same material from dictation while watching their textbooks. With the second dictation a longer portion of the sentence is dictated; and finally the entire sentence is dictated in one unit, very slowly. The second sentence is treated the same way, and then the two sentences are dictated together.

TEACHING PENMANSHIP

Penmanship drills are recommended for use with the Basic *Manual* as a means of refining improper techniques of writing that may have resulted from the early introduction of writing. The teacher's statement to the class in introducing penmanship practice may be something like this:

The more nearly your outlines resemble those in the textbook, the more legible they will be. Up to this time we have been satisfied with learning the letters and writing them so that they looked something like the ones in the book. Now we want to learn to make them more like the ones in the book.

Open your books to page 104. Notice the large model of the shorthand character for *r*. The little arrow is there to call your attention to the fact that the *r* starts with a strong curve. The same thing is true of the *l*. Watch as I write *r* and *l* on the chalk board. (Teacher writes.) Now you write *r, l, r, l* a few times. (Class writes.)

That is enough. You will get the best results in penmanship if you will spend more time *looking and seeing* than writing. Look at your *r* and *l*. Look at the ones on the chalk board. Look at the ones on page 104. Find just one fault that you can correct this time. Correct that one fault regardless of anything else. (Class writes.)

Did you correct that one fault? If so, find one more fault and let us correct that one this time. (Class writes.)

Now check your *r* and *l* again. Does it start with a deep curve? Does it end with a shallow curve? Is it level, so that if it were a saucer full of water, none of it would spill? Is the *l* more than twice as long as the *r*? Now write them again, and this time try to make them just like the ones in the book and on the chalk board.

It is a serious error to practice penmanship with the idea of writing a great many copies of the outlines in the hope that more or less accidentally some of them will be good outlines. This drill is intended to point out elements that need attention, so it is better to give more time to examining textbook and chalk-board models than to writing. The penmanship drills will usually be given in the order in which they appear in the Basic *Manual,* but the teacher who feels the need for a special type of drill may choose it at his discretion.

Shorthand penmanship is best practiced in the classroom under the teacher's supervision. It does not lend itself well to homework assignments.

MAKING ASSIGNMENTS

An assignment such as the following is of doubtful value: "Write six lines of each word in the brief-form drill." Before the sixth line, conscious direction will be missing from the repetition; and the drill will be busywork. It is generally accepted that extensive copying of connected material is more effective than repetitive intensive practice on small amounts of material, especially on isolated word lists.

The teacher is helped by the authors' suggestions to students for efficient study habits, which are attractively given in the text. The authors recommend that the student:

1. Read the word lists through, spelling the words aloud. Some teachers will want their students also to write the word lists.

2. Read the assignment through, writing on a slip of paper any words that he cannot decipher by spelling. The student should ask the teacher or other students to identify these words before class starts.

3. Copy the entire assignment through once, saying aloud each word as he writes it.

Sometimes the student will be given special drills on recall charts. Another help is a schedule of reading rates that enables the student to check his progress in increasing reading speed.

GIVING DICTATION

Writing from dictation is begun as soon as writing is begun. The first writing should be done from dictation to prevent students from drawing outlines and to accustom them to hearing words in shorthand. The classroom dictation is based on practiced homework for the first seventy lessons, for it is recommended that new-matter dictation be deferred until after the theory of the system is completed. When new matter is dictated, the words that will probably cause difficulties are previewed on the chalk board, the teacher writing as he pronounces the words.

Immediately before the dictation of practiced matter, the class reads the exercise. Then the teacher dictates for thirty to sixty seconds, asking how many got the dictation. If as many as half of the class were able to write the exercise, a second "take" of the same material is given at a faster rate. If half of the group reaches the desired standard, the third "take" is given at a faster rate. After approximately three accelerations, the teacher may drop back to a slow pace and ask the students this time to write for control of the quality of their notes. Gains made during the "spurt speed takes" can be consolidated as the longer unit of dictation is given at a somewhat slower speed than the portions.

To prevent students from merely copying from the plate and also to maintain alertness, the dictator should change an occasional simple word such as "the" for "this" or "today" for "yesterday."

In the early stages of shorthand, the dictator should give every possible help to the learner. Near the end of the course, the teacher may emulate the business dictator at his worst in order to prepare the students for any contingency. However, the dictation for speed and accuracy building is designed to focus attention on writing readable shorthand; and the teacher must help his students record what he is dictating. The following suggestions are offered to the dictator:

Use a natural, not a strained or high-pitched tone.

Avoid reading with monotonous metronomic rhythm when using a stop watch. Try to dictate in thought groups and in the shorthand phrases you are trying to make automatic with the writers. However, do not read with too much expression, as this practice diverts the attention from the writing to the meaning.

Emphasize plurals and past tenses, so that students will transcribe them correctly.

Speak distinctly and enunciate clearly. If your speech has regional peculiarities, strive to overcome them.

Practice test material before dictating it.

Dictate numbers more slowly than context material.

Before "takes" give a brief period of more rapid dictation than the "take."

Dictate sympathetically, as though you wanted students to get the dictation, not as though you dared them to get it.

Copy is counted into 20-word groups. The following table will help the beginning dictator in planning his dictation:

	RATE PER MINUTE			
	60	80	100	120
Number of seconds required for each 20-word group	20	15	12½	10
Number of 20-word groups dictated each minute	3	4	5	6

THE PATTERN FOR THE ADVANCED DICTATION CLASS

Because the problems of each lesson in advanced classes are more alike than are the problems during the elementary instruction period, it is possible to give a general pattern for dictation classes. This pattern will apply almost regardless of the text used or the exact stage of progress of the class.

The more advanced the class, the less time will be necessary for reading back homework and reading back the classroom dictation. As the class progresses, therefore, more time is available for dictation, as less time is devoted to other activities.

The following lesson pattern for advanced class dictation would be suitable for a class writing approximately 80 words a minute but not yet doing typewritten transcription. A 40-minute period might be divided approximately as follows:

MINUTES

5	Chalk-board drill on the word lists provided in the advanced text-book in use
5	Reading back and taking from dictation part of the preceding night's connected-matter homework
12	Chalk-board previews and dictation of repetitive new-matter 1-minute dictations as described in the *Teacher's Handbook to Gregg Dictation Simplified*, Second Edition. Two different 1-minute dictations can be covered in approximately 12 minutes
1	Brief-form recall drill from the chalk board or from a printed chart in the textbook
12	Two additional 1-minute repetitive dictations handled as above
4	Allowance for reading back from the 1-minute dictations during the two 12-minute dictation periods listed above
1	Recall drill from the chalk board or from printed charts in the textbook—brief forms or similar material

This 40-minute pattern can be only suggestive. It may never work out exactly the same way in any two classes. Some of the elements may be arranged in different order when the reason for the arrangement is understood.

The period opens with the drill on word lists in the textbook that is intended for homework assignments. This gives a "warm-up" at the beginning of the period and introduces new material. The next five minutes are devoted to reading back and writing from dictation the previous night's homework. This material is easier than the new dictation and should be given first to avoid an anticlimax. This drill may be completed in two or three minutes on some days; it may require as much as ten minutes on a bad day. As little time as possible should be spent on the homework.

The two 12-minute intensive dictation periods are separated by a 1-minute drill on brief forms because, if the 12-minute periods are filled with really intensive dictation, the learners need a rest in order to keep up the highest standard of effort. The four minutes allowed for reading back may be used whenever it seems best—usually divided into several short readings rather than one long one. The 1-minute recall at the end seems the best way to use that last minute just as the bell is about to ring and when sustained and intensive effort on dictation is unlikely.

The breakdown that is included here, therefore, is a good schedule but only one of many possible variations within the pattern indicated.

AN ADAPTATION OF THE SECOND-SEMESTER PLAN

One teacher of second-semester shorthand modified the above-suggested plan in a rather unconventional way with excellent results. He told the class at the beginning that it would be expected to do the usual homework automatically and without question, but that the semester's grade would depend entirely on the student's improvement in ability to take new-matter dictation at increasingly high rates. He said that the students would have an opportunity every day during the course to attempt a new-matter previewed 5-minute "take" at the rate for which each student was trying to establish a record. They were to transcribe (in longhand if a typewriter was not available and on the typewriter if it was) only the "takes" for which they hoped to establish a grade. If they thought that a transcript was done with at least 95 per cent accuracy, they could submit it for grading. After they had transcribed three "takes" with 95 per cent accuracy, they could get no further credit at that level and must progress to the next rate 20 words higher. Transcripts were made out of class on the pupil's honor, for the teacher felt that responsibility can best be developed if students are trusted. Also, he reasoned that if a student copied a transcript from another student and was able to hand in three papers reaching the desired rate standard, he would only get into trouble when he attempted to go to the next impossibly high level. Everything counted for the student, nothing against him; he was "on his own" with the burden for performance placed on him; he was working for an attainable goal; he understood what was expected; and there was no place in class for the loafer.

The lesson plan for a 50-minute period at the end of the first month looked something like this:

MINUTES

5	Oral reading from homework notes
30–35	Dictation of homework assignment, using the "pyramiding" technique
2	Chalk-board preview of new-matter 80-word "take" from *Previewed Dictation*
5	Dictation of "take" at 80 words
2	Preview of new-matter 5-minute 60-word "take"
5	Dictation of "take" at 60 words

After two months the teacher had left the 60-word level of new-matter dictation, and the "takes" were given at 80 and 100 words only. With an unusually heterogeneous group the teacher might find that three levels of dictation would be called for during the period for a short time, but that could be done with careful planning by the teacher.

The question naturally arises, "What did the 60-word people do during the 80-word dictation?" They tried to take it for a minute at the beginning, rested for a bit, and then tried to pick it up for another minute. As for the 80-word writers during the 5-minute dictation at 60 wam, they could take the dictation and try to improve the quality of their notes. Sometimes an 80-word writer was permitted to start transcribing during the 60-word dictation. In other words, students made some of the choices as to activity; and everybody worked like a beaver.

The greatest problem with this experimental class was the amount of grading required of the teacher. With everybody trying to better his own record, students often submitted so many papers that the teacher was severely taxed. However, he attempted throughout the course to develop in the students their own standards, so that few unqualifying papers were submitted. Another consideration is the amount of hard, hard work during a shorthand period when such a large block of dictation is given.

At the end of two semesters an entire college class had reached at least the 80-word level, about half had passed a few 100-word "takes," and two students were taking 120 wam. A section of the teacher's grade book on March 26 is reproduced on page 174.

The results with this class indicate an important point for the skills teacher: Let the student try his wings. How do you know that a student can't take 120 wam in two semesters of preparation if he never has a chance to try?

STUDENT	60	60	60	80	80	80	100	100	100	120	120	120
Andrews, Ralph	3/6 95	3/8 98	3/15 95	3/20 97	3/23 96	3/26 98						
Carlton, Marilyn	2/28 96	3/3 97	3/4 98	3/10 95	3/20 98	3/21 97						
Edwards, Holly Ann	3/6 95	3/8 95										
Foster, Graham	3/1 96	3/3 99	3/17 100									
Friedman, Ruthetta	2/11 98	2/15 98	2/20 97	3/2 95	3/6 98	3/17 97						

A section of the teacher's grade sheet as of March 26

CHECKING WORK

There is very little paper checking connected with teaching shorthand theory or dictation under the usual plan. The teacher takes time each day to sample homework by oral reading. He also has a check on student progress through each day's chalk-board drills and dictation of homework. However, the teacher who thinks that there is *no* paper checking will find that the quality of shorthand that his students write will rapidly deteriorate unless he has some standards to which he holds them. He should not try to regulate the size of notes written, but he should check to see that straight lines are straight, that curved lines are curved, and that circles are correctly turned.

TESTING

Many shorthand teachers give too many formal tests. They overlook the fact that the daily sampling of homework, the reading of chalk-board drills, and the ability to take class dictation are forms of testing. These three informal tests indicate the ability of the student much better than the old isolated word test, which may develop inhibitions in the writer that will seriously restrict his progress in taking dictation.

The only written test that is recommended during the learning stages of shorthand theory is an occasional timed longhand transcription test based on practiced material.

With Lessons 7–42 the authors of the *Manuals* recommend

transcription tests. The day before the test students are told that the test will be selected from two previous lessons, naming them. The students transcribe for three minutes from these assigned lessons. The authors suggest the following standards: [2]

Students may have up to five errors. To get a grade of *A*, they must transcribe 25 wam; for a *B*, 20 wam; for a *C*, 15 wam; for a *D*, 10 wam; below 10 wam, *F*.

For Lessons 43–70 the previously studied material from which the test is selected is dictated for two minutes at 50 wam. To get a grade of *A*, a student must transcribe with no errors; for a *B*, no more than two errors; for a *C*, no more than four errors; for a *D*, no more than six errors; more than six errors, *F*.

At the end of the first semester the teacher dictates from the *Manual*, without designating a special section for study, at 60 to 80 wam for two minutes. The transcripts are graded by the standards used for Lessons 43–70.

PASSING FROM LEARNING STANDARDS
TO JOB STANDARDS

The major part of the shorthand course is devoted to building shorthand speed through progression from one learning standard to the next. If the student can pass the 60-word Gregg *Business Teacher* tests with 95 per cent accuracy, he does not stay at 60 words until he can achieve 99 per cent accuracy. The 95 per cent standard is high enough for speed progression.

The job of training stenographers, however, would be incompletely done if teachers were willing to stop when their students achieve the learning standards they set. The letter with 95 per cent accuracy does not meet job standards, and some attention must be given in the course to the shift from learning standards to job requirements. This matter will be discussed in detail in the chapter on transcription, which follows; however, several points about job standards for taking dictation (not for transcribing it) require consideration here.

All office dictation is untimed, and the teacher should give some

[2] *Teacher's Handbook, Gregg Shorthand Manual Simplified*, Second Edition, pp. 89–90.

office-style dictation in his classes. If he has before him the letter to be answered on which he has outlined the main points of his reply, he will probably approximate normal dictation conditions. During this type of dictation, the teacher does not stress phrases, sound out words to help the student to think them in shorthand, emphasize word endings, or dictate with the almost metronomic rhythm that often characterizes classroom dictation. His mind is on the problem of composition. Such dictation contains revisions and corrections that the dictator wishes made. The student must learn to make these changes in such a way that they can be read back quickly and accurately. If he does not understand the correction, he should ask about it; and the dictator may redictate the portion causing confusion.

Accompanying untimed dictation practice is instruction in the proper techniques for taking office dictation. The following points should be stressed:

1. The student should be ready when the dictator starts. He should have a paper clip in his notebook to mark his place. He should have his pen filled and have a reserve pen or pencil.

2. If the dictator is interrupted, the shorthand writer should read back the last sentence dictated in order to help him regain his chain of thought.

3. The student should be trained to ask questions about the dictation if necessary and never to leave the dictator until he is sure that he can reproduce the dictation. Schools have not developed this technique, and the student is likely to try to hide the fact that he did not understand the dictation. He should learn, however, to sense the dictator's preference about the time at which to ask questions.

Some experience should be given the student in dealing with dictation containing mumbled words, errors in English, and words repeated to the point of losing their effectiveness. He should be given instruction as to the type of correction that he should make on his own initiative and the type about which he should consult the dictator.

Some attention should be given to the development of a specialized vocabulary for a particular business. The vocabulary itself should not be taught, but the student should be shown how to work out short forms for frequently used words and how to develop a list of technical words peculiar to the position.

In passing from learning standards to job standards, the shorthand student should also build ability to take sustained dictation. There seems to be almost universal approval among shorthand teachers of the 5-minute dictation test as the criterion by which the ability of a student to take dictation at a given level is measured. Yet office dictation is not of this length. The teacher should give sustained dictation over a longer period than five minutes and should encourage students to take radio dictation or to record talks and speeches. In the Business Entrance Tests (a joint enterprise of the United Business Education Association and the National Office Management Association) the dictation is given for twenty minutes with about three breaks during which the student may ask for redictation of material not understood. Teachers may adopt such practices.

Occasionally an outside businessman may dictate to the class. This motivating device gives the students a chance to take real dictation and also has the added advantage of interesting someone from the employing community in the activities of the business department.

DEVELOPING AN UNDERSTANDING OF THE VOCATIONAL OPPORTUNITIES IN THE FIELD OF STENOGRAPHY

Throughout the course, opportunities should be found for vocational guidance in the field of stenography. The advantages and disadvantages of entering the field, the local employment opportunities, traits and skills necessary for entering stenographic employment and progressing in it, and the educational background requisite for specializing within the field should be investigated and discussed. Much guidance material can be obtained through the activities of the departmental club. Field trips, readings, and talks by successful business people who used, or are using, shorthand are excellent source materials. Student interviews with business people who used stenography as an entering wedge into the business world sometimes provide personal contacts that are of more value than a group talk.

High school students are often most interested in hearing from their contemporaries, and the recent graduate who describes his job experiences is usually most effective in vocational guidance. Local chapters of The National Secretaries Association often have a speakers' bureau of successful secretaries available for high school contacts.

QUESTIONS

1. Why do beginning students often spend too much time on shorthand assignments? Give five specific suggestions of ways in which teachers can teach shorthand students to study effectively.

2. What attitude should the beginning shorthand teacher adopt toward writing on the chalk board?

3. How should chalk-board drills be arranged for most effective presentation?

4. What is the basic difference in technique between chalk-board presentation of brief forms and other words?

5. How should connected matter be read aloud?

6. How is speed developed on practiced material?

7. Give suggestions for giving class dictation.

8. List each step in the pattern suggested for the advanced dictation class. Analyze the reasons for including each portion.

9. Give five examples of learning standards in shorthand; five examples of job standards.

10. In what ways does office dictation differ from school dictation?

11. What procedures should be followed by the teacher who includes office-style dictation in his course?

12. How should the school attempt to deal with the problem of specialized vocabulary that each student will encounter when he goes to work?

13. What three informal tests characterize almost every day's shorthand class?

14. Of what should a formal test in beginning shorthand consist? Why? Should word lists be used for testing? Why?

15. How should the Gregg *Business Teacher* tests be used in dictation classes?

STUDENT ACTIVITIES

1. Introduce the first day's lesson, using either (*a*) the Functional Method, (*b*) the Basic Method with the inductive approach, or (*c*) the Basic Method with the deductive approach.

2. Present a chalk-board introduction of brief forms from one lesson.
3. Conduct a drill designed to teach students to study effectively.
4. Dictate the homework at 60 words, at 80 words, at 100 words.
5. Preview a new-matter "take" and then dictate it.
6. Conduct a speed-building drill in writing shorthand.
7. Dictate a letter as you compose it.
8. Examine or take the National Business Entrance Test in shorthand and evaluate it in terms of this chapter and what you know about business.
9. Examine all possible supplementary dictation materials: *Gregg Shorthand Dictation* (and *Handbook*), *Graded Office-Style Dictation, Dictation at In-Between Speeds, Previewed Dictation, Progressive Dictation with Previews,* and *Transcription Dictation.* Prepare a plan for their use.

BIBLIOGRAPHY

Bauernfeind, Harry B. "Shorthand Teaching Problem: Obtaining and Using Local Dictation Material," *Business Education World* (October, 1951), pp. 76–78.
Bowman, Wallace. *Shorthand Dictation Studies.* Cincinnati, South-Western Publishing Company, 1950. 655 p.
Duchan, Simon. "Can We Predict Superior Achievement in Shorthand?" *Business Education World* (February, 1953), pp. 276–277.
Grossman, Jack. *Graded Office-Style Dictation.* New York, Pitman Publishing Company, 1952. 136 p.
Leslie, Louis A., and Charles E. Zoubek. *Dictation for Mailable Transcripts.* New York, Gregg Publishing Division, McGraw-Hill Book Co., Inc., 1950. 238 p.
———. *Transcription Dictation.* New York, Gregg Publishing Division, McGraw-Hill Book Co., Inc., 1956. 420 p.
———, and Madeline Strony. *Teacher's Handbook for Gregg Dictation.* New York, Gregg Publishing Division, McGraw-Hill Book Co., Inc., 1955. 71 p.
Poulter, Max W., and D. H. Sullivan. "Vocational Aptitude Tests for Shorthand Pupils," *UBEA Forum* (December, 1950), pp. 25–27; (January, 1951), p. 25.
Tonne, Herbert A. "Letters for Office-Style Dictation," *Journal of Business Education* (January, 1950), pp. 20–21; (February, 1950), pp. 23–24; (March, 1950), pp. 30–31; (April, 1950), pp. 25–26.

————, "Who Should Take Shorthand?" *Balance Sheet* (March, 1950), p. 310.

Zoubek, Charles E. *Dictation at In-Between Speeds.* New York, Gregg Publishing Company, 1938. 345 p.

————, *Previewed Dictation.* New York, Gregg Publishing Division, McGraw-Hill Book Co., Inc., 1950. 290 p.

————. *Progressive Dictation with Previews.* New York, Gregg Publishing Division, McGraw-Hill Book Co., Inc., 1956. 320 p.

CHAPTER IX

The Teaching of Transcription

THE NATURE OF TRANSCRIPTION

THE ULTIMATE AIM OF ALL SHORTHAND TEACHING is the production of a mailable transcript. All instruction should point toward this goal; however, there is still disagreement among teachers of transcription as to the best way to achieve the mailable transcript.

Very few teachers believe that transcription should be taught from the first day of both shorthand and typewriting instruction and that typewriting for stenographers should be learned from shorthand symbols rather than from an intermediate step, the longhand copy. In other words, the student learns to typewrite *can* from the shorthand brief form *k* and not from the written word *can*. This group argues that a skill should be learned in the situation in which it will ultimately be used and that the intermediate steps, such as learning to write from longhand copy rather than from the shorthand word (the ultimate stimulus in transcription), should be eliminated.

Most teachers of transcription feel that such an approach to transcription violates one of the bases of skill building—that a skill should not be put into a problem-solving situation until it has been developed to a fairly high level. They believe that delayed transcription brings best results. But these teachers are not in agreement about the nature of transcription. One group believes that transcription is a fusion of skills already mastered; the other group feels that transcription is a new skill to be taught. When 38 leaders in the teaching of secretarial subjects were asked their opinions of the nature of transcription, they were equally divided in their answers; 18 felt that transcription is a new skill, 18 felt that it is a fusion of already acquired skills, and 2 felt that it is a combination of new and old.[1]

Transcription as a Fusion of a Series of Skills. Those who believe that transcription is a fusion of a series of skills such as typewriting, spelling, and ability to write readable shorthand feel that if the student masters these separate skills, he will be able to transcribe. During the time prior to transcription, the student is trained in writing shorthand that is legible; in typewriting and in "oral transcription," he is trained in oral spelling and punctuation of troublesome items. After a brief but careful introduction to transcription, he is given opportunity to build transcription power by daily uninterrupted periods of timed transcription at the typewriter. Discussion of English difficulties and other transcription problems is largely confined to the dictation period in the shorthand room, so that the transcription period can be freed for continuous transcription.

Transcription as a New Skill to Be Taught. Many teachers of transcription today realize that ability to write readable shorthand, to copy rapidly at the typewriter, to use English fairly well, and to spell most words correctly does not insure superior transcription ability. They know from observing the records of students in their classes that the speed typist in the group may be a slow transcriber unless he is given drill in the new skill, transcription. They know that the best shorthand writer may be a poor transcriber. They know that the best speller or the best English student may not be the best transcriber unless he acquires "know how."

Twenty-five years ago typewriting was in the "glass-wall" era; that is, a teacher would conduct a shorthand or bookkeeping class in one room while he watched his typewriting class through the glass partition separating the typewriting room from the adjoining room. Today we know that typewriting should be taught just as vigorously as any other school subject. Yet many transcription classes are still in the "glass-wall" era. There is, however, a growing recognition of the need for applying to the teaching of transcription many of the newer practices that are used in teaching typewriting and shorthand —the development of the concept of the pattern of the expert,

[1] Carlos Hayden, *Major Issues in Business Education*, p. 77.

the accentuation of technique rather than emphasis on "perfect copy," the isolation of troublesome items for special or group drill, and the right kind of repetitive practice. Teachers are now beginning to recognize that unsupervised transcription, like unsupervised typewriting, can establish such bad work habits that it may impede the progress of the learner.

Difference Between the Two Concepts. The difference between those who believe that transcription is a fusion of already existing skills and those who consider transcription a new skill is not as great as it seems at first glance. It is largely a matter of degree and of time. The "fusion" group disapproves of unsupervised transcription just as much as the "new-skill" group. Both believe in the careful introduction of transcription and the necessity for timing large blocks of work before the end of the course. Both groups favor drill in the typewriting room on such items as erasing, inserting and removing carbon packs or envelopes, arrangement of work area, and position of materials.

Those, however, who think of transcription as a new skill favor the use of many drills *in the typewriting room* to develop to a high degree the techniques that increase transcription rate and quality. They feel that such drills are teaching and are to be preferred to testing, as they would classify the everyday-and-everyday transcription of masses of dictated material without any opportunity for isolated drills to improve techniques that would increase transcription ability. They would liken the "fusion" class to the typewriting class in which many speed tests are given and long budgets assigned without provision for isolated drills to develop technique to be used in the speed tests and in the budgets.

Those who believe in much drill during the transcription period watch their classes at work. If they see that transcription is slowed down because of poor techniques in throwing the carriage, in keeping eyes on copy, in using the tabulating devices, they give drills to strengthen weak technique. They would be quick to admit, however, that isolated drill alone would not build transcription ability—that the student should have opportunity for uninterrupted periods of transcription. They would say that purposeless drill should be abandoned in favor of sustained transcription—unless it were purposeless too. They would agree that transcription rate must refer to sustained periods of transcription that involve removing and inserting paper, proofreading, and going from item to item.

The chief difference between the points of view of the "fusion" teachers and the "new-skill" teachers concerns how much uninterrupted transcription is necessary and when it should be provided. The teaching plans in this chapter are based on the theory that transcription is a new skill. They will include a number of isolated drills; however, they will also include plans for periods of sustained dictation.

The materials presented are also based on the strong conviction that results being obtained in transcription classes fall far short of the potential that could be achieved if teachers *taught* transcription, utilizing what they know of the nature of skill building. Typewriting instruction has developed tremendously in recent years; shorthand teaching has improved rapidly as we have learned more about the psychology involved, but little has been done to improve the teaching of transcription. Yet transcription skill is, after all, the basis for stenographic production. *Transcription must be taught, not merely timed.*

WHAT RESEARCH TELLS THE TRANSCRIPTION TEACHER

Within the past ten or fifteen years attention has begun to center on the development of transcription skill. Textbooks on transcription are being published, and a body of research pertaining to the nature of the difficulties encountered in the subject has been developed. Since transcription is definitely a vocational skill, the teacher should familiarize himself with studies that have been made of existing office standards in transcription. Before he can hope to prepare students for employment, he should know of the investigations that have been made in an effort to define the term "mailability" which he may hope to adopt as his criterion of satisfactory production.

What Is Mailability? Teachers glibly say that office standards should be substituted for school standards and that letters in the transcription class should be graded on the basis of mailability. To state just what "mailability" is, however, is difficult, for circumstances often determine whether a transcript should be mailed or retyped. What is acceptable in interoffice communications may not be acceptable for sending outside the organization. A letter that does not quite measure up to standards may be mailed at the end of a busy day. One need not examine a great many actual business letters to draw the conclusion that an acceptable letter in one company would not be mailed by another, that there are companies that would probably be satisfied with the work of some students whom the teacher would not be willing to recommend for stenographic work and whom he would not give a passing grade in the course.

Even though the teacher realizes that "mailability" depends on circumstances, he is helped by the generalizations made on the basis of replies received from letter dictators. According to them, a mailable letter is one that meets four criteria:

1. It follows very closely the thought of the dictation. Minor variations from the dictation are permitted, provided they do not change the original meaning of the dictator.
2. It contains no uncorrected errors, such as misspellings, typographical errors, incorrect punctuation, incorrect syllabication.
3. It looks reasonably neat. The erasures must be neatly done. Strikeovers are not permitted. Margins should be fairly even and the letter in good balance.
4. It contains no omissions, such as an entire clause or sentence in the body of the letter, or the omission of the date, the salutation, and the complimentary close.[2]

That is what 100 dictators say, and teachers should consider their standards carefully. The matter is hardly so simple, however, as just saying that these *are* our standards. They are ideals of dictators rather than existent standards, for an analysis of 550 letters actually mailed revealed that only slightly more than 50 per cent meet these requirements; half of them are "unmailable" although they are actually used to transact business. When student transcripts were evaluated by these standards, only 28 per cent were rated "mailable." [3] This research has two implications for the teacher:

[2] Sister Mary Esther Malone, *A Study of Transcription Errors of Students in Twelve Catholic Schools,* Unpublished Master's Thesis, University of Pittsburgh, 1938.
[3] S. J. Wanous, "Problems and Issues in Transcription," *National Business Teachers Association Seventh Yearbook,* 1941, p. 320.

1. He cannot accept as gospel truth all standards that businessmen report to him.
2. The percentage of mailability in schools is low, although, of course, not as low as this report would at first lead us to believe.

Balsley analyzed the transcription practices of 332 widely scattered firms and found little uniformity in practices. For instance, there were 179 different ways of recording carbon-paper notations on outgoing letters.[4] Her findings are bound to be disturbing to the transcription teacher who insists on one way and one way only for setting up the various parts of a business letter or memorandum.

What Is the Nature of Transcription Errors? Another research topic of importance to the transcription teacher before he can plan his course intelligently is the analysis of the causes of transcription errors. He cannot apply the mastery formula effectively unless he analyzes his students' difficulties. To tabulate the errors found on all papers submitted to him would, however, be too time consuming; he can profit by other teachers' analyses.

In one study of transcription weaknesses, it was found that English errors account for 55 per cent of the total errors; content errors, 28 per cent; typographical errors, 9 per cent; and letter-mechanics errors, 8 per cent.[5]

Obviously, a great deal of attention must be given to English, spelling, and proofreading along with shorthand instruction.

What Is a Satisfactory Transcription Rate? A third topic of interest to the transcription teacher concerns the determination of a transcription rate that meets office employment standards. Here again let it be said that various factors affect the answer to this question. The rate of transcription is dependent on many considerations indicated on the chart on page 187.

Because of the variations in types of material and conditions of dictation, few published statements of employment standards are available. One company that measures the output of its employees sets as a satisfactory production standard the transcription of seven letters containing eleven five-inch lines during an hour.

On the basis of his wide experience in the field of shorthand and

[4] Irol Whitmore Balsley, *Current Transcription Practices in Business Firms.* Cincinnati, South-Western Publishing Company, Monograph 86, 1954, p. 62.

[5] Wanous, *op. cit.,* p. 318.

FACTORS IN THE RATE OF TRANSCRIPTION

1. The nature of the dictation
   (Material containing problems of vocabulary, spelling, punctuation, or homonyms is transcribed more slowly than easier material.)
2. The familiarity of the transcriber with the meaning of the material
3. The speed at which the dictation was given
4. The legibility of the transcriber's shorthand
5. The amount of dictation in the "take"
   (The longer the period of dictation, the more difficult the transcription)
6. The length of the letters dictated
   (Short letters are transcribed at a higher rate than long letters.)
7. The length of the transcription period
   (It is easier to maintain a fast rate for twenty minutes than for forty.)
8. The number of carbon copies required
9. The quality of transcription which the teacher requires

---

transcription, Louis A. Leslie [6] sets the following standard for high school transcription classes:

> At the end of four semesters of shorthand and at least two semesters of typewriting, when dictation is given at 80–100 words a minute in a group of letters comprising a total dictation of 800–1,000 words, the learner should transcribe at the rate of 20–25 words a minute with 20 words as the minimum rate acceptable for credit. At least 75 per cent of the letters in any five consecutive daily transcription periods should be mailable.

What Do Transcribers Do? The trainer of transcribers should also be familiar with research relative to the activities involved in stenography. A job analysis of transcription duties of 115 stenographers and secretaries revealed that the following duties were performed by all transcribers as part of the letter transcription process:

[6] Louis A. Leslie, *Methods of Teaching Transcription*, pp. 51–52.

Arranging transcription materials
Preparing the typewriter
Writing date, address, salutation, and so forth
Reading shorthand notes, typewriting
Making corrections
Proofreading transcribed material
Addressing envelopes
Arranging finished work
Consulting references
Arranging the letter in appropriate style
Punctuating the message
Discriminating between words, spelling
Capitalizing the message
Dividing words correctly into syllables
Selecting proper correspondence form

The following additional duties were performed by more than 50 per cent of the transcribers studied:

Selecting appropriate title for the addressee
Paragraphing the message
Editing the message
Selecting the appropriate salutation, complimentary close
Deciding upon use of title for dictator

Only four of the listed duties were handled by fewer than 50 per cent of the transcribers:

Deciding upon the order in which letters are transcribed
Determining the number of carbon copies needed
Deciding upon proper file reference notations
Deciding upon appropriate subject headings [7]

Stenographers spend slightly less than one third of the working day in transcribing shorthand dictation. More time is devoted to transcription than to any other stenographic duties.

Do Stenographers Have Access to the Correspondence They Are Answering? In order to decide whether to teach students to write

[7] S. J. Wanous, "The Implications of Research Related to the Teaching of Transcription," *The National Business Education Quarterly* (Summer, 1940), p. 24.

addresses in shorthand, teachers will be interested in a survey made by Leslie.[8] He asked 641 businessmen whether they turned over the correspondence being answered to the stenographer after the dictation. More than three-fourths of the dictators (501) always gave their stenographers the letters after the dictation. The stenographer has an opportunity to get the correct spelling of the address and also to check the meaning of a doubtful item by reference to the correspondence.

Is Transcription Being Taught as a Separate Course? Finally, the transcription teacher should know something of the prevailing patterns for courses of study in the field of shorthand. A limited study reveals that 55 per cent of the schools sampled (267 of 519 schools in 4 states) have one full shorthand period *and* one full period at the typewriter every day for at least one semester.[9] When this percentage is compared with the 13 per cent reporting separate classes in transcription in a similar survey in 1934, the growth is amazing.

GOALS OF TRANSCRIPTION INSTRUCTION

Before the teacher sets the goals for his high school course in transcription, he may well consider the factors that are responsible for poor results. The presence of all or any of the elements in the chart on page 190 might result in unsatisfactory transcription.

Over-all Aim. The over-all aim of the transcription course at the high school level is to produce mailable copy at a fair rate of speed.

Subordinate Aims. The following component goals must be attained in order to achieve the over-all aim:

1. To write readable shorthand notes

   The student must be able to write shorthand notes that are readable for later, as well as immediate, transcription.

2. To improve typewriting techniques

   The student must continue to improve his typewriting techniques.

[8] Louis A. Leslie, *Methods of Teaching Transcription,* p. 136.
[9] W. W. Renshaw, "Where Do We Stand in Transcription?" *Business Education World* (May, 1946), p. 465.

Too frequently he is not studying typewriting at the time when he is learning to transcribe, and his copying rate deteriorates unless he is given drill to maintain or improve it. Also the teacher should give additional instruction in such techniques as manipulating the machine for erasing, erasing on carbons, backfeeding stapled material, erasing the error at the bottom of the page in such a way as to prevent the paper from slipping.

CAUSES FOR POOR TRANSCRIPTION ATTAINMENTS

On the Part of the Teacher

1. Failure to recognize the fact that transcription must be taught
2. Lack of understanding of the psychology of skill
3. Lack of emphasis on the necessity of producing mailable copy at the first attempt when sustained transcription is timed
4. Unwillingness to adopt timesaving techniques accepted by many businesses, such as a standardized 6-inch line, few words syllabicated at the end of the line, or short signature forms
5. Insufficient opportunity for sustained transcription after techniques have been developed
6. Failure to develop the concept that dictation is a co-operative effort, not the usual "I-dare-you-to-get-it" contest

On the Part of the Learner

1. Unthinking approach
2. Lack of responsibility for the finished product
3. Unwillingness to plan, estimate, and evaluate work
4. Disregard of the value of the dictionary or inability to use it correctly
5. Tendency to take a chance on spelling or syllabication
6. Failure to change from learning standards to job standards
7. Failure to provide self with proper materials: a desk dictionary, an eraser, paper, and so forth
8. Overdependence on the individual letter for the stimulus in typewriting

3. To co-ordinate the reading of shorthand with the typing from symbols

> The student must be taught to read in thought groups, so that he types for sense. He must be taught to read ahead in the copy while he is completing the typing from the last symbol. This is the type of training that helps to prevent the "We-have-you-letter" type of error.

4. To apply the knowledge of English, punctuation, and spelling that he already has

> Because transcription is so complex, the student is likely not to apply the principles of English, punctuation, and spelling that he supposedly knows. He will write, "A person should *way* his words," although he knows better and can make the correction as soon as it is called to his attention.

5. To develop word sense and the ability to hear word endings

> The student should become conscious of differences between such words as "ask" and "asked," "advice" and "advise," "affect" and "effect."

6. To increase vocabulary and become word conscious

> If the student does not understand the usage of a word given in dictation, he should clarify his understanding before he transcribes incorrectly.

7. To master the spelling of a basic business vocabulary

> Although there is merit in looking up the correct spelling of a word rather than spelling it incorrectly, there is more merit in knowing how to spell it without having to use the dictionary. Before a satisfactory production rate can be built, the transcriber must have mastered the spelling of the most commonly used words.

8. To recognize commonly used grammatical constructions to enable him to apply the correct punctuation to them

Inserting a comma "because it sounds better that way" is not adequate background for the stenographer. The transcriber can never learn to punctuate accurately unless he can recognize an appositive, a series, a noun clause, a participle, or a nonrestrictive clause.

9. To estimate the transcription space required for each "take" in order to assure correct placement

The student must be able to produce a mailable copy the first time he types his notes. In order to do this, he must be able to judge the number of words he usually writes in one column of his notebook. He must also have at his fingertips setups for short, medium, and long letters.

10. To arrange materials for a steady flow of work

Unless the transcriber handles his materials efficiently, he cannot attain a satisfactory production rate. Much drill should be given in the expeditious insertion and removal of carbons, erasing when preparing multiple carbons, addressing envelopes.

11. To select correct materials

The student should use the correct kind of paper for carbon copies and originals. He should discard carbon paper that will no longer produce attractive work. He should use the proper type of eraser for original and carbons and keep it clean. He should use a copyholder to position his notebook and thus avoid eyestrain. He should change a typewriter ribbon when the ink becomes too dull for legibility.

12. To clean the typewriter at the end of *each* transcription period

Since transcription involves making corrections, the typewriter should be cleaned at the end of each period and left in proper working condition for the next typist.

13. To use the dictionary intelligently

Frequently the student who looks up a word in the dictionary will make an error in transcription because of inability to understand the reference after he finds it. For instance, he may mistake a syllabication mark for a hyphen. Or he may look up the spelling of "mantel" and, finding this spelling, use it without reading the definition to discover that the word he should use is "mantle." Again, he may find that "slip-sheet" is hyphenated and not read on to learn that the verb is hyphenated but not the noun.

14.   To get the gist of the meaning of a dictated unit and to make sense in the transcript in terms of this central idea

Often the material of the dictation should be discussed with the class, so that the transcribers will understand the idea they are trying to reproduce. The unique feature of dictation is that the stenographer is asked to use another person's vocabulary in place of his own. In order to do this intelligently, he must comprehend the idea being expressed.

15.   To follow directions

When the dictation is given, instructions for transcription are given. The student should mark *at the beginning of his notes* the instructions about letter style, number of carbon copies required, order of transcription, special instructions for mailing such as "air mail," "special delivery," or "postal card."

16.   To develop responsibility for a usable final product

The student should be even more responsible for finding and correcting his errors than for transcribing in the first place. He should develop high standards, which serve him as criteria for releasing work to the instructor for grading.

CONTENT OF THE TRANSCRIPTION COURSE

The most desirable arrangement of the transcription course is to schedule it immediately following the shorthand period. The shorthand period can then be used for dictation of material to be transcribed, for all drills that do not require the use of the typewriter, and for checking papers and recording scores. As much of the transcription period as possible should be freed for sustained transcription that is timed. No set rule can be given about the amount of time that should be devoted to drill at the typewriter; that will depend on training needs as revealed by the teacher's observation of the class at work. It can be said, however, that the teacher should provide a cycle of drills for strengthening weak techniques, that they should become increasingly shorter as the course continues, and that the major part of the period should be given to timed transcription of new material.

The following outline of subject matter does not indicate the sequence of presentation, as drills are incorporated into lessons involving other items. It merely lists the types of subject matter included in the course.

I. *Analysis of Training Needs*
    A. Comparison of typewriting copying rates with transcription rates on the same copy and determination of poor typewriting techniques, both during the copying and during the transcription
    B. The measurement of shorthand reading rate (Shorthand room)
    C. Analysis of punctuation, spelling, or syllabication difficulties (partly in the shorthand room but also while typing, to check transfer of learning)

II. *Development of the Concept of the Pattern of the Expert*
    A. Reading, prepunctuation, prespelling, and possibly pretyping of troublesome words before transcription of first notes
    B. Teacher demonstration of reading and typing the transcript
    C. Student participation in unison transcription
    D. Proofreading of finished transcript

III. *Isolation of Troublesome Items (as Needed)*
    A. Drills to correct faulty typewriting habits
    B. Drills to bring transcription speed to a higher level through improved techniques on short units
    C. Pretyping of difficult words to "smooth out" troublesome sequences (A word that causes little difficulty in longhand copy may present a problem in transcription. Typing room)
    D. Drills involving the choice of correct homonyms (Homework and drill in the shorthand room are helpful, but machine-dictation drills and shorthand transcription of problem material are more valuable because it is harder to make the choices involved

while typing, especially under time, than when working alone
with pen or pencil.)

E. Drills involving common punctuation difficulties (Homework,
   shorthand classroom, and typing room)

F. Drills involving the use of frequently misspelled words (Homework and drill in both classrooms)

G. Demonstration and drill on correct techniques for inserting multiple carbons (Typing room)

H. Demonstration and drill on correct techniques for erasing on
   multiple carbons (Typing room)

I. Demonstration and drill on correct technique for reinserting
   stapled copies for correction by backfeeding and for making
   erasures at the bottom of the page without letting paper slip
   (Typing room)

J. Drills containing omission of words that students substitute to
   make sense in the transcript (Shorthand room)

K. Flow-of-work drills in which students position materials and
   insert and remove papers without typing until time required for
   operation is materially reduced (Typing room)

IV. *Student Transcription* (*Major Portion of the Course*)

A. Sources

   1. Shorthand plates (as an introduction to transcription)
   2. Notes prepared as homework (so that students become con-
      scious of the necessity for emphasizing contrasts and writing
      "self-reading shorthand")
   3. Dictated notes (usual source)
      a. Transcribed at once
      b. Transcribed after a lapse of several days

B. Types

   1. Letters, starting with the simple short forms and gradually
      proceeding to longer, more complex forms involving prob-
      lems of arrangement (usual type)
   2. Reports
   3. Office memoranda
   4. Articles
   5. Speeches
   6. Instructions to the transcriber, to be used as a basis for
      machine composition
   7. Instructions to the transcriber, to be compiled into a manual

C. Kind of Dictation

   1. Timed "takes" (most often used)

2. Untimed dictation at uneven rates
3. Dictation revised as dictator changes his mind during the "take"
4. Student requests for redictation if he does not understand an item and wants to verify it
5. Extended periods of dictation comparable to office conditions
6. Dictation by outsiders

TEACHING PLANS

Most of the teaching in transcription involves *skill building* and follows the principles of skill building set forth previously. It is undoubtedly true, however, that students have not mastered the *knowledges* necessary to accurate transcription. They must be taught to the point of mastery the background subject matter in which they are defective, such as ordinary business vocabulary, spelling, or punctuation. Of course, the purpose of the teaching of both skills and knowledges is only preparation for the ultimate objective, their *integration* into a usable product through *solution of the problems* that the dictation presents.

Applying the Psychological Principles of Skill Building. The transcription teacher will want to start his students transcribing short units that provide intensive drill with frequent relaxation periods between efforts. He will realize that, in general, his task is teaching, not testing. He will insist that the transcription rate be fairly rapid from the start—the rate that is slow enough to avoid confusions and fast enough to avoid slow, labored, unnatural movements. He will not insist upon perfect copies when he is working on technique; he is more concerned with "how" the transcription is done than with the result in the early stages.

He will set for his students only attainable goals. If the emphasis is on building transcription speed, progress will be judged in part by the student's chart for last week. If transcription is just beginning, the student will be prepared for the assigned task in such a way that he approaches it with confidence.

The teacher will check constantly for defective subordinate techniques (such as faulty shifting on the typewriter) that may be causing learning plateaus. He will, through teacher demonstration, instill in the mind of the learner the concept of the goal for which he is striving—good transcription techniques—and he will keep before the learner at all times definite objectives for each exercise assigned.

Using the Mastery Formula. The mastery formula plays an important part in the building of transcription skill. Since students have previously studied several of the skills that are integrated into the process of transcription, *pretesting* is imperative. Before drilling on techniques already known, the teacher must determine the learning needs of his students. For instance, pretesting in the spelling of the most frequently used words in business writing would indicate those requiring study. The student can then concentrate on the relatively few words he cannot spell. The same need is apparent in punctuation. Only the errors that the student commonly makes require drill, not all the material that has been taught every year since the fifth grade. Pretesting determines the difficulties that students are encountering.

When the teacher is trying to build transcription speed, the pretest is helpful. As he watches his students at work, he can check techniques that impede progress and that should be marked for special drill.

After the pretest, the teacher should *teach* the necessary material. If spelling is causing difficulty, the learner should be helped to pronounce the word in a way that will aid him in spelling it. He should be taught to spell it in isolated form, in machine dictation of context material, and finally in shorthand transcription. If nonrestrictive clauses cause difficulty—and they will—a portion of the shorthand period should be devoted to their recognition and punctuation. The student should punctuate sentences containing them and construct original sentences involving their use, so that he can learn to recognize them. After such homework and classroom drill, machine dictation and the transcription of letters loaded with nonrestrictive clauses will help to fix the construction in the student's mind.

After teaching, the teacher *tests* his results. The transcript is usually the test, as it represents the integration of the elements that were isolated for special drill. Because of the complexity of the transcription process, errors creep in that were not apparent in the learning exercise, which indicates that automatization of the skill has not yet occurred, that the student cannot use it when something else is uppermost in his thought, and that *further teaching* or drill is necessary. This is followed by *retesting*.

Introduction to Transcription. The following plan for easy progression from simple transcription to the usual pattern for the transcription class is suggested by Louis A. Leslie:[10] (Notice that two letters are timed in each drill after the first so that timing the paper change is always a factor.)

PERIOD	STEP	
1	I	Transcription of simple letter of 100–120 words from plate in textbook
		Students read and re-read letter, clarifying any problems of spelling or punctuation.
		Teacher gives machine setup.
		Students type letter without erasing errors (but they circle them in pencil to prevent development of careless habits). Students are told not to hurry but to keep the carriage moving as they read ahead in shorthand while typing.
		Students type letter a second time while they are timed. Teacher praises effort.
		No papers are collected.
2–5	II	Transcription from two letters that are dictated slowly after they have been prepared as homework
		Students transcribe untimed, then timed.
		Errors are circled in pencil.
6–10	III	Transcription of two new-matter letters that have been previewed on the blackboard
		Students transcribe untimed, then timed.
		Students make first transcript under time as soon as they seem to be ready for the transition.
After 10th	IV	Transcription of more letters of longer length and greater difficulty
		Teacher gives erasing drills until class can make erasures in 15 to 30 seconds. Students correct errors.
		Students begin to choose their own margins and placement.
		Multiple carbons are gradually introduced.
		Envelopes are required.

The Pattern for the Dictation Class. In the dictation class, which parallels the transcription class, the period will be divided somewhat like this:

[10] Louis A. Leslie. *Methods of Teaching Transcription,* Chapter VI.

MINUTES

10	Dictation for transcription
10–15	Speed drill in shorthand (1-minute repetitive practice drills described in previous chapter)
5–10	Drill on English, punctuation, spelling, and so forth as needed
10	Checking of previous day's transcripts

Drills for Building Transcription Speed. Special drills designed to improve transcription facility will be included in the classroom procedures for the shorthand room and for the typewriting room. One of the first drills that might be used is the matching drill in which students type from longhand copy, then type the same material from shorthand. Students who have fairly good typing technique will find that their transcription rate is very low at first on this type of drill because they have not yet learned how to apply to transcription the techniques that were successful in typing from copy.

In order to have a goal toward which to work, students are told to try to transcribe at least two-thirds as fast as they type from copy. If they can do this, they are probably adapting skills that they already have to the transcription skill. The matter of interpreting the transcription rate in terms of the typing rate has been badly misunderstood. To say that the transcription rate should be two-thirds of the typing rate is begging the question in terms of employment standards, as the transcription rate will vary with the nature of the conditions under which it is done. For purposes of beginning drill, however, when the student is making the change-over from longhand copy to shorthand copy, the standard is a useful one. It gives the student something to aim at. This exercise provides drill, too, in the correct form to be used in transcription. Since students have written the copy once, they should be ready to watch for matters of form. When they preread the plate, they should be permitted to refer to the typewritten copy if they are not sure of the correct way to express the shorthand. During timed transcription, of course, there will be no checking back.

The most valuable matching drill is based on unarranged letter copy rather than straight copy. The student whose straight copy rate is excellent may lose a great deal of speed while typing letters because of bad technique (such as looking up for the inside address and complimentary close). He should be given most of his timings on this practical copy and taught to automatize letter setup.

Another drill designed to build transcription speed is the repetitive copying of two letters from shorthand. It is conceded that one of the deterrents to speed in transcription—the solving of the problems of English, punctuation, and spelling, connected with the letter —will not be present when the letter is retyped. However, three values at least will be found in the repetition. The entire group is trying to type the same copy with timesaving techniques—no looking up between the date and inside address, between the address and salutation, between the salutation and body, and between the body and closing lines. If the student can cut down the time used in transcribing the letter by half a minute through using these techniques, he will probably decide to adopt them in sustained transcription. A second advantage of this drill is that it may enable the student to develop a smoother writing style. He will try for fluency in the repetition, just as he did in typewriting, and possibly get the "feel" of smooth writing when he does not fight his machine. A third value to be derived from the drill is that it gives the student a chance to try his wings. As he accelerates his rate and the teacher records his gains on the chalk board, he is surprised to find how fast he can transcribe. Of course, the rate on two letters cannot be quoted as his true transcription rate; but there is considerable merit in providing him an opportunity to discover what he can do. This drill is comparable to the "spurt speed" drills in both shorthand and typewriting.

A third drill for building transcription speed (sustained speed this time) is the flow-of-work drill. A good transcriber spends about one-third of his time on nontyping activities, but a poor transcriber spends two-thirds of his time on nontyping activities. In many cases the better organization of materials is the solution to the problem of the slow transcriber. Placing his notebook on a copyholder and arranging the dictionary, eraser, and stationery (letterheads, second sheets, carbon paper, and envelopes) for the most expeditious handling requires some experimentation with time-and-motion study. Each student should work out a pattern for himself, and the teacher should check him regularly to be sure he is following it.

Timed drills in assembling carbon packs, inserting them in the typewriter (but not typing), removing them from the typewriter, and separating them are valuable. The teacher can reduce the time allowed for the drill as improved motions are worked out. Teacher demonstrations of transcribing one letter, proofreading it, removing it from the typewriter, and inserting the next letter are also valuable.

Drills to Improve Transcription Quality. Integration has been misunderstood by many transcription teachers. When too many elements are introduced, learners are confused, not helped. For this reason, factors that cause transcription difficulty should be isolated for special drill. When spelling is being emphasized, very little special attention should be directed to other problems. When punctuation is singled out for drill, few spelling problems should be introduced.

When a topic is being given special attention, it should be presented in several situations to give adequate drill. The following sequence of learning exercises is suggested (with spelling as an example):

1. Type the words from shorthand notes until they can be written smoothly and without hesitation.
2. Type for home assignment sentences containing these words. For this work the student can proceed at his own rate.
3. Type from shorthand notes an exercise containing these words. As this is timed transcription, it is really a test.
4. In case mastery is not attained, the cycle should be retaught.

A similar plan should be used in giving drill on punctuation difficulties. If the students cannot recognize the noun clause used as the direct object so that they will omit the comma when using it, they should be taught the construction first, probably through a chalk-board presentation. Then they should prepare original sentences and a transcribed exercise containing several instances of the construction as homework, and finally they should transcribe a timed exercise containing noun clauses as a test of their mastery of the material.

A 10-minute drill on compound adjectives to precede the transcription of letters containing compound adjectives would involve the following steps:

1. Present a chalk-board exercise containing compound adjectives preceding the noun.

2. Present a chalk-board exercise containing compound adjectives following the noun.
3. Present a chalk-board example of the adverb-adjective combination requiring no hyphen.
4. Compose original sentences to illustrate all three constructions.
5. Dictate a letter containing all three constructions.
6. Transcribe.
7. Proofread.

Class drills (in the shorthand room) and homework assignments in using the dictionary efficiently should be given, so that a word can be checked in thirty to sixty seconds. These drills include exercises in determining the parts of speech (such as the difference between "advice" and "advise"), in recognizing the difference between the hyphen and the dash, and in spelling the different forms, such as the plural or the participle.

Learning from Mistakes. It is suggested that students correct all errors made on transcription papers, as they should learn from their mistakes and should not be making the same errors at the end of the course that they made at the beginning. If the error was the omission of a necessary comma, the transcriber is asked to identify the grammatical construction and give two original sentences illustrating its use. The corrections are typed at the bottom of the original letter. If the error involved incorrect spelling, the student spells the word correctly in two original sentences. If a word is incorrectly divided at the end of a line, the student writes the rule for correct syllabication and divides the word correctly twice. This method has two advantages: it provides for individual learning based on demonstrated needs, and it requires extra work on the part of those whose errors may have resulted from carelessness. In making corrections prior to the resubmission of papers, the student asks the teacher for help if it is needed.

Using Materials and Business Forms. If possible, letterheads should be used for class transcription.[11] Envelopes should be prepared for letters. At least one carbon should be made of each letter, and experience should be given in making multiple carbons until

---

[11] These are available in pads from various publishers. One publisher has a pad of master sheets of letterheads, so that the teacher can run off as many copies as needed.

they present no problem. The dictator may adopt a business-letter style for all letters to be transcribed during a given week. The following week he changes to another style.

Transcribing for Sense. Some students will transcribe whatever they have in their notes without regard for the sense of the transcript. One of the aims of the course is to develop a realization that each transcript should make sense. A drill that will help focus attention on sense is the filling in of blank spaces in a transcript with words that would make the meaning clear. For example, in the sentence, "This ———— will insure careful attention to your future requirements," the words, "practice," "procedure," or "action" might be acceptable.

At certain stages in the learning process it may be desirable for the teacher to help the student read his notes, as he may at first try to figure out the transcript in terms of what the outline looks like and not in terms of meaning. A little help along this line often pays off in the end.

Developing Timesaving Office Techniques for Transcribing. Students should be given experience in office short cuts in transcribing. In the early stages of transcribing, students are encouraged to pre-read their notes. The practice should be discontinued soon, for office transcribers do not read through their notes before typing them. The transcriber should learn to read far enough ahead in his notes to understand the thought, but he should not read the entire letter.

Some teachers set unreasonably high standards for the transcript. They should be reminded that many offices use only one letter setup and that the margins and tabulators are not changed during the day. The standard six-inch line has been adopted by a number of companies. Others urge their stenographers not to syllabicate words at the end of the line even though the margins may not be entirely symmetrical. They feel that the gain in production offsets the slightly less attractive appearance.

Another office short cut that should be adopted by the transcription class is the discontinuance of the use of the letter-placement chart. Students should have setups for long, medium, and short letters so well in mind that they can, after estimating the length of the letter by a glance at their notes, automatically set proper margins.

Proofreading. Students receive valuable experience in working together and in checking work if they proofread in pairs. Each transcriber is assigned a proofreader, and everyone is responsible for proofreading not only his own work but that of his partner, whose papers he signs. Undetected errors can then be charged against the proofreader as well as the writer. Since it is always easier to find the errors made by others, this device often helps to develop the eagle eye of the competent stenographer. Toward the end of the course, each student should be able to proofread his own work alone.

The teacher may compose his own assignments and duplicate them. The modern transcription and typewriting textbooks contain excellent proofreading exercises that may be used as suggestions.

Checking Work. Contrary to popular belief, not all work done in the transcription class should be checked. For instance, an exercise in which students are trying to write smoothly the difficult words from a list of shorthand outlines should never be checked. Neither should transcripts be checked of repetitive practice drills or drills to insure that students keep their eyes on the copy during the entire writing. These are learning drills, not tests of learning.

A second principle that the teacher should observe in connection with checking papers is that the student should become increasingly responsible for finding his errors. Of course, if the teacher hopes to give no better training than that which will prepare his graduates for positions in stenographic pools where supervisors are hired to detect errors and supervise their correction, he will not emphasize this part of training as much as he will if he wants his graduates to hold positions in which they can be trusted to proofread their own material. It is true that the teacher should do some paper checking; but he can reasonably expect that by the time the transcript has passed through the hands of two students and is given to him for approval, it will usually be in mailable form.

The third principle in connection with paper checking is that the student should do something about his errors. Merely looking at a corrected paper and noting the grade will usually not improve learning. The plan previously described for correcting errors is the one that is recommended.

Grading. Transcription standards are evolving standards. Any attempt to standardize a criterion for grading transcription indicates a lack of understanding of the nature of the growth of transcription ability and puts transcription teaching back in the realm of the "perfect copy" era in typewriting. If a teacher regards his transcription teaching as developmental, he will grade in terms of objectives only and not, necessarily, in terms of product. For instance, if a class is slow because the members look up during transcription, the teacher would give *A* to any student who did not look up, regardless of the typed result.

Some transcription teachers feel that the only justifiable basis for grading is the mailable transcript. This is true as the course progresses, but it would seem an unsatisfactory point of view in beginning transcription. The grade in transcription, just like the grade in typewriting, should be awarded in terms of the present objective. If the goal is good technique during the early stages of transcription, then the first grades might be based on a transcription technique chart.

In grading transcription, the teacher should establish a concept that there is a difference in the nature of errors. To write "$5,000,-000" for "$5,000" is obviously more serious than to write "flynig" for "flying." For this reason it is suggested that material be graded "In" if mailable and "Out" if not mailable. An error in sense, in address, in amount, or in a comma splice would throw out the letter. Substitution of "their" for "the" might not change the meaning. Teachers who favor such a plan recommend three levels in grading:

A. Mailable
B. Mailable with corrections
C. Unmailable (The letter must be rewritten.)

Other teachers feel that undetected proofreading errors should disqualify the letter, thus omitting the B level, for development of proofreading skill is one of the main objectives of the course.

In transcription the student will receive a speed grade based on transcription rate. If transcription rates are charted so that progress can be noted quickly, the teacher can assign this grade easily. In terms of class performance, he may set up a grading scale such as this for a given two-week period:

WORDS A MINUTE

A	25–29
B	20–24
C	15–19
D	10–14

At the end of two weeks the goals may be raised five words.

The grade for the number of letters mailable may be arbitrarily set by the teacher. If 25 letters are graded in a block, he may set up a scale such as the following:

GRADE	EARLY STAGES		NEAR END OF COURSE	
A	23 or more mailable		24 or 25 mailable	
B	20–22	"	22 or 23	"
C	17–19	"	20 or 21	"
D	14–16	"	18 or 19	"
F	Under 14	"	Under 18	"

Another grading scheme in which the actual percentage of letters mailable constitutes the grade works out very well toward the end of the course. For instance, if 23 of 25 letters dictated are mailable (92 per cent), the student receives a grade of 92. If 17 of the 25 letters (68 per cent) are mailable, the student receives a grade of *F*.

The above schemes do not provide for variation in the length of letters, use of carbon, typing the envelope, or any of the other factors influencing production. Leslie and Zoubek provide with one of their dictation books a grading scale for each day's assignment, which takes into consideration such items and also provides an easy word count for computing transcription rate. The grading scale for Assignment 39 is given below:

Grading Scale [12]

Points shown represent minimum complete mailability; a perfect score would be double the minimum shown.

LETTER	WDS.	PTS.	ADD. & CLOSING	PTS.	CARBON	PTS.	ENVELOPE	PTS.
230	57	1	72	1	92	1	102	1
231	92	1	107	1	127	2	137	2
232	112	1	127	2	147	2	157	2
233	132	2	147	2	167	2	177	2
234	130	2	145	2	165	2	175	2
235	161	2	176	2	196	2	206	2
236	170	2	185	2	205	2	215	2
	854	11	959	12	1,099	13	1,169	13

[12] Louis A. Leslie and Charles E. Zoubek, *Dictation for Mailable Transcripts*, p. 109.

A page from the teacher's grade book for a class using this material is reproduced on page 208. *P* means perfect (double credit) and *M* means mailable.

It is suggested that a teacher give both quality and quantity grades in transcription. A student may have an *A* in rate but a *C* in English form. If two grades are given, *A/C,* the story is much clearer to the teacher who is interested in remedial teaching than if one *B* grade were given.

The *Business Teacher* transcription tests provide a useful motivation device. Each month tests are printed for four awards if mailable transcripts of two letters are achieved:

AWARD	DICTATION RATE	TRANSCRIPTION RATE
Basic Skill	60	12
Basic Proficiency	80	15
Proficiency	100	20
Superior Achievement	100	25 with carbon copies

As a basis for the grading of the best students at the end of the year, the teacher may wish to use the National Business Entrance Tests based on 30 minutes of untimed dictation, with breaks at the end of each 10-minute period during which students may ask for redictation of doubtful items. One and a half hours are allowed for transcription.

In setting the lower level of grades, the teacher should keep in mind Leslie's minimum standard of 20-words-a-minute average transcription rate with 75 per cent mailability of any 5 consecutive days' dictation.

QUESTIONS

1. In what ways do the "fusion" teachers agree with the "new-skill" teachers of transcription? In what ways do they disagree? Which group do you favor?

2. What is meant by the statement that the teaching of transcription is still in the "glass-wall" era?

3. What is "mailability"? Why is it said that "mailability" is an ideal of dictators rather than an existent standard?

27 Number	Name *Rader, Charles*	Week Ending *Nov. 12*	Score *96*

WEEKLY TRANSCRIPTION REPORT--BLANKTOWN SCHOOL

1	2	3	4	5	6	7	8	9	10	11
Letter Number	Number of Words	Points P.	M.	Day's Total Words	Day's Total Points	Day's Trans. Speed	Week's Total Words	Week's Total Points	Week's Average Speed	Score for the Week
230	72		0				3,811	48	24	96
231	107	2								
232	127		1							
233	147		2							
234	145	4								
235	176	4								
236	185		0	959	13	24				
237	129	2								
238	105		0							
239	150		2							
240	151	4								
241	136	4								
242	168		2							
243	158		0	997	14	25				
120-38										
100-9										
244	67	2								
245	97	2								
246	118		1							
247	150	4								
248	155		2							
249	354		–	941	11	23				
250	.78		0							
251	35		–							
252	149	4								
253	187		2							
254	465		4	914	10	23				

SCORE is obtained by adding twice the week's average speed to the week's total points.

160 Minutes
Total Transcribing Time
(Take nearest average speed)

Total Words	Week's Speed
2400	15.
2480	15.5
2560	16.
2640	16.5
2720	17.
2800	17.5
2880	18.
2960	18.5
3040	19.
3120	19.5
3200	20.
3280	20.5
3360	21.
3440	21.5
3520	22.
3600	22.5
3680	23.
3760	23.5
3840	24.
3920	24.5
4000	25.
4080	25.5
4160	26.
4240	26.5
4320	27.
4400	27.5

Note: If a letter is completed but unmailable, place a zero in Column 4. If the letter was not started, place a dash in Column 2 and a dash in Column 4; if not completed, a dash in Column 4 and the number of words completed in Column 2.

Courtesy Leslie and Zoubek, Dictation for Mailable Transcripts, p. ix

Weekly transcription report for assignments 39–42

4. What does research tell us about the nature of transcription errors?

5. What factors influence transcription rate?

6. How does Leslie's standard of transcription ability at the end of four semesters of high school instruction conform to rates required for entrance into stenographic positions?

7. Of what value to the transcription teacher is the list of transcription duties? What do transcribers do?

8. Would you include all the aims of the transcription course that are listed in this chapter? Which were emphasized in your own training? Which were inadequately achieved?

9. How are the principles of skill building applied to the teaching of transcription?

10. Illustrate the application of the mastery formula to the teaching of transcription.

11. Outline a plan for the introduction of transcription and the development of a pattern for the transcription class.

12. Describe five drills that you think effective in transcription.

13. Compare the amount of time spent in nontyping activities by the good transcriber and the poor transcriber. How can the teacher achieve better organization of materials?

14. Do you favor the suggestion that students do homework exercises based on their errors on transcription papers, or do you think this is busy-work? Why?

15. Should the transcriber preread his notes?

16. How would you grade transcription classes?

STUDENT ACTIVITIES

1. Teach one of the following drills, or a drill of your own choosing, to this class for ten minutes:

A repetitive practice drill

A drill on the use of the dictionary

A drill in erasing on multiple carbons

A flow-of-work drill

A proofreading drill

A teacher demonstration of good transcription technique, including the changing of paper and starting a second letter

Introduction to transcription

2. In the light of the standards of mailability reported in this chapter, evaluate ten business letters that were actually mailed and ten student transcriptions. Compare your findings with those reported in this chapter.

3. Evaluate the transcription technique of three students whom you observe at work and recommend procedures to meet their learning needs.

4. Observe a transcription class and evaluate teaching techniques which you find.

5. Examine two current textbooks on transcription. Identify the authors as "fusion" or "new-skill" transcription teachers.

6. Examine the most recent National Business Entrance Test in Shorthand. Secure information about the number of applicants who secured the certificate. Draw your conclusions.

7. Because so many student teachers are unsure of themselves in teaching English punctuation, give yourself a checkup. Write two original sentences to illustrate each of the following:

    a. Direct address
    b. Appositive
    c. Noun clause
    d. Restrictive clause
    e. Nonrestrictive clause
    f. Compound sentence joined by a co-ordinate conjunction
    g. Compound sentence joined by an adverbial conjunction
    h. Adverbial clause in order
    i. Adverbial clause out of order
    j. Parenthetical expression

BIBLIOGRAPHY

Anderson, Ruth I., and Others. "Helping the Slow Learner in Shorthand and Transcription," *American Business Education* (May, 1954), pp. 235–242.

Balsley, Irol Whitmore. *Current Transcription Practices in Business Firms,* Monograph 86. Cincinnati, South-Western Publishing Company, 1954. 66 p.

Connelly, Mary E. "Transcription Is a Training Program," *Business Teacher* (December, 1949–January, 1950), pp. 96–97.

DeLancey, Opal H. "Applying Work Simplification to Transcription," *UBEA Forum* (January, 1951), pp. 18–19, 24.

———, "Transcription Must Be Taught," *UBEA Forum* (October, 1950), pp. 27, 39.

Forkner, Hamden L., Agnes Osborne, and James E. O'Brien. *Correlated Dictation and Transcription.* Boston, D. C. Heath Publishing Company, 1950. 545 p.

Gavin, Ruth E. "How to Set Up a Transcribing Routine," *Business Education World* (March, 1954), p. 29.

Lamb, Marion M. *Your First Year of Teaching Shorthand and Transcription.* Cincinnati, South-Western Publishing Company, 1950. 300 p.

Leslie, Louis A. *Methods of Teaching Transcription.* New York, Gregg Publishing Company, 1949. 356 p.

———, and Charles E. Zoubek, *Gregg Transcription Simplified.* Second Edition. New York, Gregg Publishing Division, McGraw-Hill Book Co., Inc., 1956. 512 p.

———, *Teacher's Handbook, Gregg Transcription Simplified.* New York, Gregg Publishing Division, McGraw-Hill Book Co., Inc., 1956. 96 p.

Murphy, Glen E. "An Analysis of the Decisions Made in Transcribing a Letter," *UBEA Forum* (March, 1950), pp. 23–24, 40.

Reynolds, Helen, and Margaret H. Ely. "Transcription—Early or Late," *UBEA Forum* (October, 1953), pp. 14–16.

Whitmore, Irol, and S. J. Wanous. *Shorthand Transcription Studies, Simplified.* (Second Edition) Cincinnati, South-Western Publishing Company, 1950. 249 p.

———, *Teacher's Handbook, Shorthand Transcription Studies Simplified.* Cincinnati, South-Western Publishing Company, 1950.

CHAPTER X

Bookkeeping in the School

HISTORY OF THE TEACHING OF BOOKKEEPING

BOOKKEEPING HAS A LONG AND VENERABLE HISTORY. The keeping of systematic and convenient records of money transactions has been traced back to the Babylonians, Egyptians, Greeks, and Romans. Double-entry bookkeeping was developed in the fourteenth and fifteenth centuries by the North Italians and is frequently called the Italian method. The treatise by Fra Luca Pacioli called "Everything about Arithmetic, Geometry, and Proportion" was published in 1494 as the first written presentation of double-entry bookkeeping. Many procedures described in this treatise had been used for several centuries, but Pacioli is usually credited with being the father of accountancy because he was the first to publish these principles. The system soon traveled to the Netherlands, England, and the rest of the world.

In the Middle Ages bookkeepers learned the trade, as did all tradesmen, by serving as apprentices. In our early colonial history we find records of private teachers giving instruction in reading, writing, and casting accounts. Later these teachers started private schools. One of the earliest of these schools was established in Plymouth, New England, in 1635 by a Mr. Morton who taught students to "read, write, and cast accounts." In 1710 we find a public school in South Carolina authorized to teach writing as well as "the principles of vulgar arithmetic and merchants' accounts." On the secondary level, the Philadelphia Academy in 1800 offered "writing, arithmetic, and mercantile accounts" in its mathematics school. The Boston

English High School, which was the first public high school in this country, included bookkeeping in its curriculum as early as 1824. As a matter of fact, bookkeeping was a required subject in Massachusetts in 1827 in every community with five hundred or more families. By the middle of the nineteenth century, most high schools in the larger cities were offering bookkeeping courses. Bookkeeping found its way into business programs on every level, from the earliest beginnings of business education right down to the present day. Bookkeeping is considered an essential phase of all business curriculums.

About twenty-five years ago, two years of bookkeeping were offered to most business students; and bookkeeping was considered a vocational course to be studied by those who became bookkeepers. The present trend seems to be toward offering one year of bookkeeping to all business majors. Capable students in the first-year course are encouraged to elect a second year of bookkeeping. While some schools offer a special bookkeeping curriculum, most of the students enrolled in bookkeeping are studying it as an important phase of their total preparation for work in the business world. The first-year course is generally taught in the tenth or eleventh year of the high school program.

Only one-fifth to one-tenth of those who now study first-year bookkeeping continue with the second-year course. The enormous dropout necessitates a change in the subject matter, so that certain phases that are vitally important for all business students are not omitted. The fact that the subject is taken as business background rather than as training for future bookkeepers also makes it desirable to give less consideration to certain topics usually presented in first-year bookkeeping. This problem of revising subject matter is considered later in the chapter.

A generation or more ago most bookkeeping in business was done by bookkeepers assisted by junior bookkeepers. This situation has changed. Now the record keeping is usually undertaken by ledger clerks; and in smaller offices much of the routine work is performed by a clerk, a stenographer, or even by the owner himself. Periodically an accountant, a professional worker, visits the establishment and completes all or most of the process of closing books and preparing statements. Bookkeeping, which was once a semiprofession, now has become on the one hand a skilled occupation and at the upper level, a definite profession.

The secondary-school bookkeeping program has not kept up with the occupational change. It still attempts to meet the problems of the old-time bookkeeper, who has become a rare occupational worker in business. It fails to recognize that accountants are trained at the collegiate level and that the instruction in the secondary schools must, therefore, be planned either to train for the kind of record-keeping activity undertaken by the beginning office worker or to provide a better understanding of business.

A carefully selected list of the activities of bookkeepers, prepared by the Pittsburgh Public Schools, is given on page 215. It is interesting to note that 75 per cent or more of today's bookkeepers neither open books nor make adjusting and closing entries. The preparation of operating and/or financial statements is sixth in rank of frequency. As a matter of fact, even this listing is not entirely valid, for most bookkeepers merely set up these statements from the work sheet that has been provided them by the accountant. Although making entries in ledger accounts is the most frequently listed activity, making journal entries is twelfth in the list.

OBJECTIVES

Before training was offered in the private business schools, bookkeeping was learned, in the main, through apprenticeship. The young office worker was rewarded for efficient service by a promotion to assistant bookkeeper although he knew nothing about keeping books. He learned by working as an assistant to the bookkeeper. He learned by doing and not by studying.

When business activity increased and the demand for bookkeepers exceeded the supply available from an apprenticeship system, private business schools began to train bookkeepers. The objective was purely vocational—to train bookkeepers. In the business office of the 1800's and early 1900's, the bookkeeper was the financial and accounting expert of the business. He was frequently the only person in the organization with any business training. Consequently, the owner turned over the management of his office and records to the bookkeeper. It was, therefore, essential for the bookkeeper to

Most Frequent Activities of Bookkeepers [1]

DUTIES	RANK	FREQUENCY
Make entries in ledger accounts	1	348
Use the telephone	2	311
Use the adding machine	3	290
Use filing system or systems	4	268
Examine and/or sort business papers	5	258
Prepare operating and/or financial statements	6	256
Prepare trial balances	7	244
Figure extensions on bills, invoices, statements	8	243
Verify and/or list information from business papers	9	196
Figure discounts	10	171
Use calculating machine	11	167
Make journal entries	12	159
Use bookkeeping machine	13	148
Type bills, invoices, statements	14	136
Use stapler	15	127
Balance cash daily	16	125
Keep inventory records	17	124
Prepare checks	18	120
Compute time records	19	118
Use transfer files	20	111
Make cross references	21	109
Prepare material for filing	22	104
Run errands	23	103

know everything about bookkeeping—from the opening entry through the preparation and interpretation of statements. Naturally, the training of bookkeepers was very broad and included an intensive study of accounting and business administration.

When high schools introduced bookkeeping, the objective remained vocational—to train bookkeepers; however, because of the change in bookkeeping activities, the high school trained bookkeeper, when he enters business, does not usually complete the entire cycle as he formerly did. Bookkeeping cannot, then, be regarded in its former vocational sense; however, many bookkeeping operations are performed by other office workers for which they should be trained. With the increased necessity for keeping adequate

[1] Duties listed by 75 per cent of 371 bookkeepers according to "A Survey of Office Duties," Pittsburgh Schools, XXIII (September-October, 1948), pp. 29–30.

records as a basis for taxation, the importance of general bookkeeping has increased. Today the aims of the course have been extended. The training of prospective bookkeepers is only one aspect of the subject.

General Aims

1. To develop a better understanding of business activities and to familiarize students with papers and forms commonly used in business transactions

2. To develop an understanding and appreciation of the values and possibilities of bookkeeping for personal needs, for vocational preparation, or for preparation for further study

3. To develop a clear and definite understanding of assets, liabilities, and proprietorship, so that business situations and changes may be correctly interpreted

4. To develop essential bookkeeping traits of accuracy, neatness, orderliness, thoroughness, and responsibility

5. To provide a comprehensive vocabulary of business and of bookkeeping

6. To teach the importance of following instructions accurately and thoroughly

Specific Aims

1. To teach students to understand the principles of double-entry bookkeeping

2. To teach the bookkeeping cycle in such a way that students understand the entire process and the relation of each step to all the other steps

3. To provide vocational training that will equip *every* business student with the practical "know how" and skills needed to perform the daily bookkeeping activities of the average business office

4. To train all business students to become *proficient* in handling the daily recording and financial routine of the average business office

5. To provide all business students with continuous review and drill in arithmetic, penmanship, and spelling, so that they will be proficient in the use of fundamentals when employed in business

6. To acquaint all business students thoroughly with business practices and procedures

7. To provide an indispensable background of practical recording experience for those students who may wish to continue the study of advanced bookkeeping and accounting

8. To provide every business student with additional vocational skills that will increase his opportunities for future occupational success and advancement

CONTENT

Bookkeeping is a textbook course, and the nature of the specific material taught depends largely on the text used. Analysis of secondary-school bookkeeping textbooks indicates that the following topics are commonly included in the first-year bookkeeping course:

1. What is bookkeeping?
2. Need for bookkeeping
    a. For the individual
    b. For a social organization
    c. For a business
3. What are the fundamental elements of bookkeeping?
    a. Assets
    b. Proprietorship
    c. Liabilities
4. What are the relationships between the fundamental elements of bookkeeping?
    a. Assets $=$ Proprietorship
    b. Assets $-$ Liabilities $=$ Proprietorship
    c. Assets $=$ Liabilities $+$ Proprietorship
5. Recording changes in the equations
    a. Use of accounts
    b. Debits and credits
    c. Balances
6. Recording typical business transactions in ledger accounts
7. Preparing simple balance sheets and profit and loss statements
8. Recording transactions through journalizing
9. Posting
10. Proving accuracy of records
    a. Footing and balancing ledger accounts
    b. Trial balance
    c. Locating errors in the trial balance
11. End-of-the-month work (Simple)
    a. Work sheet
    b. Adjusting entries

       c. Closing entries
       d. Balancing and ruling accounts
       e. Statements
       f. Postclosing trial balance
12. Practice set
13. Sales journal
14. Purchases journal
15. Cash receipts journal (two column)
16. Cash payments journal (two column)
17. Four-column cashbooks
18. Use of general journal
       a. Notes receivable
       b. Notes payable
       c. Purchase returns
       d. Sales returns
       e. Purchase discount
       f. Sales discount
       g. Correcting entries
       h. Adjusting entries
       i. Closing entries
19. Depreciation
20. Bad debts
21. Interest and discount
22. Accruals
23. Payrolls

TEACHING APPROACHES

As a rule, the bookkeeping teacher follows the approach presented in the bookkeeping textbook. It is interesting to note, however, the various plans that have been used in teaching bookkeeping at different times.

Research experiments have been conducted to test the superiority of various approaches. The available evidence seems to indicate that all methods have advantages and disadvantages. The success of any method can usually be attributed to good teaching. The best method in the hands of a poor teacher will produce poor results.

Single-Entry Approach. In the period between 1890 and 1910, most students first learned a typical single-entry system. Records were kept of assets, liabilities, and proprietorship; but no accounts were kept to show sources of profit and loss. Accounts were kept for Cash, Merchandise Inventory, Customers (Accounts Receivable),

TOPICS INCLUDED IN HIGH SCHOOL ELEMENTARY BOOK-KEEPING TEXTBOOKS AND COURSES OF STUDY

1. ACCOUNTS
   Cash
   Petty Cash
   Merchandise
   Equipment (Furniture and Fixtures, Delivery Equipment)
   Accounts Receivable
   Notes Receivable
   Supplies
   Expenses
   Proprietor's Capital
   Proprietor's Personal
   Sales
   Returned Sales and Allowances
   Purchases
   Returned Purchases and Allowances
   Accounts Payable
   Notes Payable
   Interest Income
   Interest Cost
   Sales Discount
   Purchase Discount
   Collection and Exchange
   Depreciation
   Reserves
   Accruals
   Bad Debts

2. JOURNALS
   General
   Cash Receipts
   Cash Payments
   Purchases
   Sales
   Sales Returns

Purchase Returns

3. STATEMENTS
   Trial Balance
   Work Sheet
   Balance Sheet
   Profit and Loss Statement

4. BOOKKEEPING PROCEDURES
   Debit and credit
   Journalizing
   Posting
   Taking a trial balance
   Preparing a bank reconciliation statement
   Preparing a profit and loss statement
   Preparing a work sheet
   Preparing adjusting and closing entries and posting them
   Preparing a postclosing trial balance

5. BUSINESS PAPERS
   Checks
   Invoices
   Credit memoranda
   Money orders
   Promissory notes
   Drafts
   Trade acceptances

6. ARITHMETIC
   Computation of interest
   Computation of cash discount
   Compuation of bank discount
   Computation of depreciation

Notes (Bills) Receivable, Furniture, Creditors, and Notes (Bills) Payable. Usually accounts were kept for Purchases, Sales, Expenses, or Interest. In single entry, a debit was an incoming asset, an outgoing asset, or an increase in liability or in proprietorship. An entry involved either a debit or credit but rarely both at the same time, except to record notes and certain cash receipts and payments. A sale for cash was a debit to cash only. A sale on account was a debit to the customer only. Cash disbursements for purchases or expenses were credits to cash only. The journal did not distinguish between debits and credits by position as it does in double entry. A debit account was marked *Dr.,* and a credit was labeled *Cr.* The amounts for both went into a single money column. The journal was the major record in the single-entry system. There were many types of single-entry records. As a rule, the single-entry system provided the data for constructing a balance sheet. It was quite difficult to prepare a profit and loss statement without making a detailed analysis of the journals. Any system of bookkeeping that is not a complete double-entry system may be called a single-entry system and taught as such.

The single-entry system is very rarely taught in schools today, although many small firms use some type of single-entry system. Many organizations and individuals also use single-entry records. Some accountants advocate that prospective accountants should be familiar with single-entry methods of keeping books.

The Journal Approach. When bookkeeping teachers first taught double-entry bookkeeping, they felt that the approach should be logical and follow a sequence used in actual business. They, therefore, presented the journal first, taught students how to post journal entries to the ledger, prepare the trial balance, make the adjusting and closing entries, prepare the financial statements, and develop the postclosing entries. Instruction followed in how to open a new set of books, how to reduce work by using special journals, and how to develop control over a large number of accounts through the use of subsidiary ledgers.

The Account Approach. Although the journal approach was satisfactory for adults who had some acquaintance with business, it did not work very well for the beginning student who lacked business experience; therefore, the account approach was devised and was extensively taught. In this approach students were first taught to make entries into "T" accounts as preliminary practice for making entries directly into the formal ledger. From the ledger, students then made trial balances and simple financial statements. Only after they had learned to make entries in accounts was the journal introduced as a book of original entry, where the chronological record of the business transactions is kept and through which entries can be separated into their debit and credit elements.

Soon after 1920 bookkeeping teachers became dissatisfied with the emphasis upon knowledge of bookkeeping and ability to do routine work. They felt that students knew little about the reasons for using the procedures. The balance sheet, with its various modified forms, therefore, was developed.

Balance-Sheet, or Equation, Approach. In recent years almost all secondary schools have taught double-entry bookkeeping exclusively, and the term "bookkeeping" is synonymous with "double-entry bookkeeping." The balance sheet has frequently been used as a device to explain the fundamental equations: Assets — Liabilities = Proprietorship, or Assets = Liabilities + Proprietorship. After developing the relationship between assets, liabilities, and proprietorship, the profit and loss statement is presented as a detailed report of proprietorship. The accounts necessary to record the constant changes in the fundamental elements are developed after the principles of debit and credit have been introduced. The trial balance is utilized as a check on the equality of the debits and credits in the ledger accounts. Finally, the journal is introduced to provide a chronological and complete analysis of all business transactions. This approach ignores the bookkeeping cycle until the student understands the reason for each entry and its effect on the fundamental elements. It is by far the most popular current approach to the teaching of bookkeeping.

In addition to learning bookkeeping in the schools by an analysis of the theory of debit and credit by one of the approaches named, bookkeepers may learn even today by the apprentice method. The bookkeeper in business trains his own assistants who are usually recruited from the clerical staff. The former office boy may begin by entering sales. Then he is taught the next step, and the process continues until the former clerk does the work of a regular bookkeeper.

Countless business workers have learned bookkeeping by serving as apprentices in this manner.

Many others keep books according to the instructions given them by the company that installed the bookkeeping "system." If the International Business Machines Company sets up the bookkeeping system, their directions are followed. If a firm uses the Burroughs, Dalton, National Cash Register, or McCaskey "system," the books are kept according to that particular manual of instructions. The worker learns by practice. Formalized instruction in the complete bookkeeping process is not needed to operate the "system," and a low-ability routine worker can be taught to keep records satisfactorily by this method.

ANALYSIS OF APPROACHES

The "Why" Approach. Teachers try to make arbitrary differentiation among the various so-called approaches to bookkeeping. Actually, these approaches are not so much different ways of teaching bookkeeping as they are different concepts as to the outcomes to be achieved. In general, the balance-sheet, or equation, approach emphasizes the "Why" of every entry as the basic learning element and analyzes the influence of every entry upon the fundamental equation. Does the transaction increase some assets while it decreases other assets? Does it increase assets and increase liabilities? Does it increase assets and increase capital? What other combinations of effects occur? Only after this analysis has been thoroughly understood is the student taught how to undertake the operation. For students who have some intellectual ability and curiosity, this procedure is most satisfactory. Bookkeeping is thus primarily concerned with *knowledges.*

The "How" Approach. The journal approach and, to a lesser extent, the account approach are primarily concerned with *how* to make the entry. Rules are learned rather arbitrarily, and students are shown how to make the entries either in the journal directly and then post to accounts or how to make entries to accounts first. Occasionally they are shown why these entries are made, but the *why* of the process is subordinate to the *how* to undertake bookkeeping processes. Those who favor the *how* approach are primarily concerned with developing *skill*.

Neither Extreme Desirable. Actually, no able and alert business bookkeeping teacher in a secondary school would attempt to develop completely either the *why* or the *how* of every entry to the exclusion of the other. Bookkeeping involves both knowledges and skills. Usually the teacher's first emphasis in secondary schools is upon the *why* of an entry, and therefore it is quite logical to say that most bookkeeping teachers today stress the balance-sheet approach.

When students on the secondary-school level are made to go through the formula of why every entry is made long after they have grasped the essential idea, this emphasis actually interferes with the development of their ability to make entries proficiently and efficiently. In other words, skills should be automatized, not intellectualized. Many students are often able to do better without knowing why. For them a modification of the account approach in which they first learn how to make entries and then later on why they are made in this way is more feasible. After all, for the initial worker the important thing is the skill, not the intellectualization. Far too much emphasis has been given to the general philosophy of high school subjects and not enough attention to the actual carrying out of the processes taught.

Probably an integration of the account approach and the balance-sheet approach in terms of the above discussion is the most satisfactory teaching method.

Textbooks still differ considerably on the exact sequence in which topics are taught. Some still use a general journal as the initial book through which to make the presentation; others use the cashbook; others, the sales and purchases journals; and still others the account. Some emphasize the balance sheet first and then transfer to the account. Still others start with the concept of the profit and loss statement on the theory that students should know why business operates. It makes very little difference which type of textbook or approach is used first. The manner in which the subject is taught is more important.

Actually there is no such thing as complete, whole learning of bookkeeping or any other subject because if the entire subject could be learned at one time there would be little need for classroom instruction; people could learn the work on the job. There is, moreover, rarely a possibility of avoiding completely all unlearnings. Any time a complete unit of understanding is taught in a simplified form, some unlearning is involved. When, in order to present a concept as a whole unit, it is simplified to the point where it can be grasped by the beginner, there is an oversimplification of the situation that must be corrected when the full detail is given. If, on the other hand, a small enough segment is taught so that it can be grasped in its final form, the fragment is usually so incomplete that a distorted conception of the purpose and process of the activity is created. What the bookkeeping teacher should strive for is as complete learning as possible with as little consequent unlearning as possible.

Changes in Bookkeeping Terminology. Beginning teachers are sometimes disturbed by the fact that terminology used in different textbooks varies. They do not realize that a slight variation in name is really of little importance and that the concept is unchanged. For instance, one teacher may use *Merchandise* to describe *Purchases,* or *Customers' Accounts* for *Accounts Receivable,* or *Interest Earned* for *Interest Income,* or *Interest Expense* for *Interest Cost,* or *Allowance for Depreciation* for *Reserve for Depreciation.*

In the past thirty years, teacher vocabulary has changed from the use of terms like real and nominal accounts to the substitution of temporary capital accounts. This is in many ways an effective procedure. Many teachers, however, still teach bookkeeping through the concept of real and nominal accounts and give their students an effective understanding of the fundamental processes involved. Change of terminology does not necessarily improve the procedures in teaching and learning.

The Cycle in Bookkeeping Instruction. One of the uniquely desirable qualities in the teaching of bookkeeping that should not be lost regardless of how the subject is organized and that might well be used by teachers of other subjects is the concept of the cycle method of teaching. In this method a complete but highly simplified presentation of the entire process to be taught is given very briefly. By using a cycle approach in teaching bookkeeping, teachers constantly review and re-review, learn and relearn those elements that are considered most fundamental in a constantly expanding spiral, so that at the end of a program certain fundamental elements have been gone over so thoroughly and so well that the learner cannot help having some understanding of, and ability in, the techniques used. Every time additional learnings are to be developed, they can be easily related to those learnings that have already preceded; and complete integration of subject matter can thus be achieved in a way that is not possible in many other subjects as they are now taught. This spiraling of learning is so significant that its value cannot be overestimated. It is effective, and it is exactly the same learning procedure accomplished in daily living. Individuals learn certain procedures so well by constant use of them that they become automatic. Then as they are placed in new learning positions, these learnings are easily related to the abilities previously acquired.

For example, the first time the bookkeeping cycle is worked through, the balance sheet may consist of only one asset balanced by capital. In the next cycle several assets may be added in the balance sheet, then a liability; farther along the line, a cycle will give opportunity for dividing the assets into particular types, such as current and fixed items. Finally, the student may learn the use of comparative balance sheets with percentages indicated for the various elements. This same process would be used in presenting the profit and loss statement, the division of accounts, and the introduction of the special journals for cash, sales, and purchases. Thus thorough learning of each bookkeeping concept is attained, and by constant use of all previously learned elements an unusually high degree of integration of the learnings is achieved. In bookkeeping everything can be worked into the cycle, first in simple form and finally through spiraling of learning brought into the most complex form desirable. Spiraling of learning should be accomplished in every subject. Teachers of other subjects such as English, basic business, and social studies can learn much from the competent bookkeeping teacher.

REORGANIZATION OF SUBJECT MATTER

An even more fundamental problem of the bookkeeping teacher is his constant awareness of the need for a reorganization of subject matter. Much of what is taught about complex closing, opening, reversing, and adjusting entries is of little consequence in understanding the values for which bookkeeping is taught in the secondary school at present. The basic subject matter of bookkeeping as now frequently taught is an anachronism. It served its purpose well when high school students could go out as assistant bookkeepers, but that almost never happens these days. High school graduates now use bookkeeping only incidentally in their initial jobs and are often one of several different types of recording clerks. They may also go on to a collegiate school of business and study accounting. In none of these cases is a deep understanding of the technicalities of opening, closing, and adjusting entries necessary. Yet teachers tend to overstress them and neglect to develop abilities actually needed in routine recording work.

An element in bookkeeping that needs to be emphasized is the ability to interpret bookkeeping records. Unfortunately this aspect of bookkeeping training also is usually relegated to the second year. Inasmuch as most high school students never take the second year of bookkeeping, they are left with little comprehension of the techniques that might be used in interpreting bookkeeping and other financial statements. It is most desirable that ability to interpret and to compare balance sheets be made a part of the first-year program and that technicalities of closing entries be shifted to the second year of bookkeeping or, better yet, to the collegiate level. This recommendation does not imply that high school students are going to be made auditors and bank examiners, but it must be realized that these students will use balance sheets and profit and loss statements and that they should be able to make at least elementary evaluations of them. After they have figured the percentages and ratios in financial statements, they should be referred to ratios in effect in business. These can be found in the current publications of Dun and Bradstreet, various trade magazines, and the daily newspapers.

To say that interpretation is too technical for the average student is beside the point. Undoubtedly many men and women of ordinary abilities do not know enough about bookkeeping to interpret statements; that is precisely the problem. To avoid the subject of interpretation just because it is too technical is somewhat the same as saying that a student should be given no understanding of the problems of Russia, of our military defense, or of our political organization simply because so many factors are involved that these problems cannot be completely understood by secondary-school students. The only way to give them an approach to understanding is by beginning such study in a small way in the secondary school and possibly even in the elementary school.

Bookkeeping teachers have been complaining about reduced enrollment in bookkeeping. For this they have themselves to blame. They have insisted upon continuing to teach a formalized traditional bookkeeping course instead of emphasizing (1) the use values of the subject both in orderliness and neatness of recording, (2) proper attitude toward recording, and (3) understanding of the meaning of records.

CONCLUSION

Let it be emphasized once more, however, that regardless of the reorganization that may take place in the bookkeeping program, teachers should:

1. Emphasize ability to make entries and records neatly and in an orderly way by hand, at the typewriter, and eventually at a bookkeeping machine.

2. Stress interpretation of bookkeeping records within the limited capacities of the secondary-school student

3. Eliminate, or at least reduce, the emphasis on formal opening and closing entries, work sheet, and other technical processes

4. Realize that the cycle is a unique element in the teaching of bookkeeping that they must continue to stress, spiraling the learning to the maximum of the student's capacity

QUESTIONS

1. What was the major objective of the early bookkeeping course?

2. What occupational changes have taken place recently in the field of bookkeeping?

3. What recent changes have taken place in the teaching of bookkeeping?

4. What are the present-day objectives of high school bookkeeping?

5. What are the major topics usually included in a high school bookkeeping course?

6. What are the advantages of the "journal" approach?

7. What are the disadvantages of the "account approach"?

8. Why has the "balance-sheet," or "equation," approach become so popular?

9. What changes should be made in teaching high school bookkeeping?

STUDENT ACTIVITIES

1. Prepare a brief history of bookkeeping as an occupational career.

2. Prepare a brief report on "How the Training of Bookkeepers Has Changed since 1900."

3. Read the prefaces of two or three high school bookkeeping texts and make a list of their objectives.

4. After examining the high school texts mentioned above, prepare a master list of the major topics taught in these books.

5. If you were asked to prepare a new elementary bookkeeping syllabus, what major topics in No. 4 would you include and what other topics would you add?

6. Analyze the teaching approaches used in the books examined in terms of the descriptions given in this chapter.

7. Using the textbook evaluation described in Chapter III, analyze any three high school bookkeeping texts and indicate which one you would prefer to use.

8. Consult the current and recent issues of the *Business Education Index*. Make a list of references on the material discussed in this chapter.

9. After consulting the current literature, prepare a report on "What Is Wrong with the Present Bookkeeping Course."

10. Check the current literature on record keeping. Prepare a report giving your views on this subject.

BIBLIOGRAPHY

Andruss, Harvey. *Ways to Teach Bookkeeping and Accounting.* Cincinnati, South-Western Publishing Company, 1943.

Boynton, Lewis D. *Methods of Teaching Bookkeeping.* Cincinnati, South-Western Publishing Company, 1954.

Dettman, John A. "Make Your Bookkeeping Course More Practical." *UBEA Forum,* VIII (January, 1954), pp. 26, 34.

Freeman, M. Herbert, J Marshall Hanna, Gilbert Kahn. *Teacher's Manual and Key for Bookkeeping Simplified.* New York, McGraw-Hill Book Company, Inc., 1953. 313 p.

Gemmell, James. "A Dozen Ways to Use Community Resources in Teaching Bookkeeping," *Business Education World,* XXXII (May, 1952), pp. 432–433.

Hanna, J Marshall. "Bookkeeping for the 80 Per Cent," *Business Education World,* XXVII (March, 1947), pp. 276–280.

———. "Let's Face the Facts in Bookkeeping," *Business Education World,* XXXII (September, 1951), pp. 28–30.

———, and M. Herbert Freeman. "Do You Really Teach Bookkeeping?" *Business Teacher,* XXX (May–June, 1953), pp. 232–233.

House, F. Wayne. "What Brings Success to Our Bookkeeping Students?" *Business Education World,* XXXV (September, 1954), pp. 20–21.

Leith, Harold. "The Content of the Bookkeeping Course," *Balance Sheet,* XXXIII (May, 1952), pp. 397, 403.

Martens, Helen Jordan. *Bookkeeping Requirements in Two Cities and Their Relation to High School Instruction,* Monograph 79. Cincinnati, South-Western Publishing Co., 1954, p. 27.

Rosetti, Louis J. "Bookkeeping in the State of New York," *Journal of Business Education,* XXIX (November, 1953), pp. 67–68.

Satlow, I. David. "Current Thinking in Teaching Bookkeeping," *Journal of Business Education,* XXX (October and November, 1954), pp. 22–25, 80–84.

———, "Current Thought on Teaching Bookkeeping," *Journal of Business Education,* XXXI (November, 1955), pp. 78–81.

———, "Let's Modernize the Content of Bookkeeping," *Journal of Business Education,* XXVIII (January, 1953), pp. 155–157.

———, "What about Recordkeeping?" *Journal of Business Education,* XXVII (October, 1951), pp. 72–74.

Selby, Paul O. *The Teaching of Bookkeeping.* New York, Gregg Publishing Company, 1945.

Strumpf, Benjamin E., and Alexander L. Sheff. "Bookkeeping and the High School Curriculum," *UBEA Forum,* IX (December, 1954), pp. 13–14.

Tonne, Herbert A. *Principles of Business Education.* New York, McGraw-Hill Book Company, Inc., 1954.

CHAPTER XI

Teaching Bookkeeping

BOOKKEEPING IS A SKILL SUBJECT as well as a subject developing understanding. Many of the principles that were applied in the teaching of shorthand and typewriting can also be used in building bookkeeping skills.

Many research experiments have been conducted to determine the superiority of various methods of teaching bookkeeping. An unbiased student can only conclude from the available evidence that all methods have advantages and disadvantages. The enthusiasm, ability, and experience of the bookkeeping teacher are the most important factors in determining the success of any teaching method. The following suggestions can be utilized in any bookkeeping class.

One of the basic principles of good teaching is that the presentation should go from simple to complex, from the known to the unknown. No more new items should be added to a learning situation than can be comprehended within that lesson. This is a difficult problem for the bookkeeping teacher, for in attempting to simplify learning there may be a tendency to oversimplify, so that the learning achieved is essentially unreal.

Many improvements have, however, been made in the presentation of bookkeeping in the last few years. For example, the current trend not only in high school texts but also in college texts is to present the bookkeeping cycle for the first and even second time in terms of a service business rather than a merchandising business. Thus, the difficult problem of inventory is eliminated in the first presentation of a cycle. Some of the older texts presented in the first

230

cycle the beginning inventory, purchases, and the elimination of the final inventory from the cost of goods sold. This was more than most average learners could comprehend.

Another method of simplifying the presentation of bookkeeping is to use round numbers and simple totals rather than complex and large amounts. For example, in the first presentation of a merchandising profit and loss statement the sales might be $1,000; cost of goods sold, $800; gross profit, $200; and the accumulated additional expenses, $100; leaving a net profit of $100. This simplification of figures should be characteristic whenever new learnings are to be achieved, even in the second or third practice of a particular element. Only after the process has been thoroughly mastered should more complex numbers be used. Few bookkeeping textbooks and probably even fewer teachers take full advantage of this opportunity for simplification.

The subject matter of the transactions should be kept well within the experience of the beginner in business environments. Many students are confused by the use of the term "purchase" as a synonym of the term "buy." Why not use the simpler term and use it consistently until the learning of the actual process has been well established? It is necessary to use the terms "bought on account" and "paid on account," but it is exceedingly important for the teacher to make the learners aware of the meanings of these different terms. Otherwise there is a tendency to find a false identity between the two types of transactions because the new words "on account" loom up as a more mysterious and more important term than the remainder that differentiates the transactions.

THE FIRST DAYS

Bookkeeping requires considerable written work. Much time and energy can be saved if students are seated alphabetically at the beginning of the first period. This arrangement helps in checking attendance and becoming familiar with the students. A tentative seating chart made at the end of the first day is a decided advantage in controlling the class the second day.

Many teachers start the class by asking their students why they are taking bookkeeping. The answers are sure to be interesting and varied. They can be utilized as an informal "ice breaker" to establish a friendly give-and-take spirit in the class. They can also serve to put across the idea that bookkeeping is a vital phase of business activity and that all prospective business workers need this essential training.

The teacher then introduces bookkeeping principles by using the personal possessions and present knowledge of the students to develop the fundamental elements. He starts with illustrations of personal assets such as sweaters, fountain pens, rings, and watches. He then lets the class develop its own definition of assets. The meaning and definition of proprietorship are introduced in the same way. Finally, he uses the idea of debts to put across the meaning and definition of liabilities.

FUNDAMENTAL EQUATIONS

Still using personal assets, the teacher shows the relationship between assets and proprietorship in the simple equation Assets = Proprietorship. He proves it by using small figures. He then develops the equation $A - L = P$, also using small figures. He asks whether some bright student can see another equation to express the relationship between A, L, and P. Thus he develops the very important $A = L + P$ concept. He stresses the idea that property must equal the rights to property. He uses a scale or other visual aid to impress his students with the fact that both sides of the equation must always balance. If one side increases, the other side must increase. If one side decreases, the other side must do the same. If he gets this point across, then he can feel that his students have learned the fundamental equation.

DEBIT AND CREDIT

Using the fundamental equation $A = L + P$, the teacher shows that only two things can happen to all fundamental elements—they can either increase or decrease. The "T" account is presented as a device to separate increases and decreases because it has two sides. He points out that instead of left and right, bookkeepers, in technical terms, call the left side the debit side and the right, the credit side.

Then, as in the equation, the asset balances are placed on the left, or debit, side. The class is asked how one can add to an asset in bookkeeping without using plus signs. The teacher then summarizes that asset-account balances and increases are debited. He then asks the class how they think an asset can be decreased.

After finishing with assets, the idea is developed that, since liabilities and proprietorship represent ownership, they will operate as the reverse of assets, which stand for property. He again emphasizes that the debits must always equal the credits because property equals rights to property. The teacher should spend as many periods as he finds necessary to overteach the principles of debit and credit. He tells his students that, if they learn this phase thoroughly, they are bound to succeed in this course. He teaches, teaches, and overteaches the principles of debit and credit. It will be very desirable for students to overlearn or thoroughly master this basic phase of bookkeeping. Most beginning bookkeeping teachers make the serious mistake of going too fast in the early stages of the course. Because students do not ask questions when the teacher says, "Are there any questions?" the neophyte concludes that all is well and rushes on to the next topic. He should make sure by constant review and testing, oral and written, that his students have mastered the technique of debiting and crediting before he leaves this topic to take up another.

PRESENTATION OF NEW MATERIAL

After the principles of debit and credit have been presented, the course will vary according to the textbook used. No matter what is taught, a new unit should start with a review of what the students have already learned. If the lesson today is on the trial balance, the teacher should use the ledger that students have already prepared. The accounts should be placed on the chalk board, and the reasons for making a trial balance are developed. Then with the class, the teacher starts to prepare the trial balance. The work should proceed slowly. The teacher should stop and summarize at the end of each step and again at the conclusion of the complete process. If the instruction is based on the psychology of proceeding from the known to the unknown, the teacher will not assign advance readings in the textbook. Most secondary-school students do not understand what they read in the bookkeeping textbook until the teacher has presented the material. The bookkeeping textbook should be a student guide rather than an original means of presenting new content material. Advance reading usually serves to confuse the average student rather than to instruct him. After the new topic has been presented, step by step, then the teacher can assign the reading as a review of the presentation.

ASSIGNMENTS

Hurried, last-minute, oral bookkeeping assignments are not conducive to good teaching. The subject matter is definite. The assignment should be so simple and specific that even the laziest pupil cannot use the alibi, "I didn't know the assignment." The assignment should be written every day on a designated chalk board. The specific problem or sections of problems to be completed should be listed. All directions and suggestions that may help the average student should be included. Several transactions should be started in class. If the assignment was worth making and doing, it should be checked in class the following day. The teacher should go over each step with the class, to ascertain that every student knows how to solve the problem. The teacher should walk around the room while he is checking the homework. A glance should be enough to tell him the quality of work being done by every student. Marking innumerable papers is not synonymous with good teaching. It is better to break up practice time into short periods at the beginning. The practice sets provide for integration of learning.

ANALYSIS OF TRANSACTIONS

The procedures in teaching the fundamental elements, the fundamental equations, and principles of debit and credit were described in detail in the preceding section. Typical transactions usually follow the teaching of debit and credit. Some of the typical transactions presented at this stage in many textbooks include:

1. Mr. J. Smith starts a business with Cash, Equipment, Accounts Receivable—R. Brown and B. Green. He owes money to his creditors—S. Kelly and T. Long.

2. Mr. Smith invests additional cash in his business.
3. He buys more equipment for cash.
4. He pays Mr. Kelly some cash on the amount he owes.
5. He buys more equipment on credit from Mr. Long.
6. Mr. Brown pays cash on the amount he owes.
7. A cash sale is made to Mr. Green.
8. Merchandise is sold on credit to Mr. Brown.
9. Equipment is bought for cash from Mr. Kelly.
10. Auto supplies are bought for cash.

Most beginning bookkeeping teachers are satisfied if students know how to make the entry. As was pointed out before, this procedure is satisfactory for the student who is likely to become a routine worker. However, for the student who is expected to understand the fundamental concepts and to interpret them, the entry is of less consequence at this stage of the learning process. What is very crucial is whether the pupil understands thoroughly and clearly why he makes the entry. He must appreciate what effect every transaction has on the fundamental equation. Many teachers have found the use of the following simple chart very helpful in this connection.

TRANSACTION	DEBIT EXPLANATION	DEBIT ENTRY	CREDIT EXPLANATION	CREDIT ENTRY
Bought furniture for cash	A+	Furniture	A—	Cash

The pupil is forced to reason out the transaction rather than to guess or feel the entry. Every time the teacher calls for an entry, he asks the student to explain what happened in terms of the fundamental elements. Suppose a transaction reads, "Equipment bought for cash." The student should know and say, "Debit Equipment because the asset, equipment, increases; and credit Cash because the asset, cash, decreases." If a pupil merely says, "Debit Equipment and credit Cash," there is a strong possibility that he knows "how" to make the entry, but does not know "why" he makes it that way. This lack of understanding explains why so many pupils will give an entry by saying, "Debit Cash—no, credit Cash—no, that's wrong—uh uh—debit Cash," all in one breath. They will make entries but cannot be expected to know why they make them that way unless they are constantly asked "Why? Why? Why?"

The teacher of bookkeeping uses the analysis chart in connection with all written work at this point. When he assigns a problem, he should instruct the students to prepare the analysis chart first and then make the entries in the proper accounts.

After students have spent about a week in presenting the fundamental elements, fundamental equations, debit and credit principles, and analysis of typical transactions, the teacher should prepare a written test on these items. He should not be surprised if some of the results are not so good as expected. He must go back and reteach, drill again, and then test again, until almost all students score 100 per cent on the following typical test questions. The mastery formula is called into operation.

1. Liabilities decrease on the ...... side of an account.
2. Assets increase on the ...... side of an account.
3. The balance of a proprietorship account is on the ...... side.
4. The right side of an account is called the ...... side.
5. The balance of a liability account is on the ...... side.
6. Proprietorship decreases on the ...... side.
7. The balance of an asset account is on the ...... side.
8. The left side of an account is called the ...... side.
9. Liabilities increase on the ...... side.
10. Assets decrease on the ...... side.
11. Proprietorship increases on the ...... side.
12. The fundamental elements are called ......, ..., ...
13. The simplest fundamental equation is ....
14. A second fundamental equation is ....
15. A third fundamental equation is ....
16. Bought merchandise for cash. Analyze and give entry.
17. Mr. Jones invested additional cash in his business. Analyze and give entry.
18. Mr. Jones pays Mr. Brown some of the money he owes. Analysis and entry.
19. Bought equipment on credit from R. A. Creditor. Analysis and entry.
20. Received cash on account from customer Reynolds. Analysis and entry.

While group drill is desirable, the teacher should individualize the learning materials as much as is necessary in terms of the individual interests and abilities of the class members. Mere repetition in bookkeeping, as in any other subject, is of little value. There must be conscious direction for the improvement of learning.

SUMMARY OF TEACHING SUGGESTIONS

Classroom Management

1. So much written material is handled in a bookkeeping class that it is very helpful to seat students according to some seating plan —alphabetic or numeric.

2. The bookkeeping teacher needs a student assistant more than almost any other business-subject teacher. The assistant can be used to distribute, collect, care for, and even to check some phases of the instructional materials.

3. A student assistant should also be trained to start the class promptly even if the teacher is not in the classroom. The student can carry on with one of the fast-starting devices used by the teacher at the beginning of every class period—checking assignments, arithmetic refresher, penmanship drill, or spelling review.

4. Bookkeeping is a business subject; therefore, the bookkeeping class should be conducted like a good business office. The class must start promptly. Desks should be cleared for action. Since bookkeeping is a "doing" course, student desks should always be clean of all unnecessary materials and supplies. Students should be ready and able to work without any delay.

5. Bookkeeping students should be kept busy until the period ends. Clock watchers are not popular in business offices. The teacher should, however, make certain that as far as possible the work is meaningful. Busywork is soon recognized for what it is by the students, and begets distrust of the teacher.

6. Neatness, legibility, and accuracy are important in business. They are also very important in the bookkeeping class. No work should be accepted that the student would be ashamed of claiming as his own in a business office.

7. Most business records are written on the typewriter or with a pen. The bookkeeping teacher should therefore train his students to write with a pen and on the typewriter whenever possible.

8. The teacher is able to control his class better if he is not

chained to his desk. The good teacher is on his feet and ready to move at a moment's notice to any spot where he is needed.

9. Use laborsaving devices, like rubber stamps and rating sheets, to save time and energy. The good teacher is "constructively lazy." He conserves his energy for the major job of teaching.

10. Bulletin boards and chalk boards should be utilized to the fullest extent possible.

11. Appoint one or two students to act as receptionists when visitors enter the bookkeeping room. There should be as little interruption as possible when strangers enter a class. Proceed with the class as usual. The receptionist can give the visitor a textbook and suggest where he can be seated.

12. The bookkeeping room should be properly equipped for the work to be done in it. In addition to the usual equipment found in the bookkeeping room, it is highly desirable to have adding and computing machines available and to see that they are used.

13. Daily routines are systematized, so that no time or energy is wasted. The assignment is always written on the same board. Papers are always handed in and distributed in the same manner unless there is a good reason for deviating from the set procedure.

Teaching Techniques

1. Sell the subject and yourself from the very first minute in the class to the last day of the course. Bookkeeping is important and any student can learn the subject if he *has the will* and *is willing* to put forth the effort. You must get the sales message over right from the start. Bookkeeping can be made an interesting subject if you make up your mind to put it across.

2. Accentuate the positive. Tell students what to do and how to do it rather than harp constantly on what they should not do. Don't frighten them by telling them how difficult and complicated some bookkeeping records can be.

3. Illustrate every generalization with an example drawn from previous student experience. Review previous related learnings.

4. Talk in simple terms. Until you are sure that your students understand what you are saying, use one-syllable words in prefer-

ence to longer words. Bookkeeping terminology is technical. You must translate it into simple language, at first.

5. Prepare a careful lesson plan for every class period you teach. Your teaching time is limited. You cannot afford to waste any of it by "ad libbing."

6. After each new principle has been taught carefully, give the student an opportunity immediately to apply what he has learned.

7. Make certain that there is thorough mastery or overlearning of the fundamental elements and fundamental principles. Do not worry about the bright students becoming bored by your repetition of the fundamentals. Even they can profit from this process of over-teaching that assures almost subconscious recall.

8. Teach a new unit *before* you ask students to read the text-book reference to it. Very few students can learn bookkeeping by reading a text.

9. Utilize the first few minutes of every class period for necessary remedial drills in arithmetic, spelling, and penmanship.

10. Urge students to think in terms of the fundamental elements. At the beginning of the course, they should associate cash with asset every time they mention cash. This will help them to overlearn the fundamental elements.

11. Standards of grading should be raised gradually as the school year progresses. Partial credit, which may be given for an incomplete work sheet early in the year, will not be given at the end of the term.

12. A student should be penalized only once for an error that is carried over and naturally affects other phases of the same problem.

13. The bookkeeping teacher has available and should use a variety of evaluation instruments. In the final analysis, the teacher must remember that bookkeeping is a "doing" subject; and an evaluation program is not complete without a performance test.

14. In using the "why" approach to bookkeeping, be sure to teach the "why" of every transaction. It is sometimes even more important for students to know "why" they make a certain entry than it is for them to make the correct entry.

15. Constantly point out the effect of a transaction on the fundamental elements and the fundamental equation.

Visual Aids

1. Sections of the chalk board may be permanently ruled with journal, ledger, or work-sheet forms. Permanent ruling is achieved by *etching* lines with a steel-edged rule or nail file or by painting lines. Semipermanent ruling may be made by drawing lines with chalk on a wet board. The chalk rulings should be allowed to dry before the board is used.

2. Where permanent or semipermanent ruling is not possible, try to rule the boards before you need the form. Student assistants can help with this task.

3. Columnar headings can be prepared in advance on heavy drawing paper or cardboard. These headings can be posted at the top of the board and will serve as a guide for vertical rulings.

4. If permanent or advance rulings are not feasible, obtain a portable chalk board that can be ruled in advance and reserved for use in the bookkeeping class.

5. Colored chalk can be used effectively in many different ways. A certain color may be used for each of the fundamental elements. Rulings can be made more distinctive through the use of colors.

6. Some teachers cover up sections of a board that have been prepared in advance. In teaching a work sheet, for example, only one set of columns will be shown at a time. As the presentation develops, the strip covering a set of columns is removed.

7. The principle of equal debits and credits can be illustrated graphically by drawing connecting lines to tie up debit and credit entries.

8. The most effective use can be made of a chalk board by starting at the left end and working across to the right. Important material should be retained for purposes of summary and review.

9. Charts showing the fundamental elements, equations, journals, statements, and other forms may be prepared on cardboards or window shades. Other charts may be purchased.

10. Sample blank bookkeeping forms may be obtained from local stationers. They can be mounted and pulled down from a wall holder.

11. Business forms used in local offices can be displayed on bulletin boards. Financial statements and reports can be clipped

from newspapers and magazines. They make excellent display materials.

12. One of the many ready-made accounting systems can be used for display and discussion purposes.

Practice Sets

1. The practice set provides an opportunity to integrate and apply bookkeeping principles in a school situation in as realistic a business-office manner as possible.

2. The practice set provides an opportunity for the performance of such functional bookkeeping duties as proving cash, making a bank reconciliation, preparing and checking invoices and credit memoranda, preparing payrolls and government reports.

3. The bookkeeping principles and practices included in the practice set should first be reviewed thoroughly before the set is even started.

4. The teacher should set the stage by discussing the type of business and activities for which the bookkeeping records will be kept.

5. Definite daily assignments should be made. The class should be kept together for class discussion and explanations. Students who wish to work ahead may do so, but they usually prefer to stay with the class. Some teachers work with the class as a unit in journalizing but permit students to work independently on posting.

6. The teacher should periodically audit and evaluate the work completed up to that point.

7. All business machines available in the school should be used while a class is working on a practice set.

8. The teacher should work through a practice set at least once, in order to become familiar with the rough spots and the time involved.

9. If copying is a problem, the teacher can change certain key figures.

10. At times it is possible and advisable to let groups of students work co-operatively on certain phases of record keeping. The work can be allocated on a functional basis just as is done in business.

11. Students should be required to keep a record of the number

and nature of the errors they make. This error analysis will enable each student to make a self-evaluation of his practice-set achievement.

12. The practice set provides the good teacher with many opportunities to teach related information that would never otherwise be presented. No textbook can contain all the practical details that a teacher with business experience has learned. The practice set provides the springboard for many interesting class discussions on how business does this and that.

Utilizing Community Resources

1. Students should be encouraged to obtain some bookkeeping work experience through a part-time, or co-operative, work-experience program.

2. Much bookkeeping experience can be provided through volunteer service projects for the school, town, and community organizations.

3. Recent graduates, local accountants, internal revenue officials, and businessmen can be invited to speak about bookkeeping as a career.

4. Simple surveys can be made of local bookkeeping practices, to determine types of systems, account titles, special records, and reports used.

5. The teacher may arrange class visits to local business firms to observe bookkeeping activities.

6. The teacher may arrange demonstrations of bookkeeping and calculating machines.

7. The teacher may organize and supervise a bookkeeping club, which can find many worth-while projects to justify its existence.

8. The bookkeeping teacher can extend his own bookkeeping experience by working for local firms on a part-time basis.

SPECIMEN LESSON PLANS FOR BOOKKEEPING INSTRUCTION

The following lesson plans do not follow the pattern presented in the teaching of shorthand, typewriting, transcription, or basic-business education. The purpose of changing the organization of lesson plans is to give the future teacher an acquaintanceship with as many different procedures for setting up and planning learning materials as possible. It is less necessary to present formally the purpose of a particular lesson in many phases of bookkeeping because these purposes are usually obvious. The review of previous work is made an essential phase of the lesson presentation in the plans given below. Subject matter, student activities, teacher activities, and supplies and equipment are all presented in the sequence in which they are to be used.

Lesson Plan on Introducing the Journal

Many textbooks introduce the journal after the students have learned to analyze typical transactions. The purpose of the plan is to introduce the journal and to teach students how to journalize.

1. Review the fundamental equations by placing them on the board.
2. Analyze several typical transactions and have them placed on the board.
3. Have several ledger entries placed on the board. These should be selected from the homework assignment to be checked this day.
4. *a.* Ask the class whether it has a clear and connected permanent picture of the transactions that were recorded in the ledger accounts.
   b. Ask the class if it would be easy to locate any errors that crept into the original entry.
5. Explain that, in order to have a permanent day-by-day record and history of business transactions, a daily record of all original transactions is kept. This daily record is called a *journal.*
6. The journal does not eliminate the need for the ledger entries. The ledger still provides a classified summary of the business that is obtained from the first, or original, entry made in the journal. The journal is called the *book of original entry,* while the ledger is the *book of final entry.*
7. The entry for any transaction remains the same as when it was placed directly into the ledger account. The only new thing is purely a matter of form. Illustrate the journal paper to be used. Show how it differs from ledger paper. Give each student a sheet of journal paper.
8. Journalize at the board the first transaction in the homework

assignment previously checked. Let the class make the journal entry. Point out how simple it is to journalize.

9. Make several additional entries. Let the class journalize the rest of the exercise while you walk around to help some students.

10. Summarize the major points to remember.

11. Have the class finish journalizing the exercise previously completed in ledger form.

12. Present an additional problem. Preview it and assign it for homework.

13. Ask the class to read the chapter on the journal and to answer selected questions at the end of the chapter at home.

Lesson Plan on Posting

Posting is a vital aspect of the work of a bookkeeper. In larger businesses, posting and billing are often undertaken simultaneously with the making of an original entry. It is probably unwise to complicate the process by making the student aware of this when first presenting posting, which is usually carried on in the traditional manner in most bookkeeping textbooks. However, somewhere along the line of instruction, students should be made aware of the different procedures used in posting activities and should be given an actual acquaintanceship with the many procedures that are followed.

After pupils have demonstrated their competency in making neat and correct journal entries, they are taught how to post to the ledger.

1. Use a simple problem that has been journalized.

2. Ask pupils how many accounts will be needed to transfer the entries from the journal to the ledger. Put several accounts on the board.

3. Ask a pupil to read the first journal entry.

4. Post the amount first to the appropriate ledger account. Check the amount posted against the amount in the journal. Emphasize the importance of recording the correct amount.

5. Point out that the year of the date is entered next and then the month and day. Stress the importance of the year.

6. Next comes the explanation. Tell the class that explanations are used only for opening and closing entries.

7. The next step is to put the journal page in the ledger. Explain the reason for this step.

8. The final step is to put the ledger page (folio) in the journal. Also, stress the importance of this step.

9. Give the class ledger paper, and work several entries with them. Then walk around and be sure they follow the correct procedure.

10. Assign the completion of this exercise, additional problems, reading of the chapter, and related questions.

Lesson Plan on the Trial Balance

When students have demonstrated their skill in posting accurately and rapidly, they are ready for a trial balance.

1. Use a problem that the class has journalized and posted. Ask the students whether they are positive that all postings have been made accurately and that the total debits in the ledger equal the total credits.

2. Point out that in order to be sure that the ledger is correct, a proof of its totals, or balances, must be taken. Set up a debit column and a credit column.

3. Work at the board while the students try to take a trial balance. If students have trouble, encourage them to find their own errors.

4. Point out how to find mistakes in a trial balance. Expand.

5. Point out the types of errors that do not show up on a trial balance. Expand.

6. Assign the completion of this exercise and several additional problems.

Lesson Plan on the Work Sheet

The work sheet has been placed traditionally in the program of instruction for second-year bookkeeping; however, now that most students do not take second-year bookkeeping, some textbook authors have provided a brief presentation of this significant bookkeeping instrument in the first year. Some authors present the work sheet first as a basis for setting up profit and loss statements and balance sheets and for making closing and adjusting entries. Most authors, however, fear that this complicates the procedure overmuch and therefore present the work sheet as a supplement in the later cycle rather than in the presentation of the complete cycle at some initial stage. The work sheet is a technical instrument. It is not usually assigned to a beginning worker. Many teachers of beginning bookkeeping, therefore, may wish to minimize and even completely eliminate the presentation of this topic; however, for some of the brighter students of bookkeeping it does have a real fascination. Some teachers present the work sheet as a means of maintaining the interest of these students.

1. Start with a trial balance previously completed. Have it placed on the board before class starts.

2. Point out that, though the books seem to be correct, there are some items on the trial balance that are not listed at their true value. Ask the class to search for these items. They should see that merchandise inventory, purchases, deferred expenses, fixed assets, and capital may not be correctly stated as shown on the trial balance. This creates the need for correcting entries, which accountants call "adjustments." Set up the two columns for adjustments.

3. Teach each adjustment entry separately according to the items included in the new inventories.

4. Total the adjustments and point out why they must agree.

5. Tell the class that it is now necessary to change the original trial-balance figures in line with the corrections made in the adjustments. All items not corrected are carried over as they are. The new items must also go into the adjusted trial-balance columns. The new trial balance is called the "adjusted trial balance." All future computations are made from the adjusted trial balance. Set up two columns for the adjusted trial balance.

6. Explain that all items in the adjusted trial balance are either profit and loss items or one of the fundamental elements. Students, therefore, set up one set of the columns for profit-and-loss-statement items and one set of columns for balance-sheet items. Students start at the top of the adjusted trial balance and extend every item into one set of columns or the other.

7. After the profit and loss columns have been totaled, ask the class to explain why they do not agree. Develop the idea that the difference represents profit or loss. Do the same for the balance-sheet totals. Point out that the difference between the profit and loss totals and balance-sheet totals represents the profit or loss.

Lesson Plan on Adjusting and Closing Entries

1. Place on the board a work sheet for a problem previously completed.

2. Point out that the corrections for the end of the period have been made on the work sheet. Ask the class whether these corrections have been made in the ledger. They will realize that the ledger balances remain as they were on the trial balance. Point out that the work sheet is not an integral part of the books—it is only a piece of scrap paper on which the bookkeeper computes the profit or loss for the period.

3. It is now necessary to record the corrections made on the work sheet in the books through journal entries. Use the adjustment entries on the work sheet as the basis for making the adjusting entries in the journal. Place the entries on the board. Post the entries to show their effect on the ledger.

4. Point out that it is now necessary to clear out the temporary cost and expense accounts that have already served their purpose during the current period. The March Sales account, for example, will be of no value in April. Since we want to start with a clean slate at the beginning of the new month, we close out the current period.

5. The P & L columns of the work sheet are used as the basis for making the closing entries at the board. All income items are closed out by debits to the individual accounts, while the P & L Summary is credited for the total amount. The total of the cost items is a debit to P & L Summary while the individual items are credited. The remaining profit or loss in the Summary account is closed out to the Personal or Capital account.

Lesson Plan on Special Journals

1. Use the general journal of a problem previously completed.

2. Give the class several transactions dealing with sales on account. Put the general journal entries on the board.

3. Point out that in every entry the credit to Sales remains constant, and only the debit to the various customers varies. The bookkeeper, therefore, sets aside a special section of his journal for sales. Since the credit is always to Sales, he does not bother repeating the credit but just sets up provision for the accounts debited. At the end of the period he adds up the total sales and makes one summary entry crediting sales for the full amount.

4. The debits are posted to the customer's accounts in the routine way. The credit to Sales is posted at the end of the period.

5. Point out that, in a business of some size, keeping a special journal saves considerable time and space

    a. in recording only one-half of the entry

    b. in posting only one-half of the entry

    c. in making it possible for more than one person to work on the journals.

  6. The same procedure is repeated for the Purchases journal, Cash Receipts journal, and Cash Payments journal.

It would be physically impossible in a book of this type to present the specific procedures involved in teaching all topics commonly presented in most bookkeeping classes. Sufficient techniques have been described to give the beginning teacher an understanding and appreciation of some of the methods used by successful bookkeeping teachers.

Lesson Plan on Interpretation of Financial Statements

As was indicated previously, the simple analysis of the meaning of the balance sheet and profit and loss statement is much easier to teach and much simpler to understand than it is to teach the preparation of the financial statement and the formal opening, closing, and adjusting entries. The subject has been traditionally relegated to the second year and even there has often been given only incidental attention. Everyone must at some time analyze and attempt to understand the implications of financial statements. Many who never undertake bookkeeping practices are under obligation to their firms and to their communities to make careful studies of these statements. Teachers should be encouraged, therefore, to give as much attention as is possible within their program to the utilization of the financial statement. This plan is therefore presented to help teachers provide such learning activities in elementary bookkeeping.

  1. Several days prior to the study of the analysis of financial statements have students check through the newspapers, go to the banks, and ask their parents for financial statements. Most municipalities issue financial statements in connection with their tax bills, or practically all large corporations issue financial statements. Most students, therefore, should have little difficuly in bringing in financial statements. Many of them should be able to provide a rich source of learning material.

  2. Ask good students to turn to a simple profit and loss statement in the textbook.

3. Work out with them the relationship terms of percentages between gross profit and sales, and net profit and sales.

4. Work out a profit and loss statement for a succeeding year or use one that is available in the book. Have students discuss the differentials between per cent of gross profit in one year as compared to another and the net profits in one year compared to another.

5. Develop the idea that quantity of sales must be large to reduce percentage of overhead.

6. Discuss with them such items as: cost of purchase return, cost of sales return.

7. Tell students what is meant by average inventory; demonstrate this from a profit and loss statement.

8. Have students work out the ratios for another organization giving per cents of cost compared to sales. This may be assigned as homework with the suggestion that students talk over the meaning of terms used with their parents or older brothers and sisters where appropriate.

Similar lessons should be devised for the study and analysis of the balance sheet including comparisons between different years, consideration of the degree of contingent assets, the validity of good will, the value of the working capital ratio. The learning should be fixed by actual practice.

Use should be made of picture charts and bar graphs provided by many corporations for showing the relation of cost of goods sold to wages paid, of wages paid to profits earned, and of dividends paid. Students should be encouraged to talk over these terms with their parents.

The teacher should be certain that students realize that financial statements are word pictures—that no picture is entirely correct. Comparisons should be made between photographs of people and financial statements of firms. Are they flattering, or do they fail to do justice? Caution in the interpretation of statements is vital, and oversimplification of the problem of statement analysis should not be encouraged.

QUESTIONS

1. What are the steps in the bookkeeping cycle?
2. How can the teacher stress the analysis of transactions?
3. How should the principles of debit and credit be developed?

4. How would you introduce the teaching of accounts?

5. How can arithmetic competency be improved in bookkeeping?

6. How can the teacher help students in doing their homework?

7. How should the teacher use test results in bookkeeping?

8. How can the teacher make the best use of chalk boards?

9. What other visual aids can be used effectively in bookkeeping?

10. How can the community be brought into the bookkeeping classroom?

11. What are some of the supplementary materials that can be used in bookkeeping?

12. What are the best physical arrangements for a bookkeeping classroom?

STUDENT ACTIVITIES

1. Prepare a lesson plan for the first day of your bookkeeping class. Use any textbook you desire. Teach the class for 10 minutes.

2. Prepare a lesson plan for the second day of your bookkeeping class. Teach the class for 10 minutes.

3. Prepare a lesson plan for the third day of your class. Teach the class for 10 minutes.

4. Prepare a lesson plan for the teaching of any special journal. Teach the class for 10 minutes.

5. Prepare a set of directions for handling assignments and homework.

6. Prepare a lesson plan for a practice set.

7. Prepare a list of five objective bookkeeping tests. Examine any three of these tests. Administer at least one of them in a class. Score and grade the results.

8. Prepare a list of at least five audio-visual aids available for bookkeeping. See Haas and Packer, *The Preparation and Use of Visual Aids.*

9. Resolved that: "The teaching of the work sheet in elementary bookkeeping is a complete waste of time and energy." List the arguments on both sides of the question.

BIBLIOGRAPHY

Andruss, Harvey A. "Appraising Achievement in Bookkeeping and Accounting," *American Business Education,* VI (March, 1950), pp. 135–144.

Bell, Robert P. "Planning the Bookkeeping Room," *UBEA Forum,* IX (December, 1954), pp. 16–18.

Breidenbaugh, V. E. "An Evaluation of High School Bookkeeping," *Journal of Business Education,* XXV (January, 1950), pp. 17–19.

Freeman, M. Herbert. "The Beginning Bookkeeping Teacher," *Journal of Business Education,* XXIV (November, 1948), pp. 22–24, 28.

————, and Gilbert Kahn. "The Bookkeeping Practice Set," *Business Teacher,* XXXI (April, 1954), pp. 13–14.

Garrison, Lloyd L. "Practical Suggestions for Bookkeeping Teachers," *Balance Sheet,* XXXVI (November, 1954), pp. 111–112.

Gibson, E. Dana. "Visualize Your Bookkeeping," *Journal of Business Education,* XXVII (February, 1952), pp. 253–256.

Hagen, John. "Bookkeeping Instruction Should Start Where You Find the Students," *Balance Sheet,* XXXV (October, 1953), pp. 52–53.

Hanna, J Marshall. "Methods of Teaching Bookkeeping, Using the Community as a Laboratory," *Business Education World,* XXXII (June, 1952), pp. 228–230.

————, and M. Herbert Freeman. "Do You Really Teach Bookkeeping?" *Business Teacher,* XXX (May-June 1953), p. 232.

Harms, Harm. *Methods in Vocational Business Education.* Cincinnati, South-Western Publishing Company, 1949, Chapter VII.

House, F. Wayne. "Bookkeeping Students Say Their Assignments Are Too Long, Too Hard," *Business Education World,* XXXV (October, 1954), pp. 18–19.

————. "Factors Affecting Student Achievement in Beginning Bookkeeping in High School," *Journal of Business Education,* XXIX (December, 1953), pp. 128–129.

Jacobs, Harry G. "Lining the Chalk Board in the Bookkeeping and Accounting Classroom," *UBEA Forum,* IX (December, 1954), pp. 15–16.

Kahn, Gilbert, and M. Herbert Freeman. "How to Assign Bookkeeping Homework," *Business Teacher,* XXI (February, 1954), pp. 15, 18.

————. "Bookkeeping Tests," *Business Teacher,* XXX (May, 1953), pp. 155–156.

Knost, Ralph. "A Classroom Teaching Procedure in Bookkeeping," *Journal of Business Education,* XXIV (September, 1948), pp. 17–18, 26.

Sampson, Theodore V. "Motivation for High School Bookkeeping Classes," *Balance Sheet,* XXXV (February, 1954), pp. 250–251.

Satlow, David. "Action Questions in Bookkeeping," *Business Education World,* XXXIII (May, 1953), p. 334.

Swanson, Edwin A. "Some Implications of Recent Research Related to High School Bookkeeping," *National Business Education Quarterly,* XXII (Fall, 1953), pp. 31–35.

Swanson, Robert M. "How to Use Practice Sets as a Learning Device," *Balance Sheet,* XXXVI (December, 1954), pp. 159–160, 163.

————. "What We Know About Bookkeeping and Accounting—from Research," *UBEA Forum,* VIII (April, 1954), pp. 24–25, 36.

(April, 1954), pp. 24–25, 36.

CHAPTER XII

Arithmetic in the
Business Program

THE BEGINNING BUSINESS TEACHER who is assigned to teaching business arithmetic faces an interesting but difficult task. Often he has not had sufficient training in methods of teaching to really like the subject matter. Sometimes he himself is deficient in arithmetic skill. Even if he is well trained, he finds it very difficult to understand the apparent lack of simple arithmetical skills possessed by many high school students; however, an even greater problem is the attitude of the students. Some have learned to dislike arithmetic; others, having had eight years of arithmetic in elementary school, feel they know all about it. Altogether there is a wide diversity of abilities in arithmetic skills and in the ability to apply these skills to everyday situations.

If the teacher covers the material rapidly enough to maintain the interest of the more competent students, the less qualified lag and may become lost. If he keeps his pace slow enough so that those with less arithmetical ability can really master the simpler elements, he finds that the more able students are bored.

To meet this situation, many teachers are likely to fall into the familiar pitfalls of either simply assigning exercises and hoping that mere drill will accomplish something, or of using workbook pads as a means of keeping the students busy, disregarding the uses planned for these by the publisher and author.

The fact is that many high school students have developed considerable arithmetical skill of a nonacademic variety, which they cannot translate into school terms. Many of them can make satisfactory computations in areas in which they are interested: making change in the candy store; counting up scores; and figuring batting averages. They feel adequately competent in terms of the situations they meet and therefore are not motivated to learn a skill that has little meaning to them.

TYPES OF ARITHMETIC INSTRUCTION

Several types of arithmetic may be presented in the secondary school. The first is a purely remedial type of instruction to further develop skill that may not have been achieved adequately at the elementary level; the second is a simple type of problem-solving arithmetic, similar to that taught in the elementary school; third are those aspects of arithmetic that involve business situations and relate closely to the learnings being presented in the bookkeeping classroom; and fourth are those phases of arithmetic that make use of varying degrees of algebraic solutions for problem solving. Apart from these there are, of course, the formal mathematics courses in algebra, geometry, and trigonometry that have little or no relation to the immediately utilitarian programs in arithmetic.

High school teachers habitually criticize the elementary-school teachers for the inadequate skill of their pupils in arithmetic. Such condemnation is unjust and futile. Many elementary-school pupils do develop adequate arithmetic ability, but those who fail to achieve adequate standards are the ones who stand out. Elementary-school teachers are restricted by formal courses of study that force them to work for abstract standards in some schools, and in other schools, prevent them from giving adequate attention to organized arithmetical learning experiences. All this, however, is beside the point. Secondary-school teachers must take the students as they are and do the best they can to develop their abilities. They are the ones who will be held responsible by the prospective employer.

In this chapter, therefore, the first part of the presentation will be devoted to instruction in remedial arithmetic required by a certain proportion of all students; the second part will consider the procedures for teaching the arithmetic especially required by business students.

DIAGNOSIS, THE FIRST STEP

The first step in developing adequate arithmetic ability in the secondary school, therefore, is to determine just what skills and abilities the students have and do not have. Several diagnostic tests in arithmetic that will serve adequately have been developed. Here are some of the better ones:

> Buswell-John Diagnostic Test for Fundamentals in Arithmetic. Bloomington, Illinois, Public School Publishing Company
> Compass Diagnostic Tests in Arithmetic. Chicago, Scott Foresman and Company
> Monroe Diagnostic Arithmetic Tests. Bloomington, Illinois, Public School Publishing Company
> Washburne Diagnostic Tests in Arithmetic. Yonkers, New York, World Book Company

In addition to these there are several good achievement tests [1] that can be used, if necessary, for diagnosis; but they are not so satisfactory for this purpose as tests definitely planned with this in mind. It is desirable to present a diagnostic test in arithmetic to all students in the secondary school because adequate abilities in arithmetic processes should not be limited to business students.[2] If it is not possible to administer this diagnostic test to all students as a basis for further learning, then at least those in the business program should be given the test as a group. If this also is not possible, then the teacher should present this test directly in his arithmetic class. This test should be administered exactly in accordance with the printed directions. The results of these tests will give the teacher a considerable cue for determining the deficiencies of the learners and will

[1] For example, Stamford Achievement Test, Advanced Arithmetic Test, World Book Company, Yonkers, New York.

[2] An increasing number of elementary schools give achievement tests just prior to admission to the high school. These results can often be used as guides to placement for further learning.

suggest why the errors were made. Of course, no group diagnostic test can indicate all possible causes for a failure or individual needs for further learning. These the teacher must determine individually while working with the students as they do their practice work.

For those students who fail to attain satisfactory scores in addition, the teacher should determine for each individual student the cause for the poor addition. Is it sheer carelessness? Is it lack of ability to combine numbers? For example, does the student hesitate in adding seven and six or nine and five? Does he attempt to add in combinations of numbers that are beyond his ability to grasp?

There are literally dozens of reasons why children fail to add, subtract, multiply, or divide correctly. For example, suppose you ask a student to undertake the following subtraction:

$$
\begin{array}{r}
7{,}553 \\
-2{,}321 \\
\hline
\end{array}
$$

Suppose he comes out with a result of 5,322. The cause of this may be pure carelessness. On the other hand some students can be observed to go through the process this way:

> Three from one leaves two
> Five from two leaves three
> Five from three leaves two
> And seven from two leaves five

This is utterly illogical, but children can often think the incorrect process but still come out with the correct answer. Somehow in their minds they go from the top down although actually in subtraction the lower number is subtracted from the upper number. This procedure assumes the "take-away" rather than the addition process.

Nevertheless such false processing is likely to cause errors. If this error is caught in time, it can be corrected. This false process and many other failings of this type cannot be discovered by merely looking at a test paper. The student's mental processes as he undertakes the exercise have to be analyzed.

All this takes much time; it takes effort to administer the tests and to score them; and it requires much patience to analyze them for the causes of errors. However, this work will repay itself. It makes the students aware of the errors; it gives the teacher a basis for remedial teaching; and most important, it motivates the work.

Arithmetic Necessary For All

Numerous studies have been made that indicate that the number and level of skill abilities in arithmetic required by the average adult are limited. An ability to add, multiply, subtract, and divide is fundamental. Some understanding of the relationship between aliquot parts, decimals, and per cents is desirable; but the numbers of relationships that need to be memorized are few. Adults get along well with an understanding of $\frac{1}{2}$, $\frac{1}{4}$, $\frac{3}{4}$, $\frac{1}{3}$, $\frac{2}{3}$, $\frac{1}{8}$, $\frac{3}{8}$, $\frac{5}{8}$, $\frac{1}{5}$, $\frac{1}{16}$, $\frac{1}{10}$, $\frac{1}{12}$, $\frac{5}{12}$, $\frac{7}{12}$, and a few others, and do not need to memorize such unusual fractions as $\frac{5}{16}$ or their decimal and per cent relationships. A simple acquaintanceship with ratio and proportion is probably desirable. Percentages and simple interest are so important in business life that they should probably be included, especially for business students.

Remedial Teaching

Remedial teaching will solve the problem. Every secondary school should provide a program of remedial teaching in arithmetic, not only for business students but for all students. This course should be based on thoroughly effective diagnostic testing. Those whose skills are adequate should be exempt from further learning as such; this number may vary from almost none to nearly half the students, depending on the thoroughness of the instruction received and the degree to which the skill became a part of the student's real life experience. Some of the students who show inadequacies in fundamental arithmetic skills certainly need a brief program of corrective practice. This basic learning can often be provided easily in less than a term. A study period might be used temporarily for this purpose. Many more, however, will need a more thorough program of instruction. Such students should be given full academic credit for a full program of instruction. Inasmuch as the school gives credit for four years of English instruction in high school, much of which is remedial, why deny credit for training in other meaningful skills?

Once the needs of the students have been carefully diagnosed, every effort should be made to achieve thoroughness of learning. The procedure for skills learning presented in the previous chapters is in large measure applicable to instruction in arithmetic. A uniform pattern of expertness cannot be presented by the teacher simply because all students have already achieved some degree of ability, or at worst, of inability. The teacher must, therefore, set several patterns—in some cases many patterns—and must provide for a differentiated program or practice. This practice must be meaningful for students. They will object to the same "old stuff" taught the same old way as it was in elementary school. Students need new practice materials and more direct drill.

DIFFERENTIATION IN LEARNING STANDARDS

More important even than setting up different learning materials, the teacher must set up different learning standards. It is ridiculous to assume that all students can be brought up to a particular standard of arithmetic skill, regardless of how low that standard may be. On the other hand, it is equally unjustified for the school to accept the very low standards attainable by most students for those students who can attain much higher levels. In recent years much criticism has been focused upon programs of remedial instruction. The opinion is rendered that drills presented apart from actual situations result in little or no learning.

There is little doubt that compulsory remedial learning is of little value. To assume, however, that a program without remedial instruction has any value is equally erroneous. The effectiveness of a program of remedial instruction depends on the manner in which the learnings are attained. In every operation of remedial learning, the teacher must go back to the level that the student actually has arrived at and begin from there. He must, as far as possible, make the learnings meaningful for the student by getting him to be aware of the importance of the learning, by making the learning a game, or by setting up such effective motivation that the learning will actually take place. For example, in learning to add two columns of figures, the learner may not have had practice in carrying the extra digits from the first column to the second. It might, therefore, be wise to begin in the following fashion for those who do not have adequate background.

$$
\begin{array}{r}
76 \\
38 \\
47 \\
59 \\
91 \\
24 \\
\hline
35 \\
30 \\
\hline
335
\end{array}
$$

This procedure, known as the "civil service check," is often used in business. Only after this process has been learned should the more simple procedure of carrying forward be taught.

Again, in teaching students how to add ⅔ and ⅙, it is necessary for many students to use a concrete example that gets away completely from the abstract. For example, the teacher may use a pie divided into thirds and a pie divided into sixths and show the student, the learner, that ⅔ is really the equivalent of ⁴⁄₆. Then the student can easily grasp the idea that ⁴⁄₆ plus ⅙ makes ⅚. To the person who has mastered the art of thinking in these abstractions, this seems an unnecessary and painfully roundabout way of learning. To the person who has not achieved this abstraction, it is vitally necessary. Students learn in terms of specifics rather than in terms of abstracts, and only the more able students can grasp certain abstractions from the very beginning. When the learner has grasped the elementary concept and knows why he is undertaking a particular process and how it operates, then a thorough program of mastering may be achieved. If the student, however, merely learns a particular process, the law of forgetting will start to operate immediately; consequently, the student needs a great deal of repetition resulting in overlearning. This review repetition, however, must not be merely repetition; it must be brought out in terms of new situations and with new opportunities for giving reality to the abstraction. Most people achieve mastery of an abstract process, like division or addition, apart from actual cases only after innumerable opportunities to use the process in connection with real experiences. The teacher must, therefore, apply these newly learned skills to real situations. Fortunately, daily life gives innumerable opportunities for application of those arithmetic skills that are really necessary.

The Testing Process

The testing process has often been misused in arithmetic. The teacher fails to realize how rapidly surface learning may disappear in an abstract process. He also fails to realize how much fright is involved in being tested. Many times a student could think through a process and come out with the correct result if given the opportunity and if encouraged to think in a relaxed environment. Putting an atmosphere of pressure on the student, however, encourages him to guess and to jump to wild conclusions, rather than trying to think the problems through. The tester in arithmetic, therefore, as well as in other subjects, often underestimates the actual ability of the student because the test itself is given in abstract form and because students by many years of experience have learned to guess.

Testing, obviously, is an important segment of remedial teaching. Tests should not be given, generally, as a means of instruction; but they are often necessary as markers for measuring the success of instruction and as a means of planning the line of correctional instruction to be carried on.

Problem Teaching in Arithmetic

Instruction in solving daily-life problems, such as how much insurance to buy under a given situation or whether or not to buy a house, can best be taught, in many cases, outside the formal class in arithmetic. The solution of such problems requires an integration of many understandings and skills. Some of these understandings can be attained most satisfactorily in the business-arithmetic classroom; but others will be developed better in a class in economics, in bookkeeping, in shorthand, in typewriting, in business organization, in business law, or even in business English. The development of the fundamental skills is uniquely the problem of the arithmetic classroom. The application of arithmetic skills to daily life is the problem of all classroom teachers and even more fundamentally the problem of the parent, the employer, and, of course, the student himself.

Such problem solving, when it is carried on, must be real. Unless the students understand the meaning of the problem, it is wasteful. Students cannot cope with the problem of how much insurance to buy in a given situation until they understand the principle of insurance, the limitations of insurance as a means of risk reduction, and the social values of insurance in the American economy. These problems, therefore, should be studied and analyzed when the need arises in or out of the classroom, rather than be presented formally when the topic comes up arbitrarily in an arithmetic course of study.

Many of our life activities that require the making of decisions involve arithmetic understandings; for example, should a person with an income of $5,000, with a wife and two children and considerable uncertainty as to the stability of a job, buy a house that costs $15,000 on a down payment of $2,000? The answer to this cannot be given in exact arithmetic results. So much depends on intangibles. Is society going through a period of inflation or deflation? Will the wage earner wish to move to another part of the country? Is the family likely to have more children? And many other similar elements. Such problems require an understanding of all factors involved and an ability to merge arithmetic and nonarithmetic concepts. Solving them cannot be taught as objective arithmetic. They can only be solved by merging all facts involved and then using simple arithmetic processes as aids in final decision making.

Arithmetic teachers in the elementary schools formerly spent much time on such meaningless problems as: if a train leaves New York at the same time that another train leaves Chicago, and the train from New York is traveling at 60 miles an hour and the train from Chicago at 50 miles an hour, assuming that New York and Chicago are 900 miles apart, at which point will they meet? Such problems confused the child, made him dislike arithmetic, and failed to achieve the fundamental abilities needed in daily life. Thus, although the basic arithmetic skills needed by all were very few, the elementary school often was unsuccessful in achieving them simply because the time devoted to arithmetic in considerable measure was wasted on abstract and meaningless problem solving.

Here is a problem taken from the most recent edition of a popular business-arithmetic text: Mr. Francis J. Brown invested $7,035 in stock at $67. If the stock pays 3½ per cent annually per share, find (a) the amount of the quarterly dividend check and (b) the rate Mr. Brown is earning on his investment. This problem may be a real problem for many adults just as the "meeting of the trains" problem presented previously could be a real problem for some particular individual. Nevertheless, the investment problem might be quite as abstract and meaningless to many students as the train-meeting problem if the students do not have the basis for understanding the meaning of the problem. This is the case for many students in schools at the present time.

The problem must be made meaningful to the student. If he does not know the processes of the stock market and does not realize that a share of stock at a given par value may sell at 67, then he cannot grasp the meaning of the problem in the first place. If he does not realize that 3½ per cent a share is based on par value rather than on purchase price, again he is not in a position to solve the problem. If the stock has a par value of $100, then the yield is far higher than the dividend rate, for the dividend of $3.50 is paid on par value and not on the selling price of $67. If, however, the par value is $50, then the yield is lower than the dividend rate, for the dividend now is only $1.75 though the selling price per share is still $67. It is futile to attempt to solve a problem such as this unless all parts are given and unless the student knows what it is all about. Only after the student has a rather complete grasp of the operation of financial investments, is he in the position to begin solving the problem. Then he can determine the purpose of the problem and analyze the elements for which he must seek. After that, he is in a position to determine how to solve the problem.

One of the important elements that teachers often fail to present is the common sense, the actuality, of a solution. For example, if a particular commodity sells at $60 and the student is asked to find the cost price when there has been a markup of 25 per cent on the cost price, students are likely to come to varied answers. Some will say the cost price is $45. This indicates obviously that they took the markup from the sales price rather than from the cost price as was asked. They either did not grasp the problem, did not think it through, or did not know the terminology. Others will give as the cost price $72 or $75. This obviously indicates a complete lack of common sense. For if the sales price was $60 and a profit was made, the cost price must be considerably less than the sales price.

Every experienced arithmetic teacher must have had the experience many times of finding that his students will unblushingly present a cost price higher than the purchase price in a profit situation of this type. They simply have not had the experience of using common sense. They have followed a formula incorrectly and not thought through the reality of the answer. This is pretty good evidence that the problem had no meaning to the students in the first place. This whole problem of using common sense in solving arithmetic problems is basic to evaluation. Evaluation can be carried through by doing the problem all over again, working it backward, or determining whether the answer has actual feasibility in daily life; or better yet, a combination of these procedures can be used. Unless the student has learned to use common sense and to practice evaluation, an important element in arithmetic learning has not been attained.

WHAT ARITHMETIC IS NECESSARY FOR BUSINESS USE?

Business-arithmetic teachers spend much time on such topics as: short cuts in computation, markups and markdowns, chain discounts, simple and compound interest, bank discounts, true discounts, building and loan calculations, depreciation, and good-will evaluation.

The fact is that in the business activities of most office workers and sales workers no special arithmetic skills are needed. This is particularly true of the beginning worker. Occasionally, in a specialized office, some particular process may be required; but it is impossible to present the 1,001 specialized applications of skills that might be needed. The most that can be said is that some students in the business curriculum may eventually require a higher level of ability and more facility in the same skills that are needed by all students.

THE DILEMMA OF THE BUSINESS-ARITHMETIC TEACHER

A teacher of business arithmetic is therefore faced with a serious problem. If he gives up the class in business arithmetic, the result will usually be that no instruction will be given in arithmetic. One of the usually justified complaints of businessmen, however, is that prospective business workers are not well grounded in computational skills.

Unfortunately, the high school in most school systems does not provide a program of remedial instruction, based on adequate diagnosis, for all students. High school students still take algebra, geometry, and trigonometry in the academic program, but usually receive no further instruction in simple arithmetic processes. On the other hand, the business department insists on the continuance of business arithmetic, but spends much of the time on activities that are not fruitful when the students go into the office or the salesroom.

Consequently, in many school systems, the administration loses interest in business arithmetic and drops the subject. Then after a few years the chamber of commerce and other service organizations, under the influence of some interested teacher, complain about the lack of skill on the part of graduating students; and business arithmetic is reinstated. Again after a given period the administration becomes aware of its futility, and the subject is again dropped. The explanation, of course, is rather simple. Further training in arithmetic is necessary in high school to strengthen and supplement the learnings of the elementary school; however, the subject matter usually offered in the formal course of business arithmetic does not remedy inadequacies or develop further understanding, skill, or ability in arithmetic processes.

OBJECTIVES OF BUSINESS ARITHMETIC

What then should be the objectives of business arithmetic as taught in a secondary school? They should be the same as those for any other worth-while course in arithmetic, only on a higher and possibly more adequate level than those for a preceding course. These objectives might be summarized as follows:

DESIRABLE OBJECTIVES OF BUSINESS ARITHMETIC

1. Develop further speed and higher accuracy in the fundamental processes
2. Develop facility in mental computations when practical rather than relying on written solutions
3. Acquire facility in the more usable short cuts that are of value in calculation
4. Achieve ability in problem reading, in the interpretation of these problems, and in their solutions
5. Achieve ability in estimating the common sense of an answer
6. Utilize previous learnings of business activities in other classes and develop their further understanding through the arithmetic processes; also prepare for further skills in business by developing facility in the arithmetic processes connected therewith
7. Apply these learnings of the principles of business and of arithmetic to life situations

It can be seen, therefore, that these objectives do not differ from those for any good program of arithmetic instruction, except in the degree of learning and in the thoroughness of attainment.

The procedures previously suggested in regard to a remedial program of arithmetic therefore apply equally well to the program of instruction in business arithmetic. No matter how well the remedial program of arithmetic may have been carried through, there still will be opportunities for the further development of skills in the class in business arithmetic. If a program of diagnostic testing has not been presented to the class, this should be an element of the course in business arithmetic. The data thus made available should be utilized to give improved skill as problem materials are developed.

The topics suggested above and others that might be taught in a class of business arithmetic can be found in any of the several good textbooks now available. They give opportunity for the development of further proficiency in fundamental processes. All deal with such problems as aliquot parts applied to business situations, use of graphs and percentages such as cash discount, trade discount, profit and loss, depreciation, payroll procedures. Some take up piecework, banking, bank discount, real estate tax rates, cost of premiums in insurance, short-time rates and cancellation procedures, coinsurance, arithmetic of stocks and bonds, compound interest, and financial ratios. Again the problem is to motivate the students.

Here is an example taken from a current business-arithmetic textbook.

George Kress borrowed $200 from a loan organization. He promised to repay the loan by making four monthly payments of $52.94 each. The problem is to figure the yearly rate of interest he had to pay. This is a real situation and can be made meaningful to many students because many of their parents borrow money in this fashion. Advertisements in the streetcars or newspapers make them aware that such borrowing is undertaken. Many persons will multiply $2.94 by 4 and find that their interest cost is $11.76. They will assume that this is not a great deal of interest to pay for about $200. It would seem to them to be roughly a little under $6 a hundred dollars borrowed, or about 6 per cent.

Since the money is borrowed for only four months, the interest is $35.28 for a yearly period, or three times $11.76. The student must also be aware that the $200 was not in the possession of George Kress during the entire time. By averaging the amount that Mr. Kress had for 4 months, it is found that he had the use of only an average of $125 during the period (200 plus 150 plus 100 plus 50 totals 500, divided by four, equals 125). Then we divide $35.28 by $125 to get a rate of 28.2 per cent. There are, of course, other procedures for determining interest that would result in a slightly different rate.

Students may still borrow on this basis, but the awareness that they are paying out almost one-third of the total amount borrowed in interest will make them think several times before they engage in borrowing of this type. Unless the student has the full awareness of the meaning of borrowing on a time basis and realizes the amount of interest paid, the solution of the problem is a futile process. However, when the student has learned the process, learned to use common sense in undertaking the process, and learned to evaluate his answer in terms of its reasonableness—then it is more likely that permanent learning is being achieved.

To learn this process will take anywhere from several days to several weeks with usual students depending on their motivation and previous learnings. Is it worth the time and effort? Bank clerks do not do all this arithmetic. They use an interest table. Is it necessary for Mr. Kress to know that the rate is 28.2 per cent? Will not an approximation do? For example, the intelligent student can estimate that the crude rate is 6 per cent, and he can see at a glance that the money is held for only a third of a year—that makes 18 per cent. Since he can see that the average amount possessed is only $125, or $\frac{5}{8}$ of $200, he will divide 18 per cent by 5 and multiply by 8 to get 28.8 per cent. This is more than sufficiently close to the correct sum to realize how much he is paying. Why do all the arithmetic to get absolute accuracy when even the bank clerk uses tables?

Of course, the ability to work out approximations requires thorough comprehension of what it is all about; it is not sufficient to know the procedure by rote. As we know, it is easier to teach a formula than it is to teach reasoning. Nevertheless, unless students remember the reasoning process thus used, they will soon forget the formula unless it is mastered most thoroughly; and this effort does not seem worth while. The wise thing to do, therefore, seems to teach the students how to think through approximations for many types of arithmetic problems and thereby gradually develop the art of "dead reckoning" in arithmetic situations. The teacher must ask himself in every case where considerable learning is required whether an exact answer is necessary or whether an approximation is sufficient. Probably the greatest single failure in business arithmetic is the failure to achieve mastery of the art of making intelligent approximations.

The student must be made aware that, while arithmetic processes are a skill, they involve techniques and evaluational procedures that are not typical of typing and shorthand. Of course, as soon as shorthand and typing are put to use, the ability to use common sense to evaluate one's work applies equally. Consequently, in the initial stages the skill-building process in the development of arithmetic skills follows rather closely the procedures used in teaching shorthand and typing. Possibly it would be wiser to say that arithmetic processes follow the techniques of skill building utilized in transcription more closely than those of the other skill-building subjects.

Several independent studies have been undertaken that indicate that usually students who have taken business arithmetic in high school do no better after a one-year lapse of time than those who have never had the subject. This result is assumed to show that the teaching of business arithmetic is futile, but this is an unjustified conclusion. What the studies do imply is that arithmetic taught by what has been the typical procedure is a wasteful process with a very meager result. They further imply that arithmetic instruction must be meaningful; that there must be opportunities for real learning; that the processes that are developed must be thoroughly mastered; and finally, that these steps were not achieved in business arithmetic.

THE IMMEDIATE PROBLEM OF THE BUSINESS-ARITHMETIC TEACHER

It can be seen, therefore, that if business arithmetic is to have any meaning, it must be more than disguised drill. It certainly must not be given with the intent of confusing so as to achieve supposed learning interest; and above all, it must not be presented in order to keep students busy. Yet the disinterested observer cannot help feeling that many of the activities now given in the name of arithmetic have these three objectives in mind.

The young teacher, presenting business arithmetic for the first time in a new school, may not be able to act on the suggestions given above in complete detail. It would be most unwise to attempt to remake the school program in one term. Within his classroom, he must try to come as close as possible to the program previously suggested without interfering with the work of the other teachers. He can begin with diagnosis. He can recommend exemption of a few students who show special aptitude, and he can eliminate some of the more meaningless topics, so as to emphasize mastership in the skills needed by all. Having accomplished this, he should teach thoroughly a few additional topics, such as the determination of interest by the 60-day—6 per cent method. Teachers in the higher grades to whom these students will come look for an understanding of these traditional topics and are often critical if they have not been at least touched upon.

The beginning teacher, therefore, must recognize that in dealing with a subject like business arithmetic he must try to achieve meaningful learnings; at the same time, he must have some consideration for the traditional attitudes maintained by an administration that has been accustomed to the formal program of business arithmetic.

Fortunately, there are excellent aids for the teacher of arithmetic. Some of these are suggested in the bibliography. They do not stress in sufficient detail the unique remedial teaching problem of the business-arithmetic teacher, but thoughtful application of their suggestions will be invaluable.

A NARRATIVE-TYPE LESSON PLAN

An example of a typical annual statement, slightly modified, appears on page 270. It presents sources of revenue and income and the distribution of this income. Let us assume that the students have already been working out simple ratios between turnover and sales and between income and sales. Present the data on the statement as simply as possible on the chalk board. Ask the students what per cent of profit was earned on total income. Students will at first be confused and will not be able to give a simple answer. Some of them will suggest 3 per cent, others will suggest 14 per cent, possibly some will answer 17 per cent. As a matter of fact, from the data given, they cannot tell because in this chart interest and dividends were added together.

Then indicate to students that $4,840,000 of the total interest and dividends was dividends and $1,968,000 was interest. They will then easily see that about 10 per cent of the total income was paid out as interest and approximately 4 per cent was paid as dividends. On this basis some students should be able to figure out the total earnings, which are of course the dividends paid plus the amount retained in the business, or about 7 per cent.

Then various questions should be brought up, such as: Why was the chart set up in this way? Would not the public utility ordinarily prefer to show that its dividends were smaller than its interest? Why

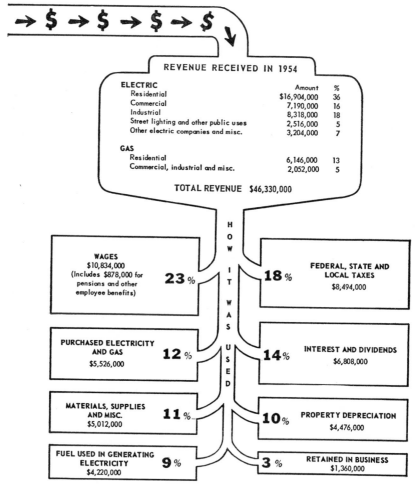

A typical annual statement in the form of a graph chart

was total profit not indicated? Why was it divided into two parts, Retained in Business and Dividends?

Finally the teacher should indicate that another ratio is far more important to the stockholders than the ratio of earnings to total income, and that is the ratio of earnings to capital. Oversimplified, the public utility had a capital of $86,000,000; and therefore the profit on capital, as compared to profit on income, was about 4 per cent which is much more realistic than the profit on earnings.

Given the capital, the profit should be drawn from the class. This experience will give the teacher a chance to indicate that in a public utility the actual public investment is very high compared to the earnings.

The teacher can then present the case of a merchandising firm wherein the ratio of sales to capital is much higher. Let us assume a merchandising firm with an income on total sales of $500,000,000 and a profit of $5,000,000 and a capital of $100,000,000. In this case the per cent of profit on sales is 1 per cent, the per cent of profit on capital is 5 per cent. This result should again of course be drawn from the students.

The teacher can then inquire which per cent of profit is usually told to the public and which per cent of profit most interests the shareholder. The purpose of this type of lesson should not be to confuse the pupils or to give them competency in developing all kinds of ratios. Rather it should make them aware of the complexity of charts of the types on page 270 and the need for caution in making judgments. After all, one of the major concerns in teaching arithmetic is to develop competency in working out relationships and recognizing the need for much data in developing these relationships. When this competency is acquired, the students will have learned something vitally significant.

QUESTIONS

1. What are some of the problems of the beginning teacher of business arithmetic?

2. Why do high school students often dislike taking a course in business arithmetic?

3. Why is homogeneous grouping more desirable in business arithmetic, for example, than in shorthand?

4. Why is diagnostic testing necessary in business arithmetic? If a formal diagnostic test is not available, what alternate procedure can be used?

5. Give several examples, other than those given in the chapter, of faulty procedures in arithmetic processes.

6. Why does the adequate teaching of arithmetic require a great deal of time?

7. How much arithmetic skill is required to get along well in daily-life activity?

8. How should the fundamental skills in addition, subtraction, multiplication, and division be taught?

9. How should the ability of adapting these arithmetic skills be developed?

10. How must the adaptation of these skills to the solution of life problems be presented in school?

11. What is the difference between the arithmetic ability required by a person who is going into business and the arithmetic ability required in daily-life activities?

12. What is the problem of curriculum placement of arithmetic in the secondary schools?

13. Why is remedial teaching necessary in arithmetic at the secondary-school level?

14. How should problem solving be taught in connection with arithmetic situations?

15. What adaptations of typical text materials must the teacher of business arithmetic make in organizing a program of worth-while teaching?

STUDENT ACTIVITIES

1. Give a diagnostic test in business arithmetic or in arithmetic to a group of your fellow students who have had business arithmetic in high school and also to a group of those who have not had business arithmetic. Try to have equal characteristics in as many other respects as possible. Compare the results, but be certain to consider factors other than business-arithmetic training that might cause differences in the results.

2. Give an achievement test in arithmetic to a group of high school seniors. Make a decision as to the extent to which they need a course in remedial arithmetic on the basis of the scores achieved.

3. Analyze in detail the content of three different texts in business arithmetic and also three elementary-school texts in arithmetic. To what extent do these two types of texts differ? To what extent is the differentiation justified? Are fundamental-skills exercises presented for remedial teaching or ignored? Are there any topics that are not justified in your opinion in terms of needs in the elementary-school text or in the high school text?

4. In co-operation with several other students, work out a plan for finding out how much arithmetic ability the average person with whom

you are acquainted really has to have. Be sure not to consider school needs. How much arithmetic ability did he have to have to purchase a home, for example, to buy his insurance, to purchase food, clothing and shelter, to get along effectively in recreational activities?

5. Make a similar analysis of the ability of at least a dozen businessmen. To what extent do they have ability superior to those of the first group you checked? To what extent would they like to have special skills and abilities that they now do not have but feel a sense of loss in not having?

BIBLIOGRAPHY

Braverman, Benjamin. "Remedial Arithmetic in High School," *Journal of Business Education*, XII (January, 1947), pp. 15–16.

Brueckner, L. J., and F. E. Grossnickle. *How to Make Arithmetic Meaningful*. New York, John C. Winston and Company, Inc., 1947.

Feuer, Isadore J. "The Fundamental Processes in Arithmetic," *American Business Education Yearbook*, XII, 1955, pp. 317–335.

Huffman, Harry. "Evaluation Techniques for Business Arithmetic," *UBEA Forum*, IX (May, 1955), pp. 28–29.

Lankford, Francis G., Jr. "Improving the Arithmetic Fundamentals of Young Adults," *UBEA Forum*, VIII (December, 1953), pp. 19–21.

Lewis, Harry. "The Arithmetic of Installment Buying," *Business Education World*, XXV (March, 1955), p. 14.

Morton, Robert L. "Remedial Learning in Arithmetic," *American Business Education Yearbook*, XII, 1955, pp. 71–124.

Orleans, Jacob S., and Emanuel Saxe. "Analysis of the Arithmetic Knowledge of High School Pupils," *Balance Sheet*, XXVI (February, 1945), pp. 203–205.

Rosenberg, Henry J. "Courses of Study in Business Arithmetic," *American Business Education Yearbook*, IV, 1947, pp. 236–246.

Rosenberg, R. Robert. "Organization and Purpose of a Business Mathematics Course," *Business Education World*, XXVI (October, 1945), pp. 82–85.

———. "What Shall We Teach in Business Arithmetic?" *Business Education World*, XXVII (February, 1947), pp. 342–344; (April, 1947), pp. 450–451.

Satlow, I. David. "What Can We Do About Arithmetic Skills of Bookkeeping Students?" *Business Education World*, XXXII (April, 1953), pp. 386–387.

Schaaf, William L. "How Can You Help Your Students Understand

Business Arithmetic?" *Business Education World,* XXXI (January, 1951), pp. 248–249.

Seldon, William. "Some Practical Suggestions for Teaching Business Arithmetic," *UBEA Forum,* VIII (December, 1953), pp. 27–28.

Sharpe, Madeline E., and William M. Polishook. "Integrating Business Arithmetic with Junior-Business Training," *Journal of Business Education,* XXI (May, 1946), pp. 15, 18.

Spitzer, Herbert. *Teaching of Arithmetic.* Boston, Houghton Mifflin Company, 1948.

Tonne, Herbert A. "A Classroom Study of Arithmetic Ability," *Journal of Business Education,* XXVIII (January, 1953), pp. 149–151.

Waks, Meyer. "Remedial Arithmetic in the Business Curriculum," *Journal of Business Education,* XXV (April and May, 1950), pp. 21–22, 25–26.

Wilson, Guy M., and Others. *Teaching the New Arithmetic.* New York, McGraw-Hill Book Company, Inc., 1951.

CHAPTER XIII

Office Practice

IT IS THE CONSENSUS OF BUSINESS EDUCATORS that a terminal course of some kind should be offered whenever possible on a secondary-school level. The major objective of the course is to give students a "feeling" of the nature of an office and the work done in it. The course as now given, therefore, integrates the various skills previously learned in business courses and elsewhere and gives the prospective worker an ability to carry through his work on the job as efficiently as possible.

A second important objective of various types of office-practice courses is to provide school training in those techniques in which it has not been possible previously to give instruction. For example, in many communities students can benefit by a considerable amount of instruction in such fields as calculating and adding machines, voice-writing equipment, duplicating machines, and the like. Moreover, in many skill-building courses it is not possible to give adequate attention to filing, filling in forms by hand and on the typewriter, telephoning, and receiving callers. Usually in courses prior to a terminal course, it has not been possible to deal adequately with office etiquette and grooming, human relations in the office, and applying for a position.

A further important objective is to maintain and improve skills learned in previous classes; for example, students who have had training in transcription may need further training in this activity and may need to learn how to integrate that skill with the other work of the office.

THREE TYPES OF OFFICE PRACTICE

Secretarial Practice. The most frequently presented course on the secretarial level is secretarial office practice. This course is based on a program of instruction in the two basic skills of taking dictation by shorthand followed by transcription. Quite frequently in this course, transcription is developed considerably further than has been possible in previous classes. The major objective of this secretarial type of course is to integrate the two basic skills with the total office environment. Some teachers are given a certain amount of office-style dictation in secretarial practice, instead of beginning this type of instruction in the transcription class. Nevertheless, the secretarial office-practice class should not be limited to instruction in activities closely or nearly related to transcription, for the competent secretary does many other things. For example, he needs to be competent in dealing with people over the telephone or at the reception desk; moreover, he should have skill at certain types of office machines, which usually cannot be developed in a transcription class.

Bookkeeping Office Practice. In a few schools, a course in office practice has been developed that relates previously learned bookkeeping activities to the total office situation. This type of office-practice course is usually built around the development of further skill in the use of adding machines and in the attainment of initial skill in the use of calculating, billing, and bookkeeping machines. Unfortunately, far too many schools that attempt to give bookkeeping office practice limit the training to instruction on machines and make very little effort to make the bookkeeping skill previously learned effective on the job.

Clerical Office Practice. Clerical office practice, as provided in some schools, is a senior-year course, which attempts to give training for the job based on a minimum of previously learned skills. Most teachers insist on a minimum prerequisite of one year of typing and probably one year of bookkeeping before they will consider a student competent to benefit by a course in clerical office practice. Such a course is planned for students who are evidently quite capable of doing office work but who are not interested either in bookkeeping or in shorthand. The course should give them sufficient skill in typical office activities to get along on a job, by integrating these activities into an actual office-practice situation. It is expected that students after taking this course will be more competent on their first job than they otherwise would be. While this type of course is offered more frequently than bookkeeping office practice, it is presented less often than secretarial practice. There is an opportunity here for the development of course material by the alert teacher.

ORGANIZATION OF OFFICE-PRACTICE COURSES

In small schools, it is necessary and is the usual practice to offer all types of office practice in one course. When only 20 or even 30 students are enrolled in office practice, it is usually wise to put the nonspecialized, the secretarial, and the bookkeeping office-practice students into the same class. The reason for this is economy. An alert teacher can provide for specialization in the areas in which the students are interested by careful planning. In large schools it is highly desirable to set up secretarial office training apart from the bookkeeping and clerical office training. The types of activities around which the work should be integrated will vary somewhat between the two types of courses. In very large schools, of course, it would be desirable to separate the clerical office training from the bookkeeping office instruction.

ELEMENTARY CLERICAL TRAINING

There is another type of clerical training that probably should not be called office practice. This type has become increasingly popular in the large metropolitan areas. This course is not primarily an integrative course, but it is usually planned for the less able students and attempts to give training that will be useful to this type of person.

The development of instructional materials for this type of course is admirable. It should not, however, be confused with a senior-year type of office-practice course. There are many students of less than average ability who cannot or will not adapt themselves to instruction in bookkeeping and shorthand. Some of these students can fit into programs other than business education; however, a considerable number of them are best fitted for routine type of office work. In many cases these students do not have an adequate background in the fundamental processes; however, usually they are not interested in further instruction in reading, writing, and arithmetic as such. These skills must, therefore, be developed further through units of instruction that are of greater interest to the students. For example, this type of clerical training usually offered in the tenth and eleventh years, and not infrequently in the twelfth year, has a major unit on writing business letters. Almost as important as the ability to write a business letter is further instruction in spelling, in sentence construction, the organization of paragraphs, and in handwriting. Similarly there is a unit of instruction in record keeping in which the major objective often is the development of further arithmetic skill.

The course in clerical training should, however, not be limited to further instruction in the fundamental processes, though to be successful the course must develop these skills further. The well-planned course in clerical training will stress the kind of typing required on the job, rather than routine typing. Such typing activity involves tabulating, typing data in special spaces on a page, filling in forms, typing information on cards, typing from rough copy. In addition the clerical training course should provide practice in the routine operation of the usual office machines, such as adding and duplicating machines of various types, and should integrate these skills into a unified understanding of the nature of work in the office.

In large metropolitan areas, this course has been unusually successful, at least in terms of enrollments. In smaller communities the teachers have not as yet seen the need for developing courses of this type. Properly taught, junior clerical practice provides certain types of students with a meaningful type of school learning. Unfortunately, in all too many schools the course does not appeal to the teachers and is little more than a means of marking time for many students until they are ready to leave school.

UNITS SUITABLE FOR A VARIETY OF COURSES

Actually any of the units included in office practice can be used by a resourceful teacher and taught in a number of classes. For instance, the unit on applying for a position might be used in advanced shorthand if no office-practice course is given. The unit on office and calculating machines could be included in a bookkeeping course. The unit on filing can be combined profitably with typewriting in an office-practice class if one is offered; or it may be used in an advanced typewriting class, if not. Once a week some attention could be given to personality development, office etiquette, or business grooming in an advanced shorthand class; and certainly inclusion of cases involving problems in human relations in the office is justified in any class worthy of being classified as "vocational."

WHAT OFFICE WORKERS DO

Probably the soundest approach to the problem of what to teach in office practice is to study what office workers do. Stenographers take dictation and transcribe; bookkeepers make journal and ledger entries and prepare financial statements. But stenographers spend more than half of their time at other office jobs, and bookkeepers also perform additional duties. Analysis of what clerks (routine office workers not in the stenographic or bookkeeping categories) do gives a clue to the office skills other than shorthand and bookkeeping that should be learned before the student is ready for an office position.

The following is a list of office duties performed by 75 per cent of 442 general clerks according to a survey: [1]

ACTIVITIES	RANK	FREQUENCY
Use filing system or systems	1	393
Use telephone	2	379
Use adding machine	3	329
Type addresses on envelopes	4	245
Make carbon copies	5	242
Use calculating machine	6	237
Copy data from one record to another on typewriter.	7	205
Verify and/or list information from business papers .	8	198
Prepare material for filing	9	193
Use stapler	10.5	192
Copy from rough draft or corrected copy on typewriter	10.5	192

[1] "Survey of Office Duties." *Pittsburgh Schools,* **XXIII** (September-October, 1948), pp. 21–22.

ACTIVITIES	RANK	FREQUENCY
Figure extensions on bills, invoices, statements	12	182
Type letters	13	180
Fold, insert letters, and seal envelopes	14	179
Type cards	15	173
Fill in printed forms on typewriter	16	170
Use follow-up files	17	162
Prepare trial balances	18	153
Examine and/or sort business papers	19	149
Prepare operating and/or financial statements	20	147
Keep inventory records	21	146
Make journal entries	22	145
Figure discounts	23	143
Compose and type letters with or without instruction as to content	24	129
Make cross references	26	125
Prepare stencil for use on duplicating machine	26	125
Receive business callers	26	125
Type bills, invoices, statements	28.5	115
Make entries in ledger accounts	28.5	115
Open, sort, and distribute mail	30	112

Another investigator [2] analyzed the duties performed by clerks in Atlanta during 756 total hours of work. He found a percentage breakdown in the time spent in various activities as given on page 281.

UNITS OF INSTRUCTION

It would seem, then, that most office-practice courses should include instruction in filing, telephoning, typewriting (unless clerical typewriting is offered as a separate course), using adding and calculating machines, duplicating, receiving callers, and handling the mail. Both studies emphasize the importance of clerical typewriting, and certainly no office-practice course can achieve vocational objectives unless typewriters are available to all students.

The business success of all students depends on their understanding of what constitutes acceptable office behavior and of what is expected of the beginning worker, so that instruction on the development of a business personality is essential. In some schools, units

[2] Parker Liles, *Some Factors in the Training of Clerical Workers.* 1947 Delta Pi Epsilon Research Award. Stillwater, Oklahoma Agricultural and Mechanical College, 1949, p. 87.

ACTIVITY	PERCENTAGE OF TIME SPENT
Typewriting	16.0
Operating adding and calculating machines	15.1
Filing	11.7
Recording	7.7
Checking	6.1
Operating posting machines	4.6
Sorting and classifying	3.5
Statistical work	2.9
Meeting public	2.7
Advanced clerical work	2.5
Telephoning	2.4
Handling the mail	2.3
Cashier	2.2
Correspondence	2.1
Clerical bookkeeping	2.0
Operating billing machine	1.9
Messenger	1.6
Operating miscellaneous machines	6.7
Miscellaneous clerical duties	6.0
Total	100.03

in office practice will include formal instruction in improving the fundamental processes of handwriting and computing by hand; in others, these skills will be stressed incidentally. Most students who seek business positions will need help in learning how to make applications.

Throughout the course, although perhaps not in a separate unit, the teacher will want to teach what is sometimes termed the "periphery skills," those little on-the-fringe tricks of the trade that increase office production: how to collate and staple (if the office-practice class has the opportunity to duplicate a number of sheets, such as for a class newspaper), how to stuff envelopes, how to seal or stamp multiple envelopes, or how to position materials for the most efficient handling.

TEACHING TECHNIQUES USED

Part of the office-practice course is devoted to teaching new skills, and the principles of skill building will still prove helpful to the teacher. In many classrooms, however, equipment is limited, so that the teaching must be done by the rotation plan. Since small groups are involved, who receive at least part of their instruction from a member of the previous group working with the equipment, the job-breakdown technique is helpful to supplement teaching and to improve demonstrations.

One of the primary objectives of the office-practice course is the development of an employable personality. It is desirable, then, that this terminal course be an activity course in which students have opportunities for developing resourcefulness and for following through on blocks or units of work that permit integration of the isolated skills learned in earlier classes. Unit planning, rather than the day-to-day assignment, is the basis for the course. In completing the units, students have opportunities to work together and to plan together so as to develop leadership and followership abilities. Finally, the course should include differentiated assignments that challenge the members of the class to work at their level of ability and interest. Techniques for teaching by the unit, by the job break-down, and by the differentiated assignment will be described; and suggestions for use of these techniques will be included in the later unit outlines.

THE JOB BREAKDOWN

During World War II, the Government was faced with the necessity for training rapidly enough office workers to handle the vast increase in paper work. The J programs were developed to help in emergency training. One of these programs was the Job Instruction 10-hour unit, which was designed to help supervisors who had no teacher training or experience to train in skills. The basic pattern of the Job Instruction program is demonstration, first at the expert level, then at the slow level, calling attention of the learner not only to the steps to be followed but also to the key point to be watched in performing that step in the operation. Later the learner tries the operation, the teacher performing with him and redemonstrating if necessary while he again stresses the key point. Sound familiar? The old mastery formula in uniform!

The greatest value of the job breakdown to the beginning teacher probably is the way in which preplanning is required. The teacher must have all equipment ready and positioned and the steps planned in logical order. The key point focuses attention on the pitfalls, and the learner is given the warning signal that will prevent his making an error. It is also useful to the student whose responsibility it is to instruct the student following him in operating an office machine; furthermore, it is very easy for the student working alone to follow a job-breakdown sheet and learn a new operation.

In some respects the job breakdown is similar to a teacher's lesson plan; in other ways it serves as a student's learning plan. It is quite similar to the job sheet that has been used for a long time in teaching vocational subjects as well as courses in the industrial and practical arts.

Like other instruments for improving learning, the job break-down—useful as it is—can be a detriment to learning if carelessly used. If the teacher merely gives the breakdown to the student and tells him to follow the steps, learning will probably be poor. Students find it difficult to read written instruction, and they do not get the incentive of the personal presentation. If the teacher has not studied the job breakdown himself and therefore fails to do the task with considerable skill, the breakdown is no substitute for the teacher's inability. Some teachers present the breakdown to one student and then expect him to teach it to a second student who, in turn, when he has learned the operation, is expected to teach it to a third. This procedure works only if kept under the constant supervision of the teacher; otherwise there is a constant loss in skill development. Detailed drawings of how the operation is carried out step by step help much to make the breakdown more useful to teacher and student alike. At least one state has adopted the job breakdown as the format for all lessons in the office-practice course,[3] largely an office-machines course in this instance.

Two job-breakdown sheets are included in this chapter on the following pages, one for filing and the other for the advanced levels of office machines in which multiplying with a constant is brought to a practical use level.

[3] Job Instruction Sheets. Office Practices and Procedures and Machines (Adding and Calculating). The University of the State of New York, The State Department of Education, Bureau of Business and Distributive Education, 1955.

A CLERICAL JOB BREAKDOWN [4]

Task: Organizing materials for filing
Operation: Coding
Equipment: Rubber finger or thumb, desk or table top, chair or stool, colored pencil or crayon, stapler, pins, plain 8½ by 11 paper of reasonably sturdy quality
Materials: Papers for filing, and, if necessary, card showing file divisions

STEPS	KEY POINTS
1. Bring papers from their temporary filing location to the cleared desk or table top. (The temporary file may be a desk drawer, an unused file drawer, or a file box or basket on top of the desk.)	1. Be alert to small papers which may slide out of the main stack. It may be wise to place papers in a folder to carry them from place to place. Hold the materials firmly in the left hand or, if they are bulky, with both hands.
2. Place the materials in the center of the cleared desk top.	2. Keep the pile even.
3. Fit rubber finger on an easily manipulated finger of the left hand.	3. Either the first or second and occasionally both fingers are rubber tipped for filing. In some offices, workers also wear rubber fingers on the same fingers of the right hand. It may feel strange at first and rather awkward, but with experience the rubber fingers become an invaluable clerical tool.
4. Separate the sheet to be read from the other sheets by sliding the left forefinger under the upper left corner of the sheet, thus raising it slightly.	4. Do not lift the sheet completely from the pile of papers.
5. Read the paper to determine the correct title or file division under which it will be filed. At the same time, bring the left forefinger to the top of the paper together with the thumb. Rest the paper between the left forefinger and thumb of the left hand.	5. The title may be a name, a location, a number, or subject depending on the filing system being used. When necessary consult the card showing the divisions of the file.
6. Pick up the colored pencil with the right hand and circle, underline, write in or otherwise indicate the title under which the article is to be filed.	6. Use a colored pencil for easily detected coding. If title or number is to be written in, it should be placed in a uniform position, usually the top third of the sheet in the right-hand corner. The written-in title should also

---

[4] This breakdown was produced by Elizabeth T. Van Derveer, State Teachers College, Montclair, New Jersey.

STEPS	KEY POINTS
	be circled or underlined for easy finding.
7. Staple or pin two or more pieces of related materials together.	7. Related materials may be first and second pages of one letter, enclosures and correspondence, incoming and outgoing correspondence for one transaction, and others. Bury the point of the pin between the pieces of material to avoid possible injury to those who handle the materials.
8. Staple short sheets (less than the customary 8½ x 11) to 8½ by 11 paper.	8. Fasten papers securely; staple top and bottom if necessary. This device prevents small papers from being pushed down or lost in the folder when actual filing takes place.
9. Move the thumb and forefinger of the left hand toward the bottom of the paper and, at approximately the center of the paper, lift it from the stack of other papers.	
10. Place the sheet face down on the desk to the left of the stack from which it was taken.	10. This will retain the original order which in some instances is important. Unless otherwise instructed, papers should be kept in original order until sorting takes place.
11. Repeat steps 4, 5, 6, 9, and 10, and if necessary 7 and/or 8 until all material to be filed has been read and coded and is ready for the sorting operation.	

OFFICE PRACTICE I (Practical Use Level)

Job Instruction Sheet No. M (A & C)-4
(Rotary Calculator)

Multiplying with a Constant

Student's Name_____Evaluation_____

Period_____Date started_____Date finished_____

Approved_____:_____
      (Instructor)   (Person for whom work was done)

Equipment: Rotary calculator, desk, chair.
Materials: Textbook or manual, paper, pencil
Directions: A constant multiplicand is a number that is to be multiplied by several multipliers, or numbers. It is a great timesaving device to hold the constant multiplicand in the machine and to multiply by the different multipliers. A very common business problem for this type of work is the payroll.

Note: If you are using fully automatic calculator, consult instructor.

STEPS	KEY POINTS
1. Position machine. Get it ready for use.	1. See Step 1 and Key Points 3a, 3b, 3c, 3d in Job Instruction Sheet 1.
2. What amount is due each employee on the following payroll summary?	

	Total hours	Rate per hr.	Net
A	42	.69	_____
B	38	.69	_____
C	52	.69	_____
D	45	.69	_____

STEPS	KEY POINTS
3. Depress repeat key. Set decimal point in answer dial and keyboard.	3. Decimal point will be placed between second and third columns as there are two decimal places in .69.
4. Depress .69 on the right of keyboard.	4. .69 is constant factor.
5. Multiply .69 by 42.	5. This will be salary due A. Answer is 28.98.
6. Write answer in space provided for it.	
7. *Do not clear keyboard or dials. Do not move carriage.*	7. Answer in lower dials is 28.98. Number in upper dials is the multiplier, 42. Number in keyboard is .69, the constant multiplicand.
8. The next number to be multiplied is 38. Change 4 in upper dials to 3 by subtraction.	8. Subtract by turning handle backward one turn on crank-driven; by depressing minus bar on electric. Number in lower dials will be 22.08. Number in upper dials will be 32. Number in keyboard will be .69
9. Move carriage one place to the left.	
10. Add until 2 in upper dials is changed to 8.	10. This will be six operations. Number in lower dials will be 26.22

STEPS	KEY POINTS
	Number in upper dials will be 38. Number on keyboard will be 69.
11. Write answer, 26.22, in space provided for it.	
12. *Do not clear keyboard or dials.*	
13. The next multiplier is 52. Change by subtraction 8 to 2 in upper dials.	13. Number in lower dials will be 22.08. Number in upper dials will be 32. Number in keyboard will be .69
14. Move carriage one place to the right.	
15. Change by addition 3 to 5.	15. Number in lower dials will be 35.88. Number in upper dials will be 52. Number on keyboard will be .69.
16. Record 35.88, the answer, in proper space.	
17. Repeat Steps 8 to 12 for the multiplier, 45.	17. Number in lower dials will be 31.05. Number in upper dials will be 45. Number in keyboard will be .69.
18. On p.____ in textbook do ____ problems.	
19. Check answers. Do problems in which there is an error.	
20. Repeat Step 18. Time yourself.	20. You should be able to do this in ____ minutes.
21. If you do not complete in time specified, repeat until you do.	
22. Take Timed Test.	22. Timed Test is ____ minutes.

Questions:

1. Why is this method of multiplication a timesaving device?
2. Name at least one type of problem in which you might have a constant multiplier.

Evaluation:

1. Were you able to do Step 18 in specified time with the first attempt?
2. If not, how many attempts were necessary to reach specified time?

Note: Attach answer sheet to Job Instruction Sheet and submit to instructor as designated.

COMMITTEE REPORTS

One of the best ways to help students learn to work together is to assign them to committees that are responsible for a project. The competition between committees that must make class presentations often causes their members to perform at a much higher level than the individual members would achieve if working alone.

A recent innovation in the use of the committee is the "buzz session." The entire class hears a talk, watches a movie or filmstrip, or reads a much-discussed and challenging article. The teacher divides the class into small groups of six or eight members. The group elects its leader, who is responsible for making a report of the conclusions or solutions reached by his group at the end of a limited discussion period. After the committee reports, the teacher can conduct a short general summarizing discussion. All members of the group participate in a "buzz session" rather than the few who would talk if the entire class stayed in one group, and the necessity for an oral report forces the pinpointing of the discussion.

THE CASE METHOD OF TEACHING

Most people will agree that people do not modify their behavior just by listening to preaching about it. To study personality only through long lists of desirable qualities of office workers is ineffectual. Office behavior can best be understood through actual cases involving choice making on the part of the worker. The student, then, who analyzes the case must work out a suggested solution based on an understanding of the principles that affect human behavior.

Most secretarial practice books contain problem material that the office-practice teacher can adapt to his class needs. Such problems as the following suggest ideas for case discussion:

In opening and reading the mail, you find a letter calling attention to the fact that an enclosure was missing from a letter that you had transcribed and mailed last week. What would you do? [5]

[5] Esther K. Beamer, J Marshall Hanna, and Estelle L. Popham. *Effective Secretarial Practices,* Third Edition. Cincinnati, South-Western Publishing Company, 1956, 666 p.

Each of two callers claims that he has an appointment with your employer at 11:30 a.m. The name of one of them is listed on your appointment record for that time. The other states that your employer met him on the street the day before and told him to come to the office at this time. Which caller would you admit for his appointment first? [6]

If the teacher is really successful with this type of teaching, students will soon supplement the textbook cases with their own problems encountered in summer or afterschool jobs. The "buzz session" can be used effectively in teaching by the case method, for it demonstrates that there is no one right answer. However, any satisfactory solution must be founded on basic principles which the students will soon bring out.

Service Projects

To give students experience in following through on a whole job, the office-practice class sometimes is used for service projects. Examples are:

Duplicating a school newspaper
Filing all student program cards
Computing class averages and student averages
Making fill-ins on form letters to all parents
Making French-fold programs for club meetings
Addressing and stuffing envelopes for a service organization
Acting as office receptionist in the school office
Telephoning to remind voters to register in order to vote in the next election
Taking dictation from various teachers to whom they are assigned

In classes using service projects, the teacher may assign proofreaders and checkers to pass on the quality or usability of the work (thus aiding students in developing their own standards). He may designate an office manager to apportion the work, checking it in and out.

One advantage of the service project is that it provides a large

[6] Peter L. Agnew, James Meehan, and Foster Loso. *Clerical Office Practice,* Second Edition. Cincinnati, South-Western Publishing Company, 1955, p. 271.

enough quantity of work to permit the teaching of periphery skills involving flow-of-work drills—which is difficult when the student has only a daily assignment to work with. Another advantage is that the work is actually used, and the student takes greater pride in work that is real. Some teachers work out a pay scheme for the service project and other office-practice projects; and instead of giving a grade, they give a certain salary for the work based on quality and quantity.

The service project is valuable if not abused. In office practice a great deal of material must be covered; and if too many projects are accepted by the teacher, he may neglect other aspects of the course. The school administrators and other teachers can become quite a problem if the teacher accepts all kinds of work in helter-skelter fashion. It is wise to set up a schedule of work that can be done as a school service in the office-practice class; however, this schedule should then be held to. The office-practice classes should never be used primarily as a service bureau, but only such work should be accepted that will serve as a means of learning for the students.

DIFFERENTIATED ASSIGNMENTS

When business-education leaders were asked their opinion of the objectives of machines training in office practice, three-fourths of them felt that it is "to provide an acquaintance with, and a little skill in operating, several machines but in addition provide a definite vocational skill on one or two machines, so that the student can function upon employment as a skilled or semiskilled business-machine operator."[7] This means that a student would receive acquaintance-ship training on all machines through undifferentiated assignments but would choose his own specialization on which he would work out differentiated assignments.

In working out units of study, the student would choose the aspect of the topic on which he would like to work and make class reports in terms of his interests and abilities. The essential material must be covered by all students, but the enrichment material would be assigned in terms of the students' interests and abilities. For instance,

[7] Carlos Hayden, *Major Issues in Business Education*, p. 67.

a boy with mechanical interests would report on how the telephone works. A girl who was considering a position as a telephone operator might prefer to work on a committee investigating vocational opportunities through reading assignments, visits to an exchange, or interviews with telephone employees.

HOW TO DEVELOP A UNIT OF STUDY

A unit of study is a departure from the familiar daily assignment and requires a different type of planning. It involves a number of closely related activities and materials, so that pupils will need several days to develop creative class presentations. The teacher must be a very skillful co-ordinator and leader, who provides the genesis of the ideas and leaves their development and the selection of activities to the pupils in terms of their interests and aptitudes.

Setting up the Objectives and Planning the Time for the Unit. In the first place, the teacher will examine the course outline and decide the length of time that can be devoted to the unit—a week, two weeks, or perhaps even a month. In many cases the time is already prescribed.

The teacher should then decide on the outcomes expected from the unit.

1. What is the absolute basic material in the unit for which every pupil is to be responsible? For instance, in a unit on "The Telephone," what would the teacher expect every pupil to know and to be able to do when the unit is completed? Of course, outcomes unrelated to subject matter will also be anticipated, such as learning how to work with other people, how to develop original and creative projects, and how to present them effectively to the entire class. In developing the unit the teacher, however, will list expected outcomes in terms of subject matter only.

2. The teacher will list enrichment outcomes that can be expected from the more able members of the class. For instance, in the unit on "The Telephone," few students would be capable of, or interested in, reporting on "Who Owns the Telephone?" and "The Relationship of the Telephone Systems"; but such a report would be within the abilities of some students.

Grading by the Contract Plan. Some teachers like to grade units by the contract plan. The advantage of the plan is that it challenges the abilities of the students who are capable of going beyond the minimum assignment, yet often are willing to stop there. Under the contract plan the following grading scheme is used:

Grade "C." The pupil covers satisfactorily the minimum assignments and can pass tests based on this material. Even if he makes a very high grade on the tests, he can get only a "C" unless he does additional work of a higher level than that required of the entire group.

Grade "B." The pupil covers satisfactorily the minimum assignments and can pass tests based on this material. In addition, he prepares and shares enrichment material with the class, completing additional assignments with a high quality standard.

Grade "A." The pupil reaches the Grade "C" level and in addition prepares and presents enrichment material representing a very high standard of research, creativity, and scholarship.

In the contract plan the burden of effort is placed on the pupil.

Selecting Materials for the Unit. Ideally the classroom is provided with a number of textbooks, brochures, and magazines related to the unit and available on open shelf to the group during the entire study of the unit. In addition, pupils are encouraged to bring in supplementary materials; but getting the unit launched involves the collection by the teacher (or by the school librarian) of a mass of material for the use of the class. In addition, most schools have a teacher assigned to the visual-aids program who will co-operate by suggesting suitable films. Kappa chapter of Delta Pi Epsilon at the University of Michigan publishes an annual evaluation of business-education films that have been appraised by several business teachers. The business-education magazines, too, have a column in which new films are described.

The resourceful teacher will have developed a file of useful materials and a bibliography of possible source materials, keeping in mind that the nearer to the high school student's interests the readings are, the more successful they will be.

Introducing the Unit. Possibly the entire first day of the unit will be spent on orientation and planning with the pupils the organization of the subsequent class periods. It is usually helpful if a *tentative* outline of the jobs to be done, together with the time allotment for each part, is given to the class at this initial session. The planning sheet should be set up so that the class can distinguish between the basic assignments for everybody and the enrichment assignments for which class members volunteer. If the committee plan of organization is used, it may be wise to explain to the group the nature of the various committees; but their volunteering for participation should be left to the second day, so that pupils can talk the unit over and make more thoughtful choices.

It cannot be emphasized too strongly that the preliminary outline of the project is tentative. As the unit is presented, additional materials may be suggested by the pupils; the creative efforts of the pupils are worth more than the teacher's inflexible suggestions. In any unit, it is suggested that the last possibility of activity be "Something that nobody else has thought of." Of course, the pupil presenting such a project should plan it with his teacher.

A day-by-day time schedule should be developed at the beginning of the unit. If Committee A is to report on the fifth day, that fact should be known from the beginning. If there is to be a speaker on the eighth day, the class should know this and make all necessary arrangements and preparations. With a duplicated tentative outline, the class can proceed in a businesslike way to commit itself for definite participation in the unit, so that everybody is working toward a final objective.

Working Through the Unit. The skillful teacher using the unit plan will spend a few minutes at the beginning of each class session in checking on difficulties that students are encountering in developing their activities. He will probably ask the various committees to give daily progress reports before the day on which their final report is due. He will give supplementary suggestions for course materials and channel the work of the group. On most days, the entire class will have basic reading assignments on which the teacher will spend some time in discussion. During the period it may be necessary to allow time for committee conferences and work sessions. It is *not* necessary that the entire group be doing the same thing at all times.

Evaluating the Unit. The written test at the end of the unit is the customary means of evaluation. In addition, the daily quiz on the assignments, which is not quite so rigid as that found in the day-by-day ordinary class session, will encourage students to prepare their homework. In addition to formal tests, though, the teacher should give full credit for the oral and written presentations by students, especially in terms of creativity and application.

SAMPLE UNITS OF STUDY

The units of study that follow are designed for flexibility. If you have three weeks for the unit on personality, you can develop it fully; if you have one week, it will have to be contracted. You may prefer making three shorter units rather than one long one. Specific materials are not suggested, for the alert teacher will want to bring current materials into his teaching. A recent article from *Seventeen* or *Glamour* will be more effective than one printed several years ago. A recent film will be more attractive than an outmoded one. One of the objectives of the unit, too, is to get students interested in collecting materials; it is their responsibility, not just that of the teacher.

No one office-practice course can possibly include all the proposed activities for groups or for individual students. This is not a curriculum guide but a chapter on methods of teaching possible materials to be included in office practice.

PERSONALITY DEVELOPMENT *

1. Film or filmstrips on qualities necessary for job success. (There are several available.) "Buzz session" with committee reports on points emphasized in film.
2. Self-evaluation sheet on job personality—one copy completed by student and another by a friend. Comparison of the two. Mapping out of personality-improvement campaign. Same test at the end of unit or end of course.
3. Bulletin-board display on two desirable personality traits by each committee.
4. Reading assignment on personality qualifications in textbooks.
5. Speaker from school placement office, "What Business Expects of the Beginning Office Worker." One student writes the letter of invitation, another acts as receptionist, another introduces the speaker and conducts

* Most of the suggested units are adapted from plans developed by undergraduate students in methods classes at Hunter College.

the question-and-answer period, and a fourth writes the letter of appreciation after the talk.

6. Class discussion. Each student chooses a person he likes and outlines why he likes him. Reports form basis for one day's class discussion. Emphasis on difference between job personality and school personality.
7. Book report. Each student reads a book on personality development. He writes up twenty points found in the book that are worth remembering, plans an attractive businesslike cover, and illustrates the report with appropriate pictures, anecdotes, and cartoons. Summaries and displays in class.
8. Class evaluation of a personality library that has been collected by the teacher and by students. Include actual rating scales used in business. Two students may make a report on such ratings.
9. Film or filmstrip on how to keep a job, with same teaching technique as in point 1, or oral reports of interview with member of family or friend on whether he ever lost a job and why.
10. Dramatization by each committee of a case study on a problem in office behavior. Solution by entire group or by committees working alone and reporting to group.
11. Report to class on success in overcoming undesirable qualities in your office personality.
12. Retest on self-evaluation sheet.

BUSINESS GROOMING

1. Self-measurement rating sheet on proper grooming. Administered at least twice during unit or during semester.
2. Film on how to be well groomed or on body care and grooming. Committee discussion and report on film.
3. Bulletin board. Each committee must prepare a bulletin board on some chosen aspect of grooming, such as make-up, clothes for the office, hair styling.
4. Reading. Each pupil must write up ten important points found in a magazine article on grooming. Class discussion.
5. Class *Vogue Magazine,* in charge of a class committee of five students. Each student in class chooses a topic on grooming that interests him and prepares a page of duplicated copy for it, including sketches, line drawings, etc. (An opportunity to integrate duplicating with another unit.) Copies of completed magazine presented to the members of class during session in which each student discusses his particular page. Copy placed on display in school library.
6. Fashion show. In order not to embarrass any member, participation is voluntary. Each student will point out a special feature of his attire worth mentioning, such as accessories, shoes, color, etc. Do's and don'ts may both be used if desired.

MEETING CALLERS

1. Panel discussion. A committee of students who have the opportunity volunteer to visit three or four companies to request some item of information, such as the clerical rating scale. (Depends on circumstances, but can be another example of integration.) They hold a panel discussion on "What Makes a Receptionist Click?"

2. On the basis of readings, each committee prepares a skit for class presentation of an imaginary problem to be faced by the receptionist. "Buzz session" solutions are reported by the chairman of each committee. (The library is on open shelf in the office-practice room—textbooks and articles contributed by teacher and students.)

3. Homework assignment involving the visitors' register. (From workbook or from a class-duplicated sheet) Homework assignment involving "While-You-Were-Away" slips. (Same source)

4. Guest speaker. A receptionist, preferably a *recent* graduate, describes the duties, traits, and problems of the receptionist. Letter of invitation written by a student, reception by a student, introduction and conducting of question-and-answer period by a student, and letter of appreciation written by a student.

5. Oral test. As a culminating unit, each student draws a slip on which is listed a problem situation that might be encountered by a receptionist. He must, with the help of a chosen classmate, enact the proper solution.

TELEPHONING

1. Check sheet to be completed by each student on his present telephone techniques. (May be prepared by students themselves as a committee assignment.)

2. Film or filmstrip on proper telephone technique. Usual evaluation procedures.

3. Panel discussion: In What Ways Does Office Telephoning Differ from Home Telephoning?

4. Talk by representative of local telephone company on improvement of telephone technique. (Members of class make arrangements as usual.)

5. Speech drill. Students practice saying letters and numbers as recommended.

6. Homework assignment on types of service and their selection, dialing (method and radius served), information services. Demonstrations by two students using practice telephones (which the telephone company in many communities will provide without charge). Criticism of voices and technique during playback.

7. Written committee solutions to ten or fifteen problem situations (from clerical and office-practice textbooks).

8. Recording of sample telephone conversations based on point 7. Criticism of actual wording and voices.

9. Homework assignment based on information contained in the front pages of the local telephone directories. Class contest on the location of telephone numbers in the local directories (if teacher can secure multiple copies from telephone company).

10. Class trip to the building switchboard, where the operator gives a demonstration.

11. Special reports on such topics as: Where Do the Wires Go? Who Owns the Telephone? What Are the Telephone Systems? What Is a Message Unit? (for urban communities only) Employment with the Telephone Company, New Developments in Telephone Equipment.

12. Understanding your telephone bill. Students bring bills to class for analysis.

13. Demonstration of emergency calls on sample telephones.

14. Oral reports. Students report on five telephone calls that they answered during the unit, criticizing the callers and the responses.

15. Homework assignment on recording telephone messages.

16. Written examination on the information aspects of the unit.

FILING

1. Student's own file folder. Each student has a vertical file folder in which he keeps all materials and units for the course. These are filed in a vertical file. On the first day of the term, student types caption for his own file folder, pastes it on the folder, and files. Students use these files at will throughout the course.

2. Bulletin board. Exhibit of filing supplies: file folders, guides, Kardex, sample captions (individual, miscellaneous, geographic, subject), out guides and folders, cross-reference sheets, etc. Teacher explains use of each during unit.

3. Exhibit. Exhibit of vertical files, numeric files, visible files in the classroom or in the school offices. Teacher explains each type.

4. Typing of file cards. Students type for alphabetizing 50 file cards, learning how to chain feed, how to invert the order of names, how to position names for easy reference, how to number cards, etc.

5. Filing of cards. Students file the 50 cards after a homework assignment on rules for alphabetizing. They check work in pairs. Teacher works with individual students on errors. Students organize into teams for timed refiling of cards. Total time of the members of a team is computed, and team having fastest total time is declared winning filing team. Each error is penalized 5 points. (Filing is a skill as well as a knowledge!)

6. Film or filmstrip on importance and methods of filing. Usual technique.
7. Filing letters. Teacher demonstrates inspection, releasing, indexing, coding, sorting, and filing of letters. Students file letters in practice set. (Practice sets may be made up in office-practice class during duplicating unit if miniature practice sets are not available. This procedure would give experience in assembling and checking.) Each letter should be numbered, so that students can complete answer sheets on sequence of letters filed. If practice set is not used, assignment may be made of a list of addresses.
8. Numeric filing. Students convert alphabetic file above to numeric file.
9. Service project. File student program cards. Set up a geographic file of students to be used for regional parents' meetings, bus routes, etc. Make files for local service-group project such as Community Chest Drive.
10. Subject file. Complete exercise on subject filing.
11. Homework assignment and class discussion. Central and decentralized files, arrangement of materials in files, taking material from files, transferring material.
12. Special demonstration of how files can be used for management control (use of color and signal systems, tickler files, tub and rotary files, visible files, etc.) by representative of company selling filing equipment. Usual student participation.
13. Test involving application of rules for alphabetizing and also information about filing procedures.

A Clerical Typewriting Unit on Personality [8] (5 Days)

(This unit is summarized from a textbook that provides a plan for the continuation of daily skill building, the performance of specific office jobs, and the preparation of a Competent Typist's Manual, which may later be used on the job.)

1. Type copy on personality for inclusion in Competent Typist's Manual.
2. Type three original copies of personality rating scale from textbook. (Last part of unarranged scale must be arranged to conform to first part.) Student is rated by self, classmate, and teacher.
3. Type receptionist's directory with appropriate headings on half sheet of paper across the narrow width.
4. Type from receptionist's longhand desk calendar the employer's appointment schedule for the following day, adding one appointment after paper has been removed from typewriter. Make carbon for self.
5. Study transcript of actual conversation with caller. Correct errors in

[8] Helen Reynolds and Eleanor Skimin. *Office Practice Typewriting.* New York, McGraw-Hill Book Company, Inc., 1954, pp. 16–25.

technique, and prepare a revised copy of a model conversation, one copy to be handed in and one copy for your Competent Typist's Manual.

SPECIAL PROBLEMS IN CLERICAL PRACTICE

Business is more and more accepting the policy that it is expeditious to hire limited-ability trained clerks rather than the academically brilliant student without specialized training who soon leaves his routine employment because it fails to challenge his level of intelligence. Clerical-practice courses are usually set up to train slow learners for routine jobs, and their teachers face special problems.

In some metropolitan schools many problem pupils have been started on their way to becoming productive workers through a clerical-practice course adapted to their level and interests. In one such school where the chairman indicated that the average IQ of the students is 75 and that most of them are discipline cases, the potentialities of the course became apparent, for no visitor would have believed either statement from casual observation.

Units must be very simple and filled with action, and the major concern is with providing opportunities for situations in which job attitude can be developed (not preached about). The teacher must be especially alert to his success or failure in "getting through" to the students, in keeping them interested in the usual office jobs and the nature of office work. Material must be simple and within the abilities of the group, whose attention span is very short.

CO-OPERATIVE OFFICE EDUCATION

Just as co-operative education is important in distributive education, it is equally desirable in office training. Unfortunately far less co-operative office training than co-operative distributive training is offered, and that which is offered is often less satisfactory. Some areas, however, are doing excellent work.

The following suggested program (adapted from the curriculum guide and course of study for secondary-school business education in North Carolina) sets up standards to be met by the school, the co-operating business firm, the co-ordinator, and the student. This program is designed for the preparation and training of office workers. It is open to students in the vocational curriculums who have had skill training. The student must have his parents' consent and a written agreement with his employer before he may enter the program.

The student who becomes a trainee spends three periods daily in school in addition to three hours devoted daily to business training on the job. He studies the required course in English, continues the development of skill in a vocational course, and devotes one period a day to an organized class with the co-ordinator for the purpose of studying problems growing out of his work experience. For all this he receives four units of credit.

The employer furnishes the co-ordinator with an outline of the office duties of the trainee and makes periodic reports concerning the trainee. The trainee receives a compensation comparable to that of a beginning worker doing similar work.

The co-ordinator's work extends over a period of ten months. He brings together in various groups all persons connected with the program: students, parents, committees, employers, supervisors, and school administrators. He visits the student on the job, has conferences with the employer, keeps systematic records, and makes reports.

An advisory committee is essential to a co-operative program. It is usually composed of two employers, two supervisory office employees, the co-ordinator, and the school principal. Its chief functions are to help in the selection of training firms and offices, to advise about training policies, to assist in promotional work, and to evaluate the program.

STANDARDS FOR CO-OPERATIVE OFFICE TRAINING

The School. 1. A laboratory classroom equipped for office training should be available for co-operative office training, the number and specific types of office machines to be determined by a survey of local businesses. The items listed on page 301 are suggested as minimum equipment.

Library tables and chairs
Bookcases
Co-ordinator's desk and chair
Duplicating machines
Dictaphones
Calculators
Adding machines

Typewriters
Chalk board
Bulletin boards
Blackout shades
Access to projector and screen
Storage space for students' materials

2. The school should provide a centrally located conference room for privacy in interviewing students and for conferences with businessmen. This room should be equipped with suitable office furniture and supplies to give it a businesslike appearance.

3. The school should provide an outside telephone connection for the co-ordinator.

4. The school should provide for car or travel allowance to meet the co-ordinator's expenses in supervising his area.

5. The school should assist the co-ordinator in giving information to the public concerning the program.

The Business Firm. 1. The business firm should have sufficient real work for a minimum of 15 hours of weekly employment.

2. The office work should be varied, so that the trainee will have a knowledge of office procedure as well as a mastery of specific skills upon completion of a year's work experience.

3. The business firm should provide adequate facilities for office work.

4. The business firm should encourage harmonious relationships among its employees.

5. The co-ordinator should be interested in working with people.

6. The co-ordinator should have initiative, imagination, and resourcefulness.

7. The co-ordinator should have a pleasing appearance and poise in talking to individuals and community groups. He should be able to handle newspaper publicity and make effective contacts by telephone and correspondence.

The Student. 1. The student should be at least sixteen years of age.

2. The student should be able to obtain a health permit to work.

3. The student should be a senior.

4. The student should have a desire to work.

5. The student should have a neat appearance.

6. The student must possess acceptable general personality traits.

7. The skill of the student should have reached a marketable standard.

QUESTIONS

1. What are the three objectives of the office-practice course? What possible class-organization plans might be developed for achieving these objectives?

2. What clerical duties are performed most often? In your opinion, do existing office-practice courses with which you are familiar prepare workers to perform these duties? What units should be included in such a course?

3. Give three examples of situations in office practice where principles of skill building would be followed. Give three examples of new techniques.

4. What are the unique features of the job breakdown? How is it used in teaching office-practice units?

5. How are committees organized for effective participation in office practice?

6. How can the case method be used in developing desirable office attitudes and behavior?

7. To what extent should classes participate in service projects?

8. In what way does the teaching problem of the teacher of clerical practice differ from that of the teacher of other types of office practice?

9. What are the outstanding characteristics of co-operative office practice as outlined in the chapter?

STUDENT ACTIVITIES

1. Develop completely a unit in office practice, indicating details of timing, specific library and film materials to be used, techniques, etc. You may use one of the skeleton outlines in this chapter, or you may develop a completely new one. Duplicate your unit, so that each member of the class may have a copy for his plan book. If you plan the unit for clerical-practice students, make the necessary adjustments.

2. Examine all available textbooks and work kits in clerical type-writing. Prepare a class report on their content and suggested methodology.

3. Teach the class for 10 minutes in some periphery skill, using the job-breakdown sheet as the basis for your lesson.

4. Teach the class for 10 minutes using the case method. (You will not have time for a complete discussion.)

5. Develop a master plan for a one-semester office-practice class of 22 pupils for whom you have available the following equipment: miniature filing sets for all, typewriters for all, telephone directories for all, one stencil duplicator, one fluid duplicator, four voice-writing transcribing units, four calculators, four adding machines, two demonstration telephones. Plan for some units in which the rotation plan is used and for some in which all students participate at the same time. Examine all available office-practice, and clerical-practice textbooks and state and city courses of study as aids in your planning.

BIBLIOGRAPHY

Agnew, Peter L. *Typewriting Office Practice*. Cincinnati, South-Western Publishing Company, 1950. 29 p. instruction plus supplies.

———, James Meehan, and Foster Loso. *Clerical Office Practice*. Cincinnati, South-Western Publishing Company, 1955.

———. *Secretarial Office Practice*. Cincinnati, South-Western Publishing Company, 1955.

Beamer, Esther, J. Marshall Hanna, and Estelle L. Popham. *Effective Secretarial Practices*. Cincinnati, South-Western Publishing Company, 1956.

Collins, Marian. "Handbook for Office Practice Teachers," *Journal of Business Education,* November, 1953, p. 83.

———. "Management Techniques for the Office Practice Teacher," *UBEA Forum,* February, 1953, pp. 22–24.

Connelly, Mary. "Successful Unit Planning in Clerical Practice," *UBEA Forum*, February, 1952, p. 7.

Cook, Fred. "An Effective Office-Practice Course for the Small High School," *National Business Education Quarterly,* May, 1954, pp. 25–30.

Eisen, Norman. 4 articles in the *Business Education World* on office practice: "Methods in Office Practice: Objectives and General Program," September, 1951, pp. 32–33; "How to Organize the Rotation Plan for Instruction in Office Practice," October, 1951, pp. 67–69;

"Methods in Office Practice: the Instruction on Calculating Machines,' November, 1951, pp. 124–126; "Methods of Teaching Office Practice: What to Do about the Duplicators," December, 1951, p. 173.

Etier, Faborn. "Integrating Office Skills and Knowledges," *UBEA Forum,* November, 1954, pp. 14–15.

Felter, Emma. "Adjusting to Vocational Life Through Clerical Practice," *American Business Education,* March, 1953, pp. 147–151.

————. *Personal and Clerical Efficiency, Basic Course.* New York, Gregg Publishing Division, McGraw-Hill Book Company, Inc., 1949.

————. *Personal and Clerical Efficiency, Advanced Course.* New York, Gregg Publishing Division, McGraw-Hill Book Company, Inc., 1950.

————. "Secretarial Practice and Clerical Practice—They Are Different and Yet Alike," *Business Teacher,* February, 1950, pp. 153–155.

Frisch, Vern. *Applied Office Typewriting—A Practice Set in Clerical Typewriting.* New York, Gregg Publishing Division, McGraw-Hill Book Company, Inc., 1955. 44 p. instructions plus forms.

Friedman, Sherwood, and Jack Grossman. *Modern Clerical Practice.* New York, Pitman Publishing Company, 1953.

Gregg, John Robert, Albert Fries, and Margaret Rowe. *Applied Secretarial Practice,* Fourth Edition. New York, Gregg Publishing Division, McGraw-Hill Book Company, Inc., 1957.

Huffman, Harry. *Business Education World,* 10 articles in a series on clerical practice: "What Should We Teach in a Clerical Practice Course?" May, 1953, pp. 440–442; "Who Should Study Clerical Practice?" June, 1953, pp. 486–488; "14 Principles to Follow in Setting up a Clerical Practice Course," September, 1953, pp. 16–17; "How Much Filing in Clerical Practice?" October, 1953, pp. 17–18; "How Much Arithmetic in Clerical Practice?" November, 1953, pp. 16–17; "How Much Duplicating in Clerical Practice?" December, 1953, pp. 19–20; "How Much Typing in Clerical Practice?" January, 1954, pp. 11–12; "How Much Office Routine in Clerical Practice?" February, 1954, pp. 9–10; "How Much Calculating Machine Instruction in Clerical Practice?" March, 1954, p. 13.

Kahn, Gilbert, and Theodore Yerian. *Progressive Filing,* Sixth Edition. Also Practice Materials and Workbook Exercises. New York, Gregg Publishing Division, McGraw-Hill Book Company, Inc., 1955.

Stroop, Christine. "Developing Correct Work Habits in Clerical Office Training," *UBEA Forum,* February, 1954, pp. 17–18.

Tonne, Herbert A. "Two Types of Clerical Training," *Journal of Business Education,* May, 1950, p. 7.

CHAPTER XIV

Teaching Distributive Education

ONE OUT OF EVERY EIGHT employed persons in the United States today distributes some form of goods and services. About 50 per cent of high school graduates enter some form of employment in the distribution field, and annually at least a quarter of a million young people get their initial jobs in some form of merchandising work. Yet when high school students were questioned about their choices of a vocational field, 85 per cent indicated that they had planned to enter a profession. Actually the American economy will support only about 5 per cent of workers in the professional category. This shows that young people have false notions about their employment possibilities.

It is desirable, then, to guide more people into such fields as distribution, where they have the greater opportunity, and to prepare them for satisfying careers in that field. Teachers and guidance workers must sell more students the idea that work in the field of distributive education is worth while and that excellent opportunities for good income and for satisfying service are to be found there.

Seventy-four per cent of the total economic effort was devoted to production in 1870, and only 26 per cent to distribution. Now manufacturing has become so efficient that only 48 per cent of our total effort is devoted to manufacturing and production and 52 per cent to distribution. Any significant improvement in the living conditions of the American people will probably require better distribution service. This means that business needs improved distribution techniques and, even more important, better trained workers.

In an economy of free enterprise selling is the dynamo that
stimulates and motivates economic activity. To the extent that selling fails to be effective, the economy of free enterprise will fail.
Unfortunately, there always have been some salesmen who have
looked upon their work as a means of hoodwinking the consumer.
Such activity is not selling; it is chicanery.

WHAT IS GOOD DISTRIBUTION?

Real merchandising is the art of making people aware of their
needs and then helping them buy the needed articles intelligently.
It is not based on sympathy buying; it is based on rendering service.
The salesman, therefore, must know his product, know his customer,
know the market, and have fundamental integrity. Selling runs the
gamut of human activity; certain aspects of it are among the lowest
paid services and others among the most highly paid services. Salesmen work in small stores and in tremendous department stores;
they serve behind counters, and they call on customers in their
homes. They work for others and are individual enterprisers. They
work for a flat salary and on a commission basis. Some sell merchandise that requires little or no knowledge of the goods and service to be sold. Others require a highly technical understanding of
their product or service in order to be good salesmen.

Distribution costs have increased in the United States for many
reasons. One of the most important is that by spending more effort
on distribution more goods are sold. To the extent to which this is
so, the increase in the cost of distribution is thoroughly justified.
Another important reason is that manufacturers not only are concerned about selling a product, but they also want to be sure that
people will know how to use it and will be satisfied with it after purchase. Manufacturers, therefore, spend additional money and effort
on "keeping the merchandise sold." To the extent to which this
service helps the consumer get more out of the merchandise he buys,
the added effort in distribution is worth while to the consumer.

All this would make one assume that schools would exert more
effort on wise distribution training than on any other vocational
training. Yet fewer than 75,000 students are receiving some form of
sales or distributive education in the high schools, whereas about

a million high school students are studying shorthand and bookkeeping. This maldistribution of enrollment has continued for many years in spite of the fact that high school graduates have far greater opportunities for employment in some phase of saleswork than in either shorthand, bookkeeping, or even in general clerical work.

REASONS FOR FAILURE TO TEACH DISTRIBUTION

1. One of the main reasons for the lack of instruction in distributive education is the poor training that most teachers have had for teaching merchandising. Teachers who lack experience are not likely to achieve successful training. The teacher's inability to make training in distributive education practical is the basic reason for failure to give good merchandising training in most communities.

2. Much of what is called salesmanship is really only practical psychology. This technique can often be developed more easily in relation to other subjects than salesmanship, for the subject matter of this course is usually outside the practical experience of many younger students.

3. Many schools have failed to enlist the co-operation of department stores and especially of the smaller shops in giving their training.

4. The fundamental reason for failure is the inability of teachers to make the work attractive, although there are many opportunities for doing so. As long as teachers give merchandising courses in a formalized manner, students will not be willing to elect them. Whenever teachers have given merchandising training in a realistic manner, the course has been unusually successful.

REASONS FOR POOR TEACHING

Here are some reasons why distributive education is not well taught.

1. A good salesman knows innumerable details about the merchandise he is selling; however, such a tremendous variety of material and service is sold that it is impossible for any single person to know in advance everything that he is likely to sell.

2. It is difficult to determine the particular ability required in

salesmanship. Some salesmen spend great effort on sheer sales pressure. Others deliberately go out of their way not to pressure a prospective customer. The formal steps in selling are good as a means of generalizing sales technique, but they do not apply exactly in specific given situations.

3. Those engaged in distribution work do hundreds of different jobs. They take cash; do the final processing of the work in the shop; check merchandise; correspond; serve as telephone operators, adjusters, casing clerks and supervisors, credit managers, floor managers, buyers, comparison shoppers, elevator operators, delivery workers, package wrappers and package sorters, markers, stock clerks, wrappers of various types, advertising workers, advertising artists, layout men, display artists, sign writers, and window trimmers.

It can be seen, therefore, that it is impossible for the high school to give specific training in all distributive occupations.

WHAT CAN BE TAUGHT IN PRESERVICE DISTRIBUTION TRAINING?

The transfer of skills from a general situation to a specific job is difficult. Nevertheless, knowledge of limited marginal vocational value can be obtained in distributive courses when they are taught by teachers with broad experience who present their work in a realistic fashion. Salesmanship tends to become a course in general principles in many schools. The student, however, needs specific training in selling. The best that can be done, therefore, in high schools where distributive training is offered on a preservice basis is to offer a single course that deals with the general principles of selling but applies them as much as possible to actual sales situations in the school, such as getting advertising for the school magazine, selling tickets for the annual school play and for athletic events, participating in the sales and distribution service of a cafeteria, carrying on demonstration sales activities in the actual classroom, and the like.

It is usually unwise to offer formal courses of selling in such general form that they are primarily valuable to the consumer. Courses in consumer education are useful, but they should be taught under that label rather than under the guise of salesmanship. Undoubtedly, much of what is taught in courses of salesmanship and advertising is useful to the student as a consumer; but if such subjects are offered as consumer education, they should be so labeled rather than surrounded by fictitious job values. The confusion of consumer values and job values defeats the purposes of both consumer education and distributive education. The best way to teach students how to sell is to give them actual training in selling and in related aspects of distributive education. This is best known as the work-experience program or co-operative work training.

CO-OPERATIVE TRAINING

Solution to the problem of combining theoretical and practical education seems to depend on some form of co-operation between school and business. In business education, co-operative training has been most effective in retail selling.

In order to give an impetus to training for distributive occupations, the George-Deen Act was passed by Congress in 1936. Under this act a little over a million dollars of Federal funds were allocated to this training. Local programs were inaugurated for training high school students on a co-operative basis and for in-service training of workers engaged in some form of distribution. The funds were used to implement training programs and to provide state supervisors for the program. Federal funds were matched by local funds for the payment of salaries to co-ordinators. About twenty times more adults receive on-the-job distributive training than do high school co-operative students. In 1946 the George-Barden Act was passed. It practically doubled Federal aid available for distributive education.

Under this plan the trainee may work in a store for half a day under supervision of a co-ordinator and on the other half day receive training in school. Another plan is to have the student work in the shop one week and go to school the next week. Under this plan an alternate student is in school while the first worker is on the job and vice versa. Under the Federal Act, co-operating workers receive the same hourly pay as full-time workers doing the same type of work.

With the increase in number of such courses, certain techniques and procedures for administering the program have evolved. Today's co-operative work experience is, consequently, a far step forward from the rather haphazard arrangement by which students got experience by doing voluntary work in the school office, going downtown to help during the rush season, or mimeographing the songs for the PTA meeting.

To obtain Federal aid, the school authorities should consult the state division for vocational education for information about requirements for such assistance.

Some of the school units provided in the co-operative program are:

Orientation (including how to apply for a job, record sales, wrap merchandise, and conform to rules of the store in which the student is placed)

Salesmanship (including actual demonstrations and the preparation of a merchandise manual)

Buying Goods (including determination of what to buy, markets, services of buying offices, techniques, and terms)

Receiving and Marking Goods (including pricing, coding, stock work, routing, and so forth)

Store Arithmetic (including computation of invoices, open-to-buy, stock turnover, markup, and markdowns)

Stock Control (including inventory and unit control)

Color, Line, and Design (including basic principles necessary for effective selling, such as attractive color combinations, lines that minimize height, or appropriate groupings)

Textiles (including sources, manufacturing processes, techniques for identifying, synthetics, and so forth)

Display (including grouping, lighting, backgrounds, and so forth, with considerable experience in building displays)

Advertising (including media, evaluation of numerous advertisements, visits to newspaper offices, writing of advertisements)

PROBLEMS IN CO-OPERATIVE EDUCATION

There are difficulties involved in co-operative training as there are in all other kinds of human relations. (1) Businessmen are not always willing to co-operate, and (2) some school administrators do not like the variation from the regular program, and (3) parents sometimes object. Yet the values are so great that these minor difficulties should not be permitted to impede the program. Some educators regard co-operative training as a cure-all for all ills and shortcomings of vocational training. This exaggerated evaluation of co-operative training is not justified; yet without some form of co-operative training, distributive education has comparatively little real justification in a secondary-school program.

Communities like Boston, Los Angeles, New York, Philadelphia, and many smaller communities have worked out fine programs of distributive co-operative training for a limited number of students. In contrast with this system, however, many more schools offer some form of co-operative training that cannot be reimbursed by the Federal Government because the co-operative workers receive no compensation and for several other reasons. Some of these programs are very worth while in spite of their failure to meet the exact Federal requirements. Many more, however, are less satisfactory. No adequate treatment of the techniques of supervising students and of handling the classwork connected with distributive education can be given in this brief presentation.

TEACHING PROCEDURES

No program of training in distributive education can be successful if it uses formal school methods. Here, above all, the student learns to do by doing. Discussion is of use, but the real learning comes by demonstration and by actual experience in selling. Based on such actual experience, discussions of the techniques used and conferences as a basis for remedial work are useful and helpful. In order to make distributive education worth while, there must be adequate equipment. The teacher of distributive education should have display windows, bulletin boards, actual store fixtures, cash registers, a considerable amount of merchandise, adding machines, wrapping paper and twine in adequate quantity, and the like. Unless the types of facilities actually used in stores are available in the classroom, the teaching of sales training is likely to be a poor imi-

tation of distributive training rather than meaningful job training.

The "pattern of the expert" cannot be followed in minute detail
in teaching distributive education. The reason is obvious—selling
and the activities related to it are not primarily skills. To the extent
to which they are skills, moreover, they are far too complex to
present a uniform pattern. Nevertheless, much of the skill-building
procedure presented previously can be followed. A demonstration
of how an expert would sell a commodity is a good means of introducing a particular learning unit. If recognition is given to the extent
to which different sales workers may be successful with different
procedures, it is helpful to have students attempt model sales presentations similar to those of the instructor. It is most important to dis-
courage slavish imitation.

Many of the elements used in teaching understanding and attitudes, such as the techniques used in presenting the basic-business
subjects, are also ideal for teaching merchandising subjects. The
student's attempt to carry out the pattern of the expert should rarely
be criticized by the instructor. The class should arrive at its opinion
through discussion, and recommendations should be based on conference procedures. In the final analysis, the test in merchandising
subjects is the ability to sell, to set up an advertising display, to dress
a window, to wrap a package, to make change, and similar actual
merchandising activities.

In teaching merchandising, therefore, the instructor should use a
combination of skill-building techniques and methods of teaching as
used in the basic-business subjects. It is essentially desirable to make
use of community resources in teaching merchandising subjects.
When the class works with a particular commodity, it is often easy to
obtain the help of a competent businessman in the community. Invite
him to the classroom and give the students the main characteristics
of his merchandise. Here, for example, is a lesson plan for the study
of gold merchandise as a buying commodity. A word of caution is in
order: no teacher can reasonably expect to encompass *all* of these
materials in the framework of but *one* 40-minute lesson.[1]

---

[1] Arnold Scolnick, "Consumer Education Based on Experience," *Journal of
Business Education,* XXVII (January, 1952), p. 208.

TOPIC

Gold Jewelry

AIM

To acquire consumer information that will help us to buy gold jewelry intelligently.

MOTIVATION

1. Several ads that were brought to class (as part of pupils' homework assignment) are read to the class.
2. Key words appearing in the ads are placed on the blackboard.
   a. 14 Karat
   b. gold filled
   c. rolled gold plated
   d. gold plated
3. Trade terms inscribed in the pupils' gold jewelry are placed on the blackboard.
   a. 14 K.
   b. G. F.
   c. R. G. P.
   d. G. P.
4. Questioning by the teacher to determine the extent to which these terms are understood by the pupils.

DEVELOPMENT

1. Why do we use gold for jewelry?
2. How is it used commercially?
3. What kind of gold do we use for jewelry?
4. What do we mean by solid gold?
5. Define alloy. (Learned in previous lesson.)
6. Define karat. (Contrast with carat learned in Precious Stones unit.)
7. What does 12 K gold mean?
8. What does 1/20 12K gold filled mean?
9. What does 1/40 12K rolled gold plated mean?
10. What does the term gold plated mean?
11. What is gold leaf?
12. How can we as consumers be certain that the inscription in the jewelry is true?

SUMMARY

1. Distinguish between solid gold and 14 K gold.
2. Distinguish between 1/10 10K G.F. and 1/30 14K R.G.P.
3. Compare gold plated and gold leaf.
4. In what way(s) will a knowledge and understanding of these terms help you as a consumer?

APPLICATION

You have a choice of buying one of the following graduation rings:
   a. 10K gold ring
   b. 1/10 14K gold filled ring
   c. 1/40 10K rolled gold plated ring.
Which one would you buy and why?

HOMEWORK ASSIGNMENT

1. Bring to class three newspaper ads on gold jewelry.
2. Underscore the technical terms appearing in the ads.
3. Explain the technical terms underscored.

The local jeweler can easily be persuaded in most cases to come to the classroom to give a presentation. Usually he needs some guidance in what to tell the students. This lesson plan will help him to decide what to teach. By planning a little in advance you can have the class prepared to ask proper and intelligent questions as a means of adequate motivation.

In addition businessmen can be invited to the classroom to give direct information to the group about such jobs as buyer, traffic manager, advertising manager, outside salesman. Businessmen can help students prepare themselves for the initial interview. In basic sales training the use of an evaluation sheet by which the pupils may judge the sales competency of the various main-street merchants and their salesmen is of great assistance. Ask the students to make personal visits to the stores. This helps the students evaluate sales techniques and to understand more about what the customers want from salesmen. Then when the students get on the job, they will not make the same errors. By evaluating selling techniques as buyers, students can see what they will have to do when they get to the job of selling on the other side of the counter.

Actual door-to-door sales experience—such as selling magazines, Christmas cards, and the like—helps to increase the horizon of the students and gives them an easily obtained and varied sales experience.

One interesting procedure in teaching textiles is to have the various similar textiles, such as silk versus rayon, cotton versus linen, set up in a debate situation. Each team looks up the information on both his and the opponents' fiber and prepares to debate it in class. Thus the entire class can learn about the textile and do research usually neglected by the students, even in their home assignments. This procedure should, of course, be definitely limited; otherwise it becomes monotonous.

In learning the various weaves, it is suggested that each student buy a hand loom or make his own hand loom out of cardboard. These hand looms can usually be bought for less than half a dollar in low-priced variety stores. If they are not available, the manager or owner can obtain them if the class will buy a sufficient number.

This procedure gives the students experience in recognizing and understanding the advantages and disadvantages of the various types of weaves. We learn to do by doing, not by talking.

Field trips to various local stores, while dealing with the unit on store setup, help develop better understanding; so do trips to local factories, when textiles or nontextiles are being studied. These trips give far better visual information of many things than can possibly be taught in class.

Window displays can be made practical by having a window display in the rear of the classroom or, even better, in the hallway so that other students can see the display. The instructor and students should dress the window. When students are more proficient, they should go into the shops of the community and dress their windows. Many storekeepers will be glad to co-operate if only for the sales promotion value. This is particularly true at certain festive times of the year, such as Halloween.

A school store helps make meaningful all the units of work, if it is operated by the students and if it is closely co-ordinated with the work of the distributive-education class. Unit control, cashiering, and many other activities should be carried on by the students.

Many distributive-education programs are made far more meaningful to the students themselves, to the school as a whole, and to the community if fashion shows are presented when dealing with the unit on fashions. This procedure helps create a better understanding of fashions and also gives the students supplementary opportunity to sell tickets, advertising space, and the like in the fashion-show program. By these activities teachers can make the study of advertising and layout thoroughly realistic. Each student's approach to a respective advertising buyer should be made with an actual ad "tailor made" for the particular merchant. Students will thereby see how much easier it is to sell merchants something if the ad to be sold is easy for the merchant to take. If the merchant must make the ad himself, the difficulty of selling the ad is greatly accentuated. Students in this way are given an opportunity to understand that selling is not merely a matter of talking with people; they will realize that careful planning is required to see to it that the service to the merchant is meaningful. They will also see the need for follow-up after the sale has been made.[2]

IN-SERVICE DISTRIBUTIVE EDUCATION

In-service courses are given to workers on the job. Trainees may include managers and operators of all kinds of stores, department heads and supervisors, purchasing agents and buyers, salespeople, store service workers, and others who come in contact with customers. Courses are usually short and intensive and are often of a highly specialized nature. Typical courses offered in various sections of the country are Meat Retailing, Fitting and Selling Shoes, Credits and Collections, Fabric Analysis, Human-Relations Training, Job-Instruction Training, Building Tourist Trade, Counter Display, Gift Wrapping, Salesman's English, Sales Problems of Commercial Laundries, and Tax Problems for Retail Stores.

DISTRIBUTIVE TEACHER REQUIREMENTS

Naturally, the experience factor is given great weight when qualifications of teachers of distributive education are considered—especially if the co-ordinator is teaching employed persons. Teachers with adequate academic requirements for certification have lacked adequate practical store experience, and qualified teachers for the field have been scarce. Yet this type of teaching position affords a contact with the public and an opportunity to participate in the business life of the community that appeals to many people who would find regular classroom work monotonous. If a person is interested in qualifying for a position in distributive education, he should ask his state supervisor of vocational education for a statement of requirements for certification, and he should be sure that the training he is receiving meets these specifications. Certainly his best procedure is to begin at once to build up, along with his college credits, an experience record in the field of distribution, probably in over-the-counter selling. Prospective teachers who like people and enjoy working with them should give serious consideration to distributive education as an area of service.

[2] Joseph Hecht, High School, Poughkeepsie, N. Y., gave some of the suggestions presented in this section.

QUESTIONS

1. Why do most high school students wish to become professional workers though job opportunities are much more frequent in distributive work?

2. What proportion of our economic efforts is devoted to production as compared to distribution? What was the proportion in 1870? Why has the proportion changed?

3. What are the characteristics of good merchandising as compared to uneconomic and undesirable merchandising?

4. Why have distribution courses increased so much in the United States in the last ten years?

5. Why are so few courses in merchandising taught in the secondary schools? Can you indicate any reasons other than those given in this chapter?

6. What phases of merchandising training can be taught in high schools on a preservice basis?

7. What are the outstanding characteristics of co-operative training?

8. What are the major elements in the George-Barden Act?

9. What are some of the problems of co-operative distributive education?

10. To what extent are in-service courses in distributive education more adequate than those on a preservice basis? Why is this so?

11. What are the desirable characteristics and certification requirements for teachers of distributive education?

STUDENT ACTIVITIES

1. Look up the details of the George-Barden Act.[3] Talk them over with some experienced teacher of distributive education both in co-operative work in the high school and on the adult level. On this basis work out a program for reorganizing the Act and making it even more workable. Give your reasons for suggested changes.

2. Read five recent articles on distributive education. What do you discover from these articles that is not present in this chapter? What differences of opinion are expressed? With which do you agree? Why?

3. Plan a detailed project in distributive education for a community that at present does not have a program of co-operative distributive education. Determine the opportunities, teacher requirements, the oppor-

---

[3] Administration of Vocational Education (Revised). Vocational Education Bulletin No. 1. United States Office of Education, Washington 25, D. C., 1948.

tunity for co-operation with businessmen, and the cost. Submit these elements as a brief for establishing a program.

4. Obtain the merchandising program of five different high schools. Analyze these and evaluate them in terms of their strong points and their deficiencies. How would you reorganize these programs?

5. Obtain the merchandising or distributive-education curriculums for five different universities and colleges that offer such programs. Evaluate them in terms of their efficiencies and deficiencies. Suggest means of improvement. In what way do they differ from the secondary-school programs in merchandising? Are these differences justified?

6. Study several different in-service programs in distributive education. Obtain your information from at least two different states. Compare and contrast the methods of procedure. Evaluate these programs in terms of achievement and cost.

7. Go to at least a dozen retailers who are evidently quite successful and get their opinions on the value of distributive education for
  a. High school students
  b. High school graduates
  c. The merchants themselves
  d. Salesmen
  e. Small shop owners
  f. Sales workers in department stores

Do the opinions of these retailers warrant an increased program of distributive education?

BIBLIOGRAPHY

Axelrod, Nathan. "Selecting Students for Distributive Education," *Journal of Business Education,* XXI (June, 1946), pp. 15–16.

Banks, Murray. "Teaching Merchandise Information," *Journal of Business Education,* XXI (January, 1946), pp. 24–25.

Blackler, William R., and Others. Distributive Occupation Issue, *UBEA Forum,* II (April, 1948).

Beckley, Donald. "Co-operative Retail Training in Retrospect," *Business Education World,* XXVI (April, 1946), pp. 422–423.

Craf, John R. "Employment Opportunities in Department Stores," *Journal of Business Education,* XXI (April, 1946), pp. 13–14.

Dame, Frank, and Others. "Improving Learning and Achievement in Merchandising and Distributive Occupations," *American Business Education Yearbook,* II, 1945, pp. 192–216.

Haas, Kenneth B. *Distributive Education.* New York, Gregg Publishing Company, 1949.

Hoffman, Aaron. "Conference Method in Distributive Education," *Balance Sheet,* XXVII (January, 1946), pp. 184, 214.

Kneeland, Natalie, and Louise Bernard. "Student Activities in Distributive Education," *Business Education World,* XXXIII (February, 1953), pp. 289–290.

Krawitz, Myron. "How We Built Distributive Education in Atlantic City," *Business Education World,* XXXIII (May, 1953), p. 448.

––––––. "This Is What We Mean by Distributive Education," *Journal of Business Education,* XXI (November, 1955), pp. 65–66.

Lee, Beatrice. "School Store," *American Vocational Journal,* XX (May, 1945), p. 24.

Morsey, Royal J. "Salesmanship—Co-operative versus Traditional," *Journal of Business Education,* XX (May, 1945), pp. 18–20.

Newcomb, Mary. "Suggestions for Teaching Retailing Fundamentals," *Journal of Business Education,* XXII (June, 1947), p. 30.

Polishook, William M., and Sarah Saphir. "A Digest of Contemporary Thought in Distributive Education," *Business Education World,* XXX (May, 1950), pp. 458–461.

Scolnick, Arnold. "More D. E. Students Through Better Display," *Business Education World,* XXXV (January, 1955) pp. 24–25.

Shapiro, Ruth. "Pre-Employment Retail Training in Secondary and Vocational Schools," *American Business Education Yearbook,* I, 1944, pp. 30–34.

Stoner, James K. "Small-Store Bookkeeping System and Practices," *Journal of Business Education,* XXX (January and February, 1955) pp. 167–168, 209–210. *See also* Dr. Stoner's column on "Training for Retailing" in the 1955 issue of the *Business Education World.*

––––––. "Training for Retailing," *Business Education World,* XXXV (September, 1954), p. 42; (October, 1954), p. 30; (November, 1954), p. 58.

Taylor, Robert R. "Opportunities in Merchandising," *Balance Sheet,* XXVIII (January, 1947), pp. 198–199, 225.

Turse, Paul L. "What Do You Mean by Distributive Education?" *Journal of Business Education* XXXI (October, 1955), pp. 27–28.

CHAPTER XV

The Basic-Business Subjects

BASIC-BUSINESS EDUCATION is a more recent term for general-business or social-business education. Included in basic-business education are: introduction to business (also known as elementary business training, junior-business training, general business and so forth), economic geography, economics, business law, consumer education, business organization, advanced or senior business, and sometimes merchandising subjects when the marketing aspect is emphasized. Leaders in business education, in dealing with the objectives and major purposes of business education, uniformly stress the importance of basic, general, or social business education. They indicate that, without an understanding of the fundamental principles of business, techniques are valueless. Only when the prospective worker in business has an understanding of business as an economic institution can he render his best service in that field. *Basic-business education* is that phase of business education in which the understanding and ability needed to get along well in business are developed.

If the citizen has a sound grasp of the functions of business in our social and economic system, he is more likely to be a good member of the community. An understanding of business and how it serves the community, plus an ability to use the services of business, is a fundamental element in good education. Basic-business education is a cardinal element in all sound educational programs since it includes all the nonspecialized skill phases of business education.

320

THE DILEMMA OF BASIC-BUSINESS EDUCATION

The fact is, however, that in the average high school, business teachers are not well prepared to teach basic business, nor are they interested in it. Consequently, they often do a less satisfactory job of teaching it than they do of teaching the skill subjects. This situation need not exist. Actually, the basic-business subjects should be more fascinating; and, instead of avoiding them, business teachers should be eager to teach them because they deal with human problems and not skills and drills. It should be easier to interest students in basic business than in skill subjects. Basic-business subjects can be made more meaningful to teachers and students.

In most schools, the basic-business subjects are taught incidentally to the teaching of the technical business subjects—shorthand, typewriting, and bookkeeping. The teacher-training programs followed by most prospective teachers also emphasize shorthand, typewriting, and bookkeeping because teacher trainers are usually enthusiastic about skill subjects, which they teach well. Oftentimes, however, the business teacher has had little training either in subject-matter content of the basic-business courses or in how to teach them.

The beginning teacher, then, is rather at a loss in organizing teaching materials because he has not had much help in planning to teach the basic-business subjects. Nevertheless, because he is the latest addition to the faculty, he is often assigned to teach these less popular courses, which he does not enjoy and does not understand. He, consequently, turns the course into a semester of business arithmetic or record keeping or, even worse, into some type of busywork and looks toward the day when he will be relieved of teaching it.

Historically, too, the basic-business subjects are secondary to the "Big Three." When business education was introduced into the public secondary school, many private business-school teachers were taken over by the public secondary-school systems. In the private business schools, business law, business arithmetic, and economic geography were taught for brief periods between the major subjects as a means of giving relief and variety to an otherwise intensive preparation in shorthand, typewriting, and bookkeeping. The private-school teachers carried their ideas over into the public schools, and this tradition of teaching "side branches" has persisted.

The tendency to look upon the basic-business subjects as incidental to the job-training subjects is unfortunate. As was pointed out before, basic-business subjects are taught for two purposes: (1) as an element in the education of all high school students in order to help them make better use of the services of business and to help them understand business as a major segment in community life, and (2) as a prerequisite to the skill subjects in order to give students the ability to make better use of these skills on the job through an understanding of the functions of business that are facilitated by these skills. In attempting to attain both objectives in all basic-business courses, a confusion of goals results. Fortunately steps are being taken to remedy this difficulty. A program for improving the status of basic business is presented at the end of this chapter.

INTRODUCTION TO BUSINESS

The most commonly taught basic-business subject in junior and senior high school is the introduction-to-business course. It has many other names such as junior-business training, general business, business science, fundamentals of business, and business practice.

It is usually taught as the first or introductory course in the business curriculum, either on a required or elective basis. In some schools it is offered to all students. It is usually found in the ninth- or tenth-year program and is generally taught a full year. In some schools it is a one-semester course alternating with business arithmetic.

Introduction to business has had an interesting history. In 1919 Frederick G. Nichols, in a survey of junior commercial occupations, discovered that junior workers—those under seventeen years of age—were not employed as bookkeepers and stenographers. He, therefore, advocated the establishment of a course in junior clerical training for those students who left school to take jobs and also for those who remained in school and would later study advanced courses in business.

Nichols's study had considerable influence in the creation of junior-business courses, although several had been given before his book was published. This type of junior clerical training, however, was not long retained in the curriculum.

The second phase in the development of junior business was characterized by a tendency to imitate the junior high school survey course, particularly the one in general science. Just as the early teaching of general science included a little physics, chemistry, biology, and astronomy, so a composite course in business training at first included a smattering of almost every subject in the business program.

Some topics were highly encyclopedic and not too well integrated; nevertheless, this new conception of general business marked a definite advance. Attempts were made to develop courses of study for the program dealing with the functions of business. One of the most significant of these was the syllabus for Introduction to Business for the State of New York, published in 1930, which still exerts considerable influence over existing courses in the field.

A third type of course should be mentioned. In many junior high schools, brief exploratory exposures are offered to students to aid them in selecting their senior high school curriculums. Several interesting programs have been set up to provide exploratory experiences based on business offerings. Typewriting, shorthand, bookkeeping, and distributive education are included. Usually an effort is made to attain some integration of subject matter by using office practice as an element common to all units. It should be realized that these samplings are not given to achieve primary learnings but rather to provide acquaintanceship with the type of subject matter in various business courses, so that students may choose their senior high school curriculums wisely. It is debatable whether a person can form an intelligent choice based on a six- or eight-weeks exploration.

Goals of Introduction to Business. Basic business as now conceived by alert teachers has several major objectives:

1. It aims to give students an elementary understanding of business and to show that this aspect of human endeavor has, like other social institutions, both desirable and undesirable characteristics.

2. It delineates the manner in which business services may be used and attempts to make the student a more skillful user of these services.

3. It emphasizes a guidance program. It answers such questions as: What are the various business occupations that a boy or girl may enter? What is an accountant? How much salary does he get? What kind of train-

ing should be given? What is the tenure in this kind of position? What are its desirable and undesirable features? What are the opportunities for women in accountancy and other occupations?

4. It serves as an introduction to other courses in business.

It will be seen from this statement of objectives that elementary business training is not a job-training subject. It is differentiated sharply from office or clerical practice, a subject that integrates previously learned job skills. Office practice is usually offered in the upper years of the senior high school; junior business in the junior high school.

TOPICS IN BASIC-BUSINESS TEXTBOOKS

BASIC-BUSINESS ABILITIES

What business is	Business forms
How to get a job	Insurance
Guidance in business	Business law
Banks	Reference books
Business ethics	Purchasing
Thrift	Elementary arithmetic
Use of advertising	Managing and organizing
Methods of payment	

COMMUNICATION

Mail	Travel
Telephone	Sending money
Telegraph	Radio

RECORD KEEPING

Personal budgets	Cashbook
Filing	Elementary bookkeeping

OCCUPATIONAL MATERIAL

Billing clerk	Messenger or office boy
Cashier's clerk	Salesclerk
File clerk	Shipping clerk
Ledger clerk	Stock clerk
Mail clerk	

This tabulation shows that some junior-business texts still emphasize occupational material that has doubtful value to junior high school students in terms of the present economic situation. Minimum-age laws keep these students in school. Further analysis of the texts shows that there is no clear agreement on the amount of time that each topic should receive. Topics are still too often treated as isolated units by some authors, and little evidence of sequence can be found.

The texts usually consider the more general business information first and discuss vocational topics later, if at all. This treatment of the subject—which consists of a mélange of bookkeeping, arithmetic, vocational material, and a smattering of business practice—creates the impression that the course is in a formative stage, although it has already been in existence for thirty years. Until junior business acquires content material in keeping with its objectives, the average instructor will teach a little about many things; and, as a consequence, students will benefit but little from the course.

Junior business, in some degree, duplicates the work in many communities of economic citizenship, a ninth-grade social study. The development of an advanced business-training course affects the subject matter in the junior course, for a careful gradation of the subject matter is necessary in order to avoid gross overlapping. The tendency toward socializing the bookkeeping course may also necessitate changes in the content of junior-business training.

While it is difficult to estimate the number of students studying junior business, there is little doubt that it ranks fourth in enrollment after typewriting, bookkeeping, and shorthand. The large enrollment may be explained in part by the fact that the subject is offered early in the curriculum and is treated in some junior high schools as a core-curriculum subject.

CONSUMER EDUCATION

It has not yet been determined which department or departments should offer consumer education, and this problem constitutes a major handicap in developing such courses. Educators are generally agreed, however, that in our present economy elements of consumer education are essential. Some feel that consumer education should

not be confined to one course but should permeate the entire curriculum. Others realize that unless responsibility for teaching the
material is placed in certain departments, the needed subject matter
will not be presented and that which is everybody's business will be
nobody's business.

Most high school courses in consumer education are sponsored
by the business department; some, by the home-economics and
social-science departments. In some schools the work is offered
jointly by several departments. In other places consumer material is
taught by merchandising teachers, who often use it for vocational
purposes. Unless such courses are carefully planned, duplication is
inevitable when several departments are offering units of consumer
education.

Perhaps the outstanding phase of consumer-education courses is
the discussion of how to buy articles such as automobiles, housefur-
nishings, building materials, clothing, drugs, fuel, and the like. Some
of this learning material probably belongs in the home-economics
department; but if it is offered there, boys usually do not have the
benefit of the instruction.

Some phases of consumer education seem to belong more appropriately in the business department because most instructors have
the necessary background for teaching the subject matter. The following topics can be handled by business teachers:

> Consumer financial problems, such as banking, credit, personal ac-
> counting and budgeting, installment buying, investing
> Consumer organizations—state, governmental, and private
> General buying problems, such as the use and evaluation of ad-
> vertising
> Problems of price
> Elimination of waste in consumption
> Improvement of standards
> Weights, grades, and measurements

Although textbooks for consumer courses have been published
recently, it is doubtful whether these courses should be developed
entirely around textbook material. One of the greatest difficulties in
teaching consumer education is to bring the subject matter into the
consciousness of the high school student, because it more directly

affects adults. To make the subject something more than mere theory and to introduce contemporary material having real significance requires ingenious planning on the part of the teacher. Certainly the growth of consumer education in the secondary schools is indicative of a trend toward subject matter that is more realistic and more attuned to the daily life of the students.

ECONOMICS

Until recently, high school economics consisted of an oversimplified survey of the supposedly basic principles of the subject. On the high school level, the student should be introduced to the study of economic life by means of word pictures, concrete situations, and definite problems, rather than by abstract rules and principles. Whatever theoretical material is involved should be presented in terms of practical situations and only as a means of relating the situation to the student's present or future experiences.

Essentially, the high school should strive to make the student economically literate. He should not be taught the old-time theoretical explanations for economic activity. If students can be made to realize that people are largely conditioned by environment and not by the arbitrary theories formulated in economic texts, the school will have performed a great service.

High school students usually do not enjoy economic theory. They can understand factors like labor and its problems, the role of the businessman and why he serves us, and government in business. The so-called institutional approach emphasizes the problems of these factors and how we may go about solving them. By dealing with the current economic situations in the student's own life, the teacher gives the student a concrete basis for understanding the economic activities of the community.

ECONOMIC GEOGRAPHY

In many schools that offer economic geography, the subject is a required course for business students and an elective for others. This would seem to be more a matter of tradition than the facts justify. A course in general geography might well be offered to all students since geography is of utmost importance in shaping human destiny.

No matter whether general or economic geography is taught, the subject is too often presented as a mass of unrelated facts about commodities and how they are produced. Geography must be a study of relationships among facts and an understanding of their meaning to human welfare, if the course is to be justified. Too often teachers make the subject little more than a textbook course, for they themselves have little understanding of or interest in it. Even though excellent texts have been published in recent years, no geography course is likely to be worth while if it is limited to recitation from a textbook.

BUSINESS LAW

A good course in business law should emphasize the use and understanding of the nature of business law rather than technical details. Courses in business law are required for business students only; yet all students are in some respect students of business and will, in the course of events, meet situations in which legal knowledge is necessary.

The faults of some high school courses in business law arise chiefly from the attempt to summarize in one semester the technicalities covered in the three-year professional program in a law school. As long as the subject is taught in this way, it will not be of much help in strengthening one of the weakest links in our social system.

A high school course in law must be made useful to the individual student and can point the way toward improvement of the legal system.

Some of the purposes of a high school course in law are:

1. To familiarize the student with some of the basic principles of law, emphasizing those that are significant in business.

2. To train the student in the use of those elementary business and legal forms that may be used without the aid of a lawyer.

3. To acquaint the student with the organization, jurisdiction, and functioning of courts.

4. To inspire in the student respect for law and constituted authority.

5. To awaken in the student a realization of the inadequacies of our present legal system and a desire to correct these weaknesses.

6. To make the student realize when he should consult a lawyer.

BUSINESS ORGANIZATION

The primary aim of a course in business organization is to give the student a picture of the component parts of the economic structure in general and of business enterprise in particular. The relationships among the functions of business—such as buying, banking, paying—and the various business processes by which these functions serve us as consumers constitute the subject matter of the course. The content should be organized so as to describe the processes of both large-scale and small-scale business operations and should take into consideration the home as well as government. An outstanding fault of some courses as now given in the high school is that they are taught like college subjects designed to prepare students for managerial positions, although high school graduates do not enter managerial jobs.

There are many possibilities for correlating business organization with other business subjects. The topics treated in business organization and in marketing are similar to a large extent and form an excellent combination for a year's unit of work, possibly in the eleventh year. Together they serve as a solid foundation for the economics course in the twelfth year. Where it is impracticable to devote a full year to marketing and business organization, the essential elements of both may be combined into a one-semester course.

ADVANCED OR SENIOR BUSINESS TRAINING

The organization of the advanced business course for the eleventh or twelfth year is one of the recent developments in basic-business education. Its growth has been particularly rapid since 1935. The elementary business course is an introductory course only and does not give an adequate understanding of the functions of business. The advanced business course grew out of the inadequacies of other business-education courses. At first, the content and the instructional material of the advanced business course were vague and duplicated some of the material in other subjects. Improved course outlines, better texts, and more adequate teaching materials are now available. Some of the content is taken from courses in marketing and business organization and management. Moreover, the nature of the material is becoming better understood; and better methods are being developed.

If the advanced business course gives the student a better understanding of marketing problems, it will perform a useful service to the entire community. The advanced business course should also show the relationship of the various positions in typical firms. Some employees are of primary importance to the company, while some merely facilitate the performance of other employees. The salesman, for example, is one of the vital factors in many businesses. The salesman's stenographer, however, is primarily valuable as she facilitates his work.

The advanced business course should, moreover, give the prospective employee an understanding of the function of the personnel department and its importance to him. To do this, the schools should give students a broad perspective, in which everyone's niche is made clear.

Still another objective of the course is to emphasize the need of planning in all types of business: personal, individual, corporate, and national. On the other hand, advanced business should not incorporate the content of formal bookkeeping, although some consideration of the subject, particularly its personal-use values, is worth while.

Advanced business should avoid duplicating the content of the elementary business course. For example, topics such as communication and travel belong in the latter course; management, risk reduction, and marketing belong in the former. Ninth-grade students are not ready for a meaningful and detailed study of these topics. Possibly the most effective way to differentiate elementary basic business from the more advanced course is in terms of approach. In the elementary course, the emphasis should be put on the solution of personal problems. In the advanced course, the learnings may be organized in terms of the solution of problems that are met by the worker in business and more particularly by the small-business owner. Seventeen- and eighteen-year-olds are thoroughly job and income conscious. They are soon bored by personal use competencies. These management problems must, however, be kept simple. High school seniors are not ready to cope with problems of high finance.

RECOMMENDATIONS

It is agreed quite generally that some of the content of the basic-business subjects is of such fundamental importance that it should be taught to all.

The courses should be taught in the business department by experienced teachers, rather than by those who are only giving the course under protest. Most business teachers, by training and experience, should be better qualified to teach these subjects than their social-studies colleagues.

It is obvious by now that many problems are involved in the teaching of the basic-business subjects—problems of curriculum, sequence of courses, subject-matter content, articulation between departments and courses, faculty, and student personnel. How can these problems be solved?

1. Recognize the general educational value of much of the content of the basic-business subjects and freely and willingly co-operate with the teachers of social studies, English, mathematics, science, and home economics in integrating into a core curriculum those phases of social-business education that are significant to all students.

2. Build the basic-business subjects around those phases of basic-business education that are not significant to all students but are nevertheless vitally important subject matter for business students.

Many phases of occupational intelligence needed by those going into business have not been treated adequately in school. Subject matter that will develop such occupational business understanding but that is not uniquely job-skill training is the core subject matter of basic-business education.

3. Develop sequences of basic-business subjects. Basic-business education has suffered because the subject mater is not taught in

any sequence. Students can study business law without having had bookkeeping, geography, or even elementary business training. Each subject is treated as an isolated unit. The teacher must go back to the fundamentals; and therefore, the treatment of subject matter must remain elementary. This results in boring the more able students who have gone through the process several times. The necessity for remaining on a superficial level results in low standards and soon causes the able students to become disinterested. A well-planned sequence of learning is, therefore, needed.

4. Develop a corps of enthusiastic, well-trained teachers of the basic-business subjects who have something to contribute to their classes. Only when the material is well taught can the courses be meaningful.

QUESTIONS

1. What is the origin of the basic-business subjects in the high school?

2. To what extent are they similar to business subjects taught in college?

3. What are the purposes of general business or introduction to business?

4. How has the content of the subject changed since it was first introduced?

5. "General business has an assured and permanent place in the school program." Evaluate this statement.

6. "Some understanding of law is important for all; and therefore, all students should take business law." Comment on this statement.

7. "Salesmanship can be justified only if students get selling jobs as a result of taking the courses." Do you agree?

8. To what extent can business organization in the high school serve as an integrating subject in bringing together the various aspects of business taught in separate courses?

9. How extensively is senior business training now being taught? Explain.

10. What is the present dilemma of the basic-business program? How could business educators correct this weakness?

11. What are some of the difficulties in improving the program of general or basic-business education?

STUDENT ACTIVITIES

1. Set up the specific objectives for a basic-business course to be taught to all ninth-grade students.

2. Make an outline for the content of the basic-business course described above.

3. Prepare some proposals to improve the program of basic-business subjects.

4. Make an outline of the content of a high school economic-geography text.

    a. Analyze the content as to its value for *all* students.

    b. Analyze the content as to its value for all business students.

5. Prepare a list of consumer-education topics that should be taught to all business students. (Use a consumer text as a basis for your solution.)

6. Make a detailed list of economics topics that should be taught to *all* business students.

7. Prepare a list of business-law topics that should be taught to *all* students.

8. Make a list of salesmanship topics that should be taught to *all* students.

9. Make a list of the salesmanship topics that should be taught to *all* business students.

10. Set up the specific objectives for a course in senior business training to be taught to *all* twelfth-grade students.

11. Make an outline for the senior business-training course.

BIBLIOGRAPHY

Douglas, Lloyd V. "Basic-Business Room Equipment," *American Business Education Yearbook*, V, 1948, pp. 191–196.

Freeman, M. Herbert. "General Business Education in the Small High School Program," *National Business Education Quarterly*, XXII (May, 1954), pp. 18–24, 38.

Graham, Jessie. "A Program for Social-Business Education," *Journal of Business Education,* XXIII (February, 1948), pp. 13–14.

Harms, Harm. *Methods in Vocational Business Education.* Cincinnati, South-Western Publishing Company, 1949, Chapter IX.

Muse, Paul F. "Social-Business Education as Revealed by Significant Educational Studies," *American Business Education Yearbook,* II (December, 1945).

Nanassy, Louis C. "Economic Education in Elementary Schools," *National Business Education Quarterly,* XXII (March, 1954), pp. 15–29.

Price, Ray G. "Need for Basic Business Education as Revealed by Significant Educational Studies," *American Business Education Yearbook,* II (December, 1945), pp. 95–97, 100.

————. "A Five-Year Statewide Basic-Business Program," *UBEA Forum,* VIII (May, 1954), pp. 36–37.

Russell, Raymond B. "Evaluation of the Basic-Business Education Program," *National Business Education Quarterly,* XXII (December, 1953), pp. 26–30.

Slaughter, Robert E. "Courses of Study in Social-Business Education," *American Business Education Yearbook,* IV, 1947, pp. 257–278.

Tonne, Herbert A. "The Fundamental Problems of Basic-Business Education," *UBEA Forum,* II (March, 1948), pp. 34–36.

————. "Preparing Teachers of Basic-Business Education," *National Association of Business Teacher Training Institutions,* June, 1948, pp. 19–22.

————. "What Brand of Economics Shall We Teach?" *Balance Sheet,* XXXVI (February, 1955), pp. 247–248, 252.

————. "What Is Happening to Junior-Business Training?" *Journal of Business Education,* XXI (November, 1945), pp. 19–20.

Zelliot, Ernest A., "Planning the Basic-Business Rooms," *American Business Education Yearbook,* V, 1948, pp. 127–132.

CHAPTER XVI

Procedures in Teaching
Basic Business

UP TO THIS POINT emphasis has been placed primarily on skill-building techniques. While all learning procedures are fundamentally similar, procedures for attaining understanding differ considerably from techniques for developing skills. As a basis for differentiating these two types of procedures, a brief restatement of skill-building techniques is given here to make the comparison and differentiation clearer.

STEPS IN BUILDING SKILLS

1. *Motivation.* The teacher motivates the students by indicating the importance of the skill and by showing the relative ease with which skill can be acquired if proper procedures are used.

2. *Demonstration.* The teacher demonstrates correct or expert procedures. He definitely avoids trial-and-error learning.

3. *Practice.* The student practices, first under careful observation and then, as he gives evidence of ability, with less and less supervision. In providing this practice, the teacher utilizes drill material that will emphasize correct procedures. If he finds individual students following wrong practices, he immediately corrects them. He minimizes consideration of why such procedures are correct or incorrect. He is concerned with results, not with causes.

4. *Testing.* The teacher tests when observation shows that some

degree of mastery has been attained. These tests are both diagnostic and achievement measures.

5. *Remedial Practice.* The teacher provides remedial practice when he discovers student weaknesses. He may remotivate and re-demonstrate as preliminaries to corrective practice. This process of remedial teaching goes on to the point of mastery. It will be recalled that mastery involves not merely the ability to perform, but the ability to perform so proficiently that the procedure is auto-matic.

6. *Articulation.* The teacher articulates mastery of the skill and ability to use the mastery in the job situation. Every possible use of a skill is made in a variety of situations. Thus, a higher level of mas-tery is attained and ability to use the skill in out-of-class situations is achieved.

It can be seen from this summary that if the teacher is an expert, if he has a sympathetic understanding of the students, and if he knows how to diagnose errors, the process is fairly definite. This is not true in the basic-business subjects, although the fundamental steps are quite similar.

The steps that may be followed by the teacher of basic-business subjects in preparation to giving an understanding of these subjects include:

1. *Motivation.* The teacher of basic-business subjects must also motivate his teaching. As the subject matter is intangible and social rather than individual, the motivation, however, must be developed on a broader basis. The teacher of typewriting can show the value of his skill in school and on the job. The teacher of basic-business subjects, who is planning to develop an understanding of the man-agerial relationships, cannot assure the students of the same tangible results. The outcomes are important and valuable, but they may seem remote to some students.

2. *Selection of Content.* Teacher-student planning is much more characteristic of the basic-business subjects than it is in the skill-building subjects. Even in the basic-business subjects the teacher usually selects the key topics, having in mind the interests of the students. The problems around which learnings are to be built may often be selected by the students in discussion; the teacher, how-

ever, may vary the sequence of topics to fit the students' current interests. It is usually necessary for the teacher to have appropriate problems available whose solution will result in attaining the learnings to be achieved by the class.

In the presentation of the unit, the teacher must be adept in interesting students to the extent that they feel that the learnings to be attained are desirable. This goal is not always possible; however, to the extent to which students accept the teacher's selection of content, this step has been accomplished well. If the teacher realizes that there is little or no student acceptance of the unit, then it would be wiser to reconsider the topic either by modification of the learnings, or by the selection of a different topic.

The content of the basic-business subjects differs from the skill subjects in that it is less specific. Attitudes are less important in the initial levels of skill building than they are in the basic-business subjects. While some knowledge is important in buying, for example, the effectiveness of learning should be measured by the extent to which attitudes toward buying have improved. Has the student acquired greater care in buying? Is he conscious of buying too much at a time? too little? Has the student analyzed the cost of a credit purchase? Is he going to take proper care of an implement? A teacher could, for example, center much of the course work on the development of *justified faith* in a business environment. Teachers should help students learn when to have faith in others and when to withhold it, as both a careless giving or withholding of faith is unsound. Of course, this attitude is never learned perfectly, but can be improved in all of us. Young people especially need help in improving their attitudes. The improvement of a person's ability to have justified faith in others could easily be made the unifying element in a course in basic business. Justified faith is needed in buying, selling, managing, banking—in fact in all business functions. Moreover, it should be an outcome of almost all other courses. It can, therefore, be a means of integrating all school learnings with out-of-school environment. Neatness might be a trait that some teachers would prefer to justified faith, but it lacks the depth and permeating quality so characteristic of justified faith. Other attitudes that might be used are business courtesy, industriousness, and dependability. Of course, many teachers may want to use the development of two or more attitudes around which to unify their work.

3. *Analysis of Previous Learnings.* Either as a part of motivation or as a segment of the teaching-learning process, the students and the teacher must find out how much they know about the unit that is being studied. In a subject like shorthand, at least at its initial learning level, the students know nothing about the subject. In every unit of basic business, however, even the least academic student knows something, though his knowledge may be incorrect. Some students already know quite a bit and have developed some good attitudes in the unit of learning.

Formal and informal pretesting of some kind is important, first to motivate the students toward further learning, and second to find out what students already know about the unit. Knowing the competencies of the various students in the class is important, so as to avoid duplication and to serve as a basis for further learning. Formal tests have some value, but they almost always emphasize isolated facts. Group discussion and teacher questioning usually give a far better understanding of the level of student competency.

4. *Presentation.* This step can, to some degree, be compared with the demonstration given by the skills teacher. The teacher of basic-business subjects may merge the presentation of a unit with the motivation of learning for that unit. The teacher of basic-business subjects cannot demonstrate the understanding or attitude he is trying to develop as easily as the instructor of typing can demonstrate the unit procedures. The teacher of basic-business subjects who is presenting a unit indicates the scope of the unit, its importance, and the sources of learning materials for it. He delimits the unit and shows its relationship to the other units. Just as the skills teacher in this level of teaching is the center of attention, so the teacher of basic-business subjects is justified in taking the center of attention in the learning process. Instead of a simple demonstration of how to do, the teacher shows the students how to learn, why the learning is important, and where to get the facts needed for learning.

Even when students work out their own units and select their own learning materials, the teacher still is important in keeping the attention of the learners focused upon the goal of the learning activity.

The basic-business teacher may use any one or more of many possible techniques in presenting a new unit.

a. He may present the new content in the form of a practical problem to be solved by an individual: *What would your father do if he needed $300 for an emergency operation?*

b. He may present it as a problem requiring group action: *Almost every month a bicycle is stolen from the school grounds. What can we do to reduce our possible loss?*

c. He may present it as a problem requiring group discussion: *The suggestion has been made that we take a trip to Washington, D. C. What transportation problems must we consider?*

d. He may present it as a problem needing deliberation: *According to the "business cycle theory," how long will our present era of prosperity probably continue?*

e. He may present it as a problem needing investigation: *How much does it cost a young married couple to live in Hometown?*

f. He may use a combination of these techniques that call for group discussion, group deliberation, and group action.

The teaching techniques in the skill subjects, on the other hand, stress individual action. They depend on intensive drives for new goals followed by periods of consolidating the new skills. This means a great deal of time spent on drill, review, time-clock and performance standards.

5. *The Assignment.* The teacher may be justified in spending an entire class period in presenting a new unit and in working out with his students the plans for developing it. The assignment in basic-business subjects presents a real challenge to the teacher. In starting a unit of work, the assignment may cover the work of several days and present an over-all view of the material. In fact, the assignment of a new unit may be looked upon as part of the teaching process and may justifiably take as much as an entire class period. After this detailed presentation, an immediate assignment covering the next day's lesson may be given. In this way, the students are given a knowledge of the assignments to come as well as definite and immediate aid in preparing the next day's work.

Assignments should be definite. For the teacher to tell his class to study about what is happening to prices is so indefinite that neither the student nor the teacher can be satisfied with the results. If he asks for at least six difficulties that the student's family faces in planning its buying of fall clothes, the student will have some basis on which to proceed. A list of specific questions tends to prevent the students from doing aimless reading or questioning. Unless they know what is expected of them, they are very likely to become confused by a mass of material and fail to discover the relative values of the various statements read.

6. *Learning Activity.* The activity that results in student learning in the basic-business subjects is quite different from that found in the business skills. In typewriting practice, the student imitates as faithfully as possible the examples set by the teacher, using the drill material supplied. In studying a unit in the basic-business subjects, however, a variety of procedures is used. For instance, if the study of the Pan-American Highway is presented as a unit for integrating a variety of learnings about economic geographic conditions in North and South America, the students would read selectively, participate in small discussion groups, study maps, and possibly develop various small projects.

The teacher's function in a unit of this type is to help students obtain materials, differentiate between important and unimportant materials, see relationships that might not be apparent to the student, and eliminate waste effort if proper reading materials have been selected.

It is trite to repeat that students learn to do by doing. Yet this basic principle is often forgotten in basic-business subjects. In school learning student activity is relatively easy to attain; however in a basic-business subject, it is so easy to talk, with occasional interpolations from students, that the teacher may simply fail to provide himself with terminal facilities. Stimulating, meaningful student activity is the foundation for this phase of learning. It is difficult to make listening a meaningful activity for learners. Planning charts, handling commodities, discussing the topic with other students, asking questions, solving problems, organizing ideas on paper so that others can understand them, and similar activities are more likely to be meaningful than mere listening. On the other hand, listening at times can be very useful, while student discussion can be pointless. To be meaningful, all activity must lead directly or indirectly to greater competence and more complete understanding of the goal for which the unit is being studied. Activity without a goal is mere busywork.

7. *Evaluation.* Testing in the basic-business subjects is very different from that in skill subjects. The few facts and incidental skills to be mastered can be checked in much the same manner as they would be in shorthand and typing. The fundamental mastery to be attained in a unit of study like that of the Pan-American Highway would be an understanding of the psychological and economic importance of the highway to all American peoples in terms of the influence of this link on Pan-American solidarity, world peace, Pan-American trade, international trade, educational advancement, and the like.

Achievement of understanding, rather than mastery of knowledge, cannot be measured by true-false tests or even by the usual type of essay test. It is necessarily a subjective process. This is one reason why so many business teachers are reluctant to teach these subjects. They like the definiteness and the finality with which grades can be given in the skill subjects. Yet, everyone would agree that these fundamental understandings, attitudes, and abilities are more important than skills as such. The fundamental test of mastery must be the ability to demonstrate it in a use situation. In any discussion of Pan-American relationships, can a student intelligently evaluate the importance of the Highway? Does the student read the newspaper more meaningfully as a result of studying this unit? Such evidences as were indicated are not tangible, yet only as students attain these types of ability can they be considered as being truly educated.

Testing in the area of basic-business subjects is a real challenge to the teacher. Results should be made as objective as possible; but, no matter how far the teacher goes, the result will continue to be a human and personal outcome. That is the delight and trial of any important humanistic teaching. Objectivity is desirable; but when it results in loss of validity in order to achieve objectivity, the value is lost. The teacher must make certain that the standards to be attained are not superficial merely because they are objective. This is a serious danger, because if the standards are so subjective and variable that anyone, regardless of interest or effort, can pass the course, then the unit will soon be labeled a "snap" by the students as well as by the teacher.

8. *Remedial Teaching.* On the basis of the diagnosis made from the test results, a program of remedial activity is planned to overcome the errors, misunderstandings, and incompetencies discovered. In general, the remedial teaching program will follow the pattern given in steps one to four. Students probably must be remotivated, for the original motivation will undoubtedly have worn thin. A representation of the unit is probably also in order to make students aware of the weaknesses discovered in their learnings. The practice must be followed through. Emphasis should be given to helping individual students undertake those activities that will give them the competency they failed to attain previously. After remedial teaching, the students should again be tested to check upon their achievement. This may result in a second period of remedial activity; or provision may be made for improved understanding of the present unit in the study of some related unit that follows. Possibly redefinition of objectives may also be in order, for results show that the level of understanding desired is in some degree beyond the range of some or all of the students.

9. *Articulation.* The fundamental test of success in teaching the basic-business subjects is found in the articulation of the understanding acquired in one unit with other understandings and competencies. Teachers perennially complain about the failure of students to have any adequate comprehension of negotiable instruments. The teachers in bookkeeping, for example, complain that students who have had elementary business training know no more about negotiable instruments than those who have never had the course. Where this complaint is justified, failure to achieve real mastery of negotiable instruments in elementary business training is evident.

If a student is able to pass a test in negotiable instruments with an "A" grade in the ninth grade, but cannot utilize his abilities in the tenth grade, then obviously the subject was not mastered. This is probably caused by (*a*) teaching too many units a semester, and (*b*) therefore, teaching them superficially.

As indicated previously, a student who learns merely to the level of initial learning soon forgets what he has studied. If he has overlearned or mastered the subject, only the law of forgetting operates, and the efficiency is still maintained. If the subject matter is worth while, numerous incidents of use of this subject matter will insure the maintenance of an adequate level of mastery.

10. *Cumulative Spiraling of Learning.* The fact that learnings are cumulative is obvious in the vocational-skills courses. As each new unit is learned, all previous learnings are given further practice. Thus there is a spiraling of learning because as each new unit of learning is mastered, previous learnings become even more thoroughly mastered. In the basic-business subjects, unfortunately, this result is not so easy to attain; and, therefore, far too much learning is presented as a self-contained unit completely unrelated to what preceded it or what will follow. This practice is unjustified. Every new learning unit in the basic-business subjects should call on previous learnings, in order to further develop the mastery of these learnings. Likewise, every new unit of learning should prepare for later units of learning in which it will be mastered more completely.

For example, suppose the first unit presented in the course in basic business is "Purchasing." In this unit students acquired a marginal mastery of the basic elements in wise purchasing such as:

a. What is the need?
b. What specifications can be provided?
c. How will payments be made?
d. In terms of total income and expenses, how much can be paid?
e. Will credit be used?
f. Where will the purchase be made?
g. How many units shall be bought?
h. Does the purchase require additional expenditures?
i. How will the purchase be shipped?
j. How shall the purchase be cared for to get best value?

Obviously these elements are oversimplified for the purpose of this discussion. These elements will be obtained from the students by careful, skillful questioning. After considerable activity, generalizations will be drawn around such elements as the ten presented above. These generalizations will be used as a basis for further activity involving purchasing, and specific activities will result in the strengthening, modification, and enrichment of the generalizations until minimum mastery has been attained. It would be most unfortunate to drop all attention to purchasing at this point, and it is entirely unnecessary to do so. Every phase of business life is related to every other phase of business. Buying is an integral aspect of most, if not all, business activity; in fact the business transaction is primarily the buying-selling process.

Let us assume that the other units around which the basic-business course revolves are:

Communication—Mailing   Insurance and Risk Reduction
Paying   Recording and Filing
Banking   Selling and Advertising
Budgeting and Saving   Managing
Travel and Shipping

It must be obvious at once that buying involves and is involved in every one of these functions of business. Buying involves oral and written communication. The unit on buying, therefore, can prepare for the unit on communication; and in the unit on communication, further learning in buying can be attained. In the same way purchasing makes use of banking, shipping, recording, and filing. Good management is just as necessary in buying as it is in every other aspect of business. Selling is the converse of buying, and therefore the vendor needs to understand the problems of the buyer. Insurance is desirable in most forms of buying, and the major problem of insurance is how to buy it wisely. It is often necessary to travel to make better purchasing possible. The relation of budgeting to buying is so obvious that it needs no amplification.

Why is it then that teachers of basic business so often neglect to attain the thorough mastery of subject matter that they find so easy to attain when teaching bookkeeping, shorthand, and typing? Possibly because they have never been made aware of the unity of business; possibly because they do not bring the new learning they are presenting to the use level? Possibly because the courses they took and the textbooks they read and used were organized as isolated learnings.

The failure to achieve cumulative learning in basic business is probably the most serious weakness in the teaching of these subjects. Fortunately the remedy is easy. Any teacher who has even a marginal competency in these subjects can attain at least partial cumulation of learning by spiraling the subject-matter mastery just as he does in the skill subjects. By relating the units of learning to each other, the dismal and all too often justified criticism of basic-business subjects—that most learnings are forgotten soon after the course is over—can be overcome. True, many petty details that were important in acquiring the fundamental masteries will be forgotten; but the fundamental understandings will have been so thoroughly mastered that they will have become an integral part of the learner and therefore cannot be forgotten.

11. *Integration.* It has been implied above that unless the learnings become a part of the student's personality, they will have little influence upon him. The attainment of this integration of learnings into the person of the student is most difficult to measure. It is what we try to get at in evaluation. However, no test of school attainment can determine with any degree of certainty whether the student will practice in non-school life what he has acquired in school. Nevertheless the teacher must constantly be alert to making the competencies acquired in the basic-business class a part of the functioning life of each student. This goal can be accomplished only in degree, but any success in this direction is worth far more than temporary success in getting a high score on petty facts in a true-false test.

SPECIFIC TEACHING PROCEDURES

There are two primary ways of teaching: (1) the *authoritative* method, essentially a teacher-centered procedure, and (2) the *developmental* method, which emphasizes student activity. Actually, every teacher uses both procedures simultaneously, so that the observer will often be at a loss to determine which particular method predominates. The authoritative or telling types of method are characterized by the lecture, the textbook, the drill, and the question and answer.

In general, authoritative procedures are less desirable because they minimize student activity and result in formal rather than lifelike learning. However, they require little paraphernalia; they seemingly avoid waste motion; and they present the work in simple form. In a final sense, there must always be a degree of authoritarianism in the teaching procedures used in the typical school. By its very nature, the school is organized to provide on a compulsory basis, if necessary, for those learnings that are not acquired satisfactorily in daily life. Nevertheless, the more closely the school can approximate life situations, the more meaningful learning will be.

In such subjects, therefore, as the basic-business subjects, it is especially desirable to go as far as possible in using developmental procedures. The smaller the class, the more equipment available, the more room available, the more understanding among teachers, students, and the administration, the more it is possible to use developmental procedures. With very large classes, little space, poor equipment, muddled understanding of objectives and poor co-operation from the administration, the teacher must necessarily tend to emphasize authoritarian methods.

The beginning teacher would usually be wiser not to go the whole way in using developmental methods. He often lacks the personal training for such procedures. The younger teacher sometimes lacks the subject-matter knowledge to free himself completely from the textbook and, quite generally, he is on trial with the administration. Extreme deviations from accepted practice may, therefore, sometimes be disastrous. It may often be wiser to wait for a year or two before utilizing the more lifelike procedures involved in the developmental processes that will achieve the kinds of learnings for which the basic-business subjects are taught.

AUTHORITATIVE METHODS

The Lecture. One of the most commonly used methods of teaching in the secondary school is the informal lecture method. It has been used quite extensively in the teaching of basic-business subjects because textbook material is usually inadequate and because other reading materials are so widely scattered that it is often difficult to direct students to them.

The lecture method was probably the earliest form of teaching used and is a primary practice in an area of teaching such as basic-business education. It has a number of serious weaknesses.

1. The lecture method is not conducive to the development of initiative on the part of students.
2. The subject matter presented in the lecture method tends to be secondhand.
3. The lecture method centers attention on the teacher rather than on the student.
4. The lecture method does not afford the student the opportunity to express himself.
5. The lecture method, by its very nature, is a process of "boring in" rather than one of basing learning on life experience.
6. The absence of student activity in the lecture method centers attention on the facts rather than on the student.
7. The lecture method tends to make teachers dogmatic.

The lecture method, nevertheless, has many desirable characteristics.

1. It saves a great deal of time.
2. It fits in well with other methods.
3. The lecture method provides easy transition from one type of classroom procedure to another; and, therefore, it serves a purpose that cannot be approximated by any other teaching procedure.
4. The lecture method also lends itself to an easy transition to the discussion method of learning, which is excellently suited to this type of subject.

In the later years of high school, students have attained a fair degree of maturity. The objections to the lecture method, which are justified in connection with the work of the lower grades, lose much of their strength when applied to students on the senior high school or junior-college level. The tendency to condemn the lecture method results from its abuse rather than from any inherent weakness.

The lecture should always be informal; and students should be given full opportunity to participate in the learning process when they fail to understand the particular explanation. The lecture, interpolated with discussion, questioning, chalk-board explanation, and slide-film presentation is very useful in motivating students to learn a particular unit. It is always an effective means for presenting the total topic to students. In indicating the area of the topic, the sources for learning, and the basic learnings to be achieved, the teacher must naturally take the center of attention. He should not hesitate to do so. It is in the process of acquiring a mastery of the objective set that the fullest opportunity for student participation can be attained.

The Textbook. The textbook method of learning has become the traditional technique of the American high school. It has many advantages for mass instruction. Some leaders in basic-business education look with fear upon the tendency to use textbooks in basic-business education. They feel that teachers using this method are likely to lean too heavily on the textbook as a guide; that they may tend to look upon the textbook as the final authority in all matters.

In an area like basic-business education, a textbook is necessarily the merest outline of what should actually go into the total learning process. To a certain extent, the splendid organization of textbooks in high schools has reduced the justification for this condemnation. Many textbooks, however, still emphasize a logical approach to a subject to the exclusion of psychological approach and development of the subject. They tend to be more concerned with the abstractions governing the subject than with the individual who is studying the book.

One of the needed improvements in basic-business education is the organization and preparation of better textbooks. If better materials were available, principals and administrators would recognize the value of this kind of subject matter and therefore would find a place for it in their school programs. It is, of course, to be hoped that teachers of basic business will never become so slavishly dependent on their text as have the teachers in so many other subjects. The textbook should be used as an aid to teachers and not as the teaching medium itself. The time-honored method of basing the daily work of the class on textbook recitation and then giving a weekly test constituting a formal check on whether the text has been studied cannot, of course, be justified.

If the use of a text results in the failure to achieve enrichment from the use of current materials, then its use will be futile. It should serve as the unifying factor that facilitates the use of varied source materials without causing confusion.

Questions and Answers. This method is, and probably will be for a long time, the backbone of classroom activity in the high school. Questioning and answering, combined with an informal type of lecturing intended to eliminate incorrect answers and to broaden the scope of the recitation, still occupy most classroom time. Obviously in an area like the basic-business subjects, the formalized use of the question-answer method is out of place if it is used merely to see that the student has mastered the teacher's presentation. The basic weakness of most questioning is its use as a means of checking whether the lecture or reading has been effective, rather than as a means of drawing out the previous knowledge of the students in terms of the present learning, thus building up a new set of abilities.

Questioning merely for questioning's sake is not to be tolerated. Every question should have some purpose in the development of the learning unit. Most important is the necessity for adapting the question as closely as possible to the individual student. The teacher should acquire as soon as possible a thorough understanding of the capacity of each student in his class. The questions should then be adjusted to the individuals. There should be questions that will be comprehensible to the weaker students, and there should be more difficult questions for the brighter ones. The meek student who is afraid to recite should be given questions that may be answered briefly. Then, as the student gains confidence, the character of the questions should be broadened. The student who wants the limelight should not, in most cases, be reprimanded directly. He can be made conscious of his desire to show off—very gradually, it is true, by being given questions that are adapted to his ability. The type of student who has this trait deeply ingrained in him needs special attention at the close of the period. He should be made to see that he is a member of a class and not the entire class.

The so-called Socratic method of questioning has considerable value in basic-business education. The questioner assumes an attitude of inquiry. By the questions asked, the teacher makes the student carry his position to its logical conclusion, in this way showing its falsity or its truth. The Socratic method is a deductive method, for the teacher bases the new learning on the previous experience of the learner, accepting the student's point of view as a starting point. Such a process is occasionally quite useful in the classroom, provided it is used with skill. Sometimes it is used to make the student look ridiculous. Such use can scarcely be justified, of course.

DEVELOPMENTAL METHODS

The Unit or Topic. One of the fundamental weaknesses in the teaching of basic-business subjects is that learning often is isolated. For example, in teaching insurance in elementary business training, students usually are presented an encyclopedic body of data about insurance that they rarely assimilate. In addition to the fact that the textbooks themselves throw a mass of facts at students, teachers accentuate this by making reading assignments that are unrelated to previous or future assignments. If insurance is considered a sound learning unit, it should be presented as a whole, beginning with the very simple facts and proceeding step by step as far as students' needs and interests are being satisfied.

Term insurance is the simplest form of insurance and the one most easily taught, yet junior-business training books usually devote very little time to this basic form of insurance at the end of the unit and frequently ignore it completely. If the facts are made simple enough and if round numbers are used, junior high school students, including students with below-average ability, can be given a simple understanding of the basic concept of term insurance in one period. In succeeding days this basic learning can be developed more fully. On the second day, for example, students can be taught the manner in which five-year term insurance operates; on the third day, straight life insurance. In succeeding periods, limited life, endowment life, and other forms might be presented. In each case the basic concept presented on the first day is used over again and is further developed.

Students may not remember everything they learn about insurance, but they will have mastered the fundamental concept of term insurance because it will have been used and reused many times. In the teaching of insurance, the students will master the concept of term insurance just as in bookkeeping the fundamental equation is utilized in every learning unit. How far the teacher goes in spiraling this learning depends on the time available, the intelligence of the students, the degree of motivation, and many other factors. Only as each unit of learning is expanded around a simple idea to be mastered will learning really take place. Such spiraling of learning around a basic concept to be mastered helps to achieve correlation with other units; for example, the relationship of term insurance to fire insurance can be made clear easily.

Basic-business education, by its very nature, requires an understanding of relationships larger than those that can be evidenced in single items of knowledge. That is why the unit plan of teaching is admirably adapted to it. The size of the unit cannot be determined arbitrarily. It must be large enough to involve concepts rather than isolated pieces of information that are acquired in daily "take-the-next-three-pages" type of assignment.

One of the serious weaknesses in the teaching of basic-business subjects is that too many units have been taught superficially. It would be better to teach fewer units and teach them thoroughly. Some teachers have succumbed to the phobia of "covering the book," so that students really master nothing. When fewer units are prescribed, there is greater opportunity for the enrichment of subject matter by means of contract assignments. Low-ability students or those with little interest can contract for a sequence of activities resulting in a lower standard of achievement than those who have greater capacity. These students should be encouraged to work for a broader understanding and greater competency.

Once a topic has been assigned, the student often is put on his own resources to find the materials to be used in completing his assignment. He is stimulated to use an index and a table of contents in various books. He must also discriminate between the important and the inconsequential in his reading, and he will develop a critical attitude toward the various statements he encounters.

Discussion and Conversation. The discussion method is probably the most natural and easygoing of all teaching methods and is a good example of a developmental type of procedure. It has the advantage of being carried on in a natural conversational tone. As this is the type of language used in daily life, it creates a more realistic situation. Discussion is one of the most common means used for settling differences intelligently. It is essentially an informal type of natural intercourse between the students and the teacher and among the students themselves.

Its effectiveness depends to a very great extent on the personality of the teacher. Speaking in ordinary tones gives evidence of the fact that the teacher has poise and does not need to adopt a formal attitude in order to maintain his status in the classroom.

The conversation method has a number of defects against which even the well-trained teacher must be on guard. Principal among these is the tendency for the discussion to ramble far from the point at issue. Discussion for its own sake is so tempting to both the teacher and the students that the desire to wander off into the trivial and irrelevant becomes almost irresistible.

Procedures for using conversational activities have been improved as a result of the job-training activities carried on during World War II. There are many excellent books and articles on conference procedures. The alert teacher should acquaint himself with the use of the conference as a device in teaching the basic-business subjects. The panel discussion, if not overdone, is also an excellent device for achieving greater student participation.

In larger classes, in which the teacher wishes to keep the whole group together as a unit, it is often desirable to have eight to twelve persons in the class utilize conference procedure. Either the teacher or some well-trained student can serve as the conference leader. When the conference terminates, the entire class may be encouraged to participate. By limiting the discussion to a small group, all points of view and all aspects of the problem can be aired, yet the aimlessness and tendency to wander that are so typical of discussion carried on by an entire class can be avoided.

These procedures for socializing the recitation have an important place in the teaching of the basic-business subjects. Learning does not take place without student activity, yet this obvious statement is almost always contradicted by classroom procedures that stress passive learning. However, the use of conference procedures, panels, and group discussion also has its limitations.

Demonstration. In those phases of business education that deal with the application of the natural sciences, the use of demonstration is invaluable. When a teacher demonstrates, for example, the differences in volume of cans or bottles of apparently the same size, the student is conscious of the techniques used to deceive consumers. When the teacher in merchandising demonstrates the tensile strength of various cloths and shows how rapidly some break under stretching, the student is made aware of the problem involved in purchasing strong material. When by actual demonstration the teacher in a consumer-education class shows the unwholesome elements found in certain foods, the student thinks more seriously about the quality of products when he goes shopping.

If the student undertakes the experiment himself, there is even a greater advantage because he assumes a personal interest in the outcome.

The Problem Project. Subject matter in the basic-business subjects should be built around problem solving. As far as possible, learning in each of the major functions of business should be organized around the solution of a series of problems. Naturally these problems should be within the ken of the students. They should not be so simple (except when introducing a unit of learning) that the solution is obvious. They must not be so difficult that their solution is not within the grasp of secondary-school students.

Motivation should usually be built around specific problems. Learning of actual content should be organized around problem solving and should result in generalization coming out of this for further problem solving. Finally, evaluation should be undertaken through the solution of problems similar to those that were used in learning.

Nevertheless problem solving should not be made a fetish. Occasionally there are specific learnings that need to be acquired outside the context of problem solving. Such learnings usually are specific skills or groups of facts that have not been learned previously or have not been learned adequately in earlier classes. When the teacher finds such deficiencies, he should teach the specific skills and facts needed, using the skill-building procedures suggested in previous chapters.

The problem project, much in use today, is a teaching procedure that leads the student to see the problems present in business life and lets him find solutions that will best remedy the difficulties. It will be noted that the method is quite informal. Assignments for homework are made in terms of problems to be solved rather than in terms of so many pages to be memorized. People in general—and students in particular—do not think just for the sake of thinking. They think in order to cope with a situation or to solve a problem. In many cases the motivation for student thinking is extrinsic; that is, it is provided by the hope of obtaining a good mark from the teacher, or, possibly, only a passing grade. Students might be more interested if work were presented to them as a series of problems. The problem method of teaching has come so prominently to the foreground within recent years that its application, its advantages, and its possible weaknesses should be considered in some detail.

The greatest point in favor of the problem method is that it permits the student to face a real difficulty. It eliminates as far as possible the mere recounting of material. It should not be thought that this method does away with the need for a teacher; in fact, the teacher is more necessary than ever, since he is now a guide to the work that is to be done. The problem method does, however, make the student and not the teacher the center of attraction. Rather than a passive listener or reader, the student is now an active searcher for the solution to his problem.

While it is in some respects unique, still the problem method should not be looked upon as a panacea for all existing weaknesses in the teaching of basic-business subjects. It is true that it does make the students undertake self-activity. It also makes them look for the essential thought on the page. It transforms classroom activity into a lifelike situation. Nevertheless, it is one thing to write about the extraordinary value of problem solving and an entirely different thing actually to use that method in a concrete classroom situation. The fact that a syllabus or a course of study is arranged in terms of questions does not insure that the teaching based on that syllabus will be of a problem-solving nature. To use the heading *How Does Business Help the Consumer?* instead of the heading *Business Helps for the Consumer* is no guarantee that the instructor teaching the syllabus will perform any differently from the way he has always taught.

While there are probably some experienced teachers who make complete use of the problem method of teaching, most teachers use it occasionally—in phases of the work that lend themselves to such treatment. Continuous use by the novice of this method of classroom instruction might result in failure. Its occasional use is to be commended. Of course, every lesson should contain an abundant amount of problem-solving material. Continuous use of problem solving, however, as the basic method of teaching might make learning too difficult for the high school student and might in many cases lead to incomplete knowledge of the subject. Intelligently used, the problem project is a very worth-while means of teaching.

The Notebook. The notebook is frequently used as a teaching device in basic-business education. While it is easy to misuse the notebook procedure and make it a mere process of copying down the teacher's supposed wisdom, it nevertheless has these decided values, which make it popular with many teachers: (1) Some students do not seem to learn what they are being taught unless they write it down. (2) A basis for review is needed by students who have not acquired the ability to use the textbook independently. (3) By means of the notebook, differentiation between important and unimportant phases of the work may be made. This advantage is especially important when certain types of textbooks are being used. The newer books, however, carefully point out items of major importance, indicating them by different types of print. With a good textbook, the differentiating value of the notebook is less important. (4) Most important of all, probably, is the fact that the notebook stimulates certain members of the class to take an interest in their work. They cannot recite well; they do poorly on tests. The notebook gives them the opportunity they need. For such students the device is unquestionably of great value.

Teachers must be careful not to permit the notebook to become a mere scrapbook composed of a large mass of miscellaneous materials, more or less related to the problem, but so poorly organized that they are useless. Children and adults love to cut and paste. They will be glad to indulge in the pastime of making picture books. Needless to say, such busywork is not education. Pictures have a place in notebooks, but they should serve a definite purpose. Otherwise they merely serve as interesting fillers.

Student Outlines. An outline is an indispensable guide for the student when the content of the textbook being used is not the same as the material being studied by the class, when emphasis is placed on different points, and, especially, when new material is being added. The teacher often follows a syllabus in which the organization and arrangement of material may differ a good deal from that of the text being used in the class. When that is the case, the outline is an excellent means of helping the students see the unity between the course of study and the textbook. Notebook material kept in the form of an outline and used to adjust the content of the textbook to the work of the class has a very definite purpose that is not achieved by the collection of scattered bits of material frequently found in the ordinary notebook. It is not always necessary to keep a consistent outline of all work of the course. When the textbook itself is properly classified and when its content follows the order used in the classroom presentation of the subject, occasional practice in making an outline is sufficient.

The teacher should not get into the habit of always giving the outline to the students. In fact, one of the best values of the outline is realized when the student has built it himself. The teacher might occasionally give the outlines to the class; but more frequently, it would be better to have the students do the work as a home or super- vised-study assignment. Then the next day several of the students might be called upon to place their outlines on the board for criti- cism and correction.

Debates. The debate furnishes zest and possibilities for display and competition. Basic-business education provides opportunity for the expression of many different philosophies of life. These differ- ences should be aired thoroughly in order that students may develop respect for the opinions of others and realize that other points of view may be just as correct as their own. For example, in a debate on the topic "Should Office Workers Unionize?" there is opportunity for the discussion of labor, management, and consumer relation- ships.

While the debate offers splendid teaching opportunities, it has a number of weaknesses, which are to a certain extent inherent. These defects make it desirable to limit classroom use of the debate. De- bating may lead to quibbling, in which the purpose of the work is obscured. The students tend to make statements and advocate principles because they help to win the debate and not because they are sound. The debate stresses many points of incidental impor- tance. Finally, it has the weakness—shared by many similar de- vices—that it utilizes the abilities of only a few members of the class.

Current Events. Current topics are frequently brought into business classes to make the subject more interesting and vital to the student. If he sees that many events going on in the world are of an economic nature and that practically all influence business, he is more likely to realize the importance of these subjects. If, added to this, he can acquire greater understanding of these events because of his knowledge of the principles of business practice, his respect for the study he is undertaking is increased.

Term Papers. Teachers occasionally require a term paper in basic-business education. Certainly if a term paper is to be required anywhere in high school, a basic-business course seems to be an excellent place for it. Serious consideration ought to be given the matter, however, before the term paper is assigned. A term or project paper is by its very nature an extended piece of organized work. High school students have had very little practice in this type of activity and, therefore, require very explicit directions. It is doubtful whether the time required for such an undertaking would be justified by the results accomplished. It is quite probable that in most cases better results would be obtained by assigning a few shorter papers.

Collateral Reading. In spite of the development of basic-business texts within the last few years, many are still rather dictionarylike. The covers of a rather small book generally enclose a vast range of subjects. As a result, the bare outlines of each topic are given in summary form. Until this condition has been remedied by teaching less material more thoroughly and until textbooks have become richer sources containing interesting illustrative material, it is necessary to require collateral reading in basic-business subjects. It is better to have reading reports made in terms of topics understood rather than in terms of pages read.

So much excellent business-education material is available in booklets, articles, and even in the daily papers that teachers can build their work around these sources. This creates a problem of selection and intelligent interpretation. Much of the material is biased; some of it is false; some of it is contradictory. This is the same situation the businessman faces in selling and buying; therefore, considerable use of such materials will give students the kind of training needed in business. Possibly business texts in the near future will be organized in terms of selected readings. This procedure has been used in other subjects with considerable success.

Field Trips. In almost every section of the country opportunities for interesting and instructive field trips relating to business activities are presented. In all the larger and many of the smaller cities, there are department stores and well-managed offices. In many communities the municipality has a testing laboratory for aid in purchasing. Within easy reach of most communities is a local wholesale food market. Markets and stores may be compared and trips made to museums of practical arts and science. Even a local sale may illustrate many aspects of the services of business. The local commercial banks should not be neglected. While almost all students are probably familiar with many of its details, a group visit will bring out many points not previously noticed.

The learning results of a field trip should almost always be presented to the whole class as a committee report. Those who made the trip have to analyze what they learned; those who stayed in school or went elsewhere get a vicarious experience and an indirect sense of participation.

GROUP DYNAMICS [1]

Experienced teachers are aware that different classes have different personalities, just as individuals have different personalities. In some classes there is considerable eagerness to learn; in others, less. In some classes there is considerable tension; in others, everything goes along quite well. Some classes get right to work; others tend to waste time. These differences may be caused by the teacher's personality; by the personalities of one, two, or three of the members of the class; or by friendships or enmities among a few members of the class.

Class relations are important in all kinds of learnings, but they are especially important in the basic-business subjects. It is important that students be serious about their work, but not too serious; that they be willing to discuss things among themselves in a friendly fashion; that they have good rapport among themselves and with the

---

[1] Some of the material for this discussion was obtained from a doctoral study by Richard Dale, New York University, 1955, "The Development of a Handbook in Group Dynamics Techniques for College Teaching of Certain Business Subjects."

teacher; that they respect the teacher but yet feel close enough to him to be able to take his advice in friendly fashion and even be able to disagree with him reasonably comfortably.

How are these good class relations achieved? The study of group relations and the improvement of these relations is known as *group dynamics*. Essentially group dynamics is a study of the interaction among members of groups, so as to help these groups to determine mutually satisfying goals and how to arrive at these goals. Business teachers can benefit by a study of how an understanding of human relations, gained through a study of group dynamics, can help achieve better class relations. Group dynamics is in part a study of principles of democracy. How do we achieve democratic practices in our classrooms and at the same time prevent the waste of time that often takes place when democratic procedures are used merely for the sake of having democratic procedures? A class is most effective if all members of the group are participating mentally and, as far as possible, physically; if they are concerned with the problems that are being discussed or the facts and judgments that are being given by the teacher; if they are interested in what their fellow students are saying; and if they are concerned with the good will and participation of other members of the class. There are certain techniques that are used to improve class interrelationships; that is, the class group dynamics.

1. Committee Work. The group procedure is used by many teachers, as it makes possible the breaking up of the class into smaller groups. Each group consists of from five to ten members and, because fewer personalities are involved, some of the more reserved members of the class may be more willing to participate; furthermore, because the teacher is not directly involved in every committee, there may be more willingness to respond. Learning through committee procedures can be used in many different phases of the basic-business subjects. For example, committees might be organized to try to solve the insurance problems of a given family; or they might be asked to suggest how the budget of a given income unit (usually a family) can be improved. Committees might be formed to solve to some degree the travel interests of an individual or a family and suggest a detailed itinerary. In a class in business law, a legal problem might be thought through by a small committee.

In a class in merchandising, the students might decide on the best technique for getting customer good will in selling a particular commodity. The possibilities for committee work are innumerable in the basic-business subjects.

Committee work is desirable because it brings about more student participation. It helps to develop a sharing of ideas and experiences and enables a group to cover a larger area of interests than would be possible for one person. Possibly more important, such procedures help bring about closer relationships among the members of the committee, by giving students some training in working together and stimulating co-operation. Consequently, interest should increase. In attaining this objective, the committee organization should allow groups of students to work on their special interests; and in this way, more work may be accomplished. Certainly it is a more democratic procedure than formal classwork. It should help students to clarify their thinking and to get real ideas from each other. It may even encourage the less energetic students to participate to some degree.

On the other hand, there is no question that committee work has its limitations. Some students use it as a way of getting out of work. Many students complain that it is too time consuming, in that it requires much preplanning. Some students argue too much among themselves, and digressions are often not controlled. Some students with poor backgrounds or limited interests do not co-operate, participate, or contribute as much as they should. Moreover, when the teacher is away, one or two individuals are likely to monopolize the meetings. It is true also that in many of our classrooms the seats that are bolted down prevent good committee activity.

These limitations can partly be overcome by the teacher, who should give considerable guidance particularly on the high school level. The teacher must encourage the election of an effective group leader to the extent possible, although even here more may sometimes be learned through an ineffective group chairman than through an effective one. Then of course there is the perennial problem of how to present the results of the group to the entire class. Should this carry-over be attained by written report or by oral report? Should the group report to the entire class? Usually the answer is

"Yes." Used with common sense, the committee techniques of learning can make a very considerable contribution.

2. Student Discussion Leaders. Discussion, particularly through the use of student discussion leaders, is another technique for improving the group relations of a class. In order to do their work correctly, such student leaders require some training. They need to be made aware of the fact that individuals who disagree need to be given some recognition. On the other hand, they need to be taught how to minimize differences of opinion that are nominal rather than real. They need to learn how to soothe the irritated person, but at the same time not to gloss over differences merely for the sake of an apparent agreement. Some writers on the improvement-of-discussion techniques suggest that consensus be aimed for rather than division among minority and majority group concepts.

The opportunities for the use of discussions with or without student leaders either for the entire class or for larger committees are endless in basic-business classes. Discussion of the meaning of every significant fact or important point of view is in order. Group discussion under the direction of students gives these students training in leadership. It often results in greater participation; moreover, shy people are sometimes encouraged to share their information with others when the presentation gets away from teacher presentation, or worse yet, teacher lecturing. Students are compelled to cope with other people's opinions and ideas. Even though students may be irritated by the misunderstanding or exaggeration of their points of view by other people, they nevertheless have become conscious of what happens to individual ideas when they are taken over by another person. This procedure can develop a sense of belonging to the group. It may develop initiative and self-confidence.

On the other hand, if the leader lacks skill and knowledge of what he is working for, the procedure can well be futile. It will be harmful, if the leader permits students to digress from the topic. Many times the class is bored by the leadership of a student. Students unfortunately will pay attention to the teacher, merely because he is the teacher, and almost as deliberately ignore the presentation and discussion carried on by a group leader, merely because he is one of them. In every class there are some students who do not want, or are not capable, to act as leaders. The procedure may make them stand out.

Yet the use of discussion through discussion leaders is so basic that some use should be made of the technique in every class, even though it may slow up classwork. It is a democratic process so frequently used in business that all students should have some experience with it.

3. Role Playing. Role playing has not been used much in business classes except in merchandising and selling. There is much value in having students act out the roles of people in business, so as to see the other fellow's point of view and the other person's ways of presenting things. Thus the observer can see his own shortcomings. Of course role playing can be used in many other situations; for example, it can be used in connection with many of the topics of basic business, such as banking and buying. The procedure is especially good in dealing with management problems either on the personal-use level or on the job level because these problems emphasize human relationships. In fact, any topic that involves better human relationships and opportunities for understanding lends itself particularly well to study through the use of the role-playing technique.

The technique is particularly useful because it can arouse interest and create a lifelike situation. Because of the increased student participation, there is more of a feeling of group unity. Of course the process gives particular opportunity for creative interests.

On the other hand, the technique of role playing can easily be overused and therefore become boring. Some students do not want to participate, and other students overplay their parts and make a comedy of something that should be serious. If the procedure of role playing is inadequately planned, much time can be wasted; and if the students do not act out their parts reasonably well, the whole process becomes something of a joke.

As in most other human-dynamics procedures, instead of taking less planning and less time, role playing probably requires more time not only on the part of the students but on the part of the teacher himself. Sometimes the students should be given a complete script of what they are going to do. Other times they should be given just a problem situation and asked to act it through in terms of what the other person says. There is opportunity also for reversing the roles; that is, to let one person act the vendor in one case and then later, the buyer. Naturally there must be opportunity to discuss the procedures used in order to determine whether the conduct and attitude of the various actors were correct in accomplishing the result hoped for. In other words, the most important result will come not from the acting or watching but from the discussion that results after a role-playing experience activity. Here is an example of a little skit that might be used in presenting the problems of buying and selling.

Instruction to Customer (a girl; if the customer is a boy, the cousin should be a girl—Cousin Mary)

You are going to spend a week end with your Aunt Jane, Uncle Tom, and Cousin Arthur. Mother has given you $3 to buy a little gift to give to the family as a whole, or if this is not possible, to Aunt Jane. Unfortunately you have neglected to make this purchase until just before you are ready to leave. The bus leaves in 20 minutes; and there is a clothing store near the bus station, the only place apparently where you can buy something. You look in the store window and see an attractive tablecloth for $2.98 that you think would serve the purpose that your mother suggested. When you go into the store, however, you find a very attractive sweater, which would be very nice for Uncle Tom, that sells for $3.50. You will be glad to spend the extra 50 cents from your own money if you think the sweater is a good buy and if you think you can "get away" with giving a gift to Uncle Tom instead of to the family.

Instructions to Salesman B

When your customer comes in, she asks you for a chance to look at the tablecloth and also at the sweater. You give her brief advice as to the quality of each and naturally try to sell her the sweater, because there is an opportunity for a little more profit. She then tells you her dilemma.

The students involved can be permitted to carry on the scene from there. How strongly should the salesperson still advise her to buy the sweater rather than the tablecloth? Should the customer give consideration to the tablecloth? Will the family appreciate a tablecloth in any case, or wouldn't the customer make a better impression with her relatives by giving one slightly nicer gift to one member of the family? The teacher may, as an alternate, work out the skit in detail himself or have a class committee fill out the details.

After the students have completed their skit, the class has an opportunity to participate either in evaluating the salesperson's merchandising technique or the dilemma of the customer in deciding to pay 50 cents more out of her precious allowance to be nice to her favorite cousin or following her mother's advice.

Numerous experiences of this type can be created. They involve careful thinking on the part of the teacher and reasonably good participation on the part of the students. Role playing gives opportunity for the thoughtful evaluation of human activity. The process focuses the group attention on a particular situation and thereby not only prevents discussion from going too far astray but, by giving a practical setting, also gives the discussion a sense of reality.

4. Student-Teacher Planning. This procedure has been used for a long time in elementary schools. It gives students an opportunity for self-determination and an insight into the problems faced by the teacher. Properly developed, this method creates better motivation and interest, because the learners have become more active participants. The procedure gives the students a feeling of belonging and therefore should develop a sense of responsibility.

On the other hand, students often plan too much for the time that is available for a unit of learning; and as any teacher will recognize, this method can easily result in a waste of time. Students often do not know their own needs, and it is difficult to reconcile the diversified interests. Nevertheless the procedure has real value and can contribute to better esprit among the students.

5. Evaluation and Student Observers. Two other procedures are often used in human-relations learning processes that should be at least considered by the basic-business teacher. Evaluation by a so-called independent observer is a useful practice at times. For example, if there is a good discussion or a good debate, one student who has some insight into human points of view could be asked to sit aside from the rest of the class to evaluate the effectiveness of the discussion. Did everybody participate? Did some person take over most of the discussion? Was there unnecessary conflict? Were the elements thought through properly? Was significant learning accomplished?

Evaluation can be either as suggested in the preceding paragraph through student observers or by the class as a whole. For example, a check list may be used to ask: Did I learn what I should have? Did I participate as much as I should have? Did one person take over too much of the discussion?

6. *General Comments on Group-Dynamics Procedures.* Learning procedures such as those described above have limited use in skill-building subjects. They can even be overdone in the basic-business subjects. However, a teacher who ignores them completely is failing to give his students the kind of learning experiences that they deserve and need in a class in basic education.

There is nothing radically new about these procedures. Good teachers have always used them to some degree; however, the emphasis upon these techniques is characteristic of the teacher who knows what is going on in the world; who is aware that we have learned something about group dynamics. The alert teacher who is interested in giving his students opportunities in line with the newer procedures for thinking, therefore, will recognize the value of group-dynamics procedures and use them as extensively as he finds them fruitful.

These procedures slow down learning. On the other hand, properly utilized, the learnings will be more effective because there will be an emotional concomitant that will go along with the learnings. We learn when we are interested. We learn when things are important to us. Group-dynamics procedures can make learning more important to students and, in so doing, learning can be made more fundamental and less superficial. This superficiality has been a basic weakness of the basic-business subjects, and group-dynamics technique can help considerably to overcome this serious limitation of learning attainment in the area of basic-business education.

QUESTIONS

1. Compare the objectives and motivation in the skill and basic-business subjects.

2. Compare the nature of the subject-matter content in the skill- and basic-business subjects.

3. How do the teaching techniques in the skill subjects differ from those used in the basic-business subjects?

4. How does evaluation in the skill subjects differ from testing in the basic-business subjects?

5. Compare teacher attitudes and preparation for teaching the skill subjects with those for the basic-business subjects.

6. What are the advantages and disadvantages of the lecture method?

7. What are the limitations of basic-business textbooks?

8. How would you use discussion and conversation methods in teaching basic-business subjects?

9. What situations in the teaching of basic-business subjects can be taught by demonstration?

10. What three debate topics could be used to good advantage in a basic-business subject?

11. What field trips could you take with a business-law class?

12. How would you use student committees in teaching economic geography?

13. What topics in consumer education could be directed by student discussion leaders?

STUDENT ACTIVITIES

1. Select either the affirmative or negative of the following topic and list your arguments. Resolved that: "The Basic-Business Subjects Are More Difficult to Teach Than the Skill Subjects."

2. You overheard a basic-business teacher discussing the satisfactions of teaching his subjects rather than the specialized skill subjects. List some of the points he might have made.

3. Compile a list of the various business subjects taught in high schools under two headings:

> *a.* Specialized Skill Subjects
> *b.* Basic-Business Subjects

4. Evaluate your own preparation for teaching the business skill subjects compared to your preparation for teaching in the area of basic-business education.

5. Compare in the latest *Business Education Index* the number of references shown for shorthand, typewriting, bookkeeping, and basic business.

6. Prepare a lesson plan to teach any topic in business law using the lecture, textbook, and question-and-answer methods.

7. Prepare a flannel board for a unit on a basic-business subject. Determine how the presentation will be used in a class project. How long will the material remain on the board? What will be done with the specimens? What presentation will follow the one you worked out?

For help in carrying out this activity, see S. W. Dry, "Felt Board for Typewriting," *Journal of Business,* XXXI (May, 1956), pp. 346–347.

8. Plan a unit in any basic-business subject utilizing several techniques in group dynamics.

9. Prepare a brief script to be used in role playing in a consumer-education unit.

10. Select any unit in a basic-business course. Prepare a list of suggested student activities under the headings:

Reading	Listening
Writing	Thinking
Speaking	Collecting
Seeing	Investigating

BIBLIOGRAPHY

Bahr, Gladys and Others. "Improving Learning and Achievement in Basic-Business Subjects," *American Business Education Yearbook,* II, 1945, pp. 308–333.

———. "An Illustration in Role Playing—Social Security." *UBEA Forum,* IX (May, 1955), p. 32.

———. "Suggested Classroom Teaching Methods and Techniques in Basic-Business Education," *Improved Methods of Teaching Business.* Cincinnati, South-Western Publishing Company, 1945, pp. 76–82.

"Basic Economic Concepts about the American Business System Which Business Executives Believe Everyone Should Know," *National Business Education Quarterly,* XXIV (October, 1955), p. 71.

"Bibliography of Free and Inexpensive Materials for Economic Education" New York, Joint Council on Economic Education, 1955.

Consumer Education Study, *Consumer Education in Your School.* Washington, D.C., National Association of Secondary School Principals, 1947, especially pp. 83–107.

Harms, Harm. "Twenty Suggestions for Improving Teaching in General-Business Education," *Balance Sheet,* XXIX (May, 1948), pp. 394–397.

Lloyd, Alan C. "Classroom Organization for Teaching Elementary Business Training," *Business Education World,* XXVIII (November, 1947), pp. 170–173.

———. "Projects in General Business," *Business Education World,* XXXV (September, 1954), pp. 23–24; (October, 1954), pp. 30–31.

————. "Student Projects in General Business," *Business Education World,* XXXIV (April, 1954), pp. 17–18; (June, 1954), pp. 35–36.

————. "General Business: Student Projects That Will Intensify Learnings," *Business Education World,* XXXIV (March, 1954), pp. 17–18.

Maxwell, Gerald W. "Try Taking a Field Trip," *Business Education World,* XXXIV (March, 1954), pp. 21–22.

Mulkerne, Donald J. "Take Them Outdoors for Economic Geography." *Business Education World,* XXXV (June, 1955), pp. 14, 33.

Musselman, Vernon A. "Try Using News to Start Units," *Business Education World,* XXXV (December, 1954), pp. 14–16.

Price, Ray G. "Try Using a Flannel Board," *Business Education World,* XXXIV (March, 1954), pp. 19–21.

Rosenblum, Irving, "Try Using an Arithmetic Bee," *Business Education World,* XXXIV (March, 1954), pp. 19–21.

Salsgiver, Paul L. "Methodology in Teaching General Business," *UBEA Forum,* II (March, 1948), pp. 31–32.

Simon, Sidney I. "The Daily Newspaper—A Living Economics Textbook," *Journal of Business Education,* XXIII (January, 1948), pp. 25–26.

Travis, Dorothy L. "Basic-Business Teaching Aids," *American Business Education Yearbook,* V, 1948, pp. 277–286.

Walker, George Thomas. "Suggestions for the Teaching of General Business," *Journal of Business Education,* XIX (October, 1943), pp. 11–12.

Zelliot, Ernest A. "Practices in Junior-Business Training," *Journal of Business Education,* XXI (December, 1945), pp. 17–18.

CHAPTER XVII

Making Basic-Business Subjects More Meaningful

BEGINNING TEACHERS are often assigned to teach the basic-business courses. Unless they have been properly prepared to teach these courses, they may have more problems with them than with the teaching of vocational-skill subjects. This is unfortunate because, if properly taught, these subjects can be fascinating to both the teacher and the students. The purpose of this chapter is to help the business teacher, inexperienced or experienced, to do a superior job in teaching these important subjects.

FIRST DAYS

How do you capture and hold student interest in the basic-business class? You do not have the natural motivation that is inherent in the promise of job opportunities and financial success in the vocational subjects. So, what do you have to offer your high school students that can compete for their interest with such attractions as the radio, television, bop, the opposite sex, and money? Why not utilize the experiences of your students as the basis for all teaching activities in the basic-business class? Every topic you present can and should be related to student interest and needs.

The very first day, for example, why start with an abstract lecture or an aimless discussion on "What Is Business?" Better get off to a good start with a pep talk selling yourself and the course. Just give them a quick preview of the many practical things to be included

369

in the course, and you will need to be less concerned about student interest and motivation. They want to know how to get along in this world of business.

Emphasize that the best way to prepare for business is to conduct this class as a business enterprise. The class must start and end promptly. Supplies must be obtained before the class begins. Desks must be cleared for action. The first job to be tackled every day will be waiting for them on a designated chalk board. They are to start work independently as soon as the starting signal (the inevitable bell) is given. They are to work independently as they would in business except under unusual conditions. The work must be done rapidly, neatly, and accurately. Outstanding work will be rewarded, while poor work will be rejected. Experienced teachers know that most students will do the kind of work they can get away with. If you let students sit around for five or ten minutes while you take the roll and get organized, they will naturally loaf, gossip, and cause you trouble. If they know that you expect them to be self-starters, they will turn on the ignition and start working.

You have now set the business stage, and the class is a going concern. What is the next motivating device? In the class in introduction to business, for example, write on the board, "Have you had any business experience?" Just watch the hands go up. As each volunteer narrates his experience, list the different kinds and the frequency of activities. This list should be summarized and recorded for comparison with a similar listing to be prepared every month to indicate student progress.

By this time the first period is almost over. How about the assignment for tomorrow? "Read pages 1 to 20. Be prepared to answer the questions on pages 21 to 23." Such an assignment is bound to kill off much of the enthusiasm you worked so hard to kindle. Try instead to extend the personal interest approach, so that it also permeates all homework activities. Write the following assignment on the chalk board.

Assignment for Tuesday
September 17, 195–

1. "My Business Activities." Describe briefly all your business experiences. If you do not remember all of them, ask your family to help you.

You might even prepare an additional list, "My Family's Business Activities."

2. "What I Know about Business." List as many items as you can remember. For example, "I Know That I Should Count My Change."

Do your best work. Use ink. Write neatly and carefully. This is a business project.

The second day you can organize your class by seating students alphabetically or according to some definite plan. Be sure to explain the business reasons for this arrangement. Business does not waste time and energy when the same goal can be accomplished automatically. Make exceptions for students who cannot see or hear well. After the class has been seated according to your plan, you will be ready to review yesterday's work. Call for volunteers to tell the class what they learned the previous day. If you use this technique every day, the better students will make a conscious effort to recall the work completed yesterday. This review should be followed with reports on the homework assignment. List on the board the points reported in connection with "What I Know about Business." You can then summarize this material and use it for comparative purposes at the end of the course. It also serves as an excellent basis for student notes.

Your next step to motivate interest is to give the students inventory tests in arithmetic and penmanship. You first explain to them that computation and handwriting are fundamental skills used constantly in business. You are anxious to help them improve these fundamental skills, hence you want them to determine their own ability at this time. The results are to be used for comparative purposes later. Students who are poor in the fundamentals should receive special remedial instruction and practice.

The skill tests are followed by a unit on self-analysis. Again you motivate the students by impressing them with the importance of human relations in all school, home, business, and community situations. Since they are anxious to be successful and popular, you won't have to worry about keeping their interest and attention.

Motivation is easy in basic business if you base all your lessons on student experiences, interests, and needs. If you merely teach so many textbook pages a day, your basic-business class will be a daily nightmare for you as well as your students. The same general procedure should be used in introducing other basic-business courses.

ADDITIONAL TEACHING TECHNIQUES

In addition to motivation, what are some of the techniques used by successful basic-business teachers? Every lesson should be planned, so that it is related to present student interests and needs. The lesson must appeal to them because they know something about the topic. Once you have captured their interest, you can extend the scope of their present needs and interests. When your students start learning about banking, do not ask, "What essential functions are performed by banks?" This is an academic question to a high school student. You can challenge his interest, however, by asking, "What would happen to you if all banks in our town closed?" He is now interested because he has a savings account or a Christmas Club account. He begins to see and understand his relationship to the banker in his community. Now that you have captured his interest, you can teach him something about his future banking needs, such as storage vaults and mortgages. Every topic can and must be tied in with student interests and needs, both present and prospective. Your students will not be bored or create discipline problems if you teach things important to *them*.

Every word you utter in a basic-business class must be understood by all your students. If you use an unusual or technical term, get into the habit of asking, "Who knows what the word 'tact' means?" Many teachers make the mistake of assuming that students understand what the teacher is saying because they remain quiet and do not ask questions. To convince yourself on this point, just ask a ninth- or tenth-grade class to explain the meaning of "tact," for example. It may be an eye opener for you. In teaching basic-business subjects, it is very easy to talk over the heads of many students. If you want to put your work across, conduct the learning in terms your class will understand. Only by patient and constant explanation of common business terms and expressions will you ever succeed in extending the business vocabulary of your students.

Stating questions in language every student understands is a big step forward in helping the student to find the correct answer. For example, a student may have difficulty in visualizing what you mean when you say, "Name the various types of banking institutions that exist in the United States." Now say, "What are the names of the banks in our town?" As you list the names on the board, underline the words "trust," "national," or "savings." The student now understands your question and has learned something about his local banks. You must always proceed from the known to the unknown. Otherwise your students may not understand what you are driving at.

There are so many techniques that are well adapted for use in basic business that the alert teacher can vary his routine from day to day. A combination lecture-discussion on one day can be followed by student reports on the next day. A quiz program on the third day can be followed by a lecture-demonstration or an audio-visual aid. A problem or project report by individuals or committees can precede a student debate, a play, a panel discussion, or an open forum. Once in a while you can bring in a local businessman as a visiting speaker or take a trip to a neighboring firm. And don't forget the possibility of using radio broadcasts, recordings, and illustrated lectures. After you have covered this cycle, you need not hesitate to start all over again. You and your students will enjoy the second round even more than the first. Learning and teaching basic business can be pleasant and effective if the teacher utilizes the many procedures available in this area.

All the teaching units in this field grow so naturally out of daily life experience that the best way to teach and learn them is through real life experiences. Learning by doing is a "natural" in this area.

A teacher with a little imagination and initiative can stimulate an energetic group of students to engage in an endless number of purposeful, interesting, and valuable educational activities. Student business activities well planned, organized, and directed add up to fun and profit for students and teacher.

SAMPLE TEACHING UNIT—CONSUMER CREDIT

The best way to illustrate the methods to be used in this area is to present plans for teaching units [1] that have been developed in this field.

---

[1] Gladys Bahr, "Attaining Objectives Through Pupil Activity in Basic-Business Education," *American Business Education Yearbook*, III, 1946, pp. 259–271.

A Plan for Teaching a Unit on Consumer Credit

General Objectives

1. To realize that consumer credit is a tool that can be used to one's advantage or disadvantage
2. To understand the growth of consumer credit and its importance in the business world
3. To learn all the facts in connection with consumer credit
4. To develop the skills of reading, writing, speaking, listening, thinking, collecting, and investigating

Specific Objectives

1. To decide when to use cash and when to use credit
2. To be able to open and use a charge account wisely
3. To know the specifications of installment buying, especially the interest cost
4. To consider whether or not borrowing money is necessary, its cost, its repayment, and its dangers
5. To be informed about the various cash-lending agencies with the particular characteristics of each
6. To determine which lending concern should best suit the needs of each consumer

Suggested Student Activities

READING

1. Read one or more of the textbook references listed in the suggested reading list in order to give you an overview of the subject.
2. Read several of the pamphlets listed as suggested reading.
3. Read reprints on consumer credit obtained from Credit Union National Association and Federal Deposit Insurance Corporation.
4. Obtain for each student a copy of the Public Affairs pamphlet, *Credit for Consumers,* by LeBaron R. Foster (Household Finance Company, Chicago, will supply reasonable quantities free). Read as a class exercise for main ideas, relating information, and summarizing thoughts.
5. Read consumer-credit advertisements in the local newspapers for installment terms of stores and for rates given by banks and small-loan companies.

6. Define terms: sales, finance companies, dollar cost, interest cost, conditional sales contract, chattel mortgage, industrial banks, small-loan companies, credit unions, unlicensed lenders, wage assignments.

7. Bring to class references on consumer credit from the school or local library. Be sure to have a complete record that may be used by the teacher, another student, at the present time or in the future. While at the library, use the *Reader's Guide to Periodical Literature.*

WRITING

1. Outline a reading reference selected from the supplementary reading list.

2. Write a review of one of the short stories told in Miss Kent's pamphlet. (See reading list.)

3. Write a letter to the Credit Union National Association, Madison, Wisconsin, for free material about the work of its organization.

4. Write to the Federal Deposit Insurance Corporation, Washington, D. C., for information about Federal credit unions.

5. Write on the topic: "Getting Married on Credit."

6. Draw a map of the United States and write in each state the usury rate, small-loan company rates. Also indicate if the state has laws governing industrial and commercial banks.

7. Write definitions of consumer-credit terms on the chalk board.

8. Show graphically the amount of money loaned by each of the money-lending agencies for a recent year.

9. Write a personal evaluation of the subject of consumer credit.

10. Draw an organization chart for a credit union that may be formed among the members of the class.

11. Write essays on: "What I Should Do If Bad Luck Prevents Me from Meeting My Credit Obligation," or "Some People Should Not Use Credit."

12. Prepare a chart to show what percentage of certain articles is bought on the installment plan.

13. Pictorialize the three C's of credit.

14. Draw a cartoon of the illegal lender.

SPEAKING

1. Prepare a debate on "Resolved, that the several states should enact legislation to regulate the business of installment selling and financing."

2. Talk to your parents about their cash and credit policies.

3. Visit a local pawnbroker, if you have a flare for adventure, and

make believe that you wish to dispose of a personal article. Report your findings to the class.

4. Dramatize this story: Joe needs to borrow money because the hospital bill must be paid before his wife may come home. His father who has dealt with illegal lenders, his pal at the factory who patronizes the credit union, and another friend who favors the local banks, give him advice.

5. Give oral reports on these topics: "My Visit to an Industrial Bank"; "Installment Costs at a Local Department Store"; "Churches and Credit Unions"; "Credit Unions at a Local Factory."

6. Present a panel on: "Pros and Cons of Installment Buying," "Use and Abuse of Consumer Credit."

7. Conduct a meeting of the board of directors of a credit union that will include reports of the credit committee, a supervisory committee, and of the secretary-treasurer of the credit union.

SEEING

1. Prepare a large picture graph for classroom use based on these facts: Of all sales, one third are credit. Of the credit sales, one third are installment and two thirds are charge accounts.

2. Arrange the bulletin board for a consumer credit display:
    Advertisements
    Clippings from newspapers and magazines
    Credit instruments
    Cartoons
    Bibliography

3. See the film *Men and Money,* easily obtained from the Household Finance Corporation, Chicago, Illinois.

4. Analyze illustrations, graphs, charts, and maps in textbooks and pamphlets.

5. Prepare a blackboard analysis on figuring costs of installment buying. Indicate arithmetical steps.

LISTENING

1. Take notes on a student's oral report. Hand in outline to the teacher.

2. Outline a ten-minute lecture given by your teacher on "Installment Credit and National Prosperity." Submit outline for suggestions and criticisms.

3. Listen to the credit manager of a local department store who may be invited to speak to your class.

4. Listen to the following recordings (Recordings Division of the New York University Film Library):

Credit Unions—The People's Bank

When You Buy on Installments

When You Borrow Money

5. Listen to one of the teachers of the high school who belongs to a teacher's credit union.

THINKING

1. Think about these questions:

Is obtaining this loan a sensible thing to do?

Am I making realistic plans for paying it off?

Am I getting it at a reasonable financial cost?

Am I steering clear of potential dangers?

2. Determine if the material written by various small-loan agencies is unbiased.

3. Recall some words and phrases that indicate propaganda for that particular concern.

4. Remember your personal blind spots about consumer credit. How did you acquire these? What are you doing to correct them?

5. Are your thoughts about consumer credit different now that you have studied this unit?

COLLECTING

1. Collect advertisements on money-lending agencies.

2. Accumulate cartoons on consumer credit.

3. Ask for credit instruments from business institutions in the community.

4. Arrange all material collected in a notebook with other activities in reading, writing, thinking, and so forth.

5. Collect statements of account, sales slip, and so forth, to show consumer's record of open-account credit.

6. Catalogue material for future reference.

INVESTIGATING

1. Compare the installment plans of various types of stores in the community; such as, department, furniture, and household appliances.

2. Talk to a local sales-finance-company manager on how to buy an automobile on time.

3. What is the interest cost when you buy a refrigerator at the local public utility?

4. Inquire about qualifications for opening a charge account in a store that is a member of the National Credit-Rating Bureau and compare these with the requirements of the corner grocery store.

5. Investigate: budget plan, thrift plan, easy-payment plan.

6. Investigate the small-loan laws in your state.

7. Find out if minors can obtain credit.

8. Find out what banks in your community have consumer departments. Obtain detailed information about their services.

9. Find out what your relatives and friends think and know about consumer credit.

Many of these activities will be combined to develop skill in reading, writing, speaking, seeing, listening, thinking, collecting, and investigating, for one often cannot be done without the other. For instance, to prepare a debate, the participating students must read, take notes, write their speeches, deliver them, draw charts to emphasize certain statistics, collect opinions, and do a great deal of thinking during the entire time of preparation and delivery. The class must listen, take notes, write or give an oral evaluation.

These student activities can be for one student, a small committee, or for the entire class.

A Plan for Teaching a Unit on Selling [2]

Selling is usually presented as a phase of several of the basic-business subjects. Here is an example of how one teacher would plan a prevocational unit on selling that emphasizes the opportunities in selling and the need for co-operation between consumer and vendor.

Purpose

From early childhood to the end of our lives we are constantly selling services. If we are not engaged in selling either goods or services, we are always busy selling ourselves or our ideas to our friends, teachers, employers, relatives, and associates. When we are not selling, we are being sold. Since selling is such an important activity in this country, all high school students should be taught the fundamental principles of selling. Can you think of any basic-business unit that can contribute more personal-use values than the unit on selling?

[2] Adapted from "A Q-SAGO Unit on Selling" by M. Herbert Freeman. *Business Education World*, XXVIII (April, 1948), pp. 484–487.

Introduction

If the teacher is "sold" on the importance of this unit, it will be easy to sell the class. Start the sales ball rolling by writing on the chalk board a few challenging questions.

You will have no difficulty in starting a lively discussion with these simple icebreakers! Every youngster in the class will have something to contribute to the verbal free-for-all. The discussion should point up the fact that selling is an important activity. The girl who persuaded her father to buy her a new coat was a good saleslady. The boy who induced his mother to let him go to the movies was a salesman. The student who obtained the leading part in the play made a sale. After convincing your class that selling plays an important part in the world of today, you have motivated them to learn the principles of selling.

Questions

The questions in the unit are designed to show the personal-use values of selling. They proceed from the known to the unknown. The first answers come so readily that the student is encouraged to continue. He begins to see that there is a strong relationship between selling and buying. He learns that the consumer has a vital interest in selling cost. He realizes that the inefficient and dishonest salesman is a social liability.

1. What is selling?
2. Are you a salesman?
3. What would happen if all merchants were to stop selling goods for a while?
4. How will a knowledge of selling help you in buying essentials?
5. Is selling a good occupation?
6. Can you talk well?
7. Would you like to earn your living as a salesman?

The questions help to correct a popular misconception that salesmen are nuisances. The student discovers for himself what would happen to his family if selling services were discontinued. For the first time, perhaps, he learns to distinguish good and bad selling.

The selling unit can also contribute to the vocational guidance of some students. Studying the status of selling as an occupation should help to correct the chain-store salesclerk notion that selling is a last-resort job.

Analyzing the personal skills and traits needed for success in selling may be the first experience for the student in self-analysis and study. It may lead, under competent teaching, to the development of desirable personality traits and characteristics.

Student Activities

The selling activities are designed to be varied, self-teaching projects. The major emphasis is on personal relationships. The students are sent out into the community to interview businessmen, shop the stores, invite speakers. Within the class they are drawn into close contacts with other students, through contests, forums and panel discussions, dramatizations and skits, debates, reports, and sales talks. Students learn how to work with people.

ACTIVITIES

1. *Poster.* Ads of services or articles advertised for sale.
   Report. Percentage of firms in your community engaged in selling and different sales methods.
2. *Visit.* Shop several stores to observe examples of selling.
   Essay. Who pays selling costs?
3. *Contest.* Specific illustrations of how selling has improved our standard of living.
   Dramatization. What happened to my family when selling became illegal.
   Forum. Consumers and selling costs.
4. *Notebook.* Select five articles purchased recently. Analyze the reason for the purchase of each item.
   Exercise. Write a sales talk for the school paper.
   Skit. How I fell for high-pressure salesmanship.
5. *Chart.* Types of selling positions.
   Poster. Number of salesmen employed in different sales jobs in our community.
   Panel. Successful selling has made America what it is today.
   Report. Compensation for selling.
6. *Report.* My speech.
   Notebook. My penmanship.
   Contest. Vocabulary quiz. Spelling bee. Oral arithmetic.
   Dramatization. Miss Careless Salesclerk and Miss Efficient Salesperson.
   Report. Steps in making a sale.

7. *Talk.* Why I want or do not want to be a salesman.
Poster. Personal traits of a successful salesman.
Poster. Good grooming.

To get along well with other people, the student must learn to analyze himself. Many students of business-training age are careless of their personal appearance. Here is the opportunity to get in some advice. Do your students need some guidance on make-up? Here is the chance. You may help to straighten out some otherwise fine youngster with improper make-up who is merely trying to copy an older sister or neighbor.

After you have had your say about personal appearance, be sure to analyze clothes. Give the class some tips on what to wear and how to wear it. When students turn in their analysis reports, don't grade and file them. Use them as the basis for class discussion. Dramatize the facts. Drive home the importance of constant self-analysis and improvement.

Today your students are reporting on "My Speech." Ask them whether they speak clearly and enunciate carefully. Do they shout and scream or speak in a whisper? Do they use slang and colloquial expressions constantly? If you improve the speech of only one student, you will have earned your salary for the day.

The dramatizations can be very fascinating teaching vehicles if you plan them carefully. Select a play-writing committee. Ask a student with writing talent to be the chairman. Give the committee a detailed plot. Outline clearly the situations you want them to create. Then tell them to utilize their knowledge of radio, movies, and television and let their imaginations run riot. Edit the tentative script to tone down the language. Rehearse the play with props. Then on with the show! Invite the head of your department and the principal to watch the Business Players present an all-star performance. The class will like the theatrical atmosphere, and you can put across almost anything when you have aroused the proper kind of interest and attention. Let them coax you into playing a minor role once in a while. It is a great morale builder when students can laugh at or applaud a teacher. Discipline problems will vanish into the wings.

In the play depicting the effects of outlawing sales, you have an opportunity to dramatize the services rendered by selling organizations. Start your performance with a scene depicting a normal, well-to-do home. The table should be set with tempting foods. The room should look very comfortable. Next present a dismal scene of cold, hunger, and want. Do not hesitate to put it on thick. (Exaggeration is the only way to get some messages across.) In the closing scene let your story return to show what can be accomplished if intelligent consumers co-operate with honest and social-minded sellers. Ring down the curtain on a happy ending. The other dramatizations called for in this unit can be produced just as effectively. Try a dramatization once, and you will be a confirmed producer ever after.

EVALUATION

It is relatively easy to test memorized information, knowledge, or skills. But how do you evaluate the acquisition of appreciations, understanding, and attitudes? Most of the standardized tests available are based on specific textbook content and are useful primarily in testing a student's ability to retain certain memorized information. They are not well adapted to a course based on student needs and interests, because the teacher may have devoted little time or attention to the textbook content. The basic-business teacher must develop much of his own testing materials.

Instead of infrequent and long formal tests, try giving short, important points covered in yesterday's work rather than a full-period examination on what is in the textbook.

Occasionally ask the students to prepare test questions and answers. Let the class select the best entries to be included in the examination. Try an open-book test once in a while. They are great fun for the teacher but not for the students.

After each unit has been completed, the students should be given an opportunity to show off what they have learned (a test). This event should be announced several days in advance. The teacher should go over the questions in a general way before the event takes place. The test should be based entirely on the material covered in class. A test is supposed to be a *teaching* and not a *punishing* device. Indicate the number of points to be allowed for each question. After the test has been marked, go over the entire examination carefully. The following unit test is offered as an illustration of the type of examination which can be used:

YOUR OPPORTUNITY TO SHOW WHAT YOU LEARNED IN UNIT II, BANKING ACTIVITIES

1. What would happen if all banks in our town closed? List all the results you can think of.   (10 points.)

2. You are interested in opening a bank account in our town or a neighboring community. Give the names of at least five different kinds of banks that are at your service. (10 points.)

3. You have decided to start a savings account. List all the points you should know about opening and keeping a savings account.
(10 points.)

4. Your father is thinking about opening a personal checking account. List the reasons you would give your father to convince him to do this.
(10 points.)

5. Your father opened a checking account. He is now ready to write checks. List the directions you would give him to follow in writing checks and keeping his checkbook. (10 points.)

6. Have you ever gone to the bank for some other reason than to open an account, to make a deposit, or to withdraw money? List as many reasons as you can for going to the bank. (10 points.)

7. Explain the meaning of the following terms
    a. To endorse a check
    b. The payee of a check
    c. F.D.I.C.
    d. An overdrawn checking account
    e. A postdated check (10 points.)

8. You have made the following deposit.

37 pennies	3 two-dollar bills
26 nickels	6 five-dollar bills
18 dimes	3 ten-dollar bills
19 quarters	1 twenty-dollar bill
6 half dollars	1 check for $25.68
9 one-dollar bills	1 check for $12.97
	1 check for $8.52

Work the following problems:
    a. Show the total amount of each denomination. (5 points.)
    b. Total the amount of specie. (5 points.)
    c. Total the amount of currency. (5 points.)
    d. Total the deposit. (5 points.)

9. Your father asks you to make a bank reconciliation from the following information:
    June 1—Bank balance and checkbook balance, $250.95.
    During June he wrote these checks: #51, $6; #52, $10; #53, $3.25; #54, $45; #55, $23.50; #56, $1.15; #57, $2.75; #58, $8.17; #59, $3.12; #60, $6.45; #61, $1.76.
On July 1 his bank statement showed a balance of $152.12 and

included these canceled checks: $6, $10, $3.25, $45, $23.50, $1.15, $8.17, $1.76. (10 points.)

The difficult element in evaluation is to test whether the learning has attained the goal set for it. The goal of basic-business learnings is to develop competencies in solving business problems in daily life. If the student was able to solve such problems adequately before he took the course, the course was futile. If the student is unable to solve business problems that come his way, then the course was futile even if he can get a perfect score on a true-false test of isolated facts. Note that the evaluative material presented above emphasizes problem solving. True, these problems require the use of facts; but the facts are to be presented in terms of actual situations.

When you have prepared the report-card grades, but before you record them, ask the students to evaluate themselves. If you have done an effective teaching job, most of your students will evaluate themselves quite accurately. At any rate it is interesting to see how your standards compare with student standards. If you have given a student a lower grade than he expected, you may want to reconcile his evaluation and yours. At least you know that he is disappointed, and you can do something about motivating him to work up to the grade he thinks he deserves. At the end of the year you should give the students an opportunity to evaluate the course. Ask them to jot down on a piece of paper what they liked about the course as well as any features they disliked. Also ask them to make suggestions for improving the course. If you have taught them effectively, you should not be afraid to ask for student evaluation. Your students know more about your teaching efficiency than anybody else—why not ask them?

SUMMARY

Here, in brief, are the basic principles to be followed in achieving more worth-while instruction in basic-business education.

1. The teacher plans all teaching around an important and fairly large unit of learning, such as insurance, buying, or banking.

2. In each basic learning unit, a few central ideas are to be thoroughly mastered by the students.

3. The teacher must be sure that students understand the importance of the subject and have as much intrinsic motivation as possible.

4. The teacher proceeds from the very simple to the more difficult. In so doing, he keeps arithmetic figures in round numbers and uses simple illustrations at the beginning. In every lesson, he goes back to the fundamental concept to be mastered. Obviously, not all elements studied will be mastered; but, as a result of repeated learning of the basic concept in many different situations, at least the fundamental idea will be retained.

5. The basic-business teacher uses a variety of procedures. He minimizes mere telling-and-showing procedures and emphasizes student activity. He must be sure, however, that the activity contributes to the attainment of the simple objective already decided upon.

6. He develops a test in terms of the simple ability or concept to be mastered. He should not glorify the memorization of picayune facts at the expense of fundamental ideas.

7. The teacher must be sure that the material to be mastered in every unit is made meaningful to the students in terms of its relation to other units of learning. The extent to which students can take the idea mastered in one unit and apply it in others is possibly the best evidence of mastery. There must be a continual further development of basic learning as each unit is studied. Thus the basic learning acquired in the first unit will have been studied many times in different situations by the end of the course. As in bookkeeping, the spiraling of learning will result in the attainment of thorough learning in the basic-business subjects.

8. The basic-business teacher teaches less more thoroughly. He avoids busywork for the sake of busywork. He does not "throw the book" at the students. Of course, in the process of learning less more thoroughly many incidental learnings are acquired. Learning in the basic-business subjects should be broad and extensive, even though much of the detailed learning may soon be forgotten. These specific learnings should, however, as far as possible, help to enrich and make more meaningful the relatively few basic understandings that have been planned for the class.

9. The problem-solving technique is thoroughly mastered in every basic-business course. Students learn to identify and isolate the problem to be solved; they consider all possible alternate solutions; they select the probable best solution; they try it out; they determine its adequacy; they follow up on the solution of the problem.

10. Attitudes and understandings are the basic learnings in basic-busi-

ness subjects. Facts and skills are needed to develop proper attitudes and understandings, but the facts and skills are means to the end rather than ends in themselves.

QUESTIONS

1. How does the introduction-to-business teacher motivate student interest the first day in class?

2. How can the introduction-to-business teacher create a business-like atmosphere?

3. How do you feel about seating students according to some definite plan?

4. What kind of student inventory tests can be given in the introduction-to-business class?

5. How do student interests and needs affect the introduction-to-business class?

6. How can the basic-business teacher use the "variety is the spice of life" technique in his daily work?

7. What are some of the student projects that can be used in teaching the first unit in the introduction-to-business class?

8. What interesting student activities can be used in the banking unit?

9. What teaching aids can be used in the telephone unit?

10. What are some of the important points to remember about evaluating basic-business units?

11. How do you feel about letting students evaluate the teacher?

STUDENT ACTIVITIES

1. Prepare a report on, "The Introduction-to-Business Course—Past, Present, and Future."

2. Using the suggested points in Chapter III, evaluate three recent introduction-to-business textbooks. Indicate the *one* you would select and tell why.

3. Make a survey of five junior and senior high schools in your area to determine the present status of the Introduction-to-Business course. Determine the course, title, grade placement, length of course, major objectives, and units covered.

4. Prepare a report on, "What All Students Should Know About Business."

5. Prepare a report on, "What All Business Students Should Know About Business."

6. Prepare a lesson plan to teach any unit to an introduction-to-business class that is open to all students.

7. Develop a good and extensive resource unit on the teaching of one of these topics:

  a. Buying a household commodity
  b. Evaluating the advertising in a national magazine
  c. Management in the home
  d. Your local business and savings banks
  e. Should we buy an automobile on time?

8. Prepare a list of the supplementary materials you would use in teaching the unit you selected for activity.

9. Prepare a short and informal test on the first topic in the unit you prepared.

10. Prepare the final test on the above unit.

BIBLIOGRAPHY

Bahr, Gladys, Issue Editor. "Evaluation in Basic Business Education," *UBEA Forum,* IX (March, 1955) Most of this issue is devoted to a series of tests, which make a serious effort at measuring competency rather than mere facts.

Christensen, Opal. "Group Planning in Problem Solving," *American Business Education Yearbook, X,* 1953.

Freeman, M. Herbert. *Basic Business Education for Everyday Living,* Monograph 74. Cincinnati, South-Western Publishing Co., 1951.

————. "Techniques for Teaching General or Basic Business," *Business Education World* (January, 1950).

"The High School Business Library," *American Business Education,* (May, 1953).

Lloyd, Alan C. "Classroom Organization for Teaching Elementary Business Training," *Business Education World,* XXVIII (November, 1947).

————. "General Business Student Projects," *Business Education World,* XXXIV and XXXV (March and June, 1954) pp. 17–18, 35, 36, (September and October, 1954) pp. 23–24, 30–31.

Malsbary, Dean R. "An Instrument to Measure Learning in Investments," *UBEA Forum,* X (November, 1955), p. 27.

Price, Ray G. "Pupil Participation in Developing Basic-Business Field Trips," *UBEA Forum,* (November, 1950).

Sasso, Enrico V. "Dramatize Good Telephone Techniques," *UBEA Forum,* (February, 1951).

Shiras, Sylvia. "An Outline for a Pupil Activity Unit on Learning to Use Money Wisely," *Business Education World* (April, 1951).

State Course of Study, *Business Education,* Part V—General Business— State Department of Education, Richmond, Virginia, 1952.

Wells, Inez Ray. "General Business Tests." *Business Education World,* XXXVI, 1955. Each issue contains a test on a phase of general business.

CHAPTER XVIII

The Beginning Teacher

IN THIS BOOK some of the basic procedures for teaching have been presented. In teaching the skill subjects, the function of the teacher as a demonstrator of expert practice has been emphasized. The need for achieving mastery of whatever is learned has been constantly brought to the foreground. The teacher should be clearly aware of those skills and facts that he believes should be mastered and of those that he teaches merely as a basis for clarifying the concepts, abilities, or understandings to be mastered. All work, therefore, should be organized constantly in terms of the fundamental elements to be mastered rather than in terms of vague areas of learning. Whenever a new unit is considered, the basic learnings that the student is to achieve and retain permanently should be foremost in the teacher's mind. In achieving these objectives the teacher is often hampered by some common weaknesses of classroom practices.

COMMON WEAKNESSES OF TEACHERS

1. *Too Much Talking by the Teacher*. The teacher should not be afraid to give informal lectures as a means of motivating a large unit of learning, as a means of indicating the scope of the unit, and as a means for giving directions. In planning every lesson, however, the teacher should check himself to see whether he has provided for student activity or whether his instructions are merely "teacher oration." In evaluating his work at the close of the day, the teacher should again check himself to see whether he has stolen the class-

COMMON WEAKNESSES OF CLASSROOM TEACHERS

1. Too much talking by the teacher
2. Meaningless and indefinite assignments
3. Correcting and not correcting papers in class
4. Limitation of work to the text
5. Lack of participation in extracurricular activities
6. Misuse of chalk board
7. Lack of planning
8. Failure to use the business environment of the community
9. Failure to consider individual differences among students
10. Excessive use of routine questions and answers
11. Failure to utilize personal experiences of students; excessive use of teacher's personal experiences
12. Ground covered too rapidly
13. Reprimands given in anger
14. Undue familiarity with pupils
15. Carelessness about discipline

---

room time from the students or whether he has really worked toward the idea of letting students learn to do by doing.

2. *Meaningless and Indefinite Assignments.* Some teachers seem to think that work for the sake of work has some inherent values, especially for others. Every assignment that is given, whether it is to be done in class or at home, should be carefully checked to see whether it can make a contribution to student learning. Many teachers complain that bookkeeping textbooks contain too few exercises. As a matter of fact, most high school textbooks in bookkeeping contain far more exercises than can possibly be utilized intelligently. Fewer exercises better prepared and more carefully analyzed as a basis for remedial teaching will be far more valuable than the vast quantities of futile busywork to which many students are now subjected. One reason why most students, whether in high school or university, dislike homework and term papers is that they cannot see the learning value of such work. If this is the case, much of the learning value of an exercise, even if it is sound, has already been lost. Better teaching and less busywork will result in more

learning. The teacher should not assign exercises in class or for homework as a substitute for his failure to work out useful teaching activities.

3. *Not Correcting Papers in Class.* Some student exercises should be corrected in class, and the careful teacher can thus skillfully provide a great deal of self-evaluation of the learning activities among his students. The teacher who spends all or most of his time after school correcting papers is likely to be a poor teacher because he will fail to get a properly balanced point of view. Inability of workers to find their own errors is one of the chief complaints employers make about present-day stenographers and typists. Teachers of stenography and typing should not diligently read and red pencil all English and typographical errors in transcripts, assignments, or tests after class hours. Instead, they should assist students to learn to proofread to detect their own errors, to use reference books, such as the dictionary if necessary, and to correct their own errors. A certain amount of paper work remains, which the teacher must do outside of class in order to record student progress. This checking should be done faithfully. Students respect the teacher who is willing to work as hard as he expects his students to work.

4. *Limitation of Work to the Text.* The teacher who makes himself a slave to the textbook is not a teacher. He is merely a drill master. No textbook can be so organized that it meets perfectly the needs of every student in the class. Work must be individualized. It must be simplified for some students and enriched for others. Textbook writers recognize this and try to encourage teachers to use the text as a means of teaching rather than as a substitute for good teaching.

5. *Lack of Participation in Extracurricular Activities.* One of the great values of school is its socializing influence. Students come into contact with others. The opportunities for contacts among students in the classroom are necessarily limited. The conversations in the cafeteria and during other odd times are fragmentary, desultory, and necessarily unplanned. Group activities with a purpose overcome these difficulties and still permit student activities without the formal control of the teacher. The very fact that extraclassroom activities take the center of interest away from the teacher and give it to the students makes them worth while. Working with students outside

the classroom may therefore be just as important as classroom activity and requires as good teaching procedures.

Business students are often likely to be less interested in extracurricular activities than others. Actually, the reverse should be true. They should be eager participants, and their association should be welcomed by other students because business students should know how to conduct various group activities. The school that limits its total program to classroom learnings leaves too great a gap between the formal learnings of the classroom and the application of these learnings to the home, the community, and especially to business.

6. *Misuse of the Chalk Board.* Many teachers fail to make full use of the chalk board. They do not realize the extent to which the visualization of learning materials helps the student to grasp meanings. A teacher who has two classes in the same subject should try to give the assignment orally to one class and to write it on the board for the second class. The difference in results will be amazing. Teachers, however, often assume that because they write outlines or other meaningless lines on the chalk board they are teaching effectively. This may be an outlet for the teacher's excess energy, but it fails as a teaching aid. The "chalk talk" is good, but the teacher must always remember that the chalk board is an aid to teaching and not a substitute for teaching. The work that goes on the chalk board should be just as carefully planned as the key questions that are to be asked or the assignment that is to be given.

7. *Lack of Planning.* No teacher can set up careful plans for five or six subjects every day, write them out in detail, check exercises, and still live a complete life. This limitation is, however, no excuse for failing to make plans. Some lessons can be planned very easily. In some cases only a few key items can be put on a card. Some lessons, however, should be planned and written out very carefully. The teacher should preserve these plans. Every term he can work out more lesson plans in detail and improve those that he has already given. Thus, every year the thoughtful teacher will acquire a larger collection of corrected and modified lesson plans. The teacher with several years of experience should be a better teacher than he was at the start of his career. One of the best evidences of this progress is a carefully worked out set of teaching plans. There are, of course, many difficulties in accumulating successful lesson plans. Teachers

are assigned many different subjects. The lesson plans that will fit one group are not effective for a group with a different type of social background and of a different intellectual level. Those that will be satisfactory for a heterogeneous group will not be satisfactory for a more homogeneous class. Nevertheless, it is easier to adapt than to start anew.

8. *Failure to Use the Business Environment of the Community.* It requires time and energy to take students to offices in the community. Frequently, the general administration objects to field trips. Businessmen will also object if the courtesy is abused. Students can be asked, however, to observe business practices in offices, stores, the school, and even the home.

9. *Failure to Consider Individual Differences among Students.* Teachers often give much attention to the students with ability and to poor students, while they ignore the average student. Even more important is the failure to recognize the personal differences among students. Not all students will react uniformly to one form of motivation or to one method of teaching.

10. *Excessive Use of Routine Questions and Answers.* The question-and-answer technique is a useful teaching device, but it must not be used as the only variation to lectures and formal drills. Some textbooks contain questions for discussion. The teacher should use these as a point of departure for carrying on the discussion and not as an end in themselves.

11. *Failure to Utilize the Personal Experiences of Students or Excessive Use of the Teacher's Personal Experiences.* Some students have had considerable business experience, far more than is credited to them by the average teacher. Their parents have had even more experience. Students like to talk about this experience, and other students like to listen to them. The teacher who monopolizes the classroom time by relating only his own business experience will soon lose the interest of his students. Nothing will antagonize a class more than the constant presentation of the teacher's job experiences, real or imaginary. The teacher need not be impersonal in his presentations, but a course should be more than a series of personal anecdotes of the teacher. Students are usually very discriminating. They do not respect a teacher who tells "tall" stories.

12. *Ground Covered Too Rapidly.* Many beginners make the

unfortunate mistake of confusing indifference with learning. Such teachers get a rude awakening after administering their first test. They find that the failure of students to reply to "Are there any questions?" does not necessarily mean that these students know the answers. Covering the textbook or the syllabus may mean that the teacher has made a fast trip over the heads of his students. It is far wiser to check whether students are learning from the very beginning than to assume that they have learned. The wisest thing is to assume that students have learned nothing unless the teacher can prove to himself that they have.

13. *Reprimands Given in Anger.* The teacher who has failed to control his class often thinks that a loud voice will settle the trouble-maker. The effect of loud reprimand is usually just the reverse—the more a teacher raises his voice, the less a class usually hears. When the teacher loses self-control, he becomes an easy mark for the mischievous student. There are times when a teacher is justified in showing his anger to the class; however, the instances should be rare. The beginning teacher should avoid showing his anger in any case. A calm voice that is just loud enough to be heard by all students is far more effective than shouting.

14. *Undue Familiarity with Pupils.* In their mistaken effort to become popular overnight, many beginning teachers court student favor by undue familiarity. Respect in the classroom must be earned. Once a high school teacher lowers the bars over which a student should never be permitted to step, he is in serious trouble. A teacher can show that he is interested in his students and likes them without becoming personal and unduly familiar with them.

15. *Carelessness about Discipline.* Closely connected with the tendency to be unduly familiar with pupils is carelessness about discipline. It is true that the old-fashioned pin-drop type of discipline is no longer countenanced in the school. Nevertheless the teacher must be certain that he has adequate attention from the students. Unless the class is paying attention to the work going on, learning is not taking place. All too frequently a teacher will give his attention to three or four students while the others are indifferent, or talking with each other or even doing the homework for other classes. The teacher must not overlook this. He must correct any such gross inattention. If necessary, he should stop the class and demand the

attention of all students. A far better procedure, however, would be to change the type of class instruction so as to get the interest of all members.

No teacher can or should expect every student to pay attention every minute of the class period, but petty mischievousness that irritates the other members of the class and distracts them from learning must not be tolerated. A little mischief carried on for a considerable period grows in momentum and becomes a major interference with classwork.

ORIENTATION TO HIGH SCHOOL STUDENTS

Like all other human beings, students can be a great joy. Life is worth living in terms of the people we know, but like all other human beings, students can be a great trial. The extent to which students are a joy rather than a trial is the extent to which a teacher will enjoy his work and the final measure of the degree to which he is successful. The basic principles of getting along with all people apply, possibly to a greater degree, to students because they are more immature and therefore the ordinary human qualities that we all possess stand out more obviously in high school students.

1. No person can be successful as a teacher unless he has a tremendous sense of humor. If a teacher took everything seriously that goes on in his classroom, his life would be a tragedy. A teacher gets along not only by his capacity to render decisions in a constructive way, but also by his capacity to look the other way. Small transgressions, small failures deserve to be ignored in students as they should be in our colleagues and relatives. Teachers must realize that, just as they themselves have small failings, their pupils will also deviate from correct practices in small ways.

2. Second in importance in getting along with students is patience. Of course a person who has a good sense of humor will have patience; but patience is a particular aspect of getting along with people. Students have a different point of view, and that of a teacher should be, and usually is, considerably more mature. A teacher often fails to realize that what is simple to him is difficult for his students and, even more important, that which is important to him because he understands it and appreciates its value is often quite unimportant to his students. Within these two basic principles for getting along with people there are a number of others that help a great deal in living with students and enjoying them.

3. The teacher should be firm once he is sure that he is right. Threatening is a futile process. The students soon learn that a threat is a meaningless thing. Firmness does not mean being dictatorial. Firmness is important after one is certain that one can enforce a judgment.

4. The teacher should be fair and treat all students alike and be especially considerate to those whom he finds trying.

5. High standards, but not unreasonably high, should be set.

6. Homework should be given that can be accomplished in the time the students have available, and work given by other teachers should be considered.

7. Credit should be given when due and, if at all possible, students should be corrected only in private.

8. Many disciplinary problems that beginning teachers have are caused by their own insistence on making situations discipline problems.

9. A teacher should be sure that there is enough work for the students to do as soon as they come into the classroom.

10. He must make certain that the work makes sense to the students and that they find it of some value.

A teacher who is successful in getting along with students will probably be successful in all other aspects of schoolwork. The beginning teacher, particularly one who has not had acquaintanceship with students of secondary-school level, may find it difficult to understand their point of view. The simplest answer is to treat them like human beings and when at all possible avoid undue bursts of temper. The teacher should avoid threatening, see to it that there is plenty of work, and not use grades as a means of discipline. The chances are that, if he does not take minor transgressions too seriously, the discipline problem will solve itself easily. If teachers get along well with people, they will get along well with students.

ORIENTATION TO OTHER TEACHERS

Second in importance to getting along with students is the ability to get along with faculty colleagues. How much the teacher should associate with the members of the faculty outside of school is a question that cannot be answered simply. The person who isolates himself from his school colleagues entirely after working hours is probably going unreasonably far. Teachers often learn to get along well and to understand each other; to tolerate each other and to give in to each other's needs and wishes by learning to be congenial human beings together. A certain amount of association with one's colleagues outside of schoolwork is, therefore, desirable. The beginning teacher especially should make a point of having friends and acquaintances not connected with the school faculty because the teacher who thinks of nothing except school is not likely to get along well in school or out of school. School, by its very nature organized in terms of service to students, is restrictive like all other institutions. The teacher, therefore, should broaden his interests and become acquainted with, and interested in, many other things.

At some faculty luncheon cafeterias, teachers penalize each other by compelling a contribution of a penny or a nickel any time anyone starts to talk "shop." The punishment possibly does not fit the crime because there are times when teachers should talk "shop" together. Fundamentally, however, the point is sound. When teachers get away from the classroom, they should think of other things than their students. Students are important, but discussing the petty details, whether Johnny was obstreperous today or whether Susie was unusually good, is not in order as a rule.

Equally undesirable is gossiping about one's colleagues or one's superiors. A certain amount of discussion about others with whom we are acquainted is desirable, and a suggestion that teachers not talk about each other or about their superiors is unreasonable. This discussion, however, can be kept on a plane of reasonableness, of courtesy, and certainly should never be malicious. Malicious gossip is bad under any circumstances. Talk that stays on the level of human interest and is an uncritical comment on personality not only can be harmless but often is entertaining and sometimes enlightening.

ORIENTATION TO ADMINISTRATION

The third important element in getting along in schoolwork is proper relationship with administration. There never has been and never will be a perfect administrator any more than there will be perfect students or perfect teachers for that matter. The reason for this is very simple—human beings are imperfect. All of us deviate more or less from perfection. One of the difficult things for us to master, and this is especially true of the beginning teacher, is the realization that other people have the right to be imperfect just because they are human beings. Teachers expect other people to tolerate their individual weaknesses and failures; and yet teachers themselves expect others rarely, if ever, to deviate.

One of the most important things, therefore, for the beginning teacher to realize is that administrators are human beings, that they make mistakes, that they scold when at times they should not, that they tend to like some people better than they do others, that they are not perfectly objective in their points of view. If a beginning teacher will start out with the realization that the administrator at times is going to be unreasonable, then a great deal of the trial and emotional upset that is caused by an actual experience of this kind is eliminated. Most administrators are in positions of authority because they do know how to get along reasonably well with people. They have been successful in getting along with students. They have learned to get along with boards of education and with parents. The beginning teacher, therefore, can presume that the usual administrator is at least as fair as most other people and probably somewhat more reasonable.

There are many things the beginning teacher can do in order to get along well with his superiors.

1. Be reasonable, courteous, considerate and thoughtful of the administrator. He likes to be treated like a human being just like everyone else. That does not mean that we have to maintain an excessive relationship of hail-fellow-well-met with the administrator. His position demands courtesy, but there is no reason why friendliness and good will cannot be mixed with considerateness and courtesy. Administrators, having been teachers themselves, find it difficult to understand aloofness, distance, and excessive formality on the part of their teachers working under their direction.

2. Follow the rules of the school. After a person has been in a school system for several years, he is in a position to evaluate their soundness or unsoundness. There are always rules in a game, and the fellow who gets along is usually the one who follows them within reason. If the rules are wrong, then the teachers and administrators jointly should correct them.

3. Don't be a nuisance. Don't send students to the administrator for

every trivial disciplinary problem that arises. Discipline is the teacher's problem and therefore, except in unusual cases, the problem should be handled within the classroom.

4. On the other hand, the principal is responsible for the work of the school; therefore, when anything happens that is out of the ordinary for which he can be held responsible, it is not only the wise thing for the teacher to inform the principal, but it is vitally necessary because if information reaches the principal indirectly rather than directly from the teacher, it is likely to be distorted. If a principal is to be faced with a problem, be sure that he has the truthful and complete story. Don't let him be faced suddenly with an unexpected situation, but let him know about it under conditions under which he can digest it and think it through. Administrators, like all other people, like to know what is going to happen to them in advance if at all possible.

5. Use supplies with discretion. Boards of education can be very critical and petty in their concern about the cost of supplies. The teacher who is indifferently careless of their use soon becomes marked by administration.

6. Be punctual with attendance records, grades, and other similar routine. They are not the most important part of schoolwork, but they are a necessary essential in every organization dealing with dozens if not hundreds of thousands of people.

7. Be sure that the room is kept in reasonable order. A little training of the students by the teacher will encourage them to leave their desks in good condition. If after a student has left a classroom and there is still an occasional scrap of paper around, the teacher should not think himself so superior to janitorial service as to ignore this. Clean chalk boards and a reasonably clean room left in as good a condition, if not better, as that in which it was found are an evidence of good breeding.

The ability to get along with students, with one's colleagues, and with the administration is far more important than one's ability to teach formal subject matter. It is true that in most cases these separate abilities cannot be isolated. A good teacher of subject matter usually is the one who gets along well with his colleagues, his students, and his administrators. Nevertheless, human relations come first; and therefore the beginning teacher should devote his best effort to adjusting himself to the people with whom he is going to work. Subject matter, if it has been well learned will, in large degree, then take care of itself.

FINDING A POSITION

During the last year of professional training, the prospective teacher is usually concerned with finding a teaching position that suits his capabilities and that provides opportunity for him to develop professionally to the best advantage. Some of the factors to be considered are:

1. Will you have helpful supervision in adjusting to your first position? Is the educational philosophy of the school in conformity with yours? Are the methods used similar to those that you have come to accept as desirable?

2. Is the school system one in which you would like to work? (During the interviewing process you may have opportunity to observe the administrators in their relations with their teachers and possibly to observe teachers in relation to each other. Sensing the climate of the job is often of paramount importance.)

3. Can you make satisfactory living arrangements that will not tax your vitality too greatly but will conserve your energies for the hard job ahead? Do these arrangements provide for what looks like a pleasant social life? In other words, will you grow both as a teacher and as a person in the environment?

4. Is the salary schedule satisfactory? The beginning teacher often looks only at the initial salary. Actually, the initial salary is often not so important as the steps.

PLACEMENT LEADS

Positions are obtained through a variety of channels: competitive examinations in large cities, college placement offices, professional organizations and associations, commercial teachers' agencies, personal contacts and unsolicited letters, and the state employment service in your locality.

Competitive Examinations. A number of large cities employ teachers through competitive examinations that are announced only when existing lists of available teachers are nearly exhausted. During emergency periods of teacher shortage special examinations are sometimes scheduled for desirable candidates when no licensed teachers are available. The National Teachers' Examination (a general examination for prospective teachers in all areas of preparation) is given twice a year in various centers over the United States. Having a score on such a standardized examination is often an asset in making application for a position, and in some school systems passing the National Teachers' Examination is a requirement for employment.

College Placement Offices. By far your best source of employment leads is your college placement office. Inexperienced candidates sometimes apply for positions "on their own" without preparing the set of credentials that serves as the basis for application through the college placement office. They do not realize that, even though they did not give this office as a source of information, the school administrator will usually request complete information on the candidate through that channel. If the applicant does not have a file in the college placement office, the administrator assumes, perhaps falsely, that the college is not backing the candidate's application. You should work closely with the college placement office. It is usually a guidance office and will discuss any problems with you and make a genuine effort to fit the person to the job. It cannot serve you effectively, however, unless you are known to the person who is usually asked for an evaluation by the prospective employer.

Most college placement offices ask the candidate to prepare a complete set of papers to be released to possible employers. These credentials include personal data, educational background in detail, student teaching experience, work experience relevant to employment as a teacher, a statement by the applicant about his experiences and interests that would increase his value to the school, and references as to the candidate's teaching ability. Even if you are not immediately available for a teaching position, it is wise to develop a set of credentials for the files in the college placement office, for you may later wish to use its services and will encounter considerable difficulty in getting references about student teaching.

The college placement office possibly has a copy of the salary schedules of schools in which you are interested and can give you other background information that will help you in making application. You will also probably find in that office information about certification requirements in various states. If you are moving to a distant city, this office may be able to give you suggestions about how to make application there. There is usually no charge for teacher placement services of colleges to their graduates.

Professional Organizations and Associations. In some states the state department of education or the state teachers' association has placement services for teachers. There is usually a small membership fee for this service, but this amount is much less than the charge of a commercial teachers' agency.

Commercial Teachers' Agencies. There are many excellent commercial teachers' agencies. If your college placement office is not giving the service that fits your needs, you may wish to register with such agencies; they also prepare a folder of credentials showing your qualifications. These agencies usually charge a fee of 5 per cent of the first year's salary. Your requirements for a position, however, may be so specialized that this fee will be money well spent in your case.

Personal Contacts and Unsolicited Letters. You may have a contact through a friend that will result in your employment. By all means, use it. Remember, however, that the employing school will probably check your credentials with the college placement office, which should be in a position to support your application through the records that you have supplied to it. For some reason you may wish to make application for a position in a district in which there is no known vacancy. An unsolicited letter may bring the desired interview. Writing such letters to all schools in a county, however, is frowned upon. Administrators are justifiably annoyed with duplicated letters of application and give them no consideration. Talk over your plans for writing unsolicited letters with the college placement office. Probably you will get some valuable suggestions as to which schools would welcome such letters and also suggestions for writing effective letters of application.

State Employment Service. The state employment service has developed a professional division and encourages candidates for teaching positions to use its services, which are free.

CREDENTIALS

When you are preparing your credentials, be very careful that they are typed in acceptable form with no errors in spelling, punctuation, or usage. Remember that these papers are your "silent salesman" and must represent you at your best. The credentials not only record your professional training but should also show you as a person, reflecting your interests and specialized abilities. All previous experiences should be carefully analyzed to see whether they can be related to your potentiality as a teacher. Experiences in extra-curricular activities show leadership qualities; working in a summer camp shows interest in children and an intention to obtain experi-ence in working with them; participating in a civic club gives a clue to your willingness to work with community groups. Merely listing such experiences sounds egotistical; relating them to your teaching ability indicates that you understand the requirements of the posi-tion. Ask yourself what you would look for in a candidate; then ana-lyze your background in terms of these requirements, and present your qualifications in a professional way. This material offers the administrator a chance to see whether you express yourself well and have imagination.

An employing official is guided by the kind of recommendation you will be given by your references. Select them carefully from among those of the college faculty who know you best and are most likely to speak well of you. Be sure to provide references from both the supervisor of student teaching and the co-operating teacher in the high school if possible. It is also wise to include a good personal or character reference. Be sure to give full information as to address and title of each reference. It is common courtesy to ask permission in advance from every person you expect to use as a reference.

In some states photographs are not permitted. In others, they are an important part of your credentials. If you use photographs, use standard application size, unmounted. Wear neat, dark, and well-tailored clothes. Avoid hats, ornate jewelry, loud shirts or ties. Do not use tinted or informal photographs. Never use group pictures. Order a supply of prints large enough to assure that you will not be left without one in an emergency. Write your name and address on the back of the photograph.

LETTERS OF APPLICATION

In writing a letter of application, the candidate should consider the following points:

1. Use standard-size typewriting paper of rag content with matching envelope. The typewriter ribbon should be well inked. Since you are applying for a position as a business teacher, your letter must be a sample of best typewriting practice. (Do not use social stationery or business letterheads from a company in which you have been working.)

2. Address the application to the proper person by name, including his title. In most schools the letter is addressed to the superintendent of schools, but in other schools employment of new teachers is the function of the assistant superintendent or of a special administrative assistant. The correct salutation is the person's name with the proper title, such as "Dear Superintendent Smith" or "Dear Doctor Smith."

3. Show that you understand the requirements of the position. To do this, try to get all possible information about the situation before applying. After you show that you understand the nature of the job, show how your qualifications fit these requirements. Do not brag, but relate your background to the job. After all, an administrator cannot evaluate your qualifications unless you set them forth in detail. Indicate that your credentials are available from the college placement office or agency. A personal data sheet to accompany the letter is often used. The letter, then, merely summarizes the points you have made in detail in your personal data sheet.

4. Make it easy for the administrator to act. Enclose a self-addressed and stamped envelope for reply. Or suggest that you will telephone at a time far enough in the future to give time for getting credentials. In the telephone conversation you may suggest that you would like to arrange an interview.

5. Return promptly, properly filled out, the forms that may be sent to you. A note of appreciation for the privilege of submitting an application is in order.

PERSONAL DATA SHEET

A personal data sheet similar to the form appearing on page 405 is usually effective. The candidate should, however, select the headings to be used in relation to his strong points. For instance, if he is not a particularly strong student, he should omit any section for "School Honors."

PERSONAL DATA SHEET

Mary Stevenson

Candidate for a position as business teacher in the Clay Public School

PERSONAL DATA

Address:	346 South High Street	Height:	5′ 4″
	Kirksville, Missouri	Weight:	115 lbs.
Telephone:	3486	Physical Condition:	Excellent
Age:	21 years	Marital Status:	Single

EDUCATION

High School: Montgomery City High School, 1948–1952
College: North Missouri State Teachers College, 1952–1956
(Eligible for Missouri State High School Certificate in Commerce)

EXPERIENCE

Salesgirl in Alexander's on Saturdays, winters of 1953–1954
Clerk in Registrar's office at KSTC 15 hours a week, 1955–1956
Dictation from three professors during secretarial-practice course, 1956

SCHOOL HONORS RECEIVED AND OFFICES HELD

High School National Honor Society
Dean's List in college every semester
Member of Freshman Orientation Committee, 1955
Secretary of junior class, 1955
President of dormitory, 1956
Pi Omega Pi (honorary business-education fraternity)

SPECIAL ABILITIES

Visual aids. Can operate opaque, 16-mm. film, and slide projectors
School newspaper production. During student teaching supervised production of mimeographed homeroom newsletter every two weeks.
Typewriting and shorthand skill. Have Gregg award for 120-wam shorthand test. Can type at 60 wam. Have passed National Business Entrance Test in shorthand and typewriting.
Business machines. Can operate SoundScriber, Mimeograph, Monroe calculator, Standard duplicator, and Burroughs adding machine.

REFERENCES

Credentials on file at College Placement Office, Room 102, Kirk Hall.
Telephone or write Dr. Hugh Albert, Director. (Telephone—7712)

PERSONAL INTERVIEW

In all probability you will be granted a personal interview if the school to which you applied is interested in you. The following suggestions may be helpful:

1. Rehearse before you go to the interview. Try to envisage what the interviewer might ask and how you would reply.

2. Know as much as possible about the situation before the interview.

3. Wear appropriate business dress, conservative make-up and accessories. Avoid sport clothes. This is a hat-and-gloves situation. You must be impeccably groomed.

4. Be on time—even a little early.

5. Take your cue from the interviewer. He will probably take the initiative in questioning; however, you will want to be sensitive to the amount of information you should volunteer in answer to questions. "Give"—but do not give too much. Many candidates talk themselves out of a job.

6. Be courteous, tactful, and good natured. You must be completely truthful and honest. Do not lose your poise.

7. Do not make promises that you cannot fulfill.

8. If your questions have not been answered during the interview, you should feel free to ask intelligent ones. The quality of your abilities can often be judged by the questions you ask; however, if your questions are concerned only with salary and hours of required attendance, you will probably not be employed.

9. Write a courteous note of thanks for the interview within a day or two.

It will be helpful to you in planning the interview if you consider the administrator's interests. He is looking for the following information:

1. Is your appearance pleasing, sensible, and wholesome?

2. Are you freakish or queer in any way?

3. Are you evasive or open, frank, and sincere?

4. Are you forward or self-effacing? too retiring?

5. Do you have sympathy and love for children?

6. Do you have an interest in teaching and in the profession of teaching in general?

7. Do you express yourself well and unhesitatingly in the field of your preparation and on questions propounded to you?

8. Do you possess initiative to carry forward the work to be done?

9. Can you be relied upon to be discreet in the discussion of school matters and your fellows in general, or are you inclined to gossip?

10. Can you take criticism without offense?

11. Do you possess the strength and force of personality and character to manage boys and girls of high school age, so as to command their respect and admiration?

12. Will you reflect credit upon the faculty and the school by your life as a citizen of the community?

13. Are you a teacher by desire or by circumstance?

14. Do you have the "human touch" in dealing with children?

CONTRACT

Until you accept a position, you are free to apply for as many positions as you wish. Once you have received a letter of appointment and have acknowledged it, you are under contract. At that time you should notify the placement office and other administrators that you are no longer available for appointment. You should complete the contract unless some unforeseeable circumstance prevents your doing so. It is not ethical to break a contract to accept a more lucrative position in another school. To do so reflects unfavorably not only on you but also upon the college in which you were trained.

PROFESSIONAL GROWTH

The real education of a teacher begins when he starts to teach. It is often said that the first school community in which a new teacher works is really paying for his training as a teacher. The successful teacher learns every day of his life. His education is never finished until he dies.

The beginning teacher will learn much from his fellow teachers, administrators, and supervisors. In addition, he may grow professionally as a result of participating in professional activities.

PROFESSIONAL ASSOCIATIONS AND LITERATURE

The new business teacher is very fortunate because he can learn much from the professional associations and literature in the field.

1. *National Associations*

Every good teacher should belong to the strong basic education groups as well as to those in his specialized field.

  a. National Education Association (NEA)
  b. United Business Education Association (UBEA)

2. *Regional Associations*

  a. Eastern Business Teachers Association (EBTA) (Active particularly in the North East)
  b. Mountain Plains Business Education Association (Affiliated with UBEA)
  c. National Business Teachers Association (NBTA) (Active particularly in the Middle West)
  d. Southern Business Education Association (SBEA) (Affiliated with UBEA)
  e. Tri-State Business Education Association (Active in Ohio, Pennsylvania, and West Virginia)
  f. Western Business Education Association (Affiliated with UBEA)

3. *State Associations*

  a. State Education Association. Every state has a general education group.
  b. State Business Education Associations. Many states have a business organization that is affiliated with the state general education group.

4. *Local Associations*

  a. City and county general education associations
  b. City, county, or area business-education associations

5. *Honorary Groups*

  a. Pi Omega Pi—Honorary business-education group
  b. Delta Pi Epsilon—Honorary graduate business-education group

6. *Professional Publications*

  a. *Balance Sheet*—Published by South-Western Publishing Company and distributed without cost
  b. *Business Teacher*—Published by the Gregg Publishing Division of McGraw-Hill Book Company, Inc., and distributed without cost
  c. *Journal of Business Education,* 512 Brooks Building, Wilkes-Barre, Pa.
  d. *Business Education World,* Gregg Publishing Division, McGraw-Hill Book Company, Inc., 330 West 42 Street, New York 36, N. Y.

e. *United Business Education Forum*—a publication of the UBEA
f. *American Business Education*—published jointly by the NBTA and EBTA
g. *American Business Education Yearbooks*—also published jointly by the NBTA and EBTA (Buy from New York University Press Bookstore, Washington Square, New York 3, New York.)
h. *Business Education Index.* An annual index of business-education publications since 1940. Prepared by Delta Pi Epsilon, Charles B. Hicks, Executive Secretary, Ohio State University, Columbus, Ohio
i. Many state and regional business-education periodicals

TEACHING AS A CAREER

One of the common faults of teachers is that they limit themselves to teaching their classes in a formal way. In order to get the most out of teaching, it is desirable to do more than teach classes. This requires organization. A good teacher plans his work and does a certain amount of checking. This can take up a great deal of time if it is not carefully organized. Careful planning, the elimination of unnecessary exercises, and getting routine things down to a system can save much time. Above all, if the teacher is to be successful, he must be interested in his profession. This means that he should read articles, go to conventions, and try to "get the feel" of his profession. It is true that many articles are dull and that the talks at many conventions simply repeat for the hundredth time what has been said before. Nevertheless, the beginning teacher can and should develop a critical and constructive attitude toward professional activities. He can become acquainted with those in positions of leadership and work out a program for self-advancement. If he finds articles dull and uninteresting, then he should write some that are meaningful. He can work out projects within his school, carry them out, and then let others know how and why they were successful. Talks and panel discussions are the necessary accessories of a convention. Conventions provide opportunities for getting acquainted with the problems of other teachers who are faced with similar situations, with writers of textbooks, and with the leaders in the field.

The beginning teacher should become acquainted with the businessmen of his local community through membership in a service club or through personal visitation. Many community organizations hold evening meetings that the teacher can attend. He can let the businessmen know what is being done, what the school problems are, and how teacher and businessmen help each other. He can listen to the businessmen's criticisms and use them where they are constructive.

GRADUATE WORK

Attending a university to obtain an advanced degree can be a meaningless and futile activity. If the student merely listens to his instructors, follows the formalities of writing term papers, then goes back to his school without making any effort to apply the concepts he may have acquired, he will have wasted his time. Even if such attendance results in an increment, the increased salary will not equal the total cost of graduate study. The teacher who attends classes after having read intelligently the current periodicals, especially articles by the instructors with whom he is likely to work, will have taken an important step in making his graduate-school experience worth while. He should get acquainted with the instructional staff and with fellow students because it is in this kind of environment that real learning takes place.

Advanced degrees are useful only as they are evidence of actual learnings. In general, the beginning teacher who expects to make teaching his career and who is sincerely interested in securing reasonable promotional opportunity should plan to obtain a graduate degree. The younger he is, provided he has had a fairly well-rounded job and teaching experience, the better. He will then be able to capitalize on his academic learnings and apply them in actual school-work. Advanced degrees are not and should not be the sole means by which promotion is obtained. Promotions should be obtained because of ability to do work at an advanced level and because of the possession of personal and job qualities that justify such promotion. Advanced degrees do help, however, in smoothing the way. All things being equal, they are evidences of achievement.

The young man who is planning to stay in teaching for only a year or two would, of course, not want to specialize in advanced work in business education. Neither will the young woman who is interested in getting married and rearing a family. Many thousands of young men and women, however, are interested in making teaching their life profession because they see an opportunity for a worthwhile and interesting life experience through such a channel.

GRADUATE COURSES

In most schools it is necessary to have an advanced degree to receive maximum income. Fortunately there are teacher-training institutions in every part of the country that grant a Master's degree upon the completion of one year (30 to 34 points) of graduate study. Usually this degree can be earned on a part-time basis, or during the summer, while the candidate is teaching.

A smaller number of universities offer graduate studies beyond the master's degree. These courses lead either to a doctorate in education, Ed.D., or to the doctor of philosophy, Ph.D., degree. These programs usually require at least two or three years of study beyond the Master's degree. Teachers who are interested in making business education a life career should seriously consider the attainment of the doctorate. The sooner they embark on this objective, the more they will profit from their training by advancement in their profession.

It is very encouraging for the beginning business teacher to know that he is engaged in an important professional career that has great promise for professional and personal growth.

OPPORTUNITIES AND LIMITATIONS IN TEACHING BUSINESS SUBJECTS

Teaching business subjects can be a dull and monotonous activity. It can also be a lifelike, really enjoyable, and reasonably profitable activity. To a great extent it depends on the teacher himself. If he looks upon teaching as a necessary evil, it will soon become a handicap and a burden. If he looks at the problems and difficulties that will inevitably face him in doing a good teaching job as hurdles to be overcome rather than as insurmountable obstacles, then these challenges can be a means of accentuating the interest in his work.

The many restrictions on a teacher's personal and social life that formerly prevailed are gradually being lifted. Teachers as a whole and especially business teachers are encouraged to participate in all normal and socially desirable community activities. In many larger communities a career in business education and marriage are not only compatible but are positively favored.

Part-time, afterschool, and summer employment are desirable and a good means of supplementing income. It should be encouraged to the extent that it does not interfere with schoolwork or advancement in one's professional career.

THE FUTURE

The sooner the teacher receives his first promotion, the more likely he is to receive promotions all along the line. This does not mean that the teacher should set all his objectives toward obtaining promotion. Many of the more able contributors to business education have been classroom teachers all their lives. Nevertheless, the kinds of activities that lead to promotion are usually those that make a teacher a more alert person and a better teacher.

In the field of business education as in any other field of human endeavor, there are many obstacles. Many try for promotion and succeed only half way. Only relatively few are fortunate in securing the best promotional opportunities. This is inevitable. But it is in the trying that interest is attained. Business education then, as a field, can be not only a means of earning a living; it can also be an interesting and worth-while adventure.

QUESTIONS

1. List the common weaknesses of classroom teaching. Do most teachers actually talk too much? even those who talk about not talking too much?

2. What are some weaknesses of classroom teaching other than those given in this chapter?

3. What are some of the teaching weaknesses of more experienced teachers as compared with those of the beginning teacher?

4. Summarize the section on orientation to high school students given in this chapter.

5. What other elements in getting along well with students must be considered in addition to those presented here?

6. Discuss the problem of getting along with other teachers. Under what conditions might one be justified in taking care of another teacher's class if that teacher is not present?

7. Under what conditions would it be justifiable to criticize another person's homeroom students?

8. Suggest some other items for getting along well with the principal and the school superintendent than those suggested in this chapter.

9. What are the usual channels for securing a teaching position? Why are credentials always important?

10. Itemize the elements on which you should check yourself before you go for a personal interview.

11. What are some of the procedures that can be used for becoming acquainted with the local businessmen?

12. How soon should a beginning teacher undertake graduate work?

13. What standard should be used in selecting a school at which one might do graduate work?

14. There is a common saying that the American school system has acquired a Ph.D. phobia. To what extent is this criticism justified? to what extent unwarranted?

15. What are some of the limitations involved in teaching business subjects as compared to teaching other subjects in the secondary schools? as opposed to work in business? Suggest some advantages and limitations other than those presented in this chapter.

STUDENT ACTIVITIES

1. Observe at least six classroom teachers of business subjects. Make a tabulation of the good points and weaknesses in classroom teaching following the items suggested in this chapter. List any others that you may find. Set up a pattern for yourself for emphasizing the good points that you found in teaching procedures and also a pattern for avoiding the weaknesses.

2. Either in your own practice teaching experience, or if necessary in a trial practice teaching procedure apart from a formal class, have some-

one observe you teach and give you an analysis of your strength and weaknesses in teaching.

3. Conduct sample interviews for a business teaching position before the class.

4. Write a letter of application for a position.

5. Talk with several high school business students and find out what they like and dislike about their teachers. Be careful to avoid particular names. What subjects do the pupils like most? Which ones do they dislike? Why? Is it because of the nature of the content or because of the kind of teacher?

6. Go to at least one and if possible more than one local, state, regional or national business-teachers convention. Discuss the value of the convention with those attending. Observe the extent to which the teachers went to the convention to listen to talks, to check up on new textbooks and new teaching materials, or to have a social visit with their associates. Make a report on the value of conventions for beginning business teachers and for you in particular. Decide how a teacher can make best use of a convention in terms of his interest in it.

BIBLIOGRAPHY

Barr, A. S., W. H. Burton, and L. J. Brueckner. *Supervision.* New York, D. Appleton-Century Company, 1947.

Briggs, Thomas, J. Paul Leonard, and Joseph Justman. *Secondary Education.* New York, The Macmillan Company, 1950.

Cooper, George K. "How To Get Yourself up in Front in Business Today," *Business Teacher,* XXXII (September-October 1954), pp. 1–2.

Douglas, Lloyd V. "Achieving Professional Stature," *Balance Sheet,* XXV (May, 1954), p. 387.

Fine, Benjamin. *Our Children Are Cheated.* New York, Henry Holt and Company, 1947.

Graves, A. D. *American Secondary Education.* Boston, D. C. Heath and Company, 1951.

Hart, Ethel. "Do You Get Along with Students?" *Business Teacher,* XXI (February, 1954), pp. 19–20.

Pumula, Ardis E. "Conservation of the Commercial Teacher's Time," *Journal of Business Education,* XX (October, 1944), p. 38.

Ryan, Robert J. "The Finest Teacher I Ever Knew," *Business Education World,* XXIII (January, 1943), pp. 309–310.

Satlow, I. David. "Why Some Lessons Don't Jell," *American Business Education,* X (December, 1953), pp. 71–75, 81.

Sellers, Clara. "Do Your Students Like Your Class?" *Business Education World,* XXXII (March, 1952), pp. 337, 353.

Sollars, Velma. "Evaluating Student Teachers in Commercial Education Course," *Business Education World,* XXVI (November, 1945), pp. 135–136.

"Suggestions for Beginning Teachers," *American Business Education,* XII (May, 1956), pp. 214–234.

Trytten, John M. "The Business Educator and Professional Relationships," *National Business Education Quarterly,* XXI (December, 1952), pp. 18–21.

Walter, John T. "Planning for a New Position," *Business Education World,* XXIII (May, 1943), pp. 517–520.

Index